The Conservation and Restoration of Ceramics

The Conservation and Restoration of Ceramics

Susan Buys, former Head of Ceramics and Glass Conservation, Victoria and Albert Museum, London

and

Victoria Oakley, Head of Ceramics and Glass Conservation, Victoria and Albert Museum, London

Routledge
Taylor & Francis Group
LONDON AND NEW YORK

First published 1993
Paperback edition 1996

First published 1993 by Butterworth-Heinemann

This edition published 2011 by Routledge
2 Park Square, Milton Park, Abingdon, Oxfordshire OX14 4RN
711 Third Avenue, New York, NY 10017, USA

First issued in hardback 2016

Routledge is an imprint of the Taylor & Francis Group, an informa business

British Library Cataloguing in Publication Data
Buys, Susan
Conservation and Restoration of
Ceramics. – (Butterworth-Heinemann
Series in Conservation and Museology)
I. Title II. Oakley, Victoria III. Series
738.1

Library of Congress Cataloguing in Publication Data
Buys, Susan
The conservation and restoration of ceramics/Susan Buys,
Victoria Oakley.
p. cm. – (Butterworth-Heinemann series in conservation and
museology)
Includes bibliographical references and index.
ISBN 0 7506 3219 4
1. Pottery – Repairing. 2. Porcelain – Repairing. 1. Oakley,
Victoria. II. Title III. Series
NK4233.B89 1993
738. 1_8-dc20 93-23174
CIP

ISBN 13: 978-1-138-17333-0 (hbk)
ISBN 13: 978-0-7506-3219-5 (pbk)

Contents

Series editors' preface

The conservation of artefacts and buildings has a long history, but the positive emergence of conservation as a profession can be said to date from the foundation of the International Institute for the Conservation of Museum Objects (IIC) in 1950 (the last two words of the title being later changed to Historic and Artistic Works) and the appearance soon after in 1952 of its journal *Studies in Conservation*. The role of the conservator as distinct from those of the restorer and the scientist had been emerging during the 1930s with a focal point in the Fogg Art Museum, Harvard University, which published the precursor to *Studies in Conservation, Technical Studies in the Field of the Fine Arts* (1932–42).

UNESCO. through its Cultural Heritage Division and its publications, had always taken a positive role in conservation and the foundation, under its auspices, of the International Centre for the Study of the Preservation and the Resoration of Cultural Property (ICCROM), in Rome, was a further advance. The Centre was established in 1959 with the aims of advising internationally on conservation problems, co-ordinating conservation activators and establishing standards of training courses.

A significant confirmation of professional progress was the transformation at New York in 1966 of the two committees of the International Council of Museums (ICOM), one curatorial on the Care of Paintings (founded in 1949) and the other mainly scientific (founded in the mid 1950s) into the ICOM Committee for Conservation.

Following the Second International Congress of Architects in Venice in 1964 when the Venice Charter was promulgated, the International Council of Monuments and Sites (ICOMOS) was set up in 1965 to deal with archaeological, architectural and town planning questions, to schedule monuments and sites and to monitor relevant legislation.

From the early 1960s onwards, international congresses (and the literature emerging from them) held by IIC, ICOM, ICOMOS and ICCROM not only advanced the subject in its various technical specializations but also emphasized the cohesion of conservators and their subject as an interdisciplinary profession.

The use of the term *Conservation* in the title of this series refers to the whole subject of the care and treatment of valuable artefacts both movable and immovable, but within the discipline conservation has a meaning which is distinct from that of restoration. *Conservation* used in this specialized sense has two aspects: first, the control of the environment to minimize the decay of artefacts and materials; and, second, their treatment to arrest decay and to stabilize them where possible against further deterioration. Restoration is the continuation of the latter process, when conservation treatment is thought to be insufficient, to the extent of reinstating an object, without falsification, to a condition in which it can be exhibited.

In the field of conservation conflicts of values on aesthetic, historical, or technical grounds are often inevitable. Rival attitudes and methods inevitably arise in a subject which is still developing and at the core of these differences there is often a deficiency of technical knowledge. That is one of the principal *raisons d'être* of this series. In most of these matters ethical principles are the subject of much discussion, and generalizations cannot easily cover (say) buildings, furniture, easel paintings and waterlogged wooden objects.

A rigid, universally agreed principle is that all treatment should be adequately documented. There is also general agreement that structural and decorative falsification should be avoided. In addition there are three other principles which, unless there are overriding objections, it is generally agreed should be followed.

The first is the principle of the reversibility of processes, which states that a treatment should normally be such that the artefact can, if desired, be returned to its pre-treatment condition even after a long lapse of time. This principle is impossible to apply in some cases, for example where the survival of an artefact may depend upon an irreversible process. The second, intrinsic to the whole subject, is that as far as possible decayed parts of an artefact should be conserved and not replaced. The third is that the consequences of the ageing of the original materials (for example 'patina') should not normally be disguised or removed. This includes a secondary proviso that later accretions should not be retained under the guise of natural patina.

The authors of the volumes in this series give their views on these matters, where relevant, with reference to the types of material within their scope. They take into account the differences in approach to artefacts of essentially artistic significance and to those in which the interest is primarily historical, archaeological or scientific.

The volumes are unified by a systematic and balanced presentation of theoretical and practical material with, where necessary, an objective comparison of different methods and approaches. A balance has also been maintained between the fine (and decorative) arts, archaeology and architecture in those cases where the respective branches of the subject have common ground, for example in the treatment of stone and glass and in the control of the museum environment. Since the publication of the first volume it has been decided to include within the series related monographs and technical studies. To reflect this enlargement of its scope the series has been renamed the Butterworth-Heinemann Series in Conservation and Museology.

Though necessarily different in details of organization and treatment (to fit the particular requirements of the subject) each volume has the same general standard which is that of such training courses as those of the University of London Institute of Archaeology, The Victoria and Albert Museum, the Conservation Center, New York University, the Institute of Advanced Architectural Studies, York, and ICCROM.

The authors have been chosen from among the acknowledged experts in each field, but as a result of the wide areas of knowledge and technique covered even by the specialized volumes in this series, in many instances multi-authorship has been necessary.

With the existence of IIC, ICOM, ICOMOS and ICCROM, the principles and practice of conservation have become as internationalized as the problems. The collaboration of Consultant Editors will help to ensure that the practices discussed in this series will be applicable throughout the world.

Preface

Ceramics conservators are required to possess an increasingly wide range of specialist knowledge: not only on everyday treatment of damaged objects, but also on subjects such as packing and handling of objects, on display techniques, and on procedures to limit damage in emergency situations. The aim of this book is to bring together this information. It is not intended to be a manual of techniques, nor can it pretend to be an exhaustive survey of the materials and methods used by past and present ceramics conservators. What it does aim to do is to present an approach to ceramics conservation that is based on an understanding and appreciation of the ceramic medium, of the materials used in its treatment, and of the ways in which the two interact. In doing so, an attempt has been made to draw together a very wide range of information, and where the amount of detail given has for reasons of practicality been small, references to further reading have been selected.

The audience for this book is intended primarily to be working conservators and students of conservation. The behaviour and treatment of ceramics of all types are based on the same fundamental principles, and it is therefore intended that the contents should be of interest to those working in all sectors of the field of ceramics conservation. There has in the past been some divergence of opinion between conservators working in commercial practice and those working in museums and similar institutions. However, these differences are becoming less apparent owing to the possibilities presented by modern materials for more satisfactory repair and restoration, coupled with a more widespread respect for the integrity of the object. Information exchange, sadly lacking in the field in the past, is growing, and a list of bodies concerned with conservation has been given in Appendix I.

The book is divided into four parts. Part One covers material which should be given due consideration before contemplating active treatment. Treatment should always be assessed in the light of the characteristics of the object in question, and for this reason, chapters have been included on the technology and deterioration of ceramics. Following on from this, the implications of these characteristics for preventive conservation are discussed, and finally methods of examination and recording are surveyed.

Part Two covers active conservation methods, and begins with a review of past materials and techniques. Then, chapter by chapter, the different stages in the treatment sequence are considered. An attempt has been made to draw attention to the questions of why treatment should be carried out at all, what it is that treatment is intended to achieve, and the criteria on which the choice of treatment should be based. Many of the details of technique are modified and developed by individual conservators to suit the way in which they work and the particular job in hand, but a basic outline of techniques in general use has been given.

It is important that the practical chapters should be read in conjunction with Part 3, which covers some of the more technical details of the materials involved in treatment, and the equipment, including health and safety equipment, required for their use. Some understanding of the nature of treatment materials and their interaction with ceramic objects is important in order to allow proper assessment of the suitability of materials for particular purposes. For this reason care has been taken to explain some of the basic principles involved in the behaviour of these materials in terms which, it is hoped, those conservators without a scientific training will find easy to assimilate. At the same time, it is intended that the information will act as a useful aid to those conservators with more experience in this area. Doubtless, there are materials and techniques in use that we have failed to mention, or materials or reports of research that have become available since the time of writing. However, it is hoped that this book will give some guidance as to the questions that must be asked before adopting such materials and techniques for use. Manufacturers of materials and equipment are given in Appendix II.

The final two chapters of the book, in Part Four, are of particular relevance to conservators with responsibility for large collections. They give information on display treatments and on emergency procedures.

The authors would particularly like to acknowledge the contribution of Professor Henry Hodges to Chapters 1 and 2.

The authors would like to thank a number of colleagues for their support and encouragement, offers of information and comments on the manuscript, in particular Dr Jonathan Ashley-Smith, Glenn Benson, Sandra Davison, Ian Freestone, Fi Jordan, Judith Larney, Graham Martin, Boris Pretzel, Dr Phil Rogers, Wendy Walker and John Watt. They would also like to thank Charles Oakley and Paul Robins for their invaluable assistance with the illustrations.

Sources of illustrations (other than those by the authors) are stated in the captions. The authors are grateful for the kind permission granted to reproduce these illustrations, and would like particularly to acknowledge the Trustees and the Conservation Department of the Victoria and Albert Museum, London.

Part One

1

The technology of ceramics

It is widely quoted that pottery was one of the first synthetic materials made by man as a result of subjecting clay to fire in order to produce an artificial stone. The discovery that clay could be used for making objects can be traced back to before the Neolithic age. The earliest ceramic artifacts that have endured the test of time for thousands of years reflect the story of civilization and the societies that made them. In many parts of the world the techniques for making utilitarian pottery have changed little from the first primitive wares, while elsewhere they have developed into a highly sophisticated industry.

An introduction to the complex subject of ceramics technology would seem incomplete without some reference to earth, water, air and fire: the basic essentials from which ceramics are derived (Rado, 1969; Fraser, 1979; Casson, 1977). The earth is mixed with water to make it workable. The resulting form is then dried in air. Finally, in subjecting it to fire, the object becomes hard and durable. Of the four raw ingredients, earth and fire exert the most important influence on the final product. The earth, as clay, a deceptively simple material (Rhodes, 1977), can possess an infinite range of variables in its composition that undergo a complex series of alterations during heating. The huge legacy of ceramic art in museums and private collections testifies to the range of possibilities that the clay and heat in combination possess.

The making of *ceramics* has been defined as the art of forming permanent objects of usefulness and/or beauty by the heat treatment of earthy raw materials (Rhodes, 1977). The state of *permanence* requires some qualifying; the permanence applies only to the material itself and not the object it forms. Within the definition an enormous range of products can be included, such as those made for industrial, scientific, architectural, structural, electronic, domestic, cult, and decorative applications. However, in the context of this book the boundaries are set to include those ceramic artifacts of an aesthetic, historical, ethnographic and archaeological nature, not including glass or enamelled metals.

Although an appreciation of ceramic objects is enhanced by, but not necessarily dependent on, an awareness of the technology behind them (Charleston, 1981), to the ceramics conservator an understanding of the technology is vitally important. Just as the enormous range of aesthetic and physical qualities displayed by ceramics is directly linked to the way in which they were made, so too is their susceptibility to different types of damage and deterioration. The conservator should be able to understand and anticipate why certain types of damage affect some ceramics. Similarly, he/she should be able to base the selection of a treatment process on a sound knowledge of how the treatment may interact with the fabric of the object, and this can only be achieved through familiarization with the technology of the material.

Clay and its origins

Clay can be found in abundance on the earth's surface. It is the product of thousands of years of intensive geological weathering of the igneous and metamorphic rocks such as granite that predominate in the composition of the earth's crust. The action of hot gases focused on the hard igneous rock resulted in its decomposition to produce a softer rock, and eventually chemical and physical breakdown into a hydrated silicate of aluminium, a clay mineral (with a definable chemical formula) known as kaolinite ($Al_2O_3.2SiO_2.2H_2O$). Kaolinite is the main and most important of the clay minerals, though it is never found in a pure state. It is usually contaminated with other clays by impurities such as iron oxide, calcareous material and other mineral decomposition products of igneous rock including quartz (Hodges, 1964). Kaolinite has an ordered crystal structure, made up of comparatively large (1.0 micron) hexagonal, plate-like crystals arranged in stacks. Another important group of clay minerals is the montmorillonites derived from basaltic rather than granitic rocks. Their composition differs from kaolinite, the ratio of silica to alumina being doubled. In addition, they also contain various other oxides including magnesium, sodium, iron and calcium. The crystals in montmorillonite are extremely small and disordered, contributing to the high plasticity of the clay. Illite is a clay mineral derived mainly from the breakdown of micas and is relatively rich in potassium. It is common in many older sedimentary clays.

Clays can be classified in various ways, though the simplest is based on origin and divides them up as either *primary* or *secondary clays.*

Primary clays, or residual clays, are those which are found at the site of their formation. They are derived from rock that has been weathered by the action of groundwater, steam and gases. Typically, deposits of primary clay will occur as irregular pockets amongst the unchanged parent rock (Rhodes, 1977). Such deposits tend to be mixed with small fragments of unaltered rock producing a coarse texture and limited plasticity. However, once sorted from the rock fragments, primary clays can be very pure. An example is china clay which comprises 98% kaolinite, and bentonite which is derived from volcanic ash. Bentonite is often added to modern ceramic bodies to impart plasticity.

Most clays rarely remain at their site of origin and are usually transported thousands of miles by water, wind or ice. During their journey, these secondary or sedimentary clays, as they are known, are exposed to an intensive, prolonged weathering process that reduces the clay into smaller particles. By a natural sorting process, the finest particles are the last to be deposited in the lower reaches of rivers, lake beds or the sea. Many impurities, such as iron, organic matter, quartz and mica, are picked up along the way; consequently clays can vary greatly in composition. Usually they consist of disordered kaolinite mixed with other clay minerals and oxides. The oxides are responsible for producing a range of different colours. Because of their fine particle size, most secondary clays are much more plastic than primary clays. Amongst the secondary clays, examples include: ball clays, red clays, earthenware clays, marls and fire clays.

Clay bodies

Originally the potter would have relied on naturally occurring clays, making little or no additions to them. However, the demands which the potter or manufacturer makes on the clay usually necessitate the addition of other materials. Such clays that have been designed for a specific purpose are called *bodies.* The usual modern recipe for a clay body is based on a careful balance of clay, fillers and fluxes. However, outside China, fluxes were rarely added to clay before the post-medieval period. The clay imparts plasticity and workability, while the fillers contribute non-plastic materials that help with shape retention during firing, and the fluxes control the fusion or hardening point of the clay body during firing. Before the clay can be worked, a certain amount of preparation must take place. Adjustments may have to be made to the recipe in order to improve the clay. Following this, the natural weathering process is continued artificially, using such processes as grinding, sieving, settling, dewatering, kneading and pounding the clay.

Plasticity and fillers

The feature that distinguishes clay from other minerals formations is the extremely small size of the particles and their ability to adsorb water chemically. When fully wetted, each clay particle becomes covered with a layer of moisture. Because of their flat shape, the moisture, known as the *water of plasticity*, causes the particles to adhere, and at the same time allows them to be moved over one another in response to pressure. In this way, the whole mass of particles provides a material that is plastic and capable of holding its shape after being deformed by pressure.

The plasticity of clay is related to its water content. If the moisture is allowed to evaporate the mass of particles becomes progressively more rigid until it can no longer be modelled (Figure 1.1). At the same time, because so much of the mass of clay is made up of water, it will shrink as it dries. Depending on the type of clay and the particle size, shrinkage can be between 5 and 17% (Rhodes, 1977; Casson, 1977). If drying is too rapid, warping and cracking may occur. To get round this problem, the clay is mixed with sand-sized material that will make the mixture more porous and will at the same time adsorb less water on the surfaces of its particles than clay would. These materials, usually called *fillers*, may include sand, finely ground rocks and shells, and even comminuted pottery, known as *grog*. Quite apart from opening up the body, these fillers may enter into the chemical structure of the wares during firing. Some fillers, such as sand may already be naturally mixed with the clay.

As a result of being hydrated, the clay particles possess a polarity, their surfaces being covered with

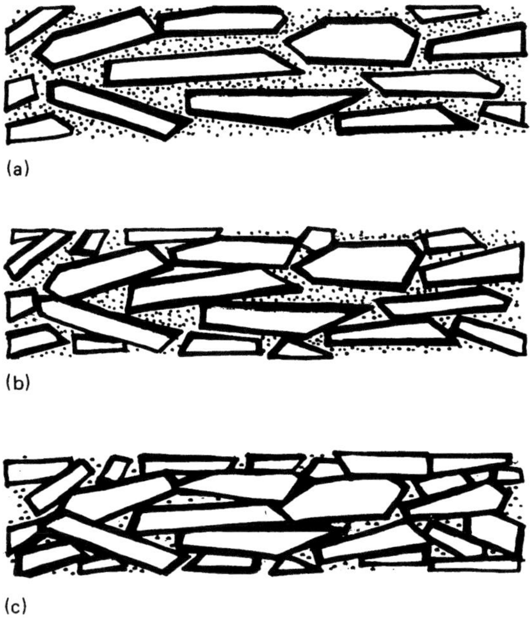

Figure 1.1 (a) Water acts as a lubricant between clay particles, making the clay soft and pliable. (b) As the water evaporates the particles are drawn closer together, producing increased friction and the clay becomes leather-hard. (c) When most of the water has evaporated, the particles can no longer move, and the resulting effect is hard, dry clay.

strong negative charges. Consequently, if the clay is mixed into water containing an alkali, the negative hydroxyl ions in the solution prevent the particles from coagulating and they will remain in suspension. In an acidic solution, however, the hydrogen ions will serve as links between the negative surfaces of the particles and they will coalesce and flocculate. Hence by adding an acidic material, as for example humus, the clay can be made more plastic, while an excessively plastic clay can be rendered less so by adding an alkaline substance such as sodium bicarbonate.

Contaminants

Naturally occurring clays are usually contaminated, most commonly with compounds of iron, usually in the hydrated state. Hence the presence of hydrated iron oxide (Fe_2O_3) gives many clays a characteristic yellow ochre colour; when heated it becomes sufficiently dehydrated and takes on the typical red colour. The presence of carbonaceous matter, generally decayed plant materials, may give some clays a very dark grey, brown or black colour. On firing, this carbon may burn out resulting in a body that is virtually white, as is the case with ball clays obtained from beneath coal measures. Some contaminants are less benign and may cause severe problems. In most kiln-fired pottery clays containing limestone or calcite inclusions (calcium carbonate $CaCO_3$), the marls, can only be used if the limestone is present as very small particles, in which case it will be rendered inert by reaction with the decomposing clay or flux. The mineral is converted to calcium oxide or calcia (CaO) during firing, releasing carbon dioxide (CO_2), and will later, months after firing, absorb water from the environment to become calcium hydroxide ($Ca(OH)_2$). If the particles are large enough, the hydration, which is accompanied by expansion, may be sufficient to push a flake of fired clay out of the pottery surface or even break the piece. Similarly, clay contaminated with fragments of plaster of Paris during shaping will suffer disruption. Such problems were usually avoided in prehistoric pottery which was fired at low temperatures so that calcite fillers like shells did not decompose.

Fluxes

In order to decrease the firing temperatures of the clay body, fluxes may be added. These form viscous liquids at high temperatures, combining with other materials such as quartz, and then cool to give glasses or glass-like materials. Examples include alkaline earth metal oxides and feldspathic materials. Calcite or whiting (calcium carbonate $CaCO_3$) in a very finely divided form can also be used as a flux.

Forming processes

There are many techniques that may be employed in making ceramic objects. They range from the most primitive methods to highly mechanized industrial processes.

The simplest way of making a vessel form is to take a ball of soft clay in one hand, and make a series of even pinches outwards from the centre while rotating the form. The hollow shape, or *pinch pot* (Figure 1.2), will have a crude and irregular finish. *Coiling* is a progression from pinching and involves forming the walls of a vessel shape using a series of clay coils. The starting point is usually a flattened pad of clay. The coils are rolled out on a flat board and gradually built up, winding round and round (Figure 1.3). Irregularities may be scraped away later using a flattened tool

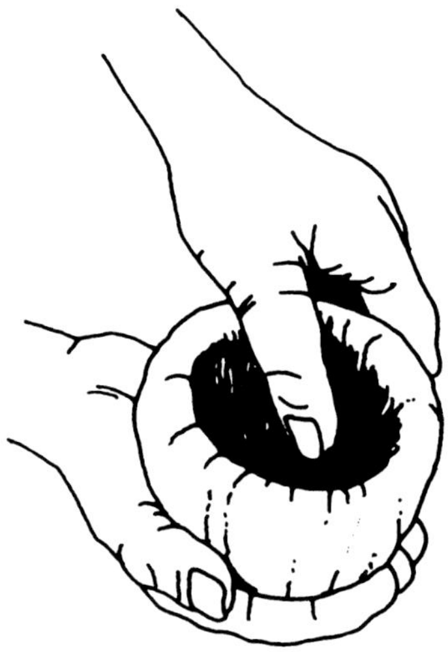

Figure 1.2 Making a simple pinch pot.

Figure 1.4 Slab building.

Figure 1.3 Coiling a pot.

or *rib*. Both pinching and coiling techniques are used to make utilitarian wares and sculptural forms.

If flat sheets of clay are rolled out, or sliced from a lump of clay, then built up to make a form, the technique is known as *slab building* (Figure 1.4). The success of the method relies on making the slabs when the clay is at the right state of plasticity. They must be allowed to dry slightly, to a *leather-hard* or *cheese-hard* consistency, before joining. In order to ensure the joins do not separate and crack during firing, the edges must be scored with a point, then wetted with slurry of clay mixed with water to cement the two parts, which are then *luted* together.

For thousands of years the technique of *press moulding* has been employed to mass produce a shape (Kingery and Vandiver, 1986). Clay is pressed into moulds made from an absorbent material such as low-fired unglazed (i.e. *biscuit*) clay, plaster of Paris, or wood. After trimming away any surplus, the clay is left in place until dried to leather-hard stage, after which shrinkage facilitates its removal. Complex forms can be assembled from a series of moulds by joining and adding pieces.

The development of press moulding techniques into a mechanized process is represented by *jiggering* and *jollying* (Figure 1.5). For making circular or cylindrical forms (such as flat ware or hollow ware respectively), a mould roughly lined with clay is rotated while a template is gradually brought towards the mould, squeezing away excess clay (Hodges, 1964).

Another type of moulding technique involves pouring a homogeneous mixture of clay or *slip* into an absorbent mould. As the water is drawn from the slip into the plaster, or biscuit clay, a thick layer of clay builds up on the inner surface of the mould. When the desired thickness has been reached, the remaining liquid slip is poured away. Complex hollow forms such as figurines can be made using the technique which is known as *slip casting*. Moulds may be made up of several pieces in order to accommodate undercuts. Components may be slip cast individually, then luted together later.

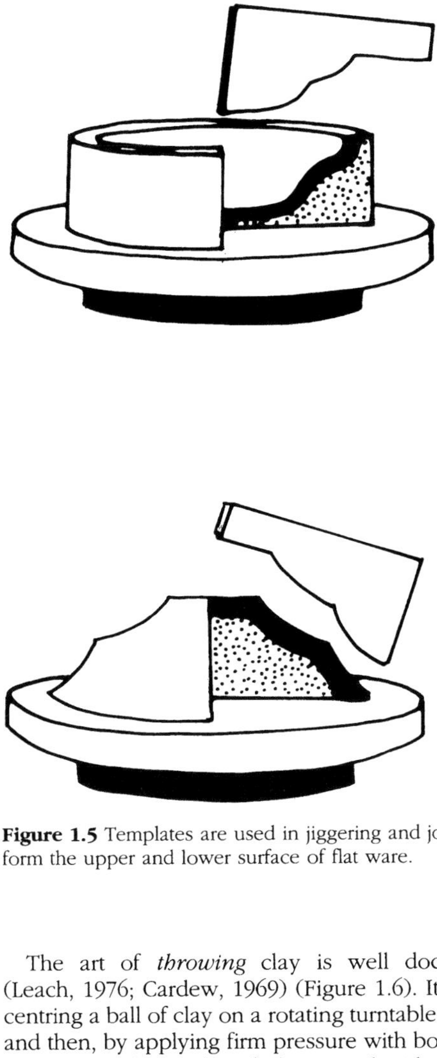

Figure 1.5 Templates are used in jiggering and jollying to form the upper and lower surface of flat ware.

Figure 1.6 Throwing a pot.

The art of *throwing* clay is well documented (Leach, 1976; Cardew, 1969) (Figure 1.6). It involves centring a ball of clay on a rotating turntable or wheel and then, by applying firm pressure with both hands, pulling up the walls of the vessel aided by the centrifugal force. Individual potters develop distinct styles and variations in their technique. The basic vessel form may be manipulated to give a range of flat and hollow shapes to which additions such as handles and spouts may be added.

Drying and finishing

It is important that most of the water content of the clay has evaporated prior to firing, otherwise steam trapped in the pores of the body may blow the pot apart. Evaporation takes place at the surface, water being drawn by capillary action from the interior of the pot. Gradually the particles shrink closer together to fill most of the spaces formerly occupied by water, until a point is reached when no more water can escape. At this stage the clay consists of a dry open framework. Some water will remain trapped in the pores and also as a film of water molecules on the surface of the clay particles.

Drying may have to be interrupted in order to *finish* the pottery. In some cases finishing may be minimal, while in others it may be quite complex. For simple pinched or coiled pots the finishing may involve scraping away all the irregularities to give a smooth and even surface. Moulded pieces that are made up of several parts can only be put together after the clay has been allowed to dry to a stage when it may be easily handled. Once the pieces are joined, seams and edges will have to be trimmed and smoothed off. Thrown pots may require some further refining by removing any excess from the outside in a process called *turning*. This involves inverting the pot on the wheel trimming away excess clay with a sharp tool, as the pot revolves to form a foot rim on the base. Handles, spouts and knobs may be luted on at this point.

The application of some types of decoration may also interrupt the drying process, utilizing the plastic condition of the clay. By incising, carving or impressing the surface, using whatever tools or objects are to hand, an enormous variety of effects can be achieved. Different coloured clays can be inlaid into grooves or impressions made in the surface (Figure 1.7). Clay shapes may also be moulded and applied onto the surface to produce a raised decoration known as *sprigging*. Slips or *engobes* can be used to coat the semi-dry pot and, depending on

Figure 1.7 A detail of inlaid white slip on a Korean box cover, partly obscured by the overlying celadon glaze (Victoria and Albert Museum, London).

Figure 1.9 A detail of sgraffito decoration where a pattern has been scratched into a layer of slip exposing the underlying body colour (Victoria and Albert Museum, London).

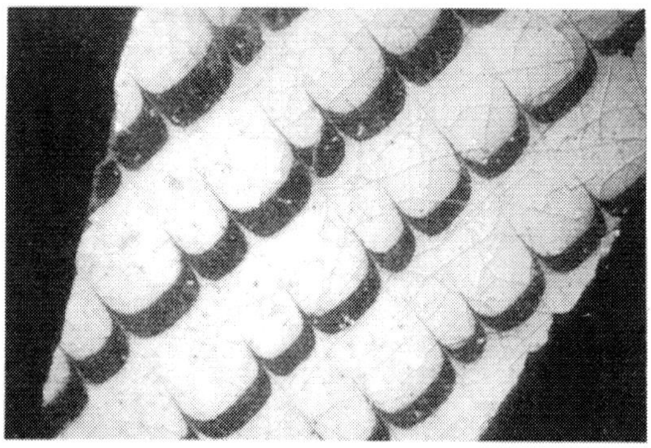

Figure 1.8 A detail of combed slip decoration on earthenware. Bands of a contrasting dark-coloured slip have been combed across the underlying slip (Victoria and Albert Museum, London).

how they are applied, whether dipped, poured or painted, different surfaces can be produced. Slips of an appropriate consistency may be used rather like icing, in order to *pipe* and *trail* lines onto the surface. Contrasting colours can be *combed* (Figure 1.8), or partially mixed at random to give swirled or *marbled* effects. *Sgraffito* is where designs are scratched through a layer of slip into the underlying body (Figure 1.9).

Firing

Although the composition of the body is the major factor in deciding the nature of manufactured wares, the *firing cycle* is of equal importance. The term 'firing cycle' implies the sequence of events from the time the raw bodies are set in the kiln, to the moment the fired objects are withdrawn. The term also encompasses the time taken to cool the kiln, the rate of temperature change, the position of the wares and any atmospheric changes that occur within the kiln. Clearly, there may be many variations in the cycle between the production of one vessel and another, but in general a number of events and stages will follow one another in sequence (Figure 1.10). An object may undergo a number of separate firings in order to achieve a certain decorative effect. The first firing or *biscuit firing* will generally be followed by a *glaze firing*, then a succession of lower-temperature firings may be necessary in order to achieve different effects such as enamels, lustres and gilding (Hamer and Hamer, 1986). It should be remembered however that before the medieval period glazed pottery was rare outside China.

With modern studio and industrial ceramics the initial rate of temperature increase is kept below 60°C per hour, in order to allow the remaining water trapped in the pores to escape gradually. Too rapid an increase may result in the sudden production of steam and could burst the body. By the time the boiling point of water is reached, most of this moisture should have evaporated. Subsequently the water adsorbed on the surfaces of the particles is driven off, again slowly. On reaching 200°C all this water should have been eliminated. Any organic material derived from vegetation should also start to break down at this stage.

Between 400°C and 600°C the chemically combined water that forms part of the molecular structure of clay is given off. The temperature increase must be gradual (100°C per hour) to prevent rapid evolution of steam and consequential damage of the object. After 500°C has been passed dehydration of the clay will be complete. The clay will now be irreversibly altered, having undergone the *ceramic change*, and

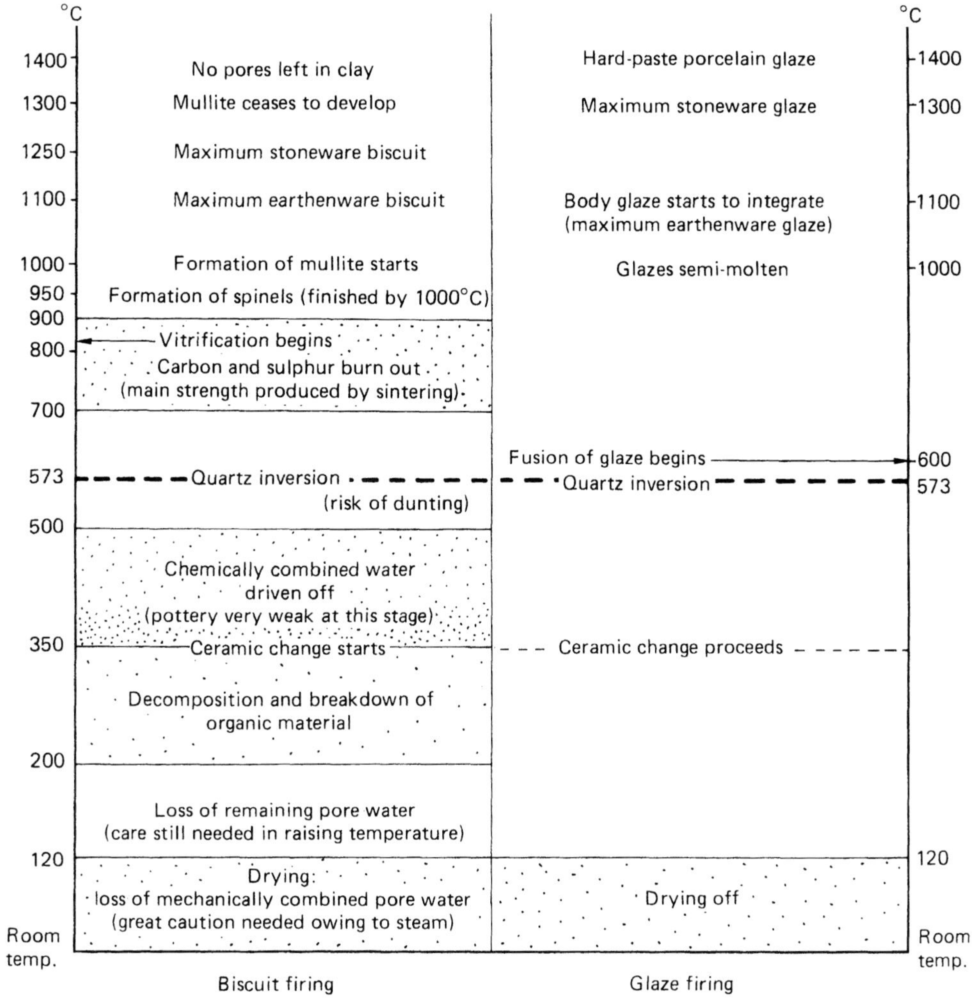

Figure 1.10 Example of possible sequences of changes that occur in kaolinitic stoneware or porcelain clay bodies during firing.

will no longer disintegrate or slake in water. In theory, the dried clay particles will be just touching each other at a few points of contact, fastened together by the process called *sintering* (Figure 1.11). Although no shrinkage will have occurred, the clay body will now be extremely fragile and porous. Somewhere between 700°C and 900°C carbon and sulphur contained in the body will *burn out* with the creation of dioxide and trioxide gases (CO, CO_2, SO, SO_2, SO_3). These are derived from carbonate and sulphate impurities, and also the organic carbon that does not burn off at lower temperatures. It is important that the burning out process is completed with no carbon or sulphur remaining, otherwise *bloating* may occur at a later stage in the firing as the trapped gases attempt to escape causing blister-like formations.

Every time a pot undergoes heating or cooling a reversible alteration occurs at 573°C, at which point any quartz present in the body will undergo inversion. This involves a molecular rearrangement in its crystalline structure, resulting in a slight increase in volume (2%), or shrinkage of the same amount on cooling; cracking or *dunting* may occur unless the temperature is carefully controlled. This is the commonest cause of cracks during firing (Rhodes, 1977). Between 600°C and 800°C calcite (calcium carbonate $CaCO_3$) is converted to quicklime (calcium oxide CaO) and essentially all the iron in the body is by now oxidized to anhydrous red iron oxide (Fe_2O_3). The body may have shrunk, and will have attained maximum porosity. Consequently wares allowed to cool from this temperature (800°C to 900°C) will be as

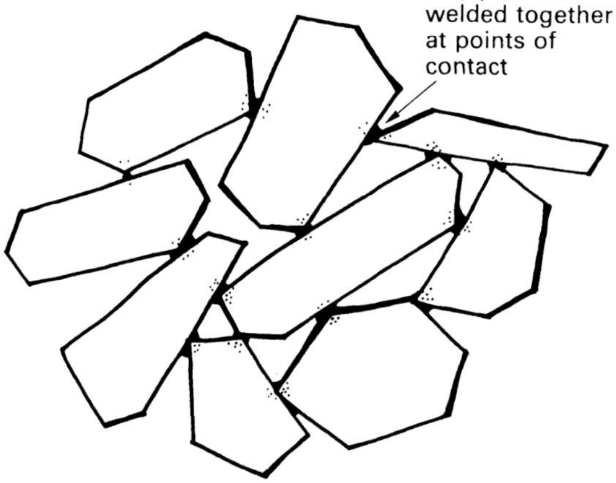

Figure 1.11 Sintering: the clay particles are secured to each other at points of contact. Although the pot is extremely fragile at this stage, sintering provides enough support to hold the object together.

red as all the iron compounds in the body allow and highly porous. Biscuit firings tend to be within the range 950°C to 1100°C, depending on the properties of the body and the strength required.

Vitrification starts to occur around 800°C as the fluxes and free silica in the clay body start to melt and fuse. If this were allowed to progress indefinitely, the body would eventually fuse completely to form a glass. At 950°C the formation of *spinels* starts; these are the double oxides of various metals, usually magnesium, iron and aluminium, derived from the clay matter. They are short-lived in the firing sequence, and by 1000°C they have been totally absorbed into the subsequently formed glass. They are of relevance in this context since their presence in a mineralogical section can sometimes indicate the firing temperature of the wares from which the sample was taken.

From now on as the temperature increases, the fusible components of the clay body continue to melt, filling the pores and dissolving the particles that they surround. In stoneware and porcelain clays the formation of the mineral *mullite* starts at about 1000°C within the amorphous regions caused by the decomposition of the clay minerals. Mullite, alumino-silicate ($3Al_2O_3.2SiO_2$), forms as sub-microscopic needle-shaped crystals that grow and elongate within the glassy matrix knitting the structure together and strengthening it. By 1300°C this metamorphosis is complete, and even if the temperature were raised slightly further there would be no change in the mullite. The body now shrinks dramatically and at the same time the open pores of the original body gradually become closed, so that by the time the temperature reaches 1250°C no pores remain open.

Wares fired above 1250°C, the hard porcelains, are thus non-porous and their bodies may be seen largely as a mass of glass supported by crystals of mullite. Wares fired around 1100°C are generally not very porous and vary from white earthenwares to stonewares and soft-paste porcelains. There are, however, exceptions. Bone china, for example, is made with a body containing a high proportion of bone ash (up to 50%), which is essentially a phosphate of calcium. During firing the other ingredients, kaolin and feldspar, tend to form a glassy matrix, while the bone ash provides long slender crystals of tricalcium phosphate ($Ca_3(PO_4)_2$) which behave as a support for the body in a similar way to mullite in other wares.

So far consideration has only been given to a firing sequence where oxygen is present in the kiln. If the oxygen supply is decreased, two important factors come into play. First, the fuel may not be fully consumed and the kiln atmosphere may contain a lot of smoke, which may be deposited as soot on surfaces in the kiln. To avoid this, pottery may be enclosed in fire clay boxes, *saggars*, to prevent penetration of soot and ash. In addition, any organic matter in the body of the wares may not be fully consumed if the oxygen supply is too low, resulting in free carbon being retained as a *black core* within the ware (Figure 1.12).

The second important phenomenon induced by a low supply of oxygen is the chemical reduction of some ingredients of the bodies. Red iron oxide (Fe_2O_3), for example, may be reduced to the black iron oxide (Fe_3O_4) to a point where an otherwise red-bodied ware may become completely blackened, though strengthened by the fluxing action of the monovalent iron. In any but the crudest of structures it is possible to control the kiln atmosphere by opening or closing the vents so that the atmosphere may be oxidizing or reducing at will; this has allowed the

Figure 1.12 Detail of black core exposed within the break edge of a damaged earthenware tile (the material on the upper edge is discoloured old adhesive) (Victoria and Albert Museum, London).

production of some interesting colour contrasts, as for example classical Greek red and black wares.

Glazes

A glaze is little more than a thin layer of glass that has been fired onto the surface of the ware. It has three main functions: to strengthen the pottery, to provide an impermeable hygienic coating and to decorate the surface (Hamer and Hamer, 1986). Like glass, a glaze will contain glass-forming materials, fluxes and stabilizers. The most important glass-forming material is silica (SiO_2), which is usually derived from flint, feldspar or china clay. The fluxes, such as oxides of sodium, potassium, calcium, magnesium and lead, are added to lower the melting point of the glass-forming oxides. The glaze stabilizer is most commonly alumina (aluminium oxide Al_2O_3). Other metallic elements may be added to produce colours (Green, 1963; Shaw, 1971).

From a functional and practical point of view it is important that the glaze and body have comparable rates of thermal expansion. The *glaze-fit*, as it is known, is determined by its composition; each component has a direct effect on the expansion rate depending on the amount present. In general it is usual for there to be some stress between the glaze and body, and preferably for the glaze to be under compression. Where the relationship is not balanced, faults such as crazing, dunting and shivering may occur (see Chapter 2).

In practice, either glazes are made raw, where ingredients are ground together, suspended in water and applied to the surfaces of the wares; or they may be produced as frits, in which case the ingredients are heated until fused to form a glass and then cooled, ground to a powder and suspended in water prior to application. There are also exceptions to this general outline in which silica in the body provides the quartz of the glaze. For instance lead compounds, such as the red or yellow oxides, are sometimes applied directly to the surfaces of the dried unfired vessels. On firing, the lead forms a glaze with the silica in the body. In a similar way *salt glazes* are achieved by throwing common salt into the kiln. At high temperatures the salt volatilizes and ionizes, the sodium ions forming a glaze by reacting with the body at the surface of the pottery. Such salt glazes are often characterized by an *orange peel* appearance (Figure 1.13) .

Glaze colourants

The colour associated with glazes is achieved using a relatively small number of metallic compounds, the metallic ions generally being responsible for the colours. The behaviour of these metallic compounds – in various concentrations, under different firing conditions and temperatures, in association with other materials – produces a surprising range of effects. Five such colourants, iron, copper, cobalt, manganese and antimony, were known from antiquity, and until the range of colourants was dramatically increased in the nineteenth century, some colours were difficult to achieve. A good red colour was one of these, and copper could be made to yield a *sang-de-boeuf* only under severe reducing conditions during the cycle. In oxidizing conditions moderate amounts of iron would give yellow through ochres and browns to black (e.g. temmoku) depending on the concentration used. A bright yellow, although somewhat opaque, could also be achieved using antimony, provided the glaze contained lead, the colourant being in fact a very fine dispersion of lead antimonate. Similarly, for greens, around 3% of copper in a lead glaze would give a leaf green, while in a sodium or potassium glaze the resulting colour would be a bright turquoise-blue. The common colourant for blue was cobalt, while manganese gave mauves and purples, depending upon the quantity present. Black glazes were made by using various admixtures of cobalt, iron and manganese, while an opaque white resulted from a very fine dispersion of tin oxide in the glaze.

The eighteenth century saw the introduction of several important new colouring materials, principally oxides of chromium and nickel. Undoubtedly the most important of these is chromium oxide (Cr_2O_3) since it can be made to yield red, yellow, pink, brown or green glazes, depending on the glaze composition and the firing temperatures. Nickel oxide (NiO), while less versatile, is mainly used to make bright colours more sober. Other red and yellow colourants such as vanadium, selenium, titanium and cadmium are of

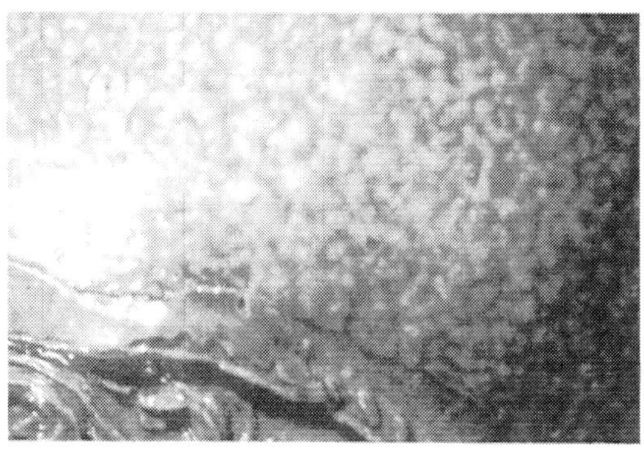

Figure 1.13 Detail of salt-glazed stoneware, showing the typical orange peel textured surface (Victoria and Albert Museum, London).

more recent introduction, as too is the use of uranium which provides a vivid yellow.

There are a number of ways in which these colourants may be applied. They may be painted directly to the surface of the wares before glazing as *underglaze colours* (Figure 1.14), or they may be incorporated in the glaze composition to produce a glaze stain or *in-glaze colour* (Figure 1.15). Alternatively, the colourant may be prepared with a frit or low-firing glaze, and applied on the already glazed surface of the ware as an *enamel* (Figure 1.16). Such *on-glaze* or *overglaze colours* are fired to relatively low temperatures around 750°C.

Colours that are applied under the glaze are less vulnerable to deterioration, since the overlying glaze must be destroyed before they are attacked. In contrast, enamels may have very poor adhesion to the glaze if the firing is inadequate and the decoration may spall away easily. Some enamels may prove to be too soft for practical purposes, making them prone to abrasion; while others may be chemically too reactive and readily attacked, for example, by alkaline cleaning materials. The low temperatures to which enamels are fired allows a wider range of colours.

Originally enamel colours were applied with a brush, as frits suspended in oil. The labour intensive nature of the technique led to the development, from the mid eighteenth century, of *transfer printing*, a process that lent itself to cheap mass production. A transfer would be made by *inking* an etched copper plate with the finely ground frit in oil, printing the image from the plate onto specially prepared paper, and then transferring this to the surface of the object. At first only a single colour was used (Figure 1.17), but by the middle of the nineteenth century full colour printing, using as many as five different etched plates, came into use.

Lustres are another type of on-glaze decoration, resulting from a low-temperature reduction firing of compounds containing copper, tin, silver, bismuth,

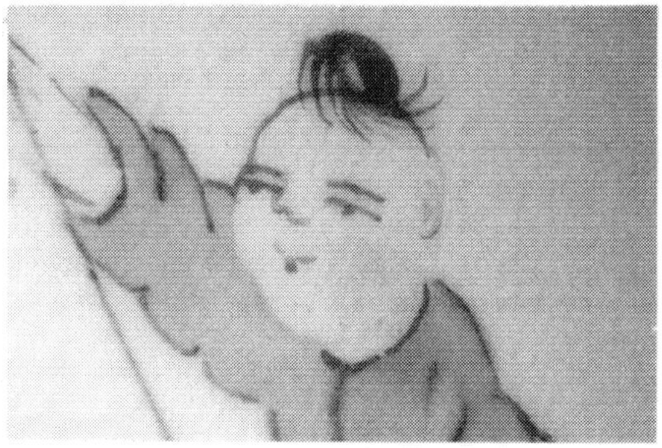

Figure 1.16 Detail of enamel decoration, fired on or over the glaze. The enamel firing is at a much lower temperature than the previous glaze firing (Victoria and Albert Museum, London).

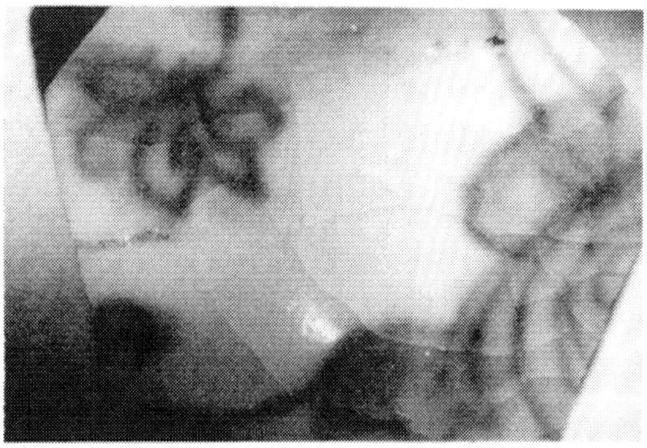

Figure 1.14 Detail of underglaze cobalt blue decoration on a fragment of oriental porcelain. The decoration would have been applied before the object was coated in glaze and fired.

Figure 1.15 Detail of in-glaze colour on a tin-glazed earthenware tile. The oxides would have been painted directly onto the freshly applied glaze surface prior to firing (Victoria and Albert Museum, London).

Figure 1.17 Detail of transfer printing on an earthenware dish (Victoria and Albert Museum, London).

gold or platinum. The end product is a very thin vulnerable film of metal overlying and adhering to the glaze. The Persian lustre wares are the result of the application of preparations containing metallic salts fired in a very strong reducing atmosphere. Copper will produce red, salmon or gold colours; gold produces reddish purple; silver yields yellowish or ivory lustres; and bismuth gives an iridescent quality to the glaze. Lustres may also be fired in an oxidation kiln, in which the colloidal metal or metallic salts are present as a suspension in a resin or oil. Carbon from the resin and oil reduces the metal which is then deposited as a thin layer.

Early examples of the use of gold as decorative on-glaze decoration have rarely survived. Until the first quarter of the eighteenth century the only gilding practised was leaf gilding, a technique comparable to the gilding of wood or manuscripts, not involving a firing stage. During the following century, a number of variants of this technique were introduced, using either ground gold leaf or a granular gold precipitated from a solution of its salts. Honey gilding was a technique in which honey was mixed with gold leaf or powder gold in order to grind up and disperse the gold particles. The gold was washed and mixed with a flux and gum prior to application and then fired. The resulting gilding, which was dull and rich in appearance, was popular at Sèvres and Chelsea. Mercuric gilding involved the use of an amalgam of mercury and gold; during a low firing the mercury would vaporize leaving a thin gold layer which could be burnished to a brassy finish. Another approach involved the use of a precipitation technique with a solution of mercurous nitrate. A far better method appeared in the early nineteenth century when it was found that a liquid preparation, previously used to produce a pink lustre, could in greater concentration give a more durable gilding (Figure 1.18). The mixture consisted of a solution of gold chloride in *balsam of sulphur* (the product of a reaction of sulphur with turpentine). The method in a more refined form is still used today, though for superior quality the use of precipitated gold powder combined with a mercury compound is still favoured (Hunt, 1980; Savage and Newman, 1976).

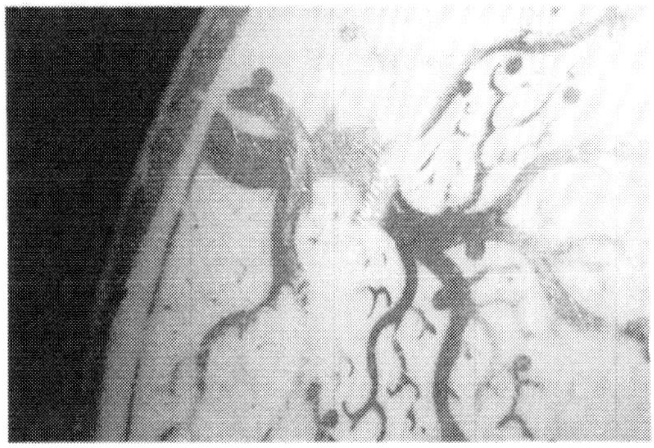

Figure 1.18 Detail of gilded decoration on the surface of a dish. The thin layer of metal is very vulnerable to abrasion (Victoria and Albert Museum, London).

Wares

One of the more confusing aspects of the study of pottery can be the wide range of ways in which various wares may be described. Thus the same vessel might be variously noted as earthenware, slipped ware, sgraffito ware, or lead-glazed ware, all of which terms may be technically correct. Furthermore, vessels made by the same techniques may be distinguished by the area from which they come, as for example Garrus ware, or by naming the makers, such as Pennsylvania Dutch ware. However in this context only the technical aspects of such nomenclature will be considered.

Wares described by shape

The simplest of these definitions must be the distinction between *hollow* and *flat wares*: flat wares being essentially flat (plates and saucers) and hollow wares having some volumetric capacity (cups and bowls). Hollow wares may be further subdivided into *open* and *closed wares*: open wares being those in which the aperture is the widest part of the vessel, and closed wares being those in which the widest part of the vessel is below the aperture (flasks, bottles and most jars).

Wares described by clay body

The term *pottery* is generally used to include all the wares derived from clay (Casson, 1977), although amongst the literature there appears to be much confusion as to whether pottery includes just earthenware (Rado, 1969) or both earthenwares and stonewares (Payton and Payton, 1981). The common major categories of ware used by most authorities are those of earthenwares, stonewares, and porcelains (Tables 1.1, 1.2). Archaeologists may choose to use texture or the size of inhomogeneities as a means of distinguishing *coarseware* from *fineware*.

Earthenware

Generally earthenware bodies are distinguished from those of stonewares by possessing a porosity of more than 5%. This is usually the result of a biscuit firing at temperatures up to 1150°C where there is a glaze, followed by a glost firing at temperatures generally

Table 1.1 General categories of earthenware (porosity >5%)

General type	*Characteristics*	*Average firing temperatures (°C)* *Biscuit*	*Glaze*	*Examples*
Raku	Porous body due to low firing temperature. Body contains much grog and fire clay in order to withstand the thermal shock of the rapid uneven glaze firing.	900 +	750–1000	Japanese tea bowls, some studio pottery, and other ceramics of ethnic origin
Common pottery	Usually made from impure clays which produce a porous, light ware, demanding thick walls to give added strength. Colours range through buff, grey, red-brown, and dark brown	600–950	800–1100	Includes unglazed ancient and primitive wares, medieval wares, some Staffordshire pottery slipwaie and also some studio ceramics, amongst others
Terracotta	Technically a type of common pottery. The word 'terracotta' is derived from the Italian for fired earth. Loosely includes unglazed low-fired bodies made from grey- or buff-coloured clay firing to red, though also includes red clays and cream firing clays	750–1050	Usually unglazed	Generally associated with sculpted and modelled clay as well as ancient Greek and Roman pottery
Tin-glazed earthenware	Low-fired, porous, soft body, coated with a lead glaze opacified with tin oxide. The unfired glaze surface is then painted with different metal oxides which fuse and blend into the glaze during firing. The body is usually of a marl or malm calcareous clay	850–1000	850–1000	*Majolica* Italian tin-glazed wares, usually with polychrome decoration. The name is derived from the route via which the technique arrived in Italy: from the Near East, then Spain and lastly Majorca *Faience* Tin-glazed earthenware usually from France, Germany or Scandinavia; originally imitating wares from Faenza in northern Italy *Delft* Traditionally a cobalt blue decoration on a white ground first made by migrant Italian potters working in Delft in the Netherlands. English delftware was made at Lambeth, Bristol and Liverpool
Fine earthenware	Usually white or off-white porous body with glazes commonly containing lead oxide. The advent of transfer printing in the mid eighteenth century lent itself to this type of popular ware	1050–1150	900–1050	*Creamware* Earthenware body with a butter-coloured lead glaze, developed in the early eighteenth century in England. The body (typically: china clay 25%, ball clay 25%, flint 35%, Cornish stone 15%) was very porous, light and fine (e.g. Wedgwood, Leeds, Whieldon) *Pearlware* Introduced early in the eighteenth century; similar body to creamware, though more durable (with additional flint and china clay). The glaze has a hint of cobalt imparting a blue tint (e.g. Liverpool, Wedgwood). Other examples: Minton and Spode

Table 1.2 General categories of stoneware and porcelain (porosity <5%)

General type	*Characteristics*	*Average firing temperatures (°C)* *Biscuit*	*Glaze*	*Examples*
Stoneware	Hard, durable, vitrified body with low porosity. Body and glaze mature at the same temperature producing a well developed glaze–body layer. Can be made from naturally occurring clays that are rich in fluxes, or from other clays modified by the addition of fluxes	950–1000	1200–1300	*Salt-glazed stoneware* has single firing at about 1150°C. The glaze is deposited as a result of vapourized salt in the kiln combining with the clay body at the surface of the pot Other examples include: ovenware, red stoneware, black basalt, jasper and some studio ceramics
Semi-vitreous and vitreous china	Basically a fine earthenware-type body with increased amounts of flux. Dense, though slightly translucent, off-white-colour, with a slightly granular fracture. The relatively low-fired glaze is soft and liable to scratching	1100–1200	950–1100	Examples include: ironstone china, flintware and white granite
Bone china	The body typically contains 50% bone ash; the remaining ingredients added in equal proportions include china clay and Cornish stone. The bone can act as a flux or a refractory depending on the amount added and the other ingredients present. The body is pure white and translucent. It is softer than hard-paste porcelain, and more durable than soft-paste porcelain	1250	900–1100	In England during the middle of the eighteenth century, Thomas Frye patented the recipe for a body that included the addition of a small amount of calcined bone as a flux. Bow was the first factory to include it in a porcelain body, then Chelsea, Derby and Worcester. The typical recipe, where half the body consists of bone ash, was developed subsequently by Josiah Spode II in the late eighteenth century Other examples include: Minton, Crown Derby and Doulton
Soft-paste porcelain	Consists of a brittle body with a high flux content which allows a lower firing temperature than that of hard-paste. The body is more porous than the hard paste, with colour varying from a translucent white to yellow, orange or brown. It fractures with a grainy sugary texture	900–1000	900–1250	Towards the end of the sixteenth century the Medici factory in Florence developed a porcelainous body with a high silica and alkali content. A similar recipe was adopted in Rouen, France (1673), then spread to St Cloud and Sèvres, and finally to England: Bow, Derby and Chelsea (amongst others) also explored its use
Hard-paste porcelain	Smooth, white, glossy, high-fired non-porous body with a glassy conchoidal fracture. The classical composition is 50%. Kaolin (white china clay), 25% feldspar and 25% quartz or flint	900–1000	1250–1400	First made in China, then developed in Europe at Meissen (1709), from where it slowly spread to the rest of Europe Examples include: Meissen, New Hall, Coalport and Spode

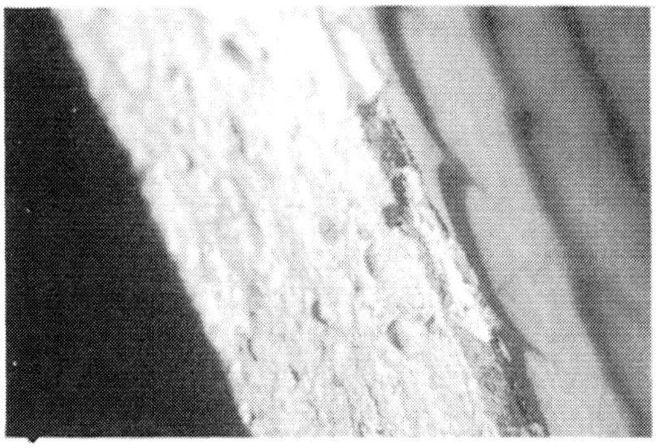

Figure 1.19 Detail of a broken edge on a piece of earthenware. The body is coarse with open pores and small coloured inclusions. The layers of slip and glaze are visible as distinct layers (Victoria and Albert Museum, London).

Figure 1.20 Detail of a broken edge on a stoneware fragment with an overlying celadon glaze. The body is more vitrified than that of earthenware, although there are still pores visible. The overlying celadon glaze is closely attached to the body (Victoria and Albert Museum, London).

below 1100°C. The lower temperatures produce a *softer* glaze and a greater range of colours. The bond between the glaze and underlying body is often poorly developed with the glaze appearing as a distinct layer in section (Figure 1.19). Earthenware bodies are generally derived from naturally occurring common clays. Other materials may be added to improve both the working and firing properties. Depending on the constituents, a range of colours including cream, yellow, buff, grey, red and brown will result after firing. Earthenwares include raku, slipware, majolica, faience, creamware and terracottas.

Stoneware

Stoneware bodies are fired to temperatures within the range 1200°C to about 1300°C, depending on the amount of flux, resulting in a vitrified almost impermeable body that is hard and strong. The body is usually grey, buff or brown in colour being composed mainly of naturally occurring clays, such as ball clay or fire clay, and modified according to the potter's requirements (Fraser, 1979). The body and glaze are usually fused in close association with a distinct body–glaze layer (Figure 1.20) an exception being salt glaze.

Semi-vitreous and vitreous chinas

The semi-vitreous and vitreous chinas slot into the sequence somewhere between the stonewares and the porcelains. They are derived from earthenwares, with an increased feldspar content. The result is a stronger and denser body (e.g. the ironstones and white granite wares). Semi-vitreous china has a low porosity, while vitreous china is almost non-porous. The biscuit firing is around 1100 to 1200°C and the low-temperature brilliant glazes mature around 950–1100°C. The ware is generally mechanically stronger than the normal hard-paste porcelain and earthenware and the density of the body results in a far better surface quality than that of earthenwares.

Porcelain

Porcelain can generally be regarded as a collective term for those ceramic wares that are white and translucent (Rado, 1969). The name is derived from the Italian *porcella* meaning 'little pig' after a Mediterranean sea shell that is white and translucent. The more important groups include porcelain, soft-paste porcelain, and bone china.

Hard-paste porcelain, or *true porcelain*, as it is sometimes referred to, is made from around 50% kaolin (white china clay), 25% feldspar (to act as a flux), and 25% quartz or flint (to stabilize the body and provide a good glaze-fit). It is fired in reduction at higher temperatures than other types of ware (up to around 1400°C). Both the glaze and the body mature together, fusing to form a distinct body–glaze layer that strengthens the form (Figure 1.21).

Historically, soft-paste porcelains were developed in an attempt to imitate the hard-paste porcelains from China. They contain more flux and are fired to a lower (or softer) temperature than the hard-paste porcelains (around 1150°C), resulting in a more brittle body with slight porosity. The body itself has a higher flux content in order to mature at a lower temperature; this in turn contributes to the brittleness of the body (Figure 1.22).

Bone china was an English development, being a type of porcelain to which bone ash is added as a flux or refractory, depending on the quantities added. The resulting body is mechanically stronger than both soft- and hard-paste porcelain. The ware is first fired to a critical temperature of 1260°C, after which its lack of

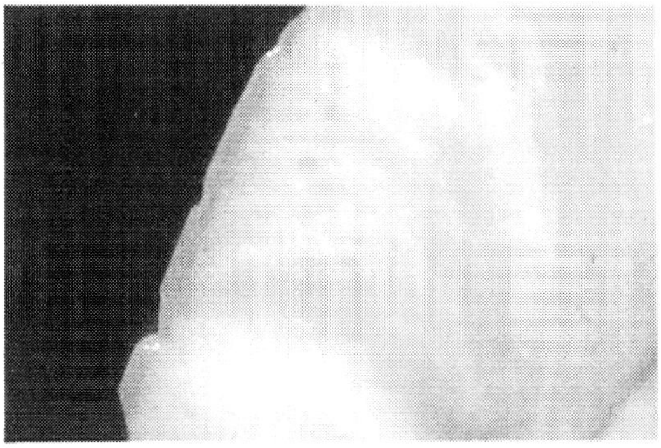

Figure 1.21 Detail of hard-paste porcelain (Victoria and Albert Museum, London).

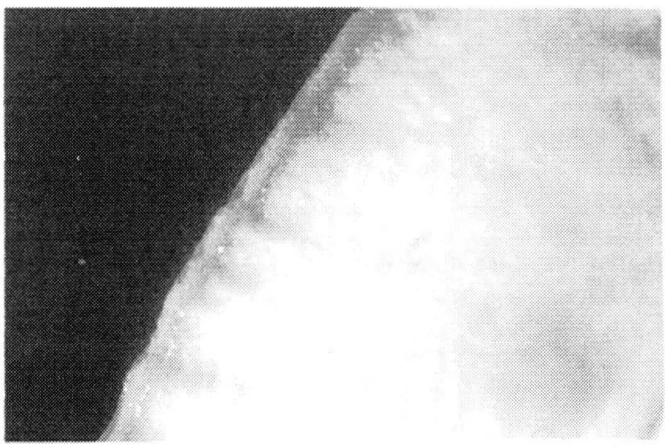

Figure 1.22 Detail of soft-paste porcelain (Victoria and Albert Museum, London).

porosity (about 0.5%) makes glaze application difficult. The lower glaze firing (1100°C) results in a greater range of colours. In addition, the softer composition of the glaze, which is lead-rich, produces a more brilliant appearance than that of hard paste porcelain due to its higher refractive index (Figure 1.23).

Wares described by decoration

Wares may also be classified according to their decoration. For example: *slipware* may describe objects with surfaces covered wholly or partly with a slip, and then usually glazed; while *slip trailed* wares are those where slip has been applied to the

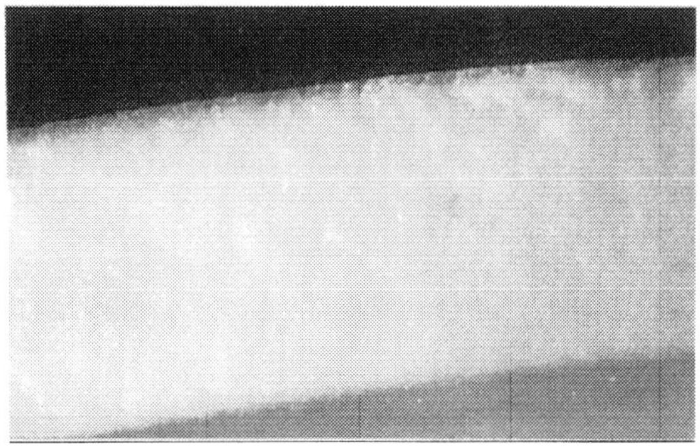

Figure 1.23 Detail of bone china (Victoria and Albert Museum, London).

surface as lines or other decorative features. *Sgraffito* wares are those where decorative devices have been cut or scratched through an overlying slip to reveal the body underneath.

Wares described by glaze

Another rather different and confusing method of describing wares is by glaze type, normally by reference to the composition of the glaze. Thus *lead glazes* are those in which the major flux is a lead compound. However the term *tin glaze* does not imply that the flux used was tin, but rather that a lead glaze has been opacified with tin oxide. Feldspathic glazes are those rich in feldspars. To some authorities feldspathic glazes should be properly included in the alkaline glazes; to others alkaline glazes are those whose composition includes any alkaline material other than feldspars. Salt glazes however, although clearly alkaline, are usually classified as a distinct type of glaze. Leadless glazes, while being free of lead, may include boron and zinc as fluxes: the former being often referred to as borosilicate glazes, the latter as Bristol glazes after the city of their origin.

There is no simple means of distinguishing visually between one glaze type and another, and such a method of description is not entirely satisfactory for what is undoubtedly a complex subject. Detailed explanation of glaze technology will not be considered here; the subject is covered in depth elsewhere (Hamer and Hamer, 1986; Wickham, 1978; Fraser, 1979; Rhodes, 1977; Rado, 1969).

2

The deterioration of ceramics

Introduction

It is in the nature of all composite materials eventually to become degraded into their basic constituents. This degradation occurs as a result of reactions, either with factors in their environment, or between the elements or compounds from which the object is made. In the case of ceramics, degradation is due almost exclusively to environmental factors, and although mechanical degradation can be rapid, chemical degradation is generally extremely slow. It is owing to this chemical stability that ceramic shards are so frequently unearthed in relatively good condition during excavations. However, as the previous chapter has outlined, the range of different types of ceramics is wide, and variations in composition, construction and firing temperature will all affect the degree to which any particular ceramic object is susceptible to individual environmental factors. In general, however, it is the lower-fired ceramics that deteriorate more easily than the higher-fired ones.

In a normal domestic or museum environment ceramics are most at threat from handling. Their fragility causes them to be very susceptible to mechanical shock, and breaks and chips will result. General domestic use or simply exposure to polluted environments may be the cause of superficial dirt or of staining within the body. Should ceramic objects be exposed to fire, flood or other major disasters it is again mechanical shock that will usually cause the most severe damage, but staining and even chemical alteration can occur. It is during exposure to hostile conditions accompanying burial that chemical alteration more frequently occurs and this may be so severe as to cause the ceramic structure to break down and crumble. Unfortunately it is also true to say that damage or the deposition of extraneous matter is not uncommonly a by-product of conservation treatment.

Some disfigurement, such as encrustations and stains, may be reversible, whilst other forms of deterioration, for example breaks and chips, can be disguised but not truly reversed. Chemical breakdown may cause deterioration that can be neither reversed nor disguised, e.g. when a glaze becomes degraded during burial. It is the concern of the ceramics conservator to prevent deterioration occurring wherever possible. Where disfigurement has already occurred one may attempt, through treatment, to return the object to its previous condition, but if this cannot be done one may, where appropriate, disguise the deterioration (see Chapter 5). It is important, therefore, that the conservator understands the ways in which ceramic objects deteriorate and the factors in their environment that affect this deterioration.

It may be helpful, before discussing deterioration, to outline some of the basic mechanical and chemical properties of ceramic materials.

Properties of ceramic materials

Mechanical strength

Mechanical strength is governed by many different factors and there is not space to cover the subject in depth in this book. The reader is referred, for further detail, to books on ceramics technology, such as Davidge (1979) and Kingery *et al.* (1975).

Mechanical strength can be measured in many different ways. Owing to their molecular structure, ceramics are strong in compression, but weak under tension. Rado (1969) cites an illustration of this high compressive strength, where eight bone china cups, one placed under each wheel, were shown to be capable of supporting the weight of a double decker bus. However, for most practical purposes, it is impact resistance that is one of the most useful measures of strength.

The factors that contribute to mechanical strength in ceramics include the porosity of the material, the crystal/glass ratio, the crystal size, the type of crystal, and the general design of the object. All these factors are governed by the raw materials used, the method of fabrication and the details of the firing process. For optimum strength a low porosity and a low glass content are necessary. This is the reason why highly porous ceramics, such as majolicas, are potted thickly. Bodies with very low porosity are often highly glassy and hence fracture easily. The glass content, a product of the fluxing of feldspathoids and free silica during firing, cannot be eliminated altogether, but bodies which sinter at a temperature well below vitrification have much more elasticity. A low crystal size, due to a low particle size of filler in the composition of the clay, will increase strength.

When considering the properties of a ceramic object, one must consider not only the body but the complete body–glaze system. The mechanical strength of an earthenware can be improved by glazing, the glaze filling surface flaws and preventing the initiation of fractures at these sites. Glazing also improves the strength of hard-paste porcelains.

Design of the object, and the method of manufacture, e.g. whether a vessel is coiled, thrown or press moulded, can have a very large influence on its strength. This is due to the fact that, owing to its brittleness, fractures in a ceramic object occur when stresses are concentrated by abrupt changes in geometry or loading. Plates with semicircular edges are much more resistant to chipping than ones with sharp edges (Dinsdale *et al.*, 1967). The angle at which a blow strikes the object is also important.

Resistance to mechanical wear

The resistance to mechanical wear is a measure of the hardness of the surface of a ceramic. In ceramic bodies this is related directly to the firing temperature and the degree of vitrification. Hence high-fired porcelains are much more resistant to mechanical wear than low-fired earthenwares. Glazes that are fired ar high temperatures are also more resistant to mechanical wear than those fired at low temperatures. However, this is due to their composition. High-fired glazes are feldspathic (hard), whereas low-fired glazes contain lead (soft). Decorative applications that are fired on at low temperatures, such as on-glaze enamels and gilding, are softer than the glaze over which they lie. They are therefore much more prone to wear.

Thermal strength

The thermal behaviour of a ceramic object will depend to some extent on its mechanical strength, and hence its ability to accommodate the stresses produced during heating and cooling. These stresses depend in turn on the thermal expansion of the particular ware. Porosity is also an important factor. The thermal strength of non-porous bodies, e.g. hard-paste porcelain, is closely related to the coefficient of thermal expansion, a low coefficient of thermal expansion producing more resistance to thermal shock. With some porous wares, the stresses produced by a high coefficient of thermal expansion can be accommodated.

The thermal behaviour of a glazed ceramic object will depend on the behaviour not only of the body but of the body–glaze system as a whole. Failure can occur in the glaze without the body being affected. The overall design of a ceramic object and the thickness of potting are important factors in its thermal behaviour. Further details on thermal behaviour of ceramics can be found in Davidge and Tappin (1967).

Cooking pots for use over fires have been used since the Neolithic period, and it is possible today to make ceramic vessels for cooking that have a very high resistance to thermal shock and can be placed directly on gas or electric hobs. These are formed from specially developed types of low-expansion hard-paste porcelain, lithia-based pottery and glass ceramics.

Porosity

Porosity is related to the temperature to which a ceramic object has been fired. The most porous bodies are those which have been fired to a temperature only just above that at which the ceramic change occurs (600°C). Porosity decreases with rising temperature as the spaces between the clay particles shrink and become filled by fluxed silica and feldspars. Bodies fired to the point at which all the spaces have been filled, e.g. hard-paste porcelain and bone china, are practically non-porous.

The porosity of earthenware objects is compensated for by the glaze coating, but if this becomes cracked or chipped, moisture can gain access to the body.

Chemical stability

Ceramic bodies fired at high temperatures generally have good resistance to chemical attack.Some bodies, glazes and on-glaze decorations are susceptible to acid attack, but in general contact must be prolonged for any appreciable deterioration to occur. Low-fired wares may retain a certain degree of water solubility, and these elements may be removed during prolonged contact with water, e.g. during burial or lengthy soaking during conservation treatment. Lead glazes in particular are prone to attack during burial and this will be discussed below.

Physical deterioration

Owing to their fragility, mechanical damage is the most common cause of irreversible deterioration of ceramic objects. It most commonly results from careless handling and packing, but may also be the result of major disasters, vandalism, frost, drying following the absorption of soluble salts, or injudicious treatment during conservation. Such damage includes minor surface abrasions, cracks, chips and breaks, glaze exfoliation and in some cases complete fragmentation of the body. As has been outlined above, certain ceramic objects will be more susceptible to mechanical damage than others. For this reason certain types of damage, for example minor glaze chips in delftwares (Figure 2.1), may be accepted as characteristic, and a conservator would not generally attempt to disguise them.

Physical deterioration will be discussed under seven headings: manufacturing defects, impact damage, abrasion, damage due to thermal shock, damage due to soluble salts, frost damage, and damage due to plant root action.

Manufacturing defects

Deterioration may occur in a ceramic object before it has been put to any use at all (Figure 2.2). There may be a number of different causes, the majority of which depend upon either a poorly formulated body, poor design and construction or careless or inappropriate firing (Fraser, 1986).

Figure 2.1 English tin-glazed earthenware posset-pot, showing minor chips and loss of glaze typical of this type of ware (Victoria and Albert Museum, London).

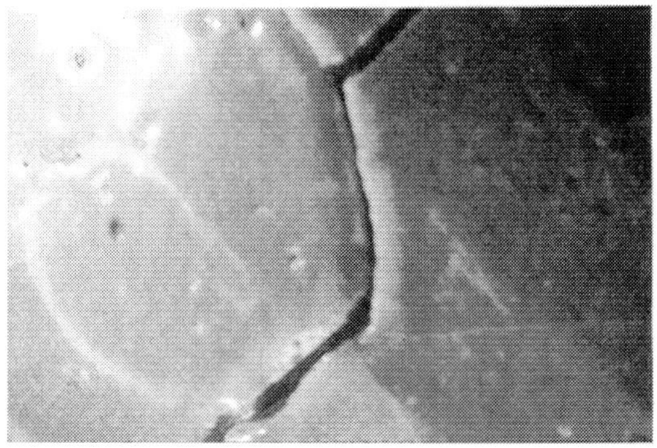

Figure 2.2 Firing crack: rounded edges of glaze show that crack took place before the glaze had set (Victoria and Albert Museum, London).

A body that contains inadequate quantities of filler and that has been allowed to dry too rapidly may well crack, while the same body fired too rapidly will equally break. Any body that has not been given an adequate drying period may suffer during firing owing to the generation of steam within it, while any body of which the cooling has been too hasty will also crack. Furthermore the composition of the body may be at fault. Thus a body containing an excess of quartz will be at risk if the rate of firing or cooling is allowed to pass too quickly through the quartz inversion temperature, in which instance the sudden expansion or contraction of the quartz may be sufficient to cause cracking or 'dunting'. Initially many of these cracks may be of only hairline character and remain undetected, but once the wares are put into service these weaknesses will sooner or later become very evident.

The crazing of glazes during and immediately after firing is a complex subject (Hodges, 1990) which can be dealt with only briefly here. Crazing is the outcome of two quite distinct phenomena: the development of strain within the glaze, and the formation of crack initiators, often no more than minute lacunae within the glaze. The cause of strain in a glaze is nearly always the higher coefficient of contraction of the glaze on cooling than that of the body to which it is applied. In potters' terms the glaze does not 'fit', and this is frequently due to wrong formulation of the glaze. It is especially true of glazes containing a high proportion of alkaline fluxes, causing a high coefficient of contraction. But it may also be the body that is at fault, as for example when it contains a high proportion of quartz. When such a body is fired to moderate temperatures much of the quartz will remain undigested, and this material, when it reaches the inversion temperature on cooling, will shrink and hence offset some of the strain building up in the glaze. Fired to a higher temperature the quartz in the

(a)

(b)

Figure 2.3 (a) Italian majolica dish showing lack of attachment of glaze to body surface. (b) Reverse of dish showing extensive loss of glaze (Victoria and Albert Museum, London).

same body may become largely vitrified, the glass will not shrink on cooling, and the strain will not be relieved. Finally strain may result from too rapid cooling of the kiln, in which case the glaze will shrink at a greater rate than the underlying body, so putting the glaze under strain.

While quantities of undigested quartz in a body may confer some benefits, as we have just seen in a glaze they may be the cause of lacunae which may serve as crack initiators. If the glassy matrix of the glaze has already begun to set by the time the quartz inversion temperature is reached, the shrinkage of the particles will result in small lacunae developing between particles and matrix, and these gaps may act as crack initiators. Crack initiators may also result from glaze devitrification – the growth of crystals in the glaze. Too much lime in the glaze batch, or too little alumina, will allow the growth of crystals, as, too, will a rate of kiln cooling that is so slow that enough time is available for crystal growth. In each case the resulting lacunae may act as initiators for crazing.

Cases have been reported, of which the proof remains uncertain, in which, after years of inactive existence, vessels have suddenly crazed. The explanation normally advanced for this phenomenon is that the body of the vessel has gradually become increasingly hydrated, and the resulting expansion has put sufficient strain on the glaze to cause crazing.

Peeling of glazes (also known as shivering or scaling) may be considered as the opposite of crazing. In this case the glaze contracts less on cooling than the underlying body with the result that adhesion between body and glaze is poor, and sections of the glaze may actually peel away from the body (Figure 2.3). The fault usually lies in an imbalance of quartz in body and glaze. If the body contains relatively large quantities of quartz, the shrinkage on cooling may be so great that the glaze is not under stress, and is therefore liable to peel off. This particular defect is a very common feature of certain classes of ware, especially Dutch and English delftwares.

The strains that develop in ceramics are often difficult to explain. Those that develop during firing are as often as not due to uneven heating in the kiln, in which case one part of the same vessel may be fired to a different temperature from another. The result may be a very visible warp, but in some cases there is no such clear evidence: although the piece may seem perfect it is, nevertheless, under considerable strain, and the merest tap may cause it to disintegrate. There are, however, wares which were clearly fired under very even conditions and yet on cooling are under considerable strain. Bone china often answers this description. If bone china accidentally becomes broken the chances are that satisfactory restoration is impossible if only because fracture has released the strain, so allowing the shards to warp to such an extent that they no longer can be made to form a neat join. Such warping has also occurred in the case of the soft paste porcelain vase illustrated in Figure 2.4.

It will often be found that vessels made of several components were manufactured by luting the pieces together with slurry. Thus, the handles of cups might have been cast in moulds and later stuck into position. The luting alone was often most unsatisfactory, and in fact what held the handle in place was the overlying layer of glaze. If the glaze should crack, the handle will perforce part company with the cup. Examples of shoddy workmanship can be found where a vessel evidently cracked and fell apart on drying. The parts were then luted together, the cracks fettled, and the

Figure 2.4 Pinxton porcelain vase with sprung cracks (Victoria and Albert Museum, London).

whole covered with a glaze sufficiently opaque to obscure the defect.

Impact damage

Owing to their fragility, objects that have been in use over a period of time will carry the scars and blemishes resulting from the purposes to which the objects have been put. Even in the museum environment damage of this sort can occur during handling, packing and storage. Chapter 3 outlines the precautions that should be taken to avoid such damage.

Depending on the friability of the ware, breakage will often be accompanied by loss of some material from along the break edge. Loss will be increased if the edges have been ground together, either due to the circumstances of the damage, e.g. if it occurred during shipment in a packing case, or due to inexpert attempts at conservation.

Major disasters, such as fire, flood or earthquake, can result in cracking, chipping and breakage. Chapter 16 outlines the ways in which damage occurs in such situations and the procedures that should be followed to minimize their effect.

During conservation, impact damage can, for example, be the result of the use of excessive force or lack of care in the use of hammers and chisels, or stone saws, to remove mortars and plaster from the backs of tiles. Careless treatment on lifting objects from archaeological sites can result in mechanical damage not only directly, but also indirectly, for example where dirt or deposits are allowed to dry and shrink, hence putting strain on the surface.

Abrasion

Dishes that have been used for serving food may be abraded by cutlery or harsh cleaning methods, and gilded or other on-glaze decoration may be particularly affected. Wear may also have occurred owing to the underside of one plate abrading the upper surface of another during washing or stacking, as glazes of the same hardness will scratch each other.

Abrasion may be caused by the use of abrasive papers, films and cloths, files, rifflers and drill burrs, when removing surface deposits or excess filling material, or smoothing down surface coatings (Figure 2.5). Although it is true to say that the lower-fired and hence softer bodies and glazes are more susceptible to damage of this nature, even hard-paste porcelain can become marked easily. Material may even be removed deliberately during conservation, for example in the drilling of rivet holes.

A somewhat unusual kind of damage is to be encountered in pottery that has been exposed to shifting sands such as dunes and some deserts. In these cases the sand acts as an abrasive, gradually wearing away the surfaces of the pottery. Depending on the length of time and intensity of the exposure the result may vary from a slight matting of the surface of the pottery to the complete erosion of the surface.

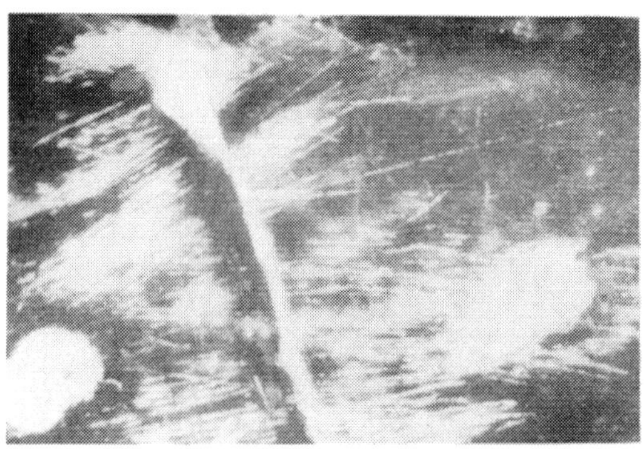

Figure 2.5 Surface of lustre ware dish showing damage caused by careless use of abrasive paper to cut back fillings in rivet holes and joint (Victoria and Albert Museum, London).

Objects excavated from marine or freshwater sites may have suffered damage through abrasion by waterborne particles.

Thermal shock damage

Thermal shock, resulting from sudden heating or cooling, can be the cause of cracking of body or glaze, or of complete fracture. All glazes exist under some degree of stress, but when an object is subjected to heating and cooling, the differences in rates of expansion and contraction of the glaze and the body may result in the glaze becoming so stressed that it cracks. Thermal shock is generally associated with domestic use, but also with fire.

Damage caused by soluble salts

One of the most damaging factors, in so far as porous pottery is concerned, is that of water soluble salts once they have been absorbed by the body of the wares, and this is especially true of salts that tend to deliquesce at high relative humidities and then recrystallize during drier periods. It is in fact the recrystallization that causes the damage, since during this process the newly forming crystals occupy a greater volume than the salt solution and exert enormous pressures on the fabric of the pottery. These may be sufficient either to cause the surface to flake off (Figure 2.6), or to effect the disintegration of the body. The speed at which the crystallization occurs will be a factor in the severity of the damage that results. This speed is dependent upon the temperature and the relative humidity of the air into which the object is introduced. Every salt has a critical relative humidity at which crystallization occurs, and the presence of more than one type of salt can affect their behaviour traits (Paterakis, 1987b). Further details of the mechanisms involved in this type of deterioration may be found in Paterakis (1987b) and Puhringer (1990). At this point it should be emphasized that this kind of damage cannot occur in the case of porcelain or completely vitrified stonewares, since neither present open pores to allow the entry of salts in solution.

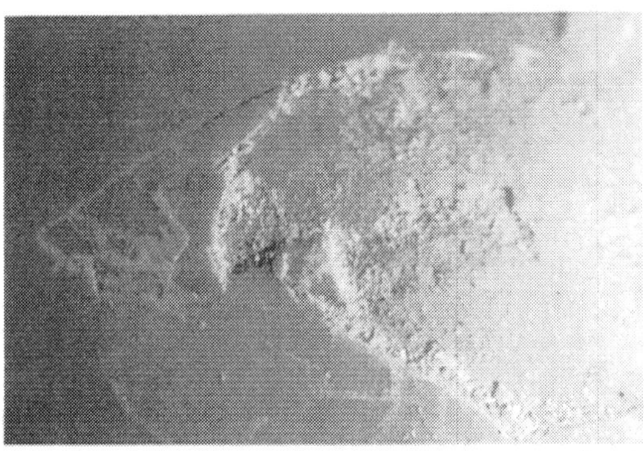

Figure 2.6 Surface of tin glazed earthenware vase, showing cracking and loss of glaze caused by salt effloresence (Victoria and Albert Museum, London).

Soluble salts most commonly associated with this type of deterioration are the chlorides, nitrates and phosphates. The presence and origins of soluble salts in the soil are discussed in Dowman (1970). Seawater is a major source of chlorides but they may also be present in urine and decaying animal tissues. Nitrates and phosphates generally originate from decaying organic matter, and phosphates are found in considerable concentrations in kiln sites owing to the presence of ash. Carbonates and sulphates are often referred to as insoluble although they are in fact slowly soluble and may be associated with this type of damage. Paterakis (1987b) lists a number of sources for these salts.

The problem may be caused by absorption of salts not only from the soil but also from food or chemicals with which a vessel has been in contact. Vessels that have been used to preserve foodstuffs in salt – fish, meat and vegetables – are cases in point, whilst cooking pots may have absorbed salts during the process of food preparation. Even vessels that were used to collect animal blood, itself a highly saline liquid, have been known to have been damaged by the salt they have absorbed. Jars that have been used for storing chemical compounds for medicinal or other purposes are also at risk.

The salts that are most damaging are, of course, those that deliquesce readily. The two most common salts of this habit occurring in nature are the chlorides of calcium and magnesium. Calcium chloride is present in considerable quantity in seawater, while magnesium chloride is invariably present in natural deposits of common salt, sodium chloride. These facts alone should be sufficient to suggest two most potentially damaging environments from which archaeologists may recover porous wares. The one is clearly seawater, and one must therefore be cautious about pottery raised from marine environments. Absorption of salts in marine environments depends on the length of immersion and the porosity of the ware (MacLeod and Davies, 1987). The second is in the case of arid and semi-arid environments, e.g. the Near East, where salt occurs naturally in the soil.

As was mentioned at the beginning of this section, the real damage is done by salt infestation when a deliquescing salt recrystallizes. It follows that the least damage will occur if the pottery is maintained in such an environment that the salts contained therein are kept either permanently damp or permanently dry. The worst possible scenario is a state in which the vessel is undergoing frequent and violent changes of humidity, as for example in a room that is excessively heated and cooled cyclically. In this context a useful precept is that what is damp should be kept damp, and pottery that is dry should be kept dry.

Several types of conservation treatment can introduce soluble salts into a porous body. These include the use of acids to remove metal stains or concretions (Figure 7.8) and the use of alkalis for removal of grease or wax. Such treatments must be followed by very thorough soaking in distilled water (see Chapter 7). A further treatment in this category, and one that should be avoided at all costs, is the use of chloride bleaches to remove stains. Chloride ions remaining in the body may form salts as the object dries, and cause the type of damage discussed above. The use of plaster of Paris or dental plaster can introduce sulphate contamination if the edges to which it is applied are not sealed, and soaking objects with old plaster restorations in water is also a danger in this respect.

Note has been made (FitzHugh and Gettens, 1971; Paterakis, 1990) of the occurrence of calclacite crystals on ceramics stored in wooden cases. It is thought that this is due to a reaction between calcium in the ceramic and acetic acid emitted from the wood in combination with residues from treatment with hydrochloric acid.

Frost damage

Another circumstance under which porous bodied wares are at risk is when they are subjected to frost. This is a phenomenon that is encountered generally only in countries in which the winters have long periods of deeply sub-zero temperatures, and is thus not likely to be met in, for example, the more temperate areas of Europe. The cause of damage is due to the formation of ice within the pores of the pottery, and normally the effect is to cause the surface, especially if glazed, to spall away from the body. Hence, if pottery becomes buried within a short distance of the surface of the soil or deposit during the rainy season it will absorb water, but when the frosts arrive the water will freeze and exert enormous pressure on the fabric of the pottery.

Damage caused by plant root action

When pottery has become softened through burial in wet conditions, plant roots may penetrate through the body causing damage in the process. This may happen particularly in the case of cremation urns interred in acid soils (Smith, in press) as the plant roots grow towards the nutrient-rich material inside the urns.

Dirt and staining

Superficial dirt, deposits and staining do not cause physical deterioration of ceramic objects. However, they do make the objects less pleasing aesthetically and, if the main purpose of an object is to be decorative, this must be looked upon as a significant type of deterioration.

Deposits may be on the surface of the ceramic or, where the nature of the ware allows, carried deeper into the interstices of the body. They may arise from use, from burial, from fire or flood, or from careless conservation treatments. Burial can result in a range of different types of staining and encrustations, depending on the circumstances and environment of the burial. Again earthenwares being porous are more prone to staining and invasive encrustations.

Food stains

Earthenware vessels and dishes that have been used for food preparation may have become stained owing to foodstuffs seeping through fractures in the glaze and being absorbed into the porous body (Figure 2.7). Greasy staining may be particularly bad if the vessel has been heated. The staining will emphasize the flaws in the glaze and may make satisfactory repair and disguise of cracks impossible. Fritwares and soft-paste porcelains are also prone to staining.

Encrustations

Where a vessel has been used as a flower vase, or has been used for boiling water, a lime deposit may have

Figure 2.7 Blue and white Turkish bowl with extensive staining, probably caused by being used to contain fatty food after it had been cracked (Victoria and Albert Museum, London).

built up on the inner surface. Other uses, e.g. as an oil lamp, may cause different types of encrustations to be built up on the surface of an object.

Ceramics recovered from archaeological sites, especially from those in which there is much fallen building material, may have become covered by concretions which are impossible to remove simply by the process of washing or light scrubbing. These concretions are usually white or off-white, but they may have become stained by other materials in the deposit such as iron compounds that will give an ochreous stain. Generally speaking, such concretions will be one of three chemical kinds – calcite (calcium carbonate), gypsum (hydrated calcium sulphate), or silica – although a concretion may be composed of varying proportions of any two or three of these compounds. Calclacite often occurs naturally in soils, although calcite and gypsum may be derived from fallen mortar and plaster by way of solution in rainwater, and their redeposition on ceramics is akin to the formation of stalagmites in limestone caves. In the cases of vitreous or glazed wares the concretion will form only on the surface of the pottery; but if the pottery is porous the chances are that the deposition will also be found in the interstices of the pottery where its removal may prove to be difficult or even impossible. The removal of silicate deposits is even more problematical. In cool or temperate climates the solution of silica in rainwater is very low, and the probability of the formation of concretions is slight: but in tropical climates the solution of silica is far greater and so, too, are the chances of silicate concretions. Since silicates do not dissolve readily in water or most mineral acids their removal may call for methods which may present unacceptable dangers for both the ceramics and the conservator. The crystallization of carbonates, sulphates and silicates is much slower than the crystallization of the more soluble salts, and is unlikely to cause any breakup of the fabric of the object.

Concretions on objects raised from marine environments may be of calcium carbonate, which is present in seawater. Exoskeletons of marine organisms, shell and sand may become encrusted on objects, obscuring them completely.

Pottery that becomes buried in a highly ferruginous deposit may sometimes be found to be covered with a concretion of iron compounds often resembling the hardpan deposits found in certain soils. Their formation is similar, too. In the upper levels of the soil, iron compounds are dissolved in rainwater, only to be deposited at lower levels in the profile. The removal of iron concretions is possibly best approached by using those methods employed to remove rust from iron objects.

Mould growth

Where the humidity is particularly high, problems with mould growth can occur on unglazed wares (Service, 1986). The spores of the moulds implicated are normally present in the atmosphere, and where there is any organic residue (including certain resins, e.g. poly(vinyl acetate) emulsion) present on the object they will start to grow when the humidity reaches a certain level. Earthenware objects are more frequently affected, owing to their porosity (Figure 2.8).

Metal staining

One of the most common types of staining in pottery from land burial is iron staining. Earthenware may absorb soluble iron compounds if it becomes buried in a highly ferruginous deposit, with the result that it becomes stained with an ochreous material. Such stains are not only disfiguring but may also be very difficult to remove. However, this may not be the end of the matter. Should pottery already stained in this manner find its way into a deposit containing decaying vegetation, there is the danger that tannic acids generated by the plants may react with the iron compounds to produce iron tannates. These cause a blue-black stain, and are chemically very similar to old fashioned iron gall ink. Such staining may be very difficult to eradicate.

Where iron rivets, dowels or other supports have been used in past repairs, these may, if allowed to corrode, produce similar staining (Figure 2.9). Green copper staining, caused by the corrosion of brass supports, may also be found.

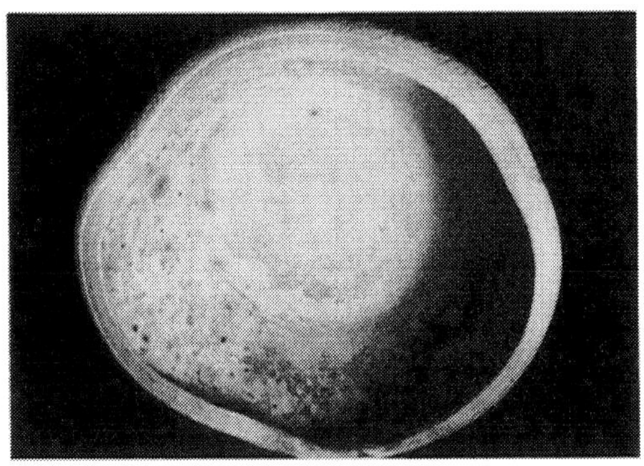

Figure 2.8 Unglazed bowl showing mould growth (Victoria and Albert Museum, London).

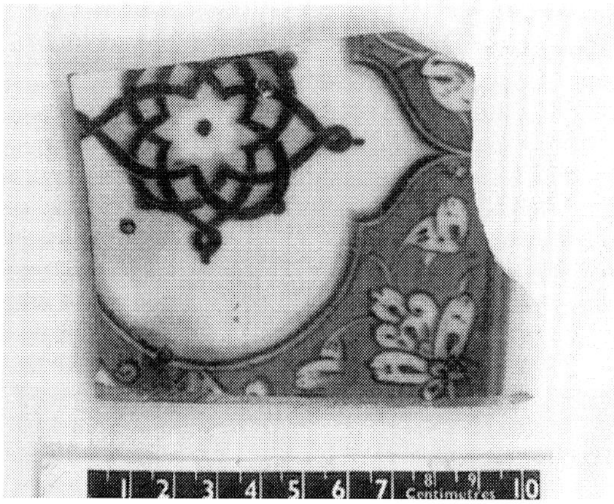

Figure 2.9 Broken piece from Turkish bowl showing iron staining around old rivet holes. The iron staining has penetrated deep into the body (Victoria and Albert Museum, London).

Deposits and stains resulting from fire

Particulate contaminants, derived from the combustion of building fabrics, furniture and furnishings, may be deposited on the surface of an object as a coating (Der Sarkissian and Goodberry, 1981; Davison and Harrison, 1987; Bogle, in press), and foams or other materials used to extinguish the fire may cause staining and deposits (Figure 2.10).

Conservation materials

Materials used in the treatment of objects may, if not carefully controlled, become deposited in areas other than those where they are required. For example, adhesives can be smeared on either side of a joint (Figure 2.11) and filling materials can spread onto the sound surface surrounding an area of loss. Such materials may pass unnoticed until, after a period of time, they begin to discolour. A common problem occurs where pressure sensitive tapes have been used which have left adhesive on the surface of the object after their removal. Not only does this adhesive discolour and become disfiguring in itself, but it may remain tacky and attract further dirt.

Injudicious marking methods can also be a cause of staining.

Figure 2.10 Group of blue and white porcelain objects showing blackening caused by fire (Courtesy of Lindsey Bogle, Amsterdam).

Figure 2.11 Sri Lankan earthenware title showing unsightly old repair using excessive adhesive (Victoria and Albert Museum, London).

Chemical deterioration

Although some minor forms of chemical deterioration may occur under the circumstances of daily household use, major chemical deterioration is generally found only in those ceramics that have been subjected to extreme conditions. Such conditions include burial in wet environments (particularly those of a highly acid or alkaline nature), fire, and exposure to certain treatment materials such as sequestering agents, or strong acids or alkalis. Under such circumstances certain fractions may be lost from the body by leaching, by reaction with acids or alkalis, or by sequestration. In the extreme circumstance of high-temperature fire, the composition of the body, glaze or enamels may be altered.

Water

Ceramics that are low fired, i.e. to temperatures around 600°C will rehydrate if subjected to wet conditions. Consequently, objects of this nature may dissolve or deform badly in wet burial conditions. Higher-fired earthenwares may contain, as body fillers, mineral particles, some of which may be soluble in water. Gypsum (hydrated calcium sulphate), and calcite (calcium carbonate), may both become dissolved in water if ceramics are allowed to remain in wet environments. Thus if earthenware containing a gypsum filler becomes buried in conditions under which water may percolate through the soil or deposit, the gypsum particles will gradually dissolve. In stagnant conditions, by contrast, because the gypsum particles soon become surrounded by a saturated solution of the salt, dissolution of the particles will be very much slower. The manner in which calcite dissolves is rather different since its solubility in pure water is very low. However, in water in which carbon dioxide has been dissolved, which is almost invariably the case in nature, a chemical reaction may occur resulting in the formation of calcium bicarbonate which is very much more soluble. Once again water percolating through the buried profile will be far more damaging than stagnant water in which carbon dioxide is soon exhausted and is not replaced.

Prolonged soaking may be used as part of a conservation treatment, for example in the removal of soluble salts or the removal of stains, and soluble fractions may be leached from low-fired pottery in the same way as during burial.

Acid attack

When the groundwater in contact with a buried ceramic is of an acid nature, any calcareous body fillers will be attacked and will wash away, leaving the object with a porous appearance. Certain glazes will deteriorate in a similar way to glass in acid conditions; the alkali modifiers in the silica network will migrate to the surface and combine with hydrogen ions from the water to form a dilute solution of either sodium or potassium (depending on the alkali modifier) hydroxide. This results in a surface layer of silica being built up and a loss of transparency of the glaze.

Certain conservation treatments, such as removal of iron stains, may involve the use of strong acids. Acids applied in these circumstances can attack calcareous body fillers in the same way as acidic groundwater and the precautions necessary when using such treatments are discussed in Chapter 7.

Ceramics that are in constant daily use may be subject to attack by acids in foodstuffs. There are four main acids responsible for this type of decay: citric acid from fruit juices, malic acid from apple juice, succinic acid present in tea, coffee and whisky, and acetic acid (vinegar). When foods containing these acids are brought into contact with fired glazes they will, in time, produce signs of attack on the glaze. The degree of attack may be so small as to be unmeasurable, but certain types of fired glaze may be attacked to a very appreciable degree resulting in a situation where toxic amounts of metallic compounds are dissolved out of the fired glaze, which may or may not show visual signs of attack. Metallic compounds of concern include selenium, barium, zinc, cadmium, antimony, and lead. Of these the latter four cause the greatest problems, particularly lead since it is such a common glaze constituent and cannot be replaced in low-temperature glazes by any other flux without affecting the glaze brilliance, craze resistance or maturing range. On-glaze enamels and transfers which contain lead fluxes may also be attacked by acids. Whilst commercial low-solubility glazes are generally more resistant, lead glazes prepared from raw lead compounds can be particularly vulnerable to acid attack, especially if underfired – yielding large quantities of toxic lead. Crystalline or 'artistic' glazes, particularly those containing metallic compounds in crystalline forms deposited on the surface of the glaze, are liable to attack, making the crystal lattice unstable. Additions of boron, raw lead, copper, potassium and sodium will increase the solubility of any lead present in the glaze whilst titanium, silica, calcium and alumina will reduce its solubility. Stoneware and porcelain glazes are less liable to attack owing to the absence of the metal fluxes and the extra resistance given by their alumina content.

Alkaline attack

Burial in alkaline conditions is more likely to affect the glaze of a ceramic than the body, although some high-fired bodies, e.g. Roman terra sigillata, can deteriorate owing to the breakdown of the vitrified silica, which behaves like glass. The deterioration of glass, and hence glazes, is faster in alkaline conditions than in acid ones. Alkalis are leached from the glassy matrix and in extreme cases the colloidal silica can become dissolved. Iridescence may result, owing to the way in which light is reflected from the laminating surface. Ultimately the surface may exfoliate. The reactions involved are moisture and temperature dependent, and hence in moist, hot climates attack will be far more severe than under cold or dry conditions. The colouring in glazes may also be affected through the leaching of alkalis, and a residue of insoluble metal salts is often left on the surface giving an iridescent effect.

Lead sulphide blackening

Under certain anaerobic conditions, decaying plant and animal tissues allow a group of bacteria to thrive that can be extremely damaging to lead glazes. These bacteria are known as sulphate reducing bacteria because their metabolism depends upon the conversion of sulphates to hydrogen sulphide. Lead glazes, especially raw glazes, may hold within the molecular network chemically available lead ions, and these will react with hydrogen sulphide to produce the black compound, lead sulphide, similar to the natural mineral galena. Since lead sulphide is not water soluble the whole glaze may become totally blackened, and any decoration associated with it completely obscured.

Sequestration

Sequestering agents may be specifically used to remove certain deposits from ceramics (see Chapter 7), and may also be present in some commercial cleaning agents (e.g. certain domestic washing powders). They are also present in commercial dishwasher powders and liquids. High-lead glazes and on-glaze decoration may be badly affected by their use (Rado, 1975).

Burial in association with animal bones may result in deterioration of lead glazes. This is due to the release of phosphate ions from the bone, which may form sequestering compounds.

Alteration due to fire

The stability of ceramics as a class of objects may be attributed to a great extent to the fact that they are subjected to high temperatures during their manufacture. It is not surprising, therefore, that if a ceramic object is subsequently heated to a similar temperature, changes in its microstructure may occur. The temperature at which any changes may occur is related directly to the firing temperatures of any particular part of the object. For this reason on-glaze decoration, which would have been fired to a comparatively low temperature, will be affected at lower temperatures than the glaze itself, and may show changes in colour or texture whilst the glaze remains unaffected. Any decoration that was applied unfired may, of course, be affected at considerably lower temperatures.

3

Preventive care of ceramics

Throughout the various specialisms in conservation the role of the conservator can be divided into two distinct areas involving either the passive or the active conservation of an object. In the former *non-interventive* type of conservation, the object is protected from decay by controlling the surrounding environment; while in the latter the conservator *actively* intervenes with the damaged object, using treatments that stabilize and halt the deterioration. Whilst a large part of the conservator's time may appear to be devoted to the active conservation of objects, emphasis should also be given to the passive conservation of objects and their protection from ever requiring active conservation.

Within museums and private collections there should be no need for a ceramic object to deteriorate except in rare circumstances. Ceramics are probably one of the most stable groups of decorative artifacts. The previous chapters have described how the various properties of individual types of ceramics are closely related to the clay used and the firing conditions to which they have been subjected. These qualities, acquired by individual objects during their manufacture, determine their particular susceptibility to certain types of damage when exposed to inappropriate and extreme conditions. The most common form of damage to ceramics occurs as a result of mechanical shock upon impact, caused by direct or indirect human intervention.

The preventive care of ceramics through their passive conservation involves guarding them against the harmful agents in the surrounding environment that pose a threat to their stability. Through an awareness of the degree of vulnerability of different types of ceramics, those potential sources of damage can be minimized when handling the objects or considering their display, storage, or packing.

Environmental requirements for ceramics

The factors within the environment that influence the rate of deterioration in ceramics include: extremes of temperature and humidity, light, particulate pollution, vibration and human intervention (Thomson, 1968). An ideal environment for the display and storage of ceramics should reduce deterioration to a minimum.

Extremes of temperature especially associated with rapid fluctuations over short periods of time can cause damage by thermal shock, or by weakening existing faults. Similarly if relative humidity is allowed to waver and alternate at levels above and below the range 40–65% changes may occur to any water sensitive materials in close association with the ceramic. A minor part can be played by light levels in the breakdown of the resins and coatings used in previous restoration treatments. Particulate pollution can disfigure ceramics, both temporarily and permanently, depending on the degree of penetration and the nature of the pollutant (Figure 3.1). Vibration can lead to damage either directly by abrasion and wear, or by glazed ceramics *creeping*, particularly on non-resistant surfaces, leading to the possibility of an object slipping from a shelf. Human intervention involving careless handling of ceramics is the major contributing factor in their deterioration, and will be considered in detail later. Finally, additional supports, backings or frames made of other materials such as metal, wood or textiles will require individual consideration for their specific environmental requirements.

The control and maintenance of the environment at a stable acceptable level, within a museum containing a *mixed collection* of objects made from a range of different materials, usually sets the parameters around the following ideals:

Figure 3.1 Temporary disfiguration of an earthenware panel by particulate pollution. The left half of the object has been cleaned to illustrate the degree of accumulation of superficial dust and dirt on the surface (Victoria and Albert Museum, London).

Temperature range 19°C ± 1°C.
Humidity range 50% ± 2% relative humidity (RH).
Ultraviolet radiation Less than 75 microwatts per lumen.
Illuminance 50-250 lux.
Filtration Pre-filter giving 98% efficiency at 5 microns (BS 6540); high-efficiency filter giving 99.97% efficiency at 0.6 microns (BS 3928).
Gases All pollutant gases should be removed.

In reality the ideal conditions are probably unrealistic goals. However, a compromise can be reached using good quality display cases. Relative humidity in display cases may be controlled if necessary, either with plant or using silica gel, to maintain the relative humidity within 40–65%, with fluctuations of no more than 5% within an hour. Temperatures can be realistically held within the range 18–25°C, and filtration of particles in the air can be 85% efficient at 5 microns. Light levels can be more easily controlled and maintained.

For the majority of ceramic objects it has to be said that the environmental parameters are not crucial. The main exceptions would be objects that are composite with organic or metal components in close association, certain objects which have been restored, and those objects contaminated by salts. Such items should be considered separately and may have to be stored in cases which can be environmentally controlled so that the relative humidity can be maintained at a suitable level.

Metal mounts, supports, rivets and dowels are susceptible to corrosion in high humidity and may also react with substances emitted from store case materials, such as wood coatings, composite wood board, sealants, paints and some furnishing materials (FitzHugh and Gettens, 1971). Occasionally some oriental ceramics are decorated with lacquered finishes that may be vulnerable to moisture. Organic materials that may be held within irregularities on the surface of ceramics, or that have been applied intentionally as decoration, can provide a nutritious medium for mould growth in conditions of high humidity.

Light levels can accelerate the discoloration and breakdown of coatings and adhesives, disfiguring and weakening the object. Some resins are known to discolour more rapidly in the dark, while others respond adversely to high light levels (Down, 1984). Old plaster fillings can be sensitive to high humidity causing salts, in particular sulphates, to be absorbed from them into porous bodies. Water soluble adhesives will also weaken in high humidity. Low-fired earthenwares, with a soluble salt content arising from a former environment such as an architectural context or burial, may be subject to cycles of salt crystallization and dissolution in fluctuating relative humidity (Figures 3.2, 3.3). Such objects will require stable conditions in order to avoid damage (Paterakis, 1987b).

Display case design

The investment of time and money in careful consideration of display case design and construction will in the long term be worthwhile. A superior case can act as a barrier to counteract undesirable conditions within a gallery, providing a more satisfactory and secure environment.

Display cases should ideally be constructed of inert materials such as metal and glass that will not emit any harmful corrosive vapours. Ceramics are

Figure 3.2 Terracotta unglazed Indian tile with salt efflorescence on the surface. The salts, which were probably absorbed in solution from a damp environment earlier in the tile's history, have now become apparent as a result of fluctuating humidity levels causing the salts to be drawn to the surface where they form crystals (Victoria and Albert Museum, London).

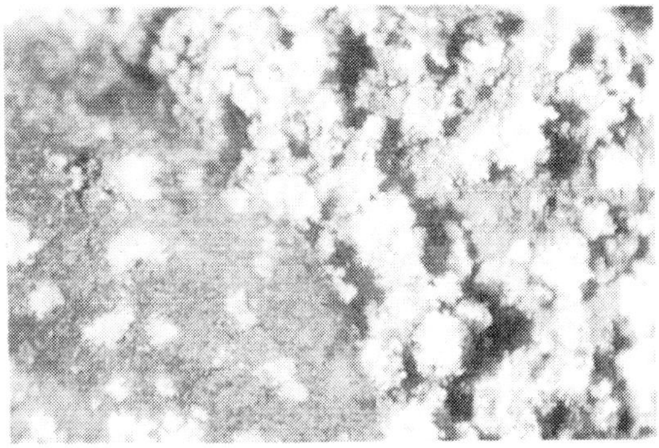

Figure 3.3 Detail of the damage caused by salt efflorescence (Victoria and Albert Museum, London).

generally resistant to many of the groups of materials that cause serious problems to objects of other media, but some reactions are known to occur (FitzHugh and Gettens, 1971). An example is the formation of formate salts after exposure of the surface of unstable glass and enamels to the formaldehyde vapours emitted from wood-chip board (Hatchfield and Carpenter, 1987). This suggests that the possibility of similar reactions occurring with degraded unstable glazes cannot be ruled out.

Figure 3.4 The interior of the case should be accessible to allow objects to be safely installed or removed (Victoria and Albert Museum, London).

If glass is to be used for the construction of a display case it should be laminated rather than toughened, to avoid any risk of damage to the contents of the case should the glass get smashed. Laminated glass will shatter but remain in position, while toughened glass will break and fall apart, scattering fragments of glass over the surrounding area. Where glass shelves are to be used, they should be strong enough to bear the weight of the objects, with secure fixings which allow the height of the shelf to be raised or lowered if necessary.

The interior of the case should be easily accessible to facilitate removal or installation of objects (Figure 3.4). The mechanism for opening the case, either by removal of a panel or by opening a door, should be simple but secure and safe. It must be possible to remove objects easily without putting them at risk by having to dismantle the case around them.

The case construction should be stable and secure. There should be no vibration which could cause damage by wear or induce creep, causing objects to move gradually to a shelf edge. If there is any possibility of creep occurring, the shelf edges should have a lip or a band of material attached to the edge which will offer resistance and restraint.

The case should be as airtight as possible, allowing minimal exchange of air to occur, ideally no more than 0.1 air exchanges per 24 hours. The internal environment will then maintain stability, and entry of pollutants in the form of dust and gases will be reduced.

Lighting should not be internal, but should be housed in a separate compartment to the objects, so that the lights may be accessed independently for maintenance. Although ultraviolet filters are not normally necessary to protect ceramics, restored objects or those that have secondary organic materials combined in close association such as mounts, supports or decorative treatments may require special consideration. It should be possible to dim each light and have the option of directing light if desired. Excessive heat build-up can occur within cases that have lights built inside the case. High temperatures may affect pieces that have been restored using thermoplastic resins, causing the resins to soften and become tacky, attracting dust and dirt and weakening joints. Such conditions as springing may also be initiated by the heat from strong lights. Where the daily routine of turning lights on and off induces cycles of temperature change, soluble salts in low-fired bodies may undergo potentially damaging changes.

If display cases are shared with organic objects, the design should incorporate space to accommodate passive humidity buffers such as silica gel in trays below the display (Figure 3.5). It should be possible to service and maintain these without disturbing the objects. The size of the compartment will depend on

Figure 3.5 A mixed media case containing objects made from different materials will demand particular environmental standards (Victoria and Albert Museum, London).

the size of the case and should be adequately sealed to minimize dust entry. Provision should also be made for the inclusion of equipment to monitor the environment within the case if necessary.

Storage of ceramics

Since it may not always be desirable or possible to display all the objects within a collection, it may be necessary to store some of them. Although stores might range in the level of sophistication from a cupboard in an office or studio area to specially designed buildings, they share the same basic aims: to safely and securely house the objects in a suitable environment.

Stores should be located so that they are easily accessible from display areas, conservation studios and curators' offices in order to minimize transfer distances. The size of the area should be related to the number of cases that will be required to house the quantity of objects; as a rough guide approximately half the floor space will be occupied by cases. Access to storage areas should ideally be via level floors, with no steps or ramps. Such irregularities are often difficult to see when carrying large boxes or baskets and cause problems when using trolleys to move objects. There should be wide double doorways, so that large containers and trolleys may, if necessary, be brought into the area. A space near the entrance can be designated as a reception area where objects can be packed or unpacked. There should be secure and stable surfaces available so that objects can be removed from the cupboards for examination or prior to transit to another part of the building. It is advisable to have a non-slip easily maintained floor-covering material laid onto a solid vibration-free surface. Ceilings should be of a height which allows for the possibility of storing large objects.

To avoid clutter and congestion within the main areas of the store, materials and equipment should be kept in a separate cupboard or side room. Items such as baskets, containers, trolleys, packing materials and gloves would also be kept in such an area and, if space and budget allow, work benches and running water might be installed.

Ideally, the store should be dust free, with a pure air supply and none of the main gas pollutants. A programme for regular cleaning of floor areas should be established to avoid build-up of dust and dirt. Other environmental requirements should be maintained as discussed earlier.

Storage cases

Cases or cupboards for storing ceramics should be strong, stable and secure. As with display cases they may be constructed of metal and glass, preferably with glass doors so that the objects can be easily observed without having to unlock the case. Adjustable shelves are useful where a wide range of objects of various shapes and sizes are to be housed. Although glass shelves within cases are helpful for viewing manufacturers' marks on the bases of objects without having to lift them, the hard transparent surface can be deceptive and can sometimes make handling and positioning objects difficult. A thin sheet of high-density polyethylene foam, cut to exactly fit the shelf size, will guard against the possibility of chipping the base of a ceramic on the hard shelf material. Objects with irregular bases that may not sit safely on such a surface should be laid down on their side and supported with cushioning if necessary.

The doors on the cases should be either sliding or hinged, with tight seals to minimize air exchange. Each door should be fitted with locks for added security. The dimensions of the cases should allow easy access; shelves that are too deep will make objects at the back of the case inaccessible. Where space is at a premium, it may be necessary to utilize ceiling height by having two tiers of cases. In such situations, stable sets of steps incorporating rigid platforms will be necessary in order to reach the cases. Although such an arrangement makes economical use of the space, it is not ideal; manoeuvring objects at a height can induce anxiety that may distract even the most experienced handlers from the task (Figure 3.6).

The ideal situation would be to have objects arranged in such a manner that no other object ever had to be moved in order to gain access to others. However, this is rarely possible, partly due to the diversity of the objects, and also because of the difficulty of designing and making shelves to fit a given area where space and budget may be limited. Small objects should be stored towards the front of the shelf, with larger pieces towards the back, making it easier to locate each item. Stacking flat objects such as tiles, plates or plaques should be avoided, as this will introduce stresses, increasing the possibility of accidents and inhibiting accessibility (Figure 3.7). If space is very limited and there is no alternative, only those objects which are sound and stable should be stacked. Each object must be separated from the one above it using layers of padding, such as tissue wads or foam discs. Tiles, small fragments and shards are best stored in a system of drawers or trays (see Chapter 15), while larger tile panels with suitable attachments can be stored vertically in a free standing rack system similar to that adopted in paintings stores.

Figure 3.6 A store devoted entirely to ceramics and glass. The problem of limited floor space has been solved by capitalizing on the high ceilings and installing two tiers of cases and additional floors on mezzanines. The arrangement, however, reduces the accessibility of the objects as shown (Victoria and Albert Museum, London).

Figure 3.7 It is inadvisable to stack flat objects such as these tin-glazed earthenware dishes. The weight of the objects may induce stress in fragile objects at the bottom of the pile. The lower objects can only be reached by unpacking those objects on top. Such a situation invites mishandling and the temptation to slide items out of the stack, putting the objects at risk (Victoria and Albert Museum, London).

When removing objects from a shelf, great care should be taken to avoid damage to adjacent objects. It is unwise to drag objects across shelves, particularly if they are heavy, as this may induce vibration and cause abrasion of the base of the object. Small objects that are liable to roll should be restrained from doing so with wedges of foam or tissue (Shelley, 1987). It is generally advisable to have two people present when moving objects on shelves. A second person can advise and direct positioning, keeping a watchful eye on potential risks from a different viewpoint.

Finally, the cases and shelves should be systematically labelled. Ideally each object should be allocated a fixed location when it enters the store. The precise store location should be recorded within the institution's information retrieval system, with any other documentation relating to the object, so that it can be quickly located when required (Padfield *et al.*, 1982).

Handling ceramics

Archaeology testifies to the fact that ceramic objects can survive for thousands of years cocooned in a stable environment, whether buried beneath layers of earth, or hidden inside a tomb. Unfortunately human intervention often plays a dominant role in their deterioration. Ideally ceramics should never be handled; they could exist indefinitely if they were left in a suitable environment untouched by humans. Although museums and private collections offer the apparent security of display cases within warded galleries managed by professional teams of curators and conservators, the displays are by no means static. It is important that these collections are accessible to allow opportunity for research and study, or for loans and exhibitions, or maintenance of galleries and displays. Any movement of an object will involve handling it in order to transfer it from one situation to another, and this immediately puts the object at risk from impact damage.

Initial considerations

Most damage which arises from handling an object is accidental and unpredictable, but the possibility of its occurrence can be reduced by good preparation and full evaluation of the circumstances. Prior to any movement of an object it is worth questioning the need for such action and considering the alternatives. The cardinal rule should be to avoid all unnecessary handling or touching (Shelley, 1987).

Planning and preparation

Once the decision has been made and the prospect of handling the object becomes inevitable, it is important to plan and prepare for the process. This should begin by considering personal effects, such as jewellery, that might catch and chip or crack ceramics; loose clothing and long hair might also snag on objects. Wearing flat comfortable shoes should minimize the possibility of slipping or tripping on polished or uneven surfaces.

Hands should be clean and dry. Cotton gloves eliminate the possibility of transferring acids and grease from the skin; however, they reduce the tactile senses, and can be dangerous when handling slippery glazed objects. The loose cotton fibres can snag on rough or flaking surfaces. There are alternative cotton gloves available commercially, incorporating PVC dots on the palm and finger pads; while these give more grip and resistance to slippage, they have the potential disadvantage of depositing polymer residues on the object's surface, which although harmless in themselves may attract dust and dirt. If gloves are to be worn, disposable vinyl, nitrile or latex gloves are probably the safest option, although they can be uncomfortable to wear for long periods unless perforations are made to the back of each glove in order to avoid the build-up of perspiration. However, clean hands should normally suffice and, if handling a number of objects, hands should be washed and dried frequently.

An examination of the object should be made prior to handling. It may be necessary to use a torch and a hand-held magnifier to assist in examination. Loose movable parts such as lids, stands, or detachable mounts should be noted, as these will have to be removed before transfer. Visible damage such as chips, cracks or breaks should be assessed. Old restorations may become more obvious and increasingly unstable with age, and old bonds should be carefully examined to make sure they are still supporting the joint. Unsound glaze on earthenwares, or flaking enamels or gilding, should be noted as these may not withstand handling or contact with packing materials. Objects made from unfired clay, or with unfired decoration, will also be fragile and will require careful handling. Loose surface material that may be of ethnographic importance should also be given careful consideration.

If the object is to be moved more than a few feet within the same building, it is safest to transport it in a padded basket, plastic container or strong box. The container should be sufficiently large to accommodate the object(s) allowing for additional padding or packing in the form of wads of acid-free tissue. The route should be checked, making sure that it is well lit and free from obstructions such as chairs, flexes, cables. Familiarity with any potential obstacles such as steps, corners, doors and lifts is important. All doorways should be wide enough to allow safe passage. Assistance can be sought from a colleague to share the load, to help open doors, and to warn others if necessary. Finally, the new location should be checked to confirm that it is ready to receive the object.

Lifting

Any detachable parts noted during the initial examination should be removed from the main object prior to lifting it. Objects made up of several components should be disassembled if necessary. Parts that appear to have been stuck in place, such as covers, should be viewed with caution; it is unwise to assume that they will remain in position during transit. The object should always be held directly below its centre of gravity, supported with one hand beneath the object, while stabilized and shielded with the other (Figure 3.8). The weakest, most vulnerable parts of ceramics are usually the protuberances such as the knop, handle, rim, spout, bocage and limbs; these

Figure 3.8 A vase being lifted with two hands. One hand takes the weight below the centre of gravity and the other supports and protects the upper part of the body and shoulder of the vase (Victoria and Albert Museum, London).

may have been damaged or restored in the past, and may not be able to support the weight of the object. Only one object should be lifted at a time, however small and light. An object should *never* be lifted over another.

There are two basic principles that the individual should bear in mind when lifting heavy objects. Firstly, the back should be kept straight, using the legs or arms as leverage. Secondly, the weight of the load should be distributed evenly. Where necessary, for large objects, special slings and hoists should be used (Williams, 1987).

Moving objects short distances in boxes or baskets

The basket or box intended to be used for transferring the object should be prepared in advance. The bottom should be lined with layers of padding such as bubble-wrap, polyethylene foam, or wads of acid-free tissue. This will act as a layer of insulation to buffer vibration or impact.

If more than one object is to be transferred using an open-topped container, they should be positioned carefully so that each one is clearly visible within the packing material. Small objects or fragments should be carried in separate trays, within the container. It is advisable to count small objects as they are placed in the trays, and then again as they are removed. Each object should be spaced so that it does not touch any other. Wads of acid-free tissue can be used as padding, and these should be packed firmly around robust objects to protect them from movement or vibration (Figure 3.9). Small white objects should be *tagged* in some way, so as to make them more obvious and less likely to be camouflaged by the surrounding white tissue. The wads should be placed more lightly around fragile objects. Objects of greatly dissimilar weight should not be packed together. The centre of gravity should be maintained at a low height in the centre of the container. Tall objects should be positioned on their sides, providing this does not stress their structure unduly. Keys, pens, or tools should be kept separately from the objects in a small receptacle within the container. No part of the object should be allowed to project over the side where it might catch or knock against something.

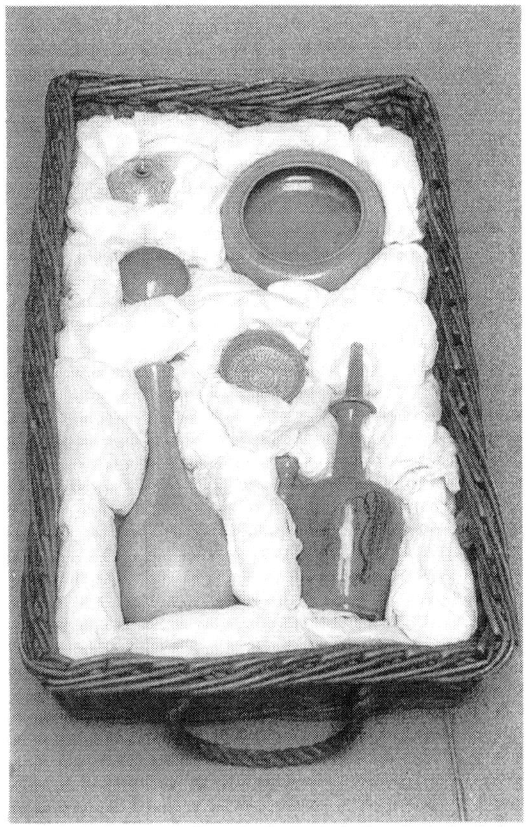

Figure 3.9 Over short journeys a basket padded with tissue wads provides a safe means of transferring ceramics (Victoria and Albert Museum, London).

Packing for longer journeys

The movement of works of art from national collections to major exhibition venues worldwide is now a common occurrence; consequently the subject of packing has become a specialist field. Such loans will require strict co-ordination to ensure that the environmental and security specifications set down as a condition of loan are complied with throughout. The subject has been covered in depth elsewhere, and the references given should be consulted for more information. Recent publications refer to some of the more sophisticated methods which are currently being researched, employing specially constructed packing cases with inner linings (Stolow, 1986; Mecklenburg, 1991). It is possible to select the best type of foam to line the transportation crate using *dynamic cushioning curves* (Richard, 1990), and also to calculate the appropriate density and thickness of foam for the object. Foam linings help to absorb the effects of shock and vibration, cushioning and protecting the object. There are numerous types of polymer-based foams available, with a range of different properties. Those selected as packing materials should be inert, closed-celled and of a suitable density. Some can be quite hard and consequently abrasive and unyielding. Such types might be ideal for more robust and durable ceramics, but they would be unsuitable for delicate pieces with fragile surfaces (Thompson, 1984). Some transportation crates are composite arrangements, involving boxes within crates, to further reduce shock; the inner box *floats* within an outer crate lined with the appropriate amount and type of foam.

Depending on whether the objects are to be transported by car, lorry, train or plane, appropriate containers and padding should be selected to give maximum protection against damage. Prior to being placed in the packing case, the object should be carefully wrapped. Generally sheets of acid-free tissue, polyethylene sheeting, or a thin lightweight microcellular foam (e.g. Jiffyfoam (Jiffy Packaging)) will provide a protective layer. For more fragile or soft surfaces such as gilding, lustres, enamels and unfired decoration, special consideration has to be given to isolating vulnerable areas from the possibility of damage by abrasion caused by wrapping materials. An object may be wrapped using tissue strips to form a cocoon around it, thus avoiding any slippage or abrasion which might rub a delicate surface (Stolow, 1986). The wrapped object may then be placed in the case, held firmly within layers of foam that have been cut to correspond with the contour of the object.

For short journeys where the packed object is accompanied throughout the journey, for example when returning objects to clients or transferring artifacts by car, the packing technique can be simple, yet effective. Strong cardboard boxes or containers should be used. If reusing boxes discarded from retailers, some indication of their durability can be surmised from the original contents described on the exterior of the box. The base or load bearing side should be secure, and if in doubt, additional strips of packing tape should be applied. The inside of the bottom of the box should be well padded with foam, tissue wadding or layers of polyethylene bubble-wrap. If packing a group of objects, a detailed list should be made before packing, mentioning any multiple parts such as covers and mounts. This list can be placed on top of the final layer of packing inside the box, rather than displayed on the exterior where it could be an incitement to theft. Each item should be wrapped separately using acid-free tissue, clean polyethylene, thin grade microcellular foam sheeting (e.g. Jiffyfoam), or clean bubble-wrap. Old newspapers should never be used; the ink will be transferred to hands and rub off onto the object. The wrapping can be secured, if necessary, with masking tape which has the advantage of being easy to remove. Labelling the outside of each wrapped item will aid recognition, and help make the unwrapping process less tentative.

Padding materials should be sufficiently yielding to protect the object from shocks, yet at the same time should hold the object in position and prevent it from settling downward and migrating to the base of the container. It may not always be possible to obtain the ideal inert padding materials, but other alternatives can be used, for example shredded polyethylene sheeting, soft polyether sponge, bubble-wrap, crumpled paper, cloth or corrugated card; even moss has been suggested (Cronyn, 1990). It is inadvisable to use cotton wool unless it is wrapped in tissue or polyethylene, to isolate it from direct contact with the object and prevent the danger of fibres snagging on glaze flakes or particles. Polystyrene peanuts should not be used as they offer very little restraint to heavy items which will gradually settle to the bottom.

Small objects should be wrapped very visibly to avoid any risk of them being discarded with the packing material. Larger objects should be cushioned, rather than wrapped (Watkinson, 1987). Intact ceramics or partially reconstructed objects may require additional internal packing to give support (Sease, 1988). When packing a large number of fragments or objects it is important to distribute the weight as evenly as possible; groups of a similar size and shape should be packed together, placing the heaviest items near the well padded bottom of the container. Each item should be separated from adjacent objects with padding, and each layer of objects should have more padding packed on top. Objects should be placed away from the sides of the case, the gap being filled by packing. As each layer of objects is filled the subsequent layers of lighter objects will be added; the last layer of objects should allow

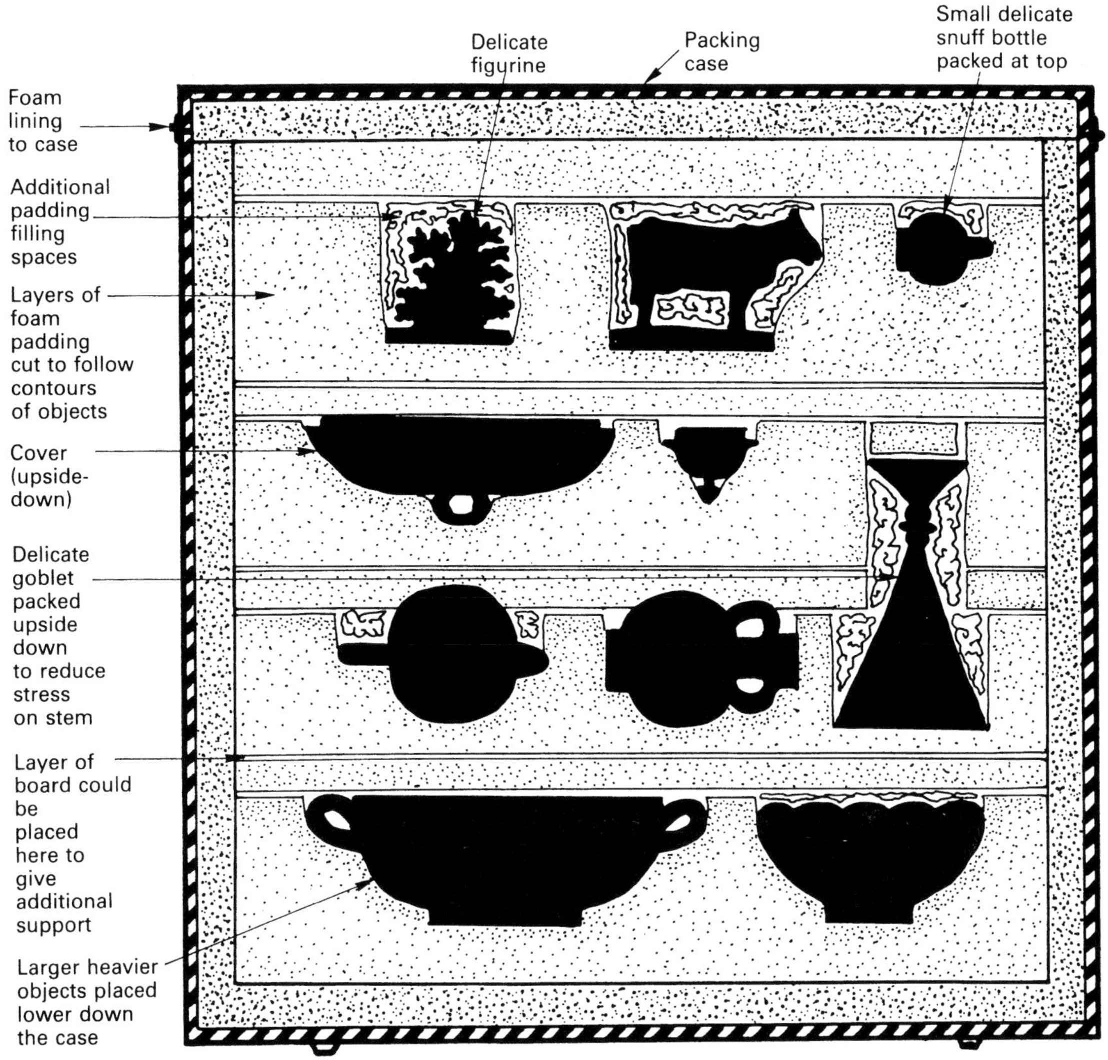

Figure 3.10 General packing for all types of ceramic (in section). The diagram shows a range of different objects packed in layers of polyethylene foam that has been cut to fit the contours of the objects. Alternatively tissue wads could be used in a similar manner.

sufficient depth above for the final packing (Figure 3.10). Where a number of whole pots are to be packed in a container, it may be necessary to insert battens of wood between them to prevent movement. Delicate objects should be carefully packed in their own container with plenty of padding material.

The top of the container should be sealed down, with labels affixed to indicate top and bottom and warn of the fragility of the contents. The addresses of both sender and recipient should also be marked.

Unloading and unpacking

Unpacking should be carried out as soon as possible after the person accompanying the container has recovered from the journey. A clear, stable surface should be made available for the objects to be unpacked onto. Each item should be carefully unwrapped, examining its condition to ensure no damage has occurred. The items should be checked against the list to make sure an object has not been overlooked, and the packing should only be discarded when all the objects have been checked. The objects should be placed gently on the prepared surface, and not near the edge of the table where they might be easily knocked. It is important to concentrate totally on the action of handling the object and not to be distracted at any stage. Distances are easily misjudged, especially on highly polished or glass surfaces which can be deceptive.

Packing archaeological finds

At some stage archaeological finds will have to be carefully packed on site in preparation for storage or for transportation elsewhere. Essentially, packing techniques and materials will be similar to those outlined in the previous section. The main aim is to prevent further damage to the fragments or objects from crushing or abrasion. In the case of objects that have been recovered from damp or wet sites, it may be necessary to provide a controlled environment of a specific relative humidity.

Ceramics that are free from salts will tolerate a wide range of humidity with little risk of damage. It is not necessary to pack them in airtight containers and it is preferable to allow some air exchange through the packing materials. Porous bodies can usually be expected to retain moisture even after lengthy drying following excavation. They should therefore be put into loose resealable polyethylene bags which have had holes punched into them, or into linen bags, in order to avoid build-up of condensation. The edges of the shards can sometimes tear or damage the polyethylene, so to avoid this, it may be advisable to place the perforated bags within other perforated bags to give added protection. Small finds should be individually packed in labelled polyethylene bags, then placed, surrounded by padding, in a plastic box (Figure 3.11). The small boxes may then be packed together in a larger box, again paying attention to adequate packing, before finally placing them in a larger container for transportation.

Ceramics that have been excavated from salt-laden soils or from marine sites should be kept wet until they can be treated in order to stop the salts from crystallizing and causing any disruption of the surface. Marine finds should be stored initially immersed in seawater in waterproof non-corroding containers. Small polyethylene boxes with tight-fitting lids may be used to carry an object over short distances by foot. However, where they are to be moved over greater distances using transport, the fragments or objects should be packed in good quality watertight corrosion-proof containers. This could take the form of a triple layer of polyethylene self-sealing bags placed inside hermetically sealed polypropylene boxes with adequate padding. Any excess air should be expelled and the containers kept cool until they reach their destination. Cushioning can be provided by large- and small-cell bubble-wrap and closed-cell foams such as Plastazote (BXL). Pearson (1987) suggests using sawdust, felt and undyed towelling fabrics or natural materials such as sphagnum moss and seaweed. All padding should be carefully assessed in terms of the potential risks of unwanted materials contaminating the objects (such as dyes, fungus or dirt), particularly if they are to remain in contact with the object over long periods of time. Wet objects should be clearly labelled with materials that are not water soluble, and which will not rot in damp conditions.

In exceptional circumstances it may be necessary to keep a ceramic object very dry in a controlled

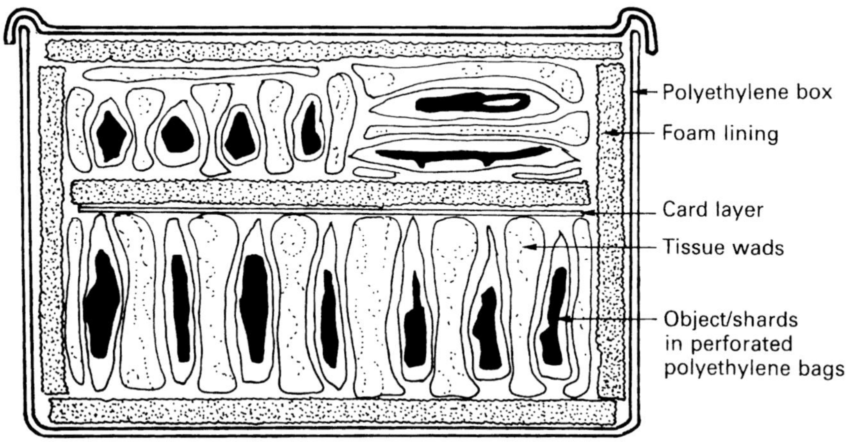

Figure 3.11 Small finds packed for transport. For humidity sensitive objects, a bag containing silica gel could be included, with a humidity indicator card placed on the inside of the box in a visible position.

environment, for example where an unstable object is held together by salt crystals that must be prevented from deliquescing and proceeding through crystallization cycles which might result in further disruption of the object. In such a situation the object will require special desiccated conditions where all the moisture has been extracted from the air using a desiccating agent such as silica gel. The object is packed in an airtight container together with an appropriate quantity of silica gel (about 1 kg of gel per 0.012 cubic metres volume). The relative humidity can be monitored using humidity strips. The gel is activated by heating to 110°C to 120°C for several hours. Its efficiency will gradually be diminished as it absorbs moisture in the sealed container, reaching a point where it will need to be reactivated again by reheating.

4

Examination and recording

A conservator may be called upon to examine an object for various reasons. The examination will usually be an investigative stage in the sequence of events that follow. Initially it will reveal the precise extent and causes of any deterioration, as well as determining the nature of the ceramic body and glaze. Such information will play an important part in deciding if conservation is necessary and in choosing the most appropriate treatment for the damaged object. Information of a complex nature might be gained from further detailed examination and analysis.

In some cases the examination will involve an assessment of the condition of the object, not necessarily with the intention of treating it. The object may be required as a loan to a special exhibition, or it might be a proposed acquisition. An expert opinion on the present condition, stability and integrity of the object may highlight weaknesses that have an important bearing on the decision of whether to lend or buy. It may well become apparent at this early stage that the costs and complexity of conserving or restoring the object, relative to its value or importance, obviate any further action.

It is important that both the activities of examining the object and recording the observations be regarded as interdependent, each being essential to the other. Examination is a pointless exercise if accurate records are not maintained. Similarly, any records must be backed up by thorough and detailed examination.

This chapter will consider the importance of examination of the object, whether purely as an assessment of its condition, or to determine the extent of damage before treatment. The numerous specialist techniques available for examination and analysis of objects and the scientific theory behind them can be extremely complex and confusing. A lack of awareness of the facilities available means that potential opportunities for further examination and research are not always recognized, and a chance to extract valuable information may well be lost. In order to help familiarize the conservator, this chapter presents a brief introductory overview of the range of the examination techniques available, together with some examples of their application. However, it is by no means intended as a practical guide to their application.

Finally, the recording of examination and treatment details will be covered in the last section of this chapter. Its importance cannot be overvalued as a continuous commitment to the preservation of the object.

Initial examination

The early stages of any conservation work generally involve an examination of the object with the naked eye, during which the conservator becomes acquainted with its characteristics (Figure 4.1). As well as assessing the condition of the object and the extent and causes of any deterioration or previous restoration, observations of colour, texture, density, hardness and porosity should not be overlooked. Such physical qualities relate to the nature of the raw materials used in the body and glazes, the firing temperature, and the method of fabrication (Shepard, 1980). All these characteristics will interact and have implications in the treatment of an object.

In order to carry out a thorough visual examination it will usually be necessary to handle the object, unless its fragility or shape makes this dangerous (Figure 4.2). A great deal may also be learned about the quality of the object through tactile examination. Its weight in relation to its size will give an indication of the density of the material, which in turn should suggest how porous the body is. By feeling and

Figure 4.1 An initial examination with the naked eye should help to determine the main characteristics and flaws in the object (Victoria and Albert Museum, London).

gauging the weight, it should be possible to distinguish, even without looking, a high-fired dense hard-paste porcelain from a low-fired porous earthenware.

An auditory examination may also be useful at this stage. This involves tapping the ceramic surface with a small implement such as a spatula, fingernail or wooden modelling tool. The resonating tone can give an indication, not only of the degree of density of the body, but also of its soundness and the presence of any flaws. A relatively small hairline crack can produce a marked dulling of the ringing tone. Unstable and insecure glazes may also be detected, by gently tapping. With experience the combination of visual, tactile and auditory senses makes the detection of some flaws seem an almost instinctive response.

A simple hand-held metal detector (such as those used by electricians to detect concealed wiring in walls) can be useful when it comes to detecting hidden dowels or rivets (Figure 4.3).

While such physical qualities as hardness and porosity are rather vague and lacking in standardization, they provide useful criteria in determining and assessing the nature of the ceramic material from which the object is made. They will also have implications in the treatment of damaged ceramic vessels.

Colour

The range of colours that are apparent in ceramic objects is the result of a combination of factors: the composition of the clay, the glazes and other decoration, together with the firing conditions within the kiln. In addition, changes in colour, whether localized on the object's surface, or generally dispersed, may be the result of foreign material from

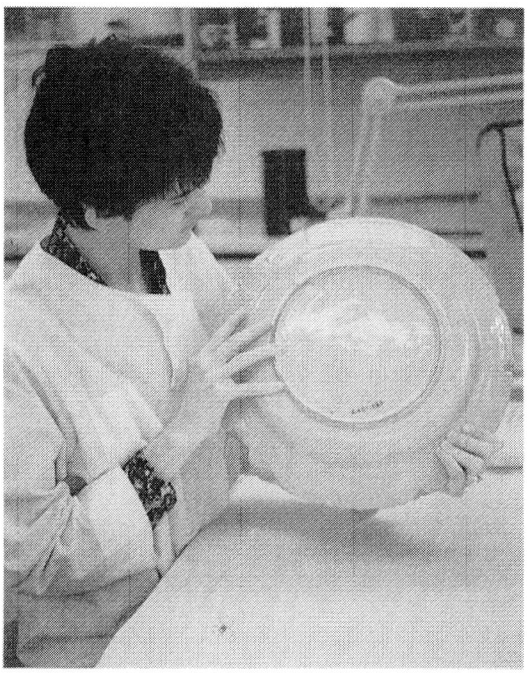

Figure 4.2 Handling the object will play an important part in assessing the extent of any damage early on in the examination process (Victoria and Albert Museum, London).

Figure 4.3 An electrician's metal detector can help draw attention to the presence of concealed dowels (Victoria and Albert Museum, London).

the surrounding environment coming into contact with the object. The extraneous material will be either deposited superficially, or absorbed and carried by moisture into the body, having gained entry at a point where the surface is not protected by a glaze. Flaws in the glaze such as crazing or cracks are capable of acting as capillaries, pulling contaminated water into the body to cause a stain. As a result, unusual or unexpected changes in colour can be an indicator of specific problems.

Some surface accretions may be of ethnographic interest to the archaeologist or historian. Mud or earth on a pot's surface may be the remains of burial material that was not removed after excavation and can give important information about the origins of the object. Residual material on the surface might also give clues about the object's use and the society to which it belonged; traces of organic products on cooking vessels may be identified, and fats absorbed by the body can be analysed (Bush and Zubrow, 1986).

Old restorations can also be responsible for changes in colour. Lacquers, coatings and resins may age and discolour with time, causing unsightly areas of inappropriate colouring on the surface of the object. Old metal rivets or dowels may corrode, particularly when exposed to moisture, the products of oxidation being drawn into the body to cause shadowing beneath the glaze. Break lines will be more obvious as adhesives age and become brittle, weakening the joint, and attracting dirt.

Colour can be accurately measured instrumentally or by reference to a colour system. While of limited application to the conservator, it may have some use in the testing of conservation materials where comparisons of colour are a critical consideration, or in describing the colour of archaeological ceramics.

Hardness

The hardness of ceramics can affect their durability or resistance to wear and damage; consequently the approach to handling and treatment will be affected. In describing the degree of hardness the Mohs scale may be used as a comparative assessment based on the known hardness of ten different minerals:

talc	(1)
gypsum	(2)
calcite	(3)
fluorspar	(4)
apatite	(5)
feldspar (orthoclase)	(6)
quartz	(7)
topaz	(8)
corundum	(9)
diamond	(10)

The test relies on the principle that the harder material will scratch the softer. The hardness of a fingernail would come between that of calcite and fluorite, while that of a needle falls between feldspar and quartz. The Mohs scale is not an accurate test, since its application is difficult to standardize and control.

Porosity

Conservation materials, such as solvents and low-viscosity resins, will readily, and in some cases irreversibly, be absorbed into a porous body, introducing the possibility of staining. Observations on the degree of porosity during initial examination will be an important factor in influencing the course of treatment and the choice of materials used.

While it may not be necessary to measure porosity for the purposes of conservation, experience in handling and treating different types of wares will increase the conservator's ability to recognize the degree of porosity. More accurate measurement involves the use of a balance and overflow-type volumeter to quantify the precise value of porosity by comparison of saturated and dry samples.

Strength

Scientists are able to measure the strength of a body under compression, or tension, or heat using complex instrumental procedures. For the conservator, it is sufficient to be aware of the characteristic and its implications in terms of the durability of an object.

Further visual examination

The hand lens

Following the initial examination of an object, the next stage could involve the use of a hand-held magnifier (Figure 4.4). This extends the powers of human observation around ten times beyond that of the naked eye, allowing the superficial qualities of the object to be seen in greater detail (Kingery and Vandiver, 1986). A local light source, such as an adjustable desk lamp, may be positioned to shine on the surface of the object at a raking angle to highlight the irregularities and textures of the surface. A sharp instrument such as a needle, held in a pin vice, or a microsurgical scalpel, can be used to probe the surface cautiously, continuing the investigation of the physical characteristics in greater detail.

Previous restoration treatments, if not immediately obvious with the naked eye, should become more apparent using a hand lens. Even the most recent treatments and so-called invisible restorations that have not undergone ageing processes should be

Figure 4.4 Simple hand-held magnifier in use (Victoria and Albert Museum, London).

detectable with a hand lens and pin at this stage. The slight differences in light transmission, or reflectance, and the subtle differences in opacity, colour and gloss, should betray so-called invisible areas of retouch or tinted fillings.

By examining damaged areas such as chips or break edges, it is possible to assess the physical characteristics of the body. With careful use of a needle, superficial dirt or deposits may be removed to expose the underlying surface. Resistance to probing and scratching with a needle helps to determine the qualities of the body. For example, softer particles of feldspar and calcite can be easily distinguished from the much harder quartz grains using a pin. The conclusion drawn from such observations will have implications in the choice of conservation treatment to be used later.

While the naked eye can make out some of the processes used in the construction of the object, low magnification will make throwing, coiling, slab building and casting more apparent. Tool marks and fingerprints, preserved in the firing process, act as clues in detecting the finer details of such processes. Manufacturing defects such as *firing cracks* should be distinguishable from post-firing cracks by studying the behaviour of the glaze at the edge of the break line. Cracks which may have occurred during firing when the glaze was still fluid will have soft, melted edges, while those occurring at cooler temperatures or after firing will have abrupt, sharp edges (Figure 2.2).

Optical microscopy

A further aid for more detailed examination is the *binocular microscope* with a magnification capability of between ×5 and ×100 (Figure 4.5). A basic portable microscope, with magnification of the order of ×10 to ×35, is ideal for use at the work bench. It can be used for close examination of the condition and structure of the object, and also for viewing treatments whilst in progress. More sophisticated instruments such as *stereo zoom trinocular microscopes* have superior optics, and can incorporate a zoom facility, as well as a third eyepiece for camera attachment (Figure 4.6). A zoom lens allows magnification to be changed without altering the focus. Such microscopes tend to be much more comfortable to use for long periods of time. The long focal length allows space for movement of instruments beneath the lens so that objects of various sizes can be accommodated on the stand for viewing. The light source is important; an adjustable fibre optic system with a dimming facility allows the conservator to select the direction of the light and the angle at which it strikes the surface of an object, so that textures and irregularities can be accentuated. Photography used in conjunction with the microscope can be an extremely useful method of documenting unusual

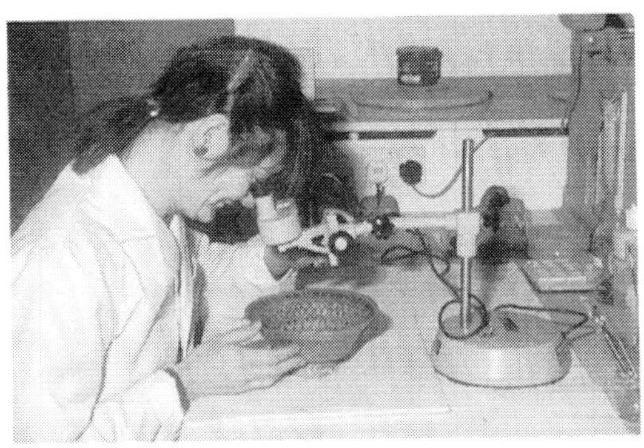

Figure 4.5 A binocular microscope (Victoria and Albert Museum, London).

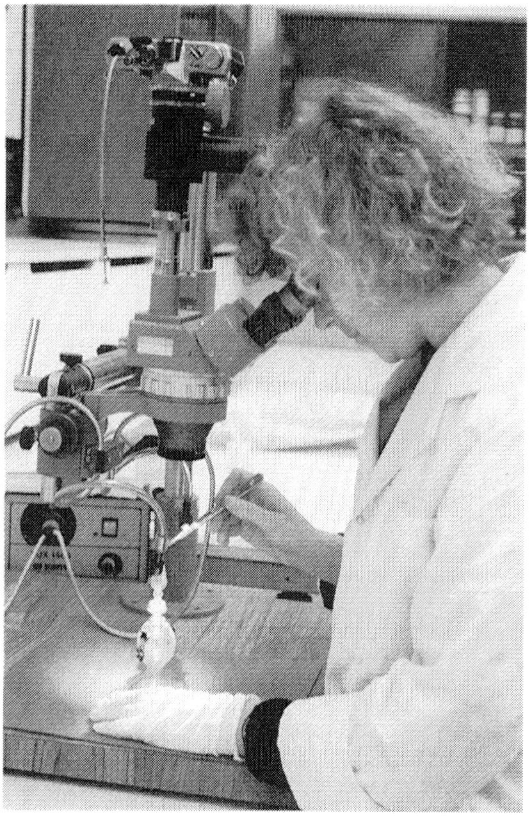

Figure 4.6 Stereo zoom trinocular microscope (Victoria and Albert Museum, London).

and interesting features. Ideally the microscope should have a built-in attachment for a camera so that the option is always available for this method of recording. Special tungsten films should be used in order to ensure correct exposure, and the risk of any vibration should be eliminated as far as possible, as a shaking camera will spoil the sharpness and detail of the image.

There are other more sophisticated types of optical microscopy techniques available (such as thin sections and electron microscopy) that help to establish more detailed information about the nature and composition of the surface of an object or sample: these will be considered later in this chapter.

Ultraviolet, infrared and X-ray aided examination

Electromagnetic radiation of those wavelengths on either side of the visible spectrum can also be used in the examination of ceramic artifacts to observe aspects of the structure of the object not usually visible under normal conditions. The wavelengths include infrared, X-ray and ultraviolet radiation. Infrared radiation has a longer wavelength than visible light and is consequently less energetic, while X-ray and ultraviolet radiation are shorter and have more energy.

Some substances, usually organic, that appear colourless in the visible light range will absorb ultraviolet light or *black light* (wavelength of 200–450 nm). Ultraviolet light can be produced artificially with a hand-held mercury vapour lamp; the light is absorbed by the surface of the object and re-emitted as fluorescence of varying intensity. The shorter, more energetic wavelengths around 250 nm tend to be most useful, although longer lengths around 400 nm may give interesting results. The individual chemical constituents on an object's surface will fluoresce as different colours revealing subtle variations in the glaze composition and any exposed body. Later additions and the presence of any restoration materials on an object may also be revealed. Hand-held ultraviolet lamps are relatively inexpensive and do not require the backup of any other sophisticated equipment (Figure 4.7). All that is needed to operate one is a dark room or a cupboard from which other light can be excluded and a source of electricity. Unfortunately it is not possible to generalize or predict the type of fluorescence that will be produced from different materials or types of ceramic owing to the variable nature of the ultraviolet radiation from individual mercury vapour lamps. Ultraviolet light, particularly the shorter wavelengths, is harmful to human tissues, and eyes should be protected from its rays. Advice should be sought from manufacturers regarding the most suitable form of protection.

Examination of the structure underlying the surface of the object is possible using X-ray and infrared radiation. These types of radiation are able to penetrate some materials to a greater or lesser extent, depending on their density, and reveal details

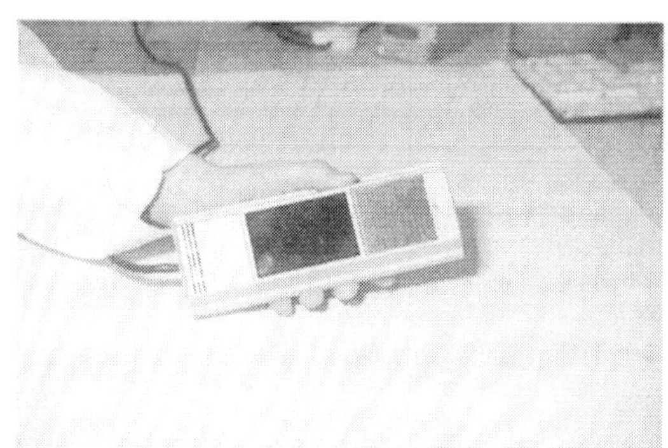

Figure 4.7 Hand-held ultraviolet lamp.

Figure 4.8 Sri Lankan tile, with unfired decoration, viewed under natural light (Victoria and Albert Museum, London).

within the matrix. Unlike ultraviolet, X-ray and infrared cannot be seen with the naked eye; image intensifiers or special sensitive film is necessary to view them. Infrared radiation is more commonly used for examination of surfaces that have become obscured for various reasons (Figures 4.8, 4.9). Decorated ceramic surfaces obscured by encrustations of salts, calcareous deposits, or carbon resulting from fire damage can be revealed under infrared radiation.

X-rays, which are of an even shorter wavelength than ultraviolet radiation, can be used to present an image of an object on a sensitized photographic plate. The energetic X-rays can penetrate materials normally opaque to visible and ultraviolet radiation to produce a two-dimensional representation of the internal three-dimensional structure, highlighting areas of different X-ray densities. Air pockets, spaces and porous areas will offer little resistance to the X-rays, allowing them to pass through the object onto the plate and produce dark, well exposed areas. Dense inclusions or any metallic components will tend to absorb the X-rays before they reach the photographic plate so that these parts appear as light underexposed areas on the negative. The different densities in the structure shown up on the X-ray plate may also give some indication of the craftsman's techniques by revealing the internal alignment and any solid components or internal armatures that might have been incorporated (Strahan and Boulton, 1988). Previous restorations including dowels, rivets, bonds and fillings, as well as any weaknesses such as internal cracks and points of stress, may also be detected using X-rays.

The interpretation of such images is by no means simple; the three-dimensional form will be presented in two dimensions, superimposing many features with no clear indication of the relative depths (Figures 4.10, 4.11). This can be overcome to a certain extent by taking several views from different angles and then comparing the various images.

If there is any doubt regarding the provenance or age of an object, it is worth remembering that the exposure of the object to X-rays may invalidate any potential results that could be obtained from thermoluminescence dating. In such circumstances it would be advisable either to avoid X-raying the object, or to consider removing a sample that could be retained for thermoluminescence dating should the need arise.

Further investigation and analysis

Further examination beyond the scope of the conservator will be carried out by scientists in a laboratory using sophisticated equipment. It is important to have a clear objective in mind before indulging in any kind of detailed examination. Usually the information to be determined relates to when, where, how and of what the object is made; any results may be used, for example, to verify the authenticity of an object.

Obviously, it is preferable if the integrity of the object is not threatened and a non-invasive method of examination is used. Techniques such as EDXRF, NAA, and EMPA can be used non-destructively if the object is small enough and sufficiently robust to be placed in the instrument's vacuum chamber. The decision whether to extract a sample or not must be weighed up against the benefits to be gained from the information that might be revealed.

The majority of the techniques outlined in this section demand that a sample is extracted from the object. The size of the sample is determined by the technique to be used; in the case of *microsamples* a small sample is removed with a diamond point, a sharp scalpel or an abrasive. Less than a millimetre of glaze or body is enough to determine the microstructure, by compositional analysis with an electron microprobe or by X-ray diffraction. Unfortunately, within one object the body tends to vary in structure and composition; one single sample is unlikely to be representative of the whole body, particularly if it is coarse. It is therefore preferable to try to obtain several samples. Some techniques demand larger samples; such *macrosamples*, for compositional analysis or thermoluminescence testing, are usually obtained by taking a small cylindrical core sample of 3 mm diameter and depth, with a water-cooled diamond core drill. They can generally be extracted from an unobtrusive part, such as a damaged area or a foot rim. Although the small hole can be filled later, it may be preferable to leave it as evidence that an analysis exists as part of the history of the object. Any extraneous materials picked up as a result of the object's use or from previous conservation treatments will distort the analysis, and so it is essential to ensure that the samples are free from such contaminants. It

Figure 4.9 The Sri Lankan tile in infrared light. The artists preliminary outlines are now visible as distinct dark lines; compare with the same tile under natural light in Figure 4.8).

Figure 4.10 Terracotta model for a tomb under natural light (Victoria and Albert Museum, London).

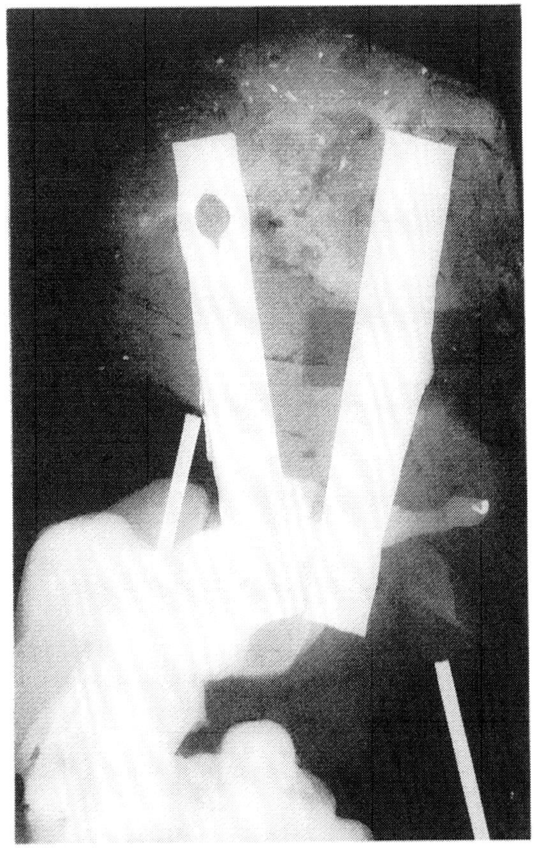

Figure 4.11 The same object as revealed by X-rays, showing areas of dense material as lighter tones. The metal components included as part of the restoration to the upper section of the model become evident. Irregularities in the plaster filling are also revealed (Victoria and Albert Museum, London).

may not be possible to be entirely confident about the absence of intrusive materials; this should be borne in mind when interpreting the results.

The conservator often has a clear idea of the type of information that he wishes to discover on behalf of the curator, archaeologist, antiquarian or just for his own research purposes. It is not always obvious how to go about getting the information, or even if it is possible. Close consultation with a scientist will be crucial to making any progress. It is also useful for the conservator to have some grasp of the testing methods available, so that he has an idea of the implications of the techniques which the scientist might suggest. There may be potential risks to the object that are not necessarily of serious concern to the scientist.

The following summary briefly considers some of the methods that the ceramics conservator may come across (Table 4.1). The techniques fall into two broad groups: those that use various forms of microscopy in order to view the characteristics and components of the surface of the sample, and those that establish the nature of the bulk composition including such details as the chemical constituents or the crystal structure. Dating techniques will be considered as the last part of this section.

Further aids to viewing the composition

Polished cross-sections

The sample is prepared by mounting it in a resin such as epoxy or polyester which is then ground and polished for examination under a microscope, normally in reflected light. Samples are usually in the range of 1–5 mm. The technique can be useful for distinguishing the structure of the body and overlying glaze or pigment layers (Figure 4.12). The different

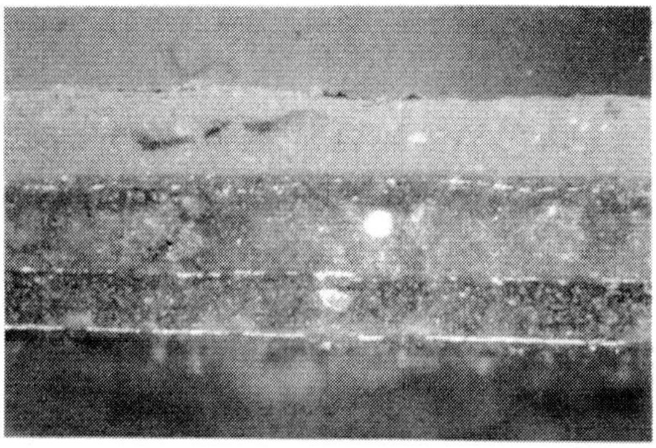

Figure 4.12 A polished cross-section, × 175, showing a sample of gilding removed from a Ming dynasty figure. The layers of pigmented lacquer separated by layers of gilding are clearly visible (Victoria and Albert Museum, London).

crystals and grains present in the body may also be identified (Kingery and Vandiver, 1986).

Thin sections

These are made from a polished sample that has been cut from either the vertical or the horizontal axis of the pot. The prepared sample is then mounted on a glass microscope slide using resin, with the polished side in contact with the glass, and then ground down to an even thickness of around 0.03 mm. The correct thickness is judged by observing the changes in the colours of the quartz crystals when viewed in polarized light using a petrological microscope. The minerals and substances present will exhibit identifiable characteristics in different types of light (Hodges, 1963).

By identifying characteristic combinations of specific minerals, fillers and other particles in a sample, it may be possible to pinpoint the source of the materials (Norton, 1958). Observations of the sections help establish how the object was made: whether it was thrown, coiled, cast, or hand-built. Such information relies on examining the orientation of the clay particles, air spaces and other inclusions. Surface decorations can be studied closely using thin sections, and conclusions drawn about the nature of slips and glazes (Woods, 1982). Firing temperatures can be assessed by examining the degree of fusion between the clay fillers and comparing it with that of a known body (Gautier, 1977).

Electron microscopes

The electron microscope offers a much greater range of resolution and magnification (× 100,000) than any optical instrument. The beam of light normally used to illuminate the object in conventional microscopes is substituted with a beam of accelerated electrons.

Scanning electron microscopy (SEM) uses a fine electron beam to scan across the surface of the sample. The release of secondary electrons can reveal

Table 4.1 Analytic techniques for examination of ceramics

Technique	*Implications for object*	*Application*
Microscopy		
Scanning electron microscopy (SEM)	Requires preparation of a sample unless object or fragment is small	Viewing surface morphology and structure
Electron microprobe analysis (EMPA)	As above	Useful for determination of spot compositions in small samples
Bulk analysis		
Energy dispersive X-ray fluorescence analysis (EDXRF)	Can be used non-destructively directly on object	Bulk analysis of elemental composition of the surface
Neutron activation analysis (NAA)	Generally uses a powdered sample though can be used non-destructively	Sensitive technique for bulk analysis of elements Particularly useful for detection and measurement of trace elements
Atomic absorption spectroscopy (AAS)	Sample destroyed during analysis	Used to quantify individual elements
Inductively coupled plasma atomic emission spectroscopy (ICP)	As above	Fast, precise, simultaneous technique to quantify individual elements
X-ray diffraction analysis (XRD)	Powder sample required	Can determine chemical compounds in crystalline substances
Dating		
Thermoluminescence dating (TL)	Macrosample required	Dating ceramics
Carbon 14 dating	Macrosample required	Occasionally used for dating ceramics

information about the surface. A suitable detector linked to a programmed computer will produce images representing the optical views of the sample with a resolution and depth of field far superior to any other method.

Although freshly broken surfaces may be examined, it is usual for a sample to be specially prepared beforehand, either by etching with acid to develop a surface texture, enabling contrasts to be observed as slight differences in the elevation of the surface, or by polishing. The sample must then be coated with carbon or some other conductive material in order to remove any charge. The high-resolution three-dimensional image gives a much more detailed interpretation of the contrasting characteristics of crystalline inclusions and their chemical variability than would be possible with other techniques. The technique allows the texture and morphology of the sample to be studied in detail. Early vitreous materials such as Egyptian blue, faience and frit have been analysed and identified as a result of studies of the microstructure revealed in the polished sections viewed with the SEM (Tite and Bimson, 1986).

SEM with back-scattered electron emissions involves the use of electrons from the beam itself that have been inelastically scattered by interaction with the sample, then collected by an appropriate detector. Contrasts are produced as a result of differences in the atomic number of the constituents, more electrons being scattered back from higher atomic number constituents. The technique can be used to clarify differences between minerals (Figure 4.13).

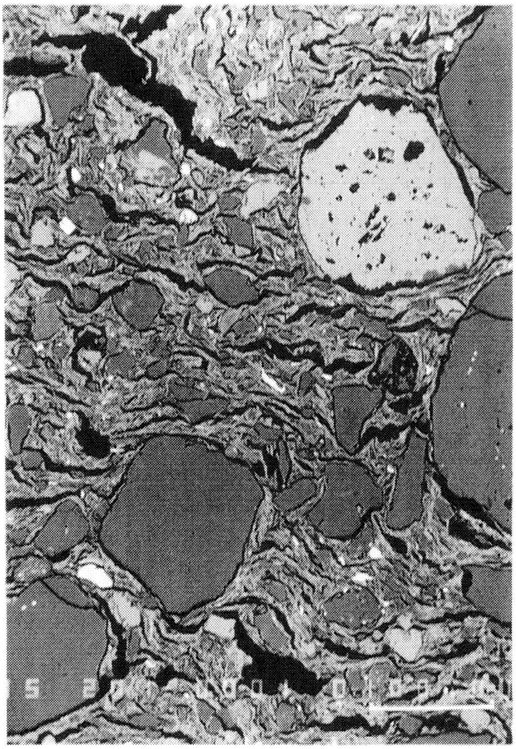

Figure 4.13 A back-scattered electron image of a polished sample taken from a terracotta bust of Henry VII (dated 1509–11) from the collection of the Victoria and Albert Museum, London. The back-scattered electron output is proportional to the mean atomic number; this makes it possible to perceive compositional differences on the surface of the sample. The image shows the larger particles of quartz and other mineral grains bonded together by a mass of fused clay; the dark areas are voids. The scale bar represents one micron (Courtesy J. Watt; Imperial College, London).

Electron microprobe analysis (EMPA)

This represents a refinement of electron microscopy in combination with energy dispersive X-ray spectroscopy, where a finely focused beam of electrons is directed onto a precise area of the object (one micron in diameter). An X-ray emission is then produced characteristic of those elements present on the surface of the sample. Quantitative identification of constituent elements which account for at least 0.1% of the composition is possible. The sample, which can be very small, is usually polished, coated with carbon (to remove the charge), mounted and then placed in the vacuum chamber of the instrument. Lighter elements, which in the past were not easily detected compared with the heavier elements (Kingery and Vandiver, 1986), can now be picked up with a suitable detector. One of the most successful applications is in determining spot compositions within extremely small samples, such as comparisons between the various phases in the weathering crusts of glazes and the unaffected layers below, or local variations within the glaze surface (Vandiver and Kingery, 1985). It has recently been used, with some success, to compare Chinese Han dynasty green lead glazes with green high lead glazes on ceramics from northern China dating from the Tang and Ming dynasties. The technique helped to identify the detailed composition of the glazes and to detect large grains of undissolved quartz suggesting that the materials used for the glaze were unfritted (Wood *et al.*, 1992).

Analysis of the bulk composition

While the various types of microscopy serve as a specialist aid to viewing the fine structure of the object, other techniques offer a means of analysing the materials and precisely determining the relative proportions of the constituents.

Energy dispersive X-ray fluorescence spectroscopy (EDXRF)

This technique is normally used to determine the elemental composition of materials, and can be used non-destructively with specially designed equipment. A small area of the surface (about 2 mm in diameter) is bombarded with high-energy X-rays. The elements within the target area respond by becoming excited, releasing secondary fluorescent X-rays. The energy of these X-rays is characteristic for each element and the intensity is related to the quantity of those elements present. Signals are immediately conveyed to an analysing instrument which assimilates and processes the information, displaying it as a spectrum on its visual display unit (Figure 4.14).

Generally, XRF instruments are able to detect all elements with an atomic number of about 11 and above, though in order to do so the sample must be placed in a vacuum chamber, which obviously puts limitations on the sample size. Instruments most suited to the examination of complete artifacts are designed without the vacuum chamber, but as a consequence are unable to detect elements with atomic numbers below 20 (or thereabouts). The method restricts analysis to the surfaces of the object, penetrating to a depth of 30–100 microns, though further examination is possible if the interior is exposed through damage, or a sample is extracted.

EDXRF spectroscopy has been successfully used in the examination of glazes. The identification of any metal oxides used as colourants in the decoration can be extremely useful as an aid to characterizing different groups of ceramics. The colouring oxides are seldom pure and the technique will detect the different elements present so that comparative assessments can be made to verify the provenance and date of particular objects.

Wood and Kerr (1992) used EDXRF to study the copper-red pigment on the decoration of Korean ceramic vessels from the Koryo and Choson periods. They made preliminary observations of the glaze colourants, comparing and contrasting them with

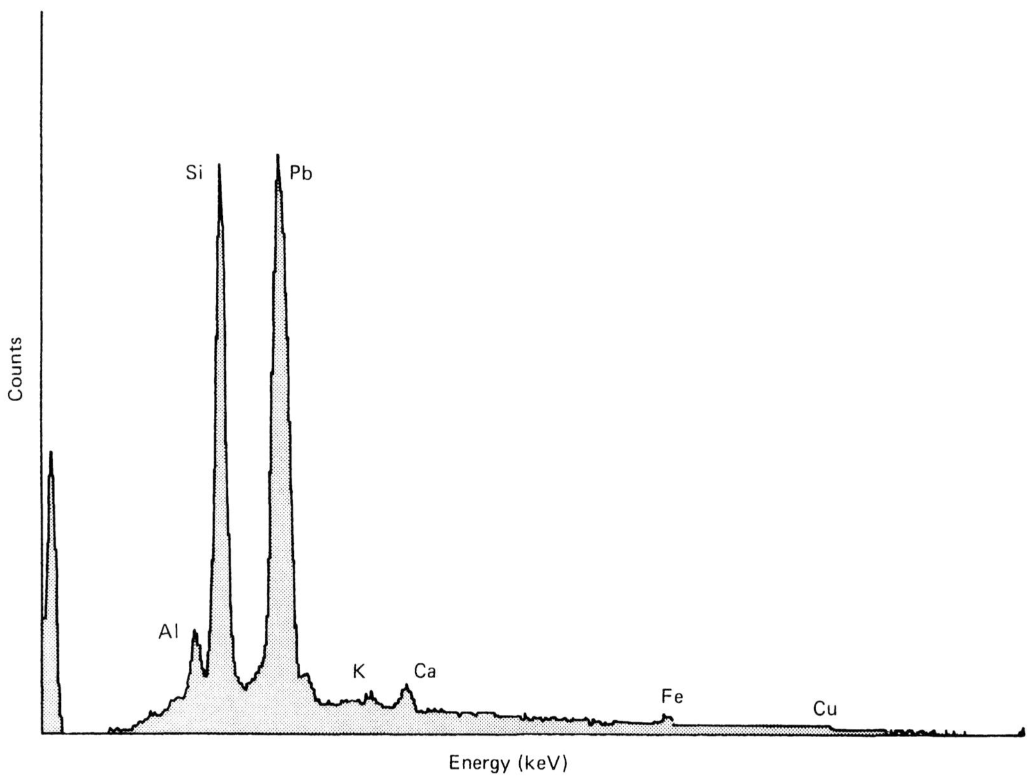

Figure 4.14 Energy dispersive X-ray spectrum of a sample of coloured lead glaze from a green-glazed earthenware Chinese jar (206 BC to AD 220) from the collection of the Victoria and Albert Museum, London. The total number of counts in each peak (plotted vertically) is proportional to the percentage of elements present. X-ray energy is plotted along the horizontal axis; each element has a characteristic energy at which a peak will occur if the element is present. The major peaks coincide at the energies that are characteristic for silica and lead with trace amounts of alumina, potassium, calcium, iron and copper (Courtesy J. Watt; Imperial College, London).

parallel groups of Chinese porcelains and drawing conclusions to suggest the techniques that might have been used to achieve particular decorative effects.

Yap (1986a) has used the technique to determine the authenticity of Chinese porcelain from the Ming and Qing dynasties. He also used the technique (1986b) in order to detect non-destructively modern fake reproductions, and by establishing the typical ratios of certain elements present in the glaze of genuine Qing ceramics a comparison could be made with the suspect objects. Foster (1987) describes a research project where the industry of Minoan faience production was studied with the aid of the analysis resulting from EDXRF.

Neutron activation analysis (NAA)

Neutron activation analysis can be used to help identify the bulk chemical composition of clay samples. It is an extremely sensitive analytical technique that facilitates detection and measurement of small quantities of a range of elements, including trace elements, present as 0.01% by weight. Trace elements do not affect the general properties of the object material; however, since they occur in very specific combinations and concentrations their occurrence may be used rather like a fingerprint. The characteristics and properties of two clay deposits from different geological sources may be very similar in general terms, but it is highly unlikely that the constituent amounts and proportions of trace elements will be exactly the same.

The technique has been used extensively by researchers as a means to study prehistoric trade routes and distributions, as well as to characterize and classify archaeological ceramics (Sayre, 1958). The examination process involves irradiating a powder sample with a neutron beam in an atomic pile, causing the individual elements to become excited and to transform into unstable radioactive isotopes. When the sample is withdrawn from the pile, the amount and type of particular isotopes present are identified by analysis of the emitted radiation. The technique can also be used non-destructively, although it has the disadvantage that the object becomes radioactive for some time (Perlman and Asaro, 1969). King *et al.* (1986) describe how the technique was applied in order to characterize geochemically 129 shards from 38 sites recovered during an archaeological survey in south-west Cyprus. Such extensive detailed research relies heavily on statistical techniques in order to establish patterns and correlations in the results. Another example of application of the technique is illustrated in the work of Topping (1986), who used it to confirm that later prehistoric pottery from the Western Isles of Scotland was probably used and made locally.

Atomic absorption spectroscopy (AAS) and inductively coupled plasma atomic emission spectroscopy (ICP)

Both these techniques involve examining the bulk properties of a substrate by passing a dilute solution of the sample through a high-temperature flame. The well established technique of AAS is used to determine the amounts of individual elements, one at a time, while the recently developed and more sophisticated technique of ICP has the advantage of simultaneous assessment of several elements with a high degree of precision and speed.

In AAS light of specific wavelength produced by a hollow cathode discharge lamp is directed towards the spray of the sample solution and absorbed by the atoms (Figure 4.15). The absorption bands of most metallic elements are known and precise quantitative analysis is possible by calibration with solutions containing known elements (Hughes *et al.*, 1976).

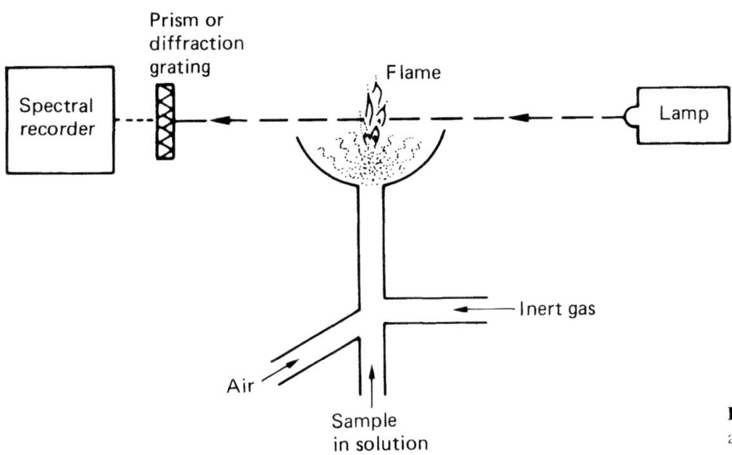

Figure 4.15 Schematic representation of atomic absorption spectroscopy.

Since the technique demands that the elements to be analysed have already been identified it tends to be used as a means of establishing the presence (or not), and amount, of specific trace elements in a sample. The results may help to confirm whether or not a ceramic sample is derived from a particular source (Burgess, 1990).

In ICP the sample solution is sprayed into a very high-temperature argon plasma which has the effect of reducing the sample to an atomic level accompanied by the emission of light that can then be analysed by a suitable instrument. The technique is particularly suited for trace element detection as an aid to ceramic characterization and provenancing.

X-ray diffraction analysis (XRD)

Most of the techniques so far described aid the identification of different elements in the composition, whereas this technique is used to determine chemical compounds in crystalline structures, present in ceramic materials. When X-rays are passed through crystalline material a unique diffraction pattern is produced. The X-rays are focused on the sample which is often prepared in powder form. The X-rays interact with the planes of atoms or molecules and are diffracted in a distinct pattern of curved lines that can be recorded photographically as a series of concentric circles. Each mineral produces a distinct diffraction pattern that can be used as a means of identification (Kingery and Vandiver, 1986; Burgess, 1990).

XRD has been used to identify the characteristics of particular clays (Williams *et al.*, 1985), as well as to study the effects of heat on clay. Bimson (1969) describes the examination of ceramics by X-ray powder diffraction using very small samples (less than 0.05 g), scraped from the object using diamond faced spatulas, files or pencils. The technique can be used to reveal information about the minerals in a clay body which may help determine the authenticity of a particular piece.

Dating methods

Thermoluminescence (TL) dating

Thermoluminescence dating may be used to determine the age of fired ceramic objects when provenance and origin are in doubt, or when historical research has failed to produce any conclusive evidence as to the age of an object (Fleming, 1971; 1974; Fleming and Sampson, 1972; Fleming and Stoneham, 1973). The technique relies on the predisposition of ceramics to contain small concentrations of radioactive substances that release nuclear energy during their radioactive decay. This energy is gradually absorbed and stored by some of the minerals present in clay. If the object is then reheated to within the range 100–400°C, the accumulated energy will be released, emitted as light or luminescence, and can be measured. The original firing of the pottery and any subsequent reheating result in the thermoluminescent clock being put back to zero again. Accurate measurement of the glow during reheating makes it possible to determine the amount of time which has lapsed since the object was last heated. Although the concept is fairly simple there are many variables to be considered; the degree of luminescence will be affected by the composition of the pottery (Cairns, 1974), the original firing temperature (Han, 1974) and also by environmental factors. Restoration or conservation treatment may affect and invalidate the accuracy of the results. If the object has been subjected to excessive heating at some point during its lifetime, or exposed to X-rays, the results of thermoluminescence may be unreliable. Usually a sample (3 mm) is taken with a diamond core drill and the age of the object can be theoretically determined to within $\pm 20\%$. Applications include the detection of fakes, where ages of 50–100 years can easily be distinguished from 300–1000 years (Fleming, 1971).

Carbon 14 (^{14}C) dating

Ceramics which contain carbon either as part of a black core, or introduced into the pores by cooking or decoration, can be ^{14}C dated, provided there is no calcite present. The technique relies on the principle that radioactive carbon is produced by the impact of cosmic rays in the atmosphere transforming a very small portion of nitrogen atoms into radioactive ^{14}C atoms. These atoms find their way, via carbon dioxide and photosynthesis, into plants and consequently animals. When an organism dies it no longer acquires further ^{14}C atoms and the ^{14}C starts to disintegrate slowly at a known rate. By comparing the radioactivity of a sample of organic material extracted from an ancient pot with a modern example, the length of time which has lapsed since the organic material of the unknown sample has ceased to be alive can be estimated. The method is rarely of practical use on ceramics owing to the inadequate quantities of carbon present. However, the carbon derived from the fuel that was used for firing some ancient pottery can be useful as a dating method (Gabasio *et al.*, 1986). The work of Johnson *et al.* (1986) suggests that the use of at least two different dating techniques will give more reliable results.

Recording

While examination forms a very necessary part of the conservation process and can provide an interesting insight into the nature and condition of the object, the information extracted is only of transitory use unless accurately recorded. Observations made when the damaged object first arrives in the studio are easily forgotten 24 hours later after an old restoration has been taken apart. Even the use of more sophisticated and elaborate methods of examination is no guarantee that the facts revealed during interpretation of the results will be remembered later.

The documentation and working records relating to both condition and treatment should be regarded as an essential element in a professional approach to conservation. Without them, valuable information about the original condition of the object and the treatment may be lost; future conservation may be unnecessarily prolonged by attempts to discover the precise nature of the previous restorer's work. The solution is to have access to accurate notes of any past work or examination. It is not unusual to be involved with undoing restorations to ceramics treated as little as 5 years previously, for example in situations where the synthetic materials used have deteriorated or the craftsmanship in carrying out the repair is of an unacceptable standard. Consequently the role of documentation becomes all the more important when we consider that it is highly likely that it will eventually be necessary for another conservator to reverse the work when adhesives and retouching lacquers have discoloured to an unacceptable level.

During the process of dismantling an old restoration, or when faced with fresh damage, the conservator is often in the privileged situation of seeing parts of the object that are not normally exposed. If a detailed examination of the object is undertaken, information will be gained which, although not relevant to the conservator, may be invaluable to others later. Accurate records of the treatment may also be useful to the curator, and may save time later if the conservator should be called upon to advise on the suitability of an object for loan or exhibition. The administration and forward planning of a small studio can be greatly helped by an efficient, reliable recording system that can be used to review output in terms of time, staffing and resources.

To aid what is undeniably a tedious task the use of notebooks or *daybooks* can prove helpful. These do not necessarily have to be immaculate, fastidiously kept journals, but should be regarded as working tools, to be constantly open at the work bench (Figure 4.16). Notes may be quickly jotted down during the course of the treatment to serve primarily as a personal prompt for later when a more detailed report on the work is written. Daybook entries might include notes, photos and sketches made during the dismantling of a previous restoration, and include details not readily apparent during the initial examination which have become clearer after practical work has been started. The type of adhesives used, whether water soluble or otherwise; the existence of any fillers; and the methods adopted to remove them should be noted. Such information,

Figure 4.16 A daybook is invaluable for jotting down notes, making diagrams, and leaving reminders that can later be transferred to treatment reports.

although seemingly obvious and unforgettable while the scalpel is still in the hand, is easily forgotten later, especially if two or three similar objects are being treated simultaneously.

In an archaeological context, where objects being excavated may require some emergency on-site treatment, the discipline of making careful records can prove invaluable later when the object eventually reaches the conservation studio. Because of the usual lack of well equipped facilities, expertise, and time, conservation work carried out in the field is often regarded as short term, aimed at preventing any further unnecessary damage occurring to the object in transit between the excavation and the studio. Recording the treatment should avoid the need to test methods to reverse unknown materials. Even the most basic of treatments, such as washing or cleaning, which have been carried out on the excavation site should be documented, particularly if they have altered the appearance of the object or its physical properties. Such treatments may have some bearing on the future condition of the object.

In some circumstances it may be useful to retain a small sample of adjacent soil with the object. If further analysis is to be carried out, as for example in thermoluminescence dating, or if unusual staining and reactions on or within the body have occurred, they might be explained by such a sample from the surrounding environment. Encrustations and any loose organic matter discovered in intimate association with an excavated ceramic vessel should also be carefully recorded and samples retained so that the opportunity for further detailed research associated with the object is not lost.

For the restorer in private practice, the discipline of keeping daybooks and records could easily be dismissed as a dispensable activity. He/she may feel that it is unrealistic to be expected to spend time keeping details of his/her work. However, the client who cares enough about his object to have it restored professionally should be given some written record of the processes employed in repairing the damage. It is the responsibility of the restorer to point out the importance of retaining the report of treatment, so that it can be retrieved later should any further examination or treatment of the object ever prove necessary.

Record cards

The general subject of conservation record cards has been widely discussed by various conservation institutions (Keene, 1983; Bradley, 1983; Corfield, 1983; Drown, 1983; Perry, 1983) in the hope of agreeing on a format that suits most requirements. Record cards are probably best designed by the users, or in close collaboration with them since individual needs will differ depending upon the conservators' circumstances, and what they wish to gain from the system. Private restorers working for themselves might have very practical reasons for adopting a simple card index system, arranged chronologically or in alphabetical order. Others may prefer to amalgamate the records with their correspondence files, or perhaps to document all relevant points in a book. Whatever the choice, it is important that the system works for those who use it.

Larger organizations such as private firms or museums have found that the sheer volume of documentation involved has lent itself to computerization as an aid towards efficiency. This has largely played a part in dictating the format of the record cards. The computerized system tends to require a more disciplined approach to terminology and order, with administrative details (such as museum number, type of object, origin etc.) being entered in a systematic manner to aid rapid retrieval. In the long term, such systems may completely remove the need for cumbersome records on paper. Actual details of treatment, by their nature, have to be more discursive and can be separated from the administrative details.

In general, records should be made using archival quality paper and inks. The format of treatment record cards should include three main sections. Firstly, a section will be devoted to the descriptive information relating to the object. Secondly, part of the card should include a space for details about the condition of the object before treatment. The last section should be for detailing the treatment stages, mentioning the processes involved and the materials used, together with their proprietary and chemical name. Then finally, it may be necessary to mention points particularly relevant to display or storage.

Labelling ceramic objects

Labelling of objects may be necessary for recording objects and for security reasons. Some form of numbering may be important for archaeological objects in order to record them as soon as they are excavated, or as soon as they are purchased by a museum. This may be a permanent or temporary number and may be marked on the object itself, on a label attached to the object, or on the container in which the object is placed.

Wherever suitable, the number should be written directly on the object. Where an object is too small to make this practical, the object may be stored in a small plastic box or bag. The box or bag can then itself be marked with the number, or a label may be stored alongside the object. Similarly, a collection of shards may be placed in a numbered container to avoid marking each shard. The pen used for marking the label itself should be as durable as possible, and work has been carried out comparing the properties of various pens available (Jones, *et al.*, 1980; 1985; Townsend, 1986; 1990; Ramsay and Thomson, 1990; Horie, 1990).

The numbering should be done in such a way that it is not obtrusive, yet so that it can be easily located and read without the need for excessive handling of the object. The number should not be applied to an unstable area, or one that is heavily encrusted, nor should it be marked on a break edge. When numbering shards, it is preferable to mark the inner surface rather than the outer one. The materials used should not cause any damage to the object and should be reversible. Although it might be preferable to make the numbering indelible for security reasons, this should be regarded as undesirable from an ethical point of view.

A small patch on the chosen area of the ceramic object should be cleaned and then primed with an application of clear resin such as 10% Paraloid/Acryloid B-72 in acetone, or 10% poly(vinyl acetate) in acetone. This will prevent the number from being absorbed into the body of a porous ware and will provide a more suitable protective surface on a glazed ware. When the application is dry, the number is applied using a drawing pen and drawing ink. Only minimum pressure should be used to avoid scratching through the sealing layer and damaging the ceramic. Alternatively the number may be painted on using a hand-held brush and pigmented acrylic paint, alkyd paint or oil paint. When this has dried a sealing coat of clear resin is applied on top of the number.

The labelling of damp objects from wet sites may not be possible using the materials so far described. Leskard (1987) suggests using Teflon strips imprinted with a Dymo labeller, or marking polypropylene paper labels with permanent waterproof felt-tip pens.

Photography as a method of recording

As a visual means of recording the condition and stages in the conservation treatment of an object, photography can be invaluable, provided it is of reasonable quality. Photographs should be regarded as a complementary aid to the interpretation of written documentation and drawings but not as a substitute. They should provide the additional level of information and detail that cannot easily be conveyed in words or sketches, such as shapes, colours, decoration and textures, as accurately as possible (Dorrell, 1977).

Unless conservators work for a large institution it usually falls upon them to take their own photographs. Although this has obvious disadvantages in terms of requiring time and a certain amount of familiarity with photographic techniques, it does allow conservators to record exactly what they want , at particular stages during the treatment, without having to interrupt work until a photographer is available.

The decision of whether to use black and white or colour film is determined by the nature of the subject matter and by personal preference, and also by expense. Black and white photography can be comparatively expensive unless darkroom facilities are available. It will show most types of damage and deterioration quite adequately, as well as offering greater archival permanence. In many situations the use of colour in photography may only serve as an added distraction to the main purpose of the photograph, though it can work out as the cheaper option, depending on the level of quality. In other situations colour photography may prove a more appropriate and satisfactory alternative, for example to illustrate colour changes caused by staining, or a discoloured old restoration, although the results may not always be a faithful reproduction of the subject. Black and white photography may also be useful in illustrating staining: by using colour filters selectively, such black and white photos can draw attention to stains or cracks of a specific colour in situations where other colours may distract from the point of the photograph.

Another dilemma may be faced in deciding whether to opt for colour prints or for colour transparencies. Prints are useful when illustrating a report, and can be filed with the documentation of the object. On the other hand, transparencies produce a sharper image and more accurate record of the colour with a sense of depth often absent from prints. Unfortunately the image that is produced on the film base itself tends to be too small and dark to see under normal circumstances. It can be enlarged by a viewing aid such as a hand-held portable viewer, or a projector and screen. Transparencies are also invaluable aids for lectures. For publication purposes they will also reproduce far better than colour prints which lose a significant degree of sharpness.

Regardless of the type of film, whether colour or black and white, the choice of film speed should be given consideration. A slower film speed – ISO 100, 50 or 25 – is preferable. These films will usually require a tripod to avoid camera shake, which will in turn enable a slow shutter speed or small aperture combination to be used. Faster films will give grainier quality, though they can be useful where lighting conditions are poor.

It is important to be consistent in the approach to photographing objects. By maintaining all the potential variables, such as lighting, type of background, measuring scale, film quality, filter, lens, height and distance, as constant as possible, the results should give reliable records. Such a standardized approach should be adopted for all photography and not just for each individual object, so that treatments and conditions can be compared convincingly. It is also worth taking several shots of the same view at various settings, to ensure a good result.

The camera

Single-lens reflex 35 mm cameras have the advantage of allowing the user to see the image of the object exactly as it appears on the film, which is not the case with view-finder cameras. They are also more versatile than other types of camera such as autofocus compact cameras, or cameras with self-developing materials (i.e. *Polaroids*), and allow a degree of flexibility in determining the end products. By varying focus, aperture, depth of field, lens, filter and other accessories, it is possible to achieve a variety of results to suit particular requirements (Bailey and Holloway, 1979).

Cameras with self-developing materials can produce a photograph within minutes. They can be useful in situations where results may be required right away, such as at the scene of an accident or disaster, or when dismantling a complex multi-component object.

Lenses

Light waves reflected from the subject pass via the lens through the *aperture* into the inside of the camera. The aperture controls the amount of the light entering by varying the diaphragm, calibrated by the *f* numbers or *stops*. When a lens is set at infinity, light waves from a distant subject converge to meet at a *focal point*. The plane on which the image comes into focus remains constant and is known as the *focal plane* and coincides with the *film plane*. The *focal length* of the lens is the distance between the focal point and the centre of the lens, usually measured in millimetres. Light waves from closer subjects converge into focus further behind the lens at the image plane. For a crisp picture the image plane must be brought to coincide with the focal plane.

The focal length of a lens determines its field of view and the size of the image in the frame. Choice of lens and hence focal length will be determined by the size of the object. Unfortunately it is not possible to achieve a completely accurate representation of the form of an object; there will nearly always be some distortion due to the limitations of the equipment (Dorrell, 1977). The images of objects with straight sides (tile panels and some vases) will suffer distortion using lenses that have a shorter focal length. A *standard lens* with focal length usually around 50/55 mm will give an image and field of view similar to what you see. A *macro lens* sacrifices maximum aperture for lens correction, allowing very close focusing up to half the real size of the subject, and is useful for detailed shots. A less expensive alternative to investing in a macro lens is either close-up filters (+1, +2 and +4) that will attach to the front of a standard lens or extension rings that are inserted between the lens and the camera body.

Depth of field

The depth of field is the distance in front of and behind the subject that is in focus. It is controlled by the aperture size: the smaller the aperture setting (at large *f* numbers), the greater the depth of field. Therefore greater care has to be taken when taking close-up detailed photographs of objects. This also has implications for the way the object or objects are positioned, as the aim should be to make all parts of the subject lie as much as possible within the plane of focus (Figure 4.17). So photographing a three-dimensional form such as a figurine can become an exacting task. For a vessel form such as a vase or jug, the camera should be positioned so as to minimize the depth of the object, making the rim appear as a narrow ellipse. This creates the impression that the base appears slightly smaller than the rim, owing to the effect of perspective. By convention spouts are shown on the left and handles on the right (Figure 4.18), arranged in such a way that the thickness of the handle is apparent (Dorrell, 1977; 1989). Problems of insufficient depth of field are typically encountered when an ordinary standard 50 mm lens is used close up, or as close as it will focus, and also when a macro lens or close-up filters are used. It is advisable when focusing at close range to check for consistent sharpness on the surrounding areas, as well as the central prism, and to focus slightly behind the nearest part of the object. It may be necessary to move the entire camera in relation to the object instead of adjusting the lens. Therefore in order to have maximum depth of field for close-up photography when using a macro lens, the aperture will have to be

(a) (b)

Figure 4.17 Photographing a three-dimensional object can cause problems when focusing, particularly if the distance from the front to the back is great. In order to ensure that all parts of the object are sharp the aperture should be set at a large *f* number. Photograph (a) was taken on *f* 2.8 at 1/125 s, resulting in only the front part of the object being in focus; photograph (b) was on *f* 22 at 1/2 s (using a tripod) in order to get all parts of the object sharp.

Figure 4.18 The usual convention for photographing objects with handles and spouts is to place the handle to the right in order to show up the form of the object. Additional close-up photography can be used to show detail in areas of interest (Victoria and Albert Museum, London).

at the smallest setting between *f* 22 and *f* 32. It will also be necessary to increase the exposure to compensate for the size of the aperture. This can be done either by reducing the shutter speed so that there is longer time for the light to fall on the film, or else by increasing the intensity of the light source.

Filters

These are circular pieces of transparent gelatin or glass in a variety of colours that may temporarily be attached to the front of the camera lens. The filter absorbs some of the colours of the light coming into the camera, making those colours nearest to it in the spectrum lighter, while darkening others that are further away; the deeper coloured filters have stronger absorptive powers. There are two main types:

Correction filters Used to improve the tonal rendering of colours and to correct faults in the lighting. They usually range from pale yellow through to green.
Contrast filters These bring out the contrasting tones of colours by absorbing one part of the spectrum almost completely. They tend to exaggerate contrasts and alter the colour in order to give added impact. They range from deep yellow, orange, green, blue and red and are normally only used for monochrome photography. The use of contrast filters in black and white photography of polychrome wares will impart greater definition to the individual colours, so avoiding a washed-out appearance.

When using filters the exposure has to be increased, as the filters tend to absorb some of the light by a filter factor. A normal *through the lens* (TTL) meter will compensate automatically for the exposure correction. It is not necessary to have a large number of filters: two would probably be enough for most work, a pale yellow and a yellow-green.

Lighting

The use of cameras, lenses, filters and film will not necessarily guarantee a perfect result unless the lighting of the object is given careful consideration. Subject matter can be deceptive, particularly when the observer has become familiar with the appearance of the object as a result of handling it and seeing it in different conditions. The eye will have perceived its own individual impression of the object, unlike the camera which records exactly what it sees, and this includes both shadows and highlights not necessarily in the detail we had hoped. An additional consideration is the effect of metamerism. This causes the phenomenon where colours appear to alter under different lighting conditions. An accurately colour-matched area of retouching may appear perfect in natural daylight, but when photographically reproduced acquires a slightly altered colour; this is especially true for shades of blue. It is caused by the difference in sensitivity of the eye compared with that of the emulsion on colour film (Staniforth, 1985).

Lighting can be used as a tool to emphasize the texture of rough unglazed surfaces and the shape of complex or simple objects (Figure 4.19). The position of the lights can be used to *model* the object by creating slight shadows. If one side receives twice as much light as the other, this should be sufficient to give the ideal level of light and shade (Figure 4.20). A

Figure 4.19 The form of this simple bowl is highlighted by use of light and shade.

single light source, or daylight, can also be used successfully in combination with a reflector, such as a white piece of card placed opposite or above to bounce light into the shadows. Similarly *hot spots* and bright reflections on glazed or burnished wares can usually be eliminated by careful use of a piece of black card to block out the light source (Figure 4.21).

Diffusing light by placing translucent material in front of the light will have the effect of making the light source appear larger so that the shadows and highlights become weaker, and detail is increased. It is important to achieve a good level of diffusion; if there is too much, there will be no shadows and the result will give a very dull and flat effect.

Light can be provided by photographic lamps or by individual adjustable flash units with incandescent bulbs. The photographic tungsten lamps are either short-life photo-floods, or more expensive longer-life photo-lamps. The floods give a soft even light balanced over an arc of 60°. Adjustable electronic flash systems are always balanced to match daylight film. However, tungsten lamps demand either special tungsten films to produce the correct colours, or the use of correction filters with daylight film. The daylight simulating lamps recommended for use in conservation studios can also assist in photographing objects and have the advantage of being easy to angle and position in relation to an object.

Consistency of lighting arrangements is extremely important if a series of photographs is to be taken to illustrate the stages during a conservation treatment. A different lighting set-up can dramatically alter the visual appearance of the object and distract from the main purpose of the photograph.

Backgrounds

A plain background can be provided by a large sheet of plain paper or fabric, pinned to a back wall

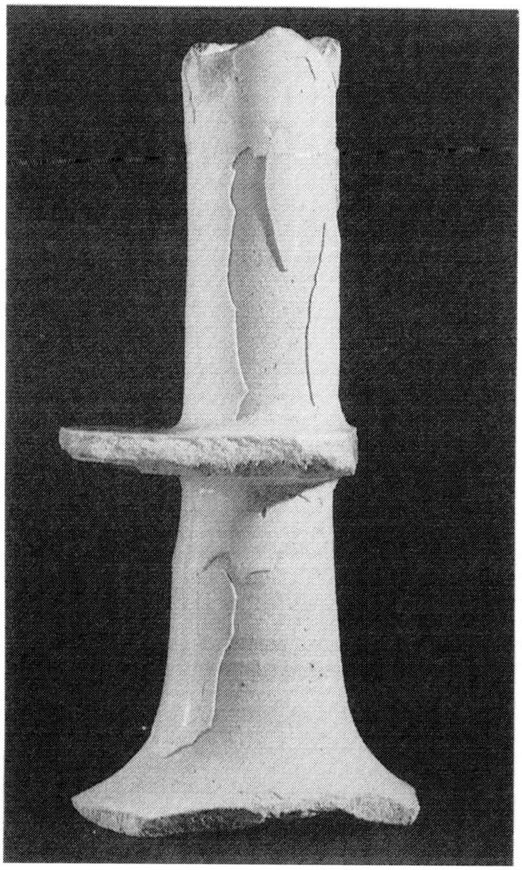

Figure 4.20 Lighting can help to highlight surface detail. The problems associated with the surface of this object are emphasized by careful positioning of lights (Victoria and Albert Museum, London).

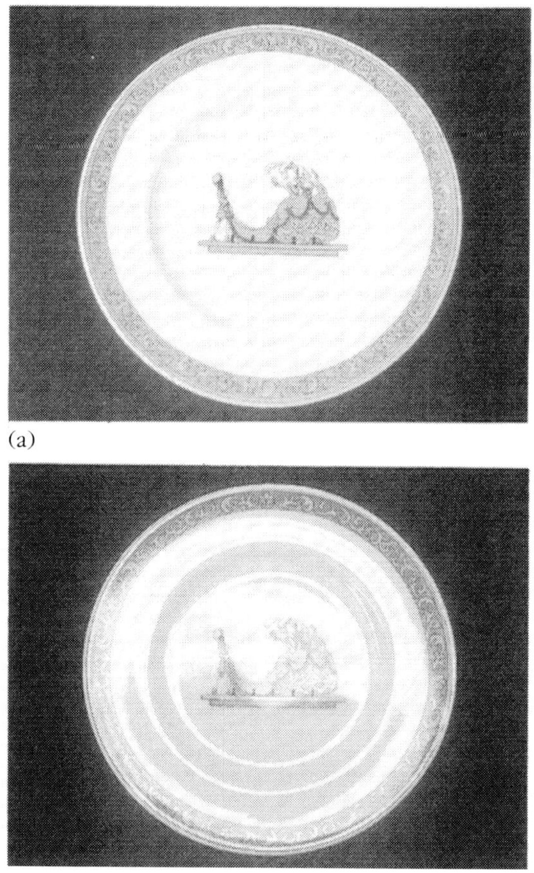

(a)

(b)

Figure 4.21 Reflections can be controlled by carefully positioning the lights or by using reflectors. Comparing (a) with (b) shows how obscuring and distracting reflections can be.

immediately behind the surface on which the object is to be situated. The background should gently curve from the vertical to the horizontal without any distracting sharp creases, and the object should be positioned well in front of it to avoid hard shadows. The colour and tone of the background should not distract from the object or hide it. As an example it would be unwise to place a creamware dish on a light or white background, particularly if the shot is to be taken in black and white. The light-coloured object would be lost on the pale ground; a darker colour of grey or brown might be a more appropriate choice. Black velvet will give a shadow-free background, while black paper tends to give a grey colour due to the individual paper fibres that reflect the light. Small objects or shards can be photographed using a copystand; if they are placed on a sheet of clear glass that has been raised above the stand itself, the background will appear out of focus and unobtrusive.

The same background colour should be used for all the shots taken during the course of the object's treatment. Incorporating a scale in the foreground will serve as a guide to the size of the object. A colour patch, although not essential, will help to standardize the colour. It consists of a strip of coloured patches with a reference scale of greys.

Part Two

5

The development of ceramics conservation

Introduction

The creation of objects from clay is one of the most ancient crafts, dating back to between 15,000 and 10,000 BC. The earliest ceramic artifacts were mainly utilitarian in nature but votive and decorative objects were also manufactured from very early times. In circumstances where ceramic objects were seen to be highly prized items, owing either to scarcity or to artistic or religious merit, it was inevitable that some form of repair and restoration of damaged objects should have developed. It is not known exactly when people started making repairs to ceramic objects, but the oldest such repairs held by the British Museum date from around 7000 BC (Williams, 1988).

Objects made from other materials, such as wood and metal, have traditionally been repaired using the same material as that from which the object was manufactured. Many of the skills involved in repair of these objects are the same as those employed in their manufacture. Although ceramic materials have been used to effect restorations to ceramic objects, they have not been used to a great extent, owing to the difficulty of analysing and matching the constituents, and because of the problems caused by alteration of the materials during the firing processes. Consequently, other materials have had to be sought as substitutes for use in restoration. The nature of these materials has varied widely, depending not only on availability, but also on whether the repair was being made to a functional object of no particular aesthetic value, or to a finer, more highly prized object.

The type of people who carried out repairs in the past varied widely. Specialized repairers have undoubtedly been in business for hundreds of years and there is even a little known poem written by Thomas Hood (1799–1845) called 'The Chinamender'. However, repairs were also carried out in the home, and early editions of Mrs Beeton's *Book of Household Management* (1861; 1915) give advice to 'the handy housemaid' on how to repair broken ceramics with glues of various types. Early repairs to many archaeological finds were probably carried out by the servants of the landowner on whose property the dig was made, but by the end of the nineteenth century conservation as a distinct discipline was beginning to take shape. Freidrich Rathgen in Berlin wrote extensively on conservation (1905) including that of clay tablets and vessels, and later Arthur Lucas produced the first English volume on conservation (1932) which included that of ceramics. Since then, the specialism of ceramics conservation has developed rapidly alongside that of conservation as a whole, and today there are specialist ceramics conservators working in museums and institutions throughout the world, as well as in private commercial practices. Several books have been published on the subject by working restorers, including Larney (1975b), Wells (1975), Whir (1977), White (1981), Evetts (1983), Williams (1983) and Wissler (1983).

Early materials

The range of bonding, filling and retouching materials that have been used in the past to repair ceramics is wide, but a brief outline of some of the more common ones follows. The evidence for their use comes partly from analysis of old repairs and partly from information recorded in ancient manuscripts and more recent books. Unfortunately, although the working practices of most conservators today include the recording of materials used, this has been a relatively recent development. In the past, such information was often considered to be a craft secret, to be jealously guarded from other conservators, who were looked upon primarily as competitors rather than fellow professionals.

Horie (1987) writes that the commonly available materials in use for repairing artifacts prior to the late nineteenth century included starch pastes, natural gums and resins, protein binders, beeswax, and fats. Materials representative of all these groups, with the possible exception of fats, have been used in the past for the repair of ceramics. Horie points out that such natural products are not easy to analyse, and may become even more difficult to analyse after ageing. To begin with they were either dissolved in water or drying oils, or heated, to make them liquid for use; it was not until the seventeenth century in Europe that solvents such as turpentine and spirits of wine were used to dissolve resins.

Bonding materials

One of the earliest forms of adhesive known was bitumen. A very durable adhesive and filler, bitumen is still found on ancient objects excavated today, including Sumarian objects from around 5000 BC. It was extracted from petroleum deposits and hence is commonly found on objects from the Middle East. In more recent times it has been used throughout the world for repairs to ceramics. By today's standards it is not a satisfactory material for use, being dark brown to black in colour, messy to apply and difficult to remove completely.

Wax and wax mixtures were widely used by the early Egyptians and Romans, and wax has been incorporated in adhesive mixtures used in this century. A wax and shellac mixture is quoted as an adhesive and support material used at the British Museum at the beginning of this century (Robson, 1988) and Khazanova (1981) reports the use of adhesive containing rosin, mummy, yellow wax and linseed oil in Russian museums. Wax is still a popular restoration material in some parts of Europe, including Italy, France and Hungary.

Protein binders in the form of gelatin (Rathgen, 1905; Thiacourt, 1868), isinglass and animal glues (Williams, 1988; Robson, 1988) have been used on ceramics since early times. Strahan and Boulton (1988) report the analysis of an adhesive found on a T'ang tomb figure as animal glue and rosin. Animal glues generally remain readily soluble in water and often soften with heat. They are therefore susceptible to environmental extremes. Of the naturally occurring resins, the one most commonly used on ceramics has been shellac. This was in use on ceramics in the Far East from the seventeenth century onwards. It is extracted from a resin excreted by South Asian insects such as *Laccifer lacca* and was applied dissolved in alcohol or heated to make it liquid. The raw resin contains an insoluble yellow dye and a water soluble red dye that was usually washed out in preparation, but if this was incompletely carried out the resin stained the ceramic badly. Staining was also caused by the burning of the shellac during heating *in situ*. Cross-linking occurs with age and causes shellac to be very difficult to remove. Koob (1984) reports that shellac is, regrettably, still in use for bonding ceramics in parts of Turkey and Greece.

Shellac has been used in combination with other materials. For example Thiacourt (1868) reports its mixture with sulphur, and Robson (1988), writing on techniques used at the British Museum in the earlier part of this century, reports its mixture with beeswax to line Bronze Age urns. Shellac has been, and still is, used as a filler and a retouching medium (see below). In the latter case a bleached form of the resin is used, and provided it is applied with care, it may be used without danger to the ceramic.

There is little evidence of starch pastes having been used alone for bonding ceramics. However, many of the adhesives used in the past were made from combinations of materials and many of these old recipes included some form of starch paste as one of the ingredients. Williams (1988) quotes several recipes for adhesives for bonding ceramics which were translated from seventeenth century Chinese manuscripts by Sayer (1951). They tended to combine materials from two or more of the categories outlined by Horie, and include the following: wheat gluten and sifted lime; glutinous rice congee and white of egg; white of egg, lime and green bamboo; mulberry tree juice.

In the nineteenth century and early twentieth century, recipes similar to the Chinese ones quoted above were current in Britain. Recipes using isinglass, gum mastic and gum ammonia dissolved in spirits of wine, rum and brandy or alternatively powdered lime, egg white, milk whey and vinegar are given in contemporary editions of Mrs Beeton's *Household Management* (1861; 1915). Other recipes can be found in contemporary writings such as Ris-Paquot (1876) and use combinations such as cheese and quicklime; shellac and rectified spirits; resin and calcined plaster and oil (Williams, 1983).

Inorganic materials have also been used in the past as adhesives for ceramics. They tend to be difficult to remove. They include Portland cement, waterglass (sodium silicate), and sulphur, which was applied in the molten state (Harris and Service, 1982).

By the end of the nineteenth century synthetic adhesives were being introduced, with cellulose nitrate adhesive being one of the first available. Rubber adhesives were also adopted for use on ceramics (Gedye, 1968) but have shown a tendency to be unstable. Discussion of the adhesives currently used by ceramics conservators can be found in Chapters 9 and 14.

An alternative approach to the use of adhesives to repair broken ceramics has been to join the pieces with mechanical bindings. A number of different methods of this type have been used including riveting, tying, and lacing. Tying involved the literal tying of a binding of reed, rope or wire around the two halves of a break and could therefore only be used on breaks in handles, stems and openwork ceramics. It did not require holes to be drilled in the ceramic, whereas lacing and riveting did (Figure 5.1). In the case of lacing the holes passed right through the ceramic and the binding material was threaded through. In the case of riveting the holes were drilled just a short way into the ceramic and did not pass all the way through. Metal laces and rivets may have been given extra stability by binding with wire, which may then have been coated with solder. These types of joining methods have been used since antiquity, with the earliest ties being made of reed or straw. The Greeks bound pots with lead ties, and early Roman vessels are found with contemporary lead rivets (Figure 5.2). Rivets were in general use in China in the seventeenth century and had spread to Europe by the nineteenth century. During this period rivets may even have been embellished, rather than any attempt made to disguise them. Riveting is still practised, albeit to a lesser extent, throughout the world today. Modern proponents of the use of rivets claim that for domestic ware, in regular use, it is the only

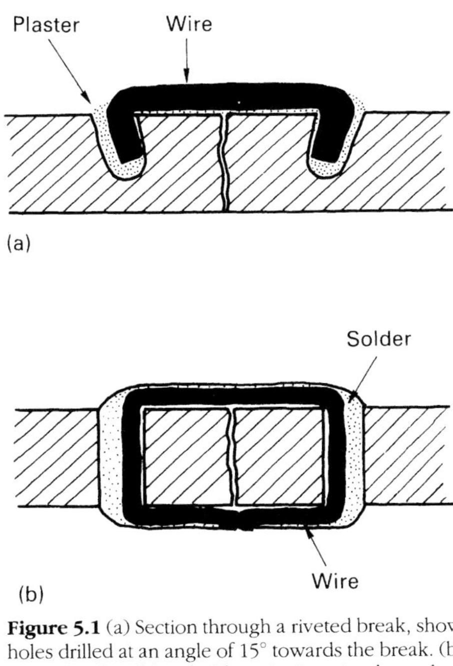

Figure 5.1 (a) Section through a riveted break, showing rivet holes drilled at an angle of 15° towards the break. (b) Section through a laced break. The wire is twisted together on the underside and the excess cut off. It is then covered with solder and filed smooth.

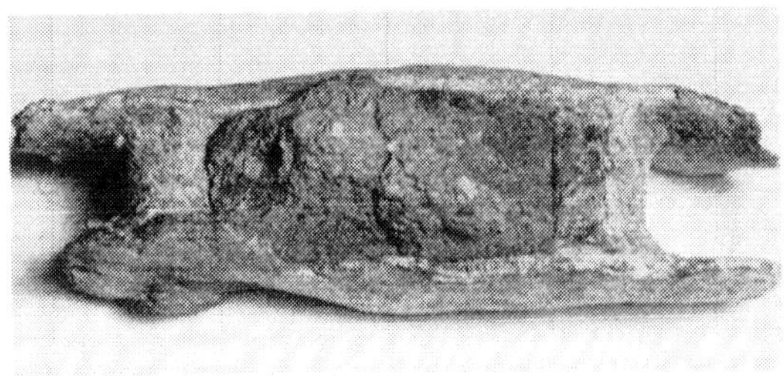

Figure 5.2 Lead rivet excavated with pottery from Roman sites at Ramsbury. Part of the pot remains, enclosed in the rivet. (Wiltshire Archaeological and Natural History Society).

method that can be guaranteed to hold the broken object together. This is probably true, but most ceramics conservators agree that the price, in terms of loss of original material and disfigurement of the object, is too high.

The contemporary techniques used for riveting, tying, lacing and binding are covered in detail in Parsons and Curl (1963). It is important for the ceramics conservator to have some knowledge of these techniques, particularly of riveting, in order to be able to reverse them safely. Basic riveting was carried out in six stages: marking out the positions of the rivets; drilling the holes; preparing the ceramic; making the rivets; pulling the rivets; and finishing off.

Rivets were positioned one near each end of a break and then at intervals of never more than two inches between these two end points. The holes were drilled at an angle of 15° from the vertical towards the break edge on either side of the break (see Figure 5.1) on lines drawn at right angles to the break. Traditionally the holes were drilled with a hand operated bow drill with a diamond tip, although more recently motor driven drills have been used. The ceramic was then thoroughly cleaned and the rivet prepared, measured precisely to the correct size. Because of the angle of the holes and the corresponding angle of the rivet legs, the rivet had to be stretched or 'pulled' into position, and once in place would fit tightly without rocking. Finally, the holes were packed with plaster of Paris and the rivets and plaster painted to make them less obtrusive.

Rivets may have been bound with wire, soldered in place, to hold them. It should not have been necessary to apply adhesive to the joint although, if the break edges were badly chipped, filler may have been applied. Good riveting was a highly skilled art and depended on careful positioning of the rivets, correctly angled and smoothly drilled holes, and precisely made and pulled rivets.

Another joining technique which was particularly common in the Victorian era, but which may still be used under special circumstances today, was dowelling. Holes were drilled into both break edges and a dowel inserted and packed in place, in the past often with plaster or shellac. Dowels made from inappropriate materials can cause damage to the ceramic through metal staining, or by expansion of metal dowels due to corrosion or by swelling of wooden ones with water absorption. In the past, dowels were sometimes made from such unlikely objects as bones, knitting needles, safety pins, needles and hair pins. Strahan and Boulton (1988), when examining Tang dynasty quadrupeds, found screws, sheet metal, drill bits and wood used as dowels. The method was also used for repairing breaks in hollow objects, where it was not necessary to drill holes, but the dowel was packed into the existing hollows. In such cases a large amount of packing material may have been necessary and it is not uncommon to find old newspapers, straw or textiles used as packing material.

Dowelling is still practised today, but is only recommended when essential to strengthen very vulnerable joints or when the object is extremely heavy. Inserting dowels involves loss of original ceramic material unless old holes can be reused, and also puts the object at risk of further damage.

A final technique that used metal to join broken pieces together was to grind out channels across the joint and fill these with molten metal. Klein (1962) gives detailed instructions on the use of molten pewter to create joints in this way. Again this involved the removal of original material.

Consolidants

It is perhaps only more recently that attempts have been made to consolidate friable ceramics. Vacuum impregnation with polyethylene glycol (Carbowax) was routinely carried out in the 1950s at the British Museum (Rosenquist, 1961; Hey *et al.*, 1960). The treatment was not satisfactory as the objects had a tendency to sweat at high relative humidities and attract dirt, and low-fired ceramics were liable to disintegrate during treatment. Soluble nylon was used extensively in the 1960s and 1970s (Gedye, 1968; Plenderleith and Werner, 1974). It was thought to be tough and durable, not to contract as it dried, and to be permeable to salts and thus allow desalination following consolidation. Soluble nylon has since been shown to cross-link, shrink, discolour, soften and attract dirt owing to its low glass transition temperature, and to flake and become insoluble (Sease, 1981). Its use as a consolidant for ceramics has been discontinued.

Filling materials

A wide range of materials and techniques have been used to restore losses in ceramic objects. In the Middle East, restorations to fritware and pottery were frequently effected using pieces taken from another ceramic object (Hogan, in press). This was often combined with filling with plaster or unbaked clay and disguised with extensive overpainting (Figure 5.3). Hogan (in press) also reports finding replacement pieces in fired ceramic material that had

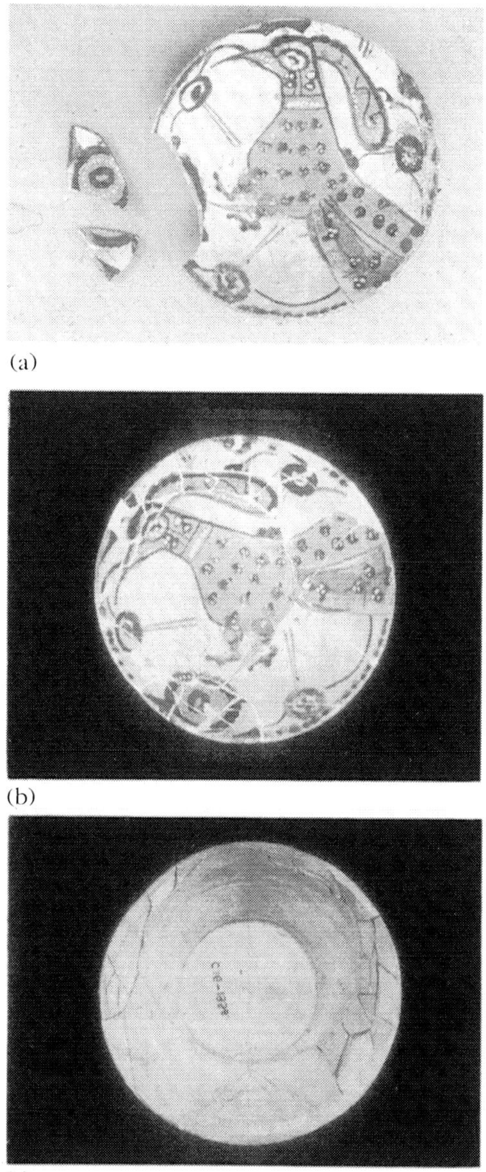

(a) (b) (c)

Figure 5.3 Bowl in which pieces from other objects have been used for repair. (a) The bowl before removal of old overpaint.(b) The old overpaint removed revealing 'foreign' pieces. These are (c) of a different thickness and body colour (Victoria and Albert Museum, London).

evidently been made for the particular damaged object. The technique of using pieces from another object was also used in China, although in these cases a fired glaze was used to disguise the 'patch' (Figure 5.4). Sayer (1951) quotes the following report from a sixteenth century manuscript:

> Old pieces of porcelain from any famous kiln such as censers lack ears or feet or if vases have damaged mouth rims one can use old bits to patch the old; and if one adds glaze and then bakes it is just the same as the old. But the colour is weak at the patch. Yet people prefer this to new stuff. And if one uses the method of blowing the glaze on to the patched part there is still less of a trace.

The technique of applying a low-firing glaze to fuse together breaks has also been used in Europe, and signed examples exist of such repairs carried out in the latter part of the eighteenth century in the south-west of England by a restorer called Coombes (Williams, 1988). This technique must have carried a high risk of the object being further damaged and owing to this it cannot be recommended.

Another technique using ceramic material has been to replace whole parts, for example limbs, with new pieces modelled or cast in clay. The replacement part was fired separately and then bonded onto the object using adhesive. The hind legs of the Tang horse in Figure 5.5 were formed in this way. The difficulty with this technique lies in allowing accurately for the shrinkage of the clay during drying and firing. Generally extensive retouching was also carried out in order to conceal the restoration. This type of repair has been carried out in this century by the Meissen factory which retains original moulds for figurines and will cast missing parts in porcelain and decorate them with the appropriate glazes and enamels.

Of the alternative materials used for making up missing parts, plaster of Paris is perhaps the most

Figure 5.4 Bowl with fired restoration (Victoria and Albert Museum, London).

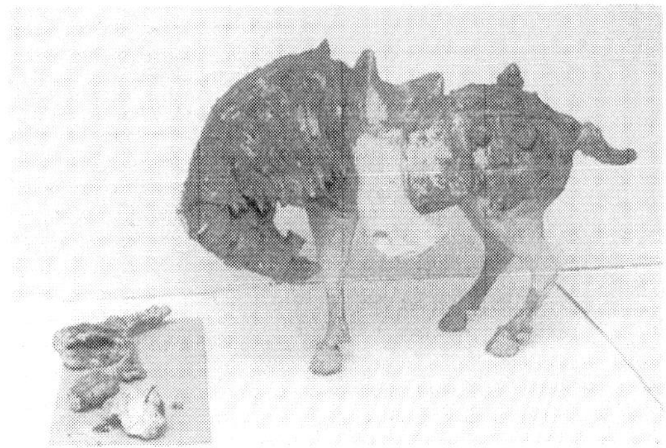

Figure 5.5 Tang dynasty figure of a horse with legs restored using fired clay. These were made separately and bonded to the horse and the joints were filled and retouched (Victoria and Albert Museum, London).

commonly found. It has been used either with or without additives such as animal glues, alum, plant gums and resins, and synthetic polymers, and with or without pigmentation. It is still widely used for fillings in earthenware objects, but one of its main drawbacks has been the possibility of contamination of porous ceramics with soluble salts. When plaster is used now, this is guarded against by first sealing the raw edges of the ceramic. A second drawback is that plaster of Paris has poor adhesive properties and in the past it has been common practice to score the edges of the ceramic to provide a better key for its attachment (Plenderleith and Werner, 1974). Klein (1962) describes a method of grinding grooves for anchoring fillings made with an unspecified material.

One of the ancient oriental methods of restoration, and one that is still practised today (Oddy, 1989), is that of using Urushi lacquer to fill damaged areas and coating it with powder gold (Figure 5.6).

Portland cement, stone, wood, cardboard, paper pulp (Figure 5.7), wax, gutta-percha and metal are amongst the other materials that have been used. Metal replacements were often executed with great skill (Figure 5.8) and were sometimes finely worked (Figure 5.9).

Retouching materials

In some cases no attempt was made to disguise the fillings, e.g. in the case of oriental gilded lacquer fillings or in cases where the repair was painted a neutral colour to avoid confusing the repairs with original material. In other cases, however, methods have been used to disguise the repair. Fillings in unglazed pottery, such as Tang dynasty tomb wares, were often disguised by smearing with unbaked clay or mud (Strahan and Bolton, 1988). A variety of

(a) (b)

Figure 5.6 (a) Gilded repair to Korean jar. (b) Gilded repair to Korean stand (Victoria and Albert Museum, London).

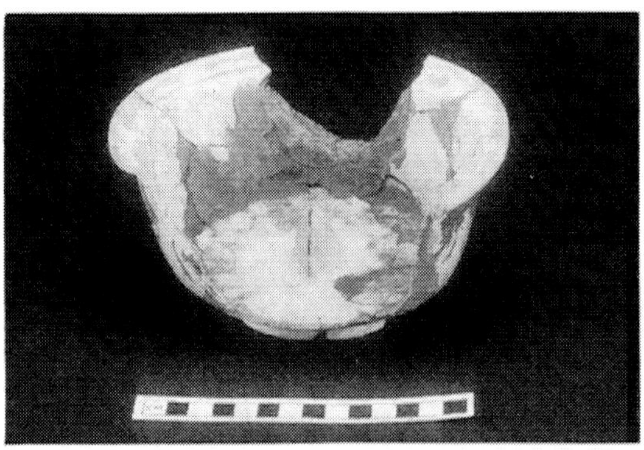

Figure 5.7 Part of a bowl with restorations made using sawdust and resin (Victoria and Albert Museum, London).

Figure 5.8 Teapot with silver mounts, made to disguise damage to spout (Victoria and Albert Museum, London).

materials have been used as media for the coating of restorations with pigments: water, skimmed milk (Plenderleith and Werner, 1974), shellac, oils and gums, and more recently synthetic polymers. Over-painting is often found to be very extensive, covering original material as well as the filling. Khazanova (1981) cites examples of vessels that have been completely coated in a mastic of 'glue' and chalk, tinted to the colour of the ceramic body, and then had the decoration repainted with varying degrees of accuracy. He also reports some vases completely coated with cellulose nitrate lacquer to give the

Figure 5.9 Turkish earthenware bottle, dating from the second half of the sixteenth century, with a silver mount on the neck which probably dates from the nineteenth century (Victoria and Albert Museum, London).

impression of an unflawed surface, a technique that has been used in this country. The problem with most of these materials used in the past, and one that is also found with many retouching media in use today, is that the colour tends to alter with age. This was due to changes occurring either in the media or in the pigments themselves, and the repairs consequently have become more obvious.

In the twentieth century, with the development of synthetic materials, there has been a proliferation of materials suitable for use in the field of conservation. A conservator is quite likely to come across unfamiliar materials used for old repairs and must apply his knowledge carefully in order to weigh up the advantages and disadvantages of leaving such materials in place on an object, and if necessary in devising ways of removing them safely. Conservators have become more aware recently of implications to their own health of the use of certain materials, and many of the solvents used in the past, for example dimethylformamide (Khazanova, 1981) and chloroform, are now considered unsafe.

Ethical considerations

Few of the old repair materials mentioned above are in use today. The reasons for this are several: many were ineffective in the long term, and some even in the short term; many were unsightly; and some even caused further damage to the object. What few of them were able to do was to restore to the damaged ceramic object its original strength and appearance in such a way that the impact of the damage and the treatment was minimal, in terms of the physical, historical and aesthetic integrity of the object. It is the strict adherence to this principle of minimizing the overall impact of damage and treatment, or indeed wherever possible preventing damage ever occurring, that signifies to today's conservators an 'ethical' approach.

The *Oxford English Dictionary* defines ethics as 'the science of morals, moral principles and rules of conduct'. In order to practise his profession in a way that cannot be criticized on ethical grounds, the conservator must have rules of conduct that extend not only to his approach to the treatment of objects but also to his responsibilities to 'the profession', to fellow conservators, other professionals, owners of objects and students of conservation.

Some of the very first guidelines for conservators were presented at the Museums' Association's Annual General Meeting in 1895 (Brown-Goode, 1895). Much has been written since then concerning ethical practice (Hodges, 1975; Ashley-Smith, 1980; 1982; Child, 1988; Corfield, 1988) and many bodies have produced their own sets of guidelines. These include the Murray Pease Report (International Institute for Conservation – American Group, 1964), *Code of Ethics and Standards of Practice* (American Institute for Conservation, 1979), *Guidance for Conservation Practice* (United Kingdom Institute for Conservation, 1981), *Code of Ethics and Guidance for Conservation*

Practice (Institute for the Conservation of Cultural Material, 1986), and *Code of Ethics and Guidance for Practice* (International Institute for Conservation – Canadian Group, 1989). These documents have been drawn up in such a way that their contents are applicable to all branches of conservation and restoration. However, it is worth examining some of the main points with special reference to ceramics.

Examination

Examination and records

All the codes of practice stress the need for adequate examination of an object before any treatment is carried out. Full documentation of any examination carried out must be made and kept as a permanent record with the object. The importance of examination in the field of ceramics conservation is discussed in Chapter 4.

Sampling

Many of the documents state that samples should only be taken from the fabric of the object when absolutely necessary in order to ensure that correct treatment is used or for other beneficial reasons. Only the minimum sample necessary should be taken and this sample should be retained as part of the record. In the case of ceramics conservation it is rarely necessary to take samples from the fabric of the object itself in order to ensure appropriate treatment. Samples are usually taken for technical and historical study.

Treatment

Necessity and extent of treatment

Owing to the possibility of further damaging an object during any intervention, several of the above documents stress that treatment should only be carried out when deemed necessary, for example, when without treatment further damage would occur to the object. Wherever possible the need for treatment should be avoided by non-intervention methods such as environmental control. It is often tempting to the ceramics conservator, when presented with an object that has been restored in the past, to dismantle all the old repairs as a matter of course. The reader is directed to the introduction to Chapter 6 for a discussion of the necessity of removal of old restorations. Another temptation is to repair every little chip, despite the fact that it may be characteristic of the ageing of the particular type of ceramic. For example, delftware is highly prone to chipping of the glaze on exposed edges and such minor chips are generally accepted and should be left untreated. In contrast, chips around the rim of a high-fired porcelain bowl might not be acceptable, and would usually be restored. The Victoria and Albert Museum Conservation Department *Code of Practice* (unpublished) states that repair of these minor flaws is unnecessary 'except where they are causing deterioration of the object, are an aesthetic obstruction or are obscuring information'. Concerning extent of treatment the ceramics conservator must ensure that each stage of the conservation process is properly carried out. For example, it may be tempting to neglect proper cleaning in the hope that subsequent fillings and retouching may hide the dirt. This approach is rarely satisfactory.

Treatment records

All codes of practice stress the importance of maintaining detailed records of treatment. This is important not only from the point of view of the possible need for reversal of treatment in the future, but also for assessment of the performance in practical conditions of the various materials used. Problems caused to the ceramics conservator by lack of records include not only general problems in identification of old treatment materials used but, for example, problems caused by undetectable dowels in joints, and lack of information about the accuracy of restorations of missing pieces and decoration. With the improvement in performance of the materials available and the corresponding possibility of making treatments more and more 'invisible', it becomes more difficult to detect previous treatments and make allowance for them. It is therefore increasingly important that good documentation practices are used. The reader is directed to Chapter 4 for information on present practices of recording information about treatments on ceramic objects.

Removal of material

Agreement that removal of original material is highly undesirable is common to all the above codes of practice. The ceramics conservator is in danger of removing original material in many of his treatment processes unless great care is taken. Mechanical cleaning of break edges or friable surfaces, washing of low-fired ceramics and abrading of filling material all carry a risk of damage to the original material. Techniques such as dowelling and riveting, and grinding and scoring of break edges, are essentially unacceptable within this limitation. In the past it was common to grind down break edges to compensate for bad bonding practices (Klein, 1962; Khazanova, 1981), and to grind flush with the surface the stumps of broken handles etc. Hogan (in press) reports serrations cut into break edges in nineteenth and early twentieth century restorations, and even as recently as the 1970s Plenderleith and Werner (1974) suggested that break edges should be scored to provide a better key for adhesives and plaster fillings. The removal of decayed glaze must also be questioned, and the possibility of the chemical removal of original components during certain treatments guarded against.

Techniques and materials

All codes of practice stipulate the use of tested materials and techniques that have minimum interaction with the object, will not interfere with future treatment, will be as durable as possible, and will be reversible with the minimum of damage. Several of them acknowledge that in certain cases these ideals cannot be realized and that the conservator must weigh up the adverse effects of treatment with the possible dangers of leaving the object untreated. Reversibility, in particular, is not always an achievable ideal (Horie, 1983; Appelbaum 1987) and the ceramics conservator will be exercised more particularly in this respect with regard to unfired or low-fired ceramics than in the case of stonewares and hard-paste porcelains. Reversibility is a particularly important factor when choosing first-aid field treatments, but its importance is also illustrated by Elston (1990) who writes of the restoration of an Attic kylix and a kanthora of which at some later stage, following initial restoration, further missing fragments were found and had to be incorporated into the object. Techniques that involve heating the object may destroy evidence for thermoluminescence dating.

Restoration and reconstruction

In most of the documents concerning ethics and codes of practice, restoration and reconstruction are treated as a means of returning to the object certain cultural, aesthetic and historical values that may have been lost with the missing material. They stress that there must be appropriate evidence for the restorations (Figures 5.10, 5.11, 5.12), and the Charter of Venice states that restoration ends where hypothesis begins (International Council on Monuments and Sites, 1966). They must be carried out only to the minimum degree necessary and must be fully documented. The objects that ceramics conservators deal with can range from single shards to multi-part, decorative objects, and from coarse, low-fired pottery to fine, high-fired porcelain. The treatment that is appropriate must be related to an interpretation of the 'purpose' of the object as seen by the present owner. A collection of shards that are held for the study and record of their mineral content will be treated very differently from a collection of shards from which it is desired to convey something about the form and appearance of the object or objects from which they came. If the object is to be returned to a state in which

Figure 5.10 Tile panel showing the church of St Mary Redclyffe, Bristol. The missing tiles have been retouched to the background colour of the existing tiles and, where appropriate, the border lines painted in. This diminishes the impact of the loss of the tiles without carrying out detailed retouching, for which there is insufficient evidence (Victoria and Albert Museum, London).

Figure 5.11 Chinese tulip vase showing restoration of upper portion. There was no direct evidence for the restoration, the proportions and shape of which were deduced from other intact objects of this type. This restoration gives information about the form of the object without disguising the fact that it is a restoration (Victoria and Albert Museum, London).

(a)

(b)

Figure 5.12 Chelsea figure group showing (a) old restoration in which the figures hold flowers. This group was known to represent a group of musicians and in (b) the old restorations have been removed and replaced with restorations based on information from another existing group. Owing to the indirect nature of the evidence upon which they were based, these restorations have been retouched in a neutral colour so that they remain readily identifiable (Victoria and Albert Museum, London).

it is possible to appreciate the full aesthetic impact that was intended by its maker then the approach may be different again. Child (1988) quotes the example of a stoneware puzzle jug in a social history collection. This was simply bonded together to prevent accidental loss of fragments and abrasion of edges and allow interpretation and display on social history grounds, but no attempt was made to fill and retouch the chips. In contrast Barov (1988) discussing the restoration of the Kyknos Krater states that

> Physically the fragments required only minimal conservation. If they had been judged notable solely for their historical worth, no further restoration would have been necessary. However, it was important also to evaluate this vase as a work of art . . . To restore some of the artistic integrity of the vase it was decided to display the fragments within a complete reconstruction of the original shape.

Mibach (1975) and Elston (1990) both point out that the geometric shapes of fragments can present visual patterns that distract from the object as a whole and that floating fragments in reconstructions can lose meaning. They therefore feel that practices such as retouching lacunae to background colours, and extrapolating regular patterns, for example replacing the concentric circles in the Attic kylix, are fully justified. The codes of practice cannot give detailed guidance on such points; however what they do dictate is that the treatment involved for any one interpretation must not exclude future treatment and presentation in a different, equally valid form.

General obligations and responsibilities

Most of the codes of practice give guidance for professional conduct towards fellow conservators, other professionals, the owners of the objects and students. They also state that the conservator has an obligation towards his own professional development but must recognize his own limitations. The field of ceramics conservation has no special requirements concerning these and the many other points covered in the code of practice documents. Along with other branches of conservation there is a growing movement towards more professionalism in the field. Former secrecy concerning materials and treatments is giving way to a freer exchange of information and, although training is still very varied and largely unformalized, several courses have been set up in the past two decades which aim to give students a fuller and more soundly based training than has been available previously. The setting up in 1984 of the Ceramics and Glass Conservation Group of the United Kingdom Institute for Conservation has also been a major step towards achieving greater professionalism in the field of ceramics conservation.

6

Removal of previous restoration materials

Introduction

In many instances the first action of a conservator after initial examination of a ceramic object is to remove materials applied during former conservation and restoration treatments. There are indeed a number of reasons why this may be desirable. Such materials may simply be unsightly, if, for example, they were clumsily applied, or if they have become discoloured (Figure 6.1). They may have been applied in such a way that they are misleading, with modelling of missing parts being spurious or with fillings or retouching too extensive, hiding original material (Figure 6.2). Included in this category are 'restorations' that have intentionally changed the appearance of the object (Figure 6.3). In other instances they may have deteriorated to a state where they are no longer effective and perhaps make handling of the object unsafe (Figure 6.4). In the worst cases, deterioration of materials can be causing damage to the object, for example, when adhesives, coatings or consolidants are shrinking and breaking up the fabric of the object, or when metal rivets are corroding and causing staining.

It is often tempting to strip off all old restorations regardless of their condition or accuracy. The effects of doing this must be carefully considered and the benefits weighed against the possible dangers, in particular that of damaging the object in the process. Old restorations may even be of intrinsic interest or aesthetic value, such as the oriental gold lacquer repairs shown in Figure 5.6(a) and (b), and the intricately chased silver replacement shown in Figure 5.8. Elston (1990) points out that certain old restorations may be important in the context of the study of the history of restoration techniques. If it is necessary to remove the restoration material for any reason, either a sample of the material, or all the

Figure 6.1 Figurine showing unsightly old repairs. The retouching medium has discoloured badly and the plaster restoration of the arm is unsound (Victoria and Albert Museum, London).

Figure 6.2 Dish showing old retouching covering a simple break. The retouching medium has been spread far on either side of the break in order to try to disguise it, and it has discoloured badly (Victoria and Albert Museum, London).

material, may be retained and stored separately so that the information it contains is not lost.

Preparation

Removal of any material should only be carried out after thorough documentation of both the condition of the object and the location and extent of the former treatment material. The safety of the object during the removal processes should always be considered, and it is essential to ensure that the object is adequately supported at all times so that, should bonds or fillings give way unexpectedly, damage will not occur. Where appropriate the object should be placed on a surface covered with a padding material, such as polyethylene foam, or supported by netting. If necessary special supports should be made such as the paper and plaster casing created around the Portland Vase during dismantling (Williams, 1989).

When removing old restorations it is generally the overpaint that is removed first. This will reveal the extent of the underlying damage and allow assessment of the old adhesive and filling materials used.

Removal of surface coatings

Areas of old overpaint may be detected in several ways. They are most obvious when they have discoloured, as in Figure 6.2, or if the original match to the colour of the ceramic was poor. Even when they match the ceramic very closely in colour, the gloss, surface texture and feel may be slightly different from the original. These subtle differences can usually be detected by the practised restorer, using, if necessary, lighting and magnification techniques described in Chapter 4.

Paint can be removed by the use of mechanical or solvent methods. Mechanical methods are preferred by many restorers as they avoid the danger of dissolved paint being drawn into the body of the ceramic or spreading onto surrounding surfaces. Any underlying fillings or bonds are less likely to be affected by mechanical removal of the overpaint than by solvent removal and the conservator has more control over the dismantling process.

Mechanical removal of overpaint

Where the underlying surface of the object is glazed, a sharp scalpel can be used to remove paint with little risk of damage (Figure 6.5). A careful check can be kept under a binocular microscope to ensure that no damage is being caused. However, great care must be taken to avoid areas where there is any onglaze decoration, such as enamels or gilding, or areas of flaking or degraded glaze, and in these areas the paint must usually be removed using solvents. Removal of hard, brittle paint layers can sometimes be achieved using air abrasive methods, but these are not commonly used on ceramic objects. Unless the paint layer is already detaching from the ceramic surface, solvent removal is usually necessary in the case of unglazed ceramics.

Solvent removal of overpaint

Where the nature of the old overpaint has not been recorded it will be necessary to test the solubility of the paint using a range of solvents applied on cotton wool swabs. Water, white spirit, industrial methylated spirits, acetone and dichloromethane (usually in the form of a commercial paint stripper) are all commonly used, but other solvents may be appropriate. Solvents that have been used in the past but whose use is now considered a health risk include chloroform and dimethylformamide (Khazanova, 1981). If there is any unfired decoration present the stability and solubility of this must also be tested and a solvent chosen for the removal of the paint which will not affect the original decoration.

When using solvents (other than water) on porous bodied ceramics some conservators pre-soak the objects in water for a few minutes to reduce their porosity. However, care must be taken when there is a possibility that underlying fillings or bonds are water soluble, as immersion in water may cause them to collapse. Pre-soaking in water is also inadvisable in the case of very low-fired or friable pottery, or objects that are suspected of containing soluble salts. The

(a)

(b)

(c)

Figure 6.3 Eighteenth century Meissen parrot which had been adapted to form a pair for another parrot. (a) Shows the old retouching removed revealing extensive filling around the neck and chest. In (b) the filling material has been removed and a firing crack running up the chest revealed. The smooth edges of the joint between the neck and the body suggested that the head had been cut off. (c) Shows the head repositioned, the joint filled and retouched. With the head at this angle the firing crack continues up from the chest into the head, confirming the correctness of this position (Victoria and Albert Museum, London).

Figure 6.4 Plate in which unsightly old repairs are breaking down, making handling dangerous (Victoria and Albert Museum, London).

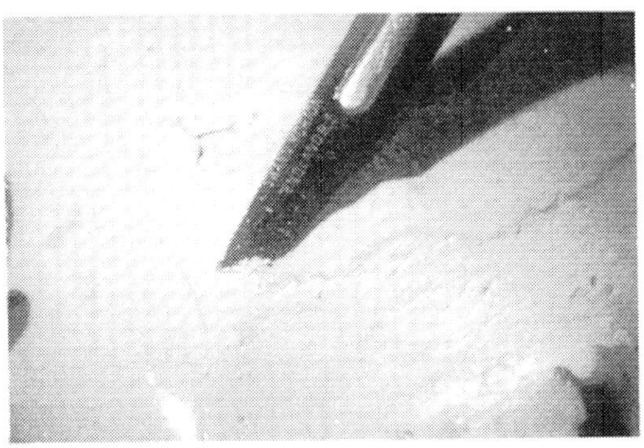

Figure 6.5 The use of a scalpel to remove old overpaint.

appropriate solvent is applied on cotton wool swabs using a swab stick, and a rolling action is used, rather than a wiping one, so that the paint is lifted up off the surface rather than pushed into it. If a paint stripper containing dichloromethane is used, this is painted onto the surface using a brush and left until the paint has bubbled up off the surface. Evaporation of the dichloromethane contained in the paint stripper can be slowed down, if necessary, by covering the application with polythene sheeting. The bulk of the paint and paint stripper may then be removed using cotton wool or paper towels and the remainder is rinsed off thoroughly using a brush and water. If necessary repeated applications are made until all the paint has been removed. Owing to the toxicity of dichloromethane, anything other than very minor applications should be carried out in a fume cupboard or in an area of local fume extraction and the necessary personal protection worn.

Removal of filling materials

Old fillings may be all that are holding the broken pieces of an object together and it must be borne in mind that their removal may result in the broken pieces coming apart. Care must therefore be taken to support an object properly when working on the fillings.

Old fillings were made from a very wide range of materials, some of which are mentioned in Chapter 5. Fillings made more recently are commonly of calcium-sulphate-based fillers or synthetic resin compounds based on epoxy, acrylic, or polyester resins. Identification is based on colour, texture, hardness and chemical reactivity; however this is not always easy as a wide variety of pigments and aggregates may have been added to the resins. In some cases large fillings may have been dowelled onto the object and if this is suspected a check can be made for metal dowels using a hand-held metal detector. As with old surface coatings, old fillings can be removed using mechanical or chemical methods.

Mechanical removal of filling materials

The use of mechanical methods may be the only practical means of removing many types of filling material. When large areas of any type of filling material are to be removed, it is usually preferable to remove the bulk of the filling using a mechanical method, even if chemical methods are used to remove the remainder of the filler that is in intimate contact with the ceramic.

Cement mortar is an example of a filler that is almost always removed mechanically. Although it can be broken down by acid treatment this is seldom practical or safe. The dangers involved in the use of acids on ceramics are discussed in Chapter 7. Judicious use of a hammer and chisel to remove the cement by gradual degrees is the method most generally used, although the risk of damaging the fabric of the ceramic is high. The risk can be reduced by padding the object well and ensuring that the chisel is angled obliquely to the ceramic surface rather than straight down at right angles to it. Plaster, which is one of the most commonly found filling materials, is also most effectively, and most safely, removed mechanically. It only softens to a limited degree if soaked in water and with porous bodied ceramics there is a danger of soluble salts being drawn from the plaster into the body of the ceramic.

Depending on the shape and location of the fillings, a variety of tools can be used for their mechanical removal. The bulk of large protruding fillings can be sawn off with a hacksaw and then the remainder removed using a scalpel or needle. Drills may be used to remove fillings where the use of a saw is not suitable, a series of holes being drilled around the perimeter of the filling and a file or hacksaw blade then being used to cut through the material between the holes. Again the removal of the material close to the joint of the filling with the object should be carried out with a scalpel or by chemical means in order to avoid damaging the break edge. Removal of fine pieces of filler from the break edge can be carried out using a needle held in a pin vice.

The dust generated during mechanical removal can be a problem in that it can work its way into the surface of unglazed objects or into cracks and other surface irregularities. Surrounding surfaces can be masked off using a masking tape, or rubber latex. Cleaning of surfaces that have become contaminated with plaster dust can be difficult. Barov (1988) describes the use of AB57, an ammonium-bicarbonate/sodium-bicarbonate solution, to remove minor deposits of plaster of Paris from the surface of pottery. Dust from some materials, in particular plaster of Paris, can be an irritant to contact lens wearers and the dust from epoxy or polyester resin fillings can also pose a health hazard. For this reason a suitable mask should be worn when dealing with such fillings.

Air abrasive and ultrasonic techniques may also be useful but can easily damage bodies and glazes.

Chemical removal of filling materials

Solvent removal of fillings is generally only used on the area of filling remaining after the bulk of the filling has been removed mechanically, or for removing very small fillings. The most commonly used solvents are water, for removing unfired clay and water soluble compositions made up with animal glue or gelatine; and dichloromethane, in the form of a paint stripper, for removing compositions based on synthetic resins such as epoxy resins, acrylic resins or polyester resins. Other solvents, in particular acetone, may be useful for removing some compositions, e.g. resin and plaster of Paris mixtures. Whenever any materials are put into solution on the surface of an object it is important to avoid the solution being drawn into the body of the object and to this end porous bodied objects can be pre-soaked in water, provided the water itself is not likely to cause damage (see following chapter).

Chelating agents such as sodium (hexametaphosphate) polyphosphate may be used to soften plaster-based fillers (Hodges, 1986) but must be used with extreme caution on low-fired ceramics or objects with on-glaze decoration, as there is a risk of damage. For discussion of the dangers of using sequestering agents on ceramics see Chapter 7.

Removal of adhesives

Removal of old adhesives can be looked upon in two stages: the first stage of separating the two halves of the joint, and the second of removing the remaining adhesive from the exposed break edges. Owing to the position of the adhesive, sandwiched tightly between the broken pieces of ceramic, mechanical means alone can rarely be employed to accomplish the first stage. Appropriate solvents, in liquid or vapour form, are used to soften and swell the adhesive and part the joint and then the remaining adhesive is removed using further solvent or mechanical methods. In cases where the adhesive is thermoplastic it may be possible to separate the joint using heat and then follow this by removal of the adhesive from the break edges by mechanical or solvent means.

Mechanical removal of adhesives

Before the joint has been separated it may be possible to remove a certain amount of adhesive by picking and cutting with a scalpel or needle. This can only be done where excessive adhesive has been used and has squeezed out of the joint onto the surrounding surfaces, or in areas that are accessible because the joint has been badly aligned or there are chips along the break edges. In rare cases it may actually be possible to remove enough adhesive in this way for the joint to be separated. Generally, however, mechanical methods are not helpful until after the joint has been parted using a solvent. Any remaining adhesive can then be removed from the break edges either by further applications of solvent or by picking or cutting with a scalpel or needle. The latter may be preferable to solvent removal as there is less risk of spreading the adhesive in solution onto surrounding surfaces or into the body of a porous ceramic. Care must be exercised when using mechanical methods of removal in order to avoid scratching the ceramic or removing particles of body or glaze.

Solvent removal of adhesives

Selection of the appropriate solvent for removal of an adhesive is based on identification of the adhesive. Where there are records of the former treatment this is obviously made much simpler. However colour, hardness and other physical properties, together with their solubility in a range of solvents, will enable identification of most adhesives. Where excessive adhesive has been used a sample can be removed for testing. A list of the most commonly encountered adhesives follows, with identifying characteristics and detailed discussion of methods of removal. However, there are some general points that can be made.

In order for the adhesive in the joint to be sufficiently softened, the solvent, in the form of a liquid or a vapour, must usually be in contact with the adhesive for some time. The length of time will depend on the solubility of the adhesive in the particular solvent and the thickness and tightness of the joint. Small objects may be completely submerged in solvent. Solvent may be applied to larger objects on cotton wool swabs, or using poulticing materials such as blotting paper. Alternatively, thixotropic formulations can be used, e.g. by mixing the solvent with carboxymethyl cellulose or Laponite RD. In order to slow down the evaporation of the solvent the object may be covered in polythene sheeting. If a highly volatile solvent such as acetone is being used, the object can be placed in an atmosphere of the solvent inside a sealed container. This can be quite simply carried out by placing the object, suitably supported, together with a beaker of the appropriate solvent inside a sealed polythene box.

There are several precautions that should be observed in order to avoid causing damage when removing old adhesives, especially from low-fired ceramics. Where the object is very low fired or unfired or there is any unfired decoration or gilding present, spot tests should be made to ensure that the solvent used will not cause any damage. Porous bodied objects may be pre-soaked in water to prevent adhesive in solution being drawn into the body provided the water itself is not likely to cause damage. If the object is sufficiently large or delicate that unsupported collapse of the bonds may result in damage then support must be provided. This can range from a simple prop such as crumpled tissue paper, a tied mesh or gauze bandage or bag, to a more intricate form of support such as gauze or fabric applied with a resin that will not be affected by the treatment to remove the old adhesive. Only gentle pressure should be applied to the joints to try to part them, as stronger pressure, applied before the adhesive has softened sufficiently, may result in a thin layer of the body being torn away with the adhesive (Figure 6.6) or a fresh break occurring elsewhere.

The following notes give some guidance on identification of adhesives, and particular points that should be borne in mind when removing each type. Where identification is not possible it will be necessary to make tests using a range of solvents to find the most appropriate one.

Figure 6.6 Broken edge of medieval floor tile showing the way in which material has torn away from the other half of the joint when the joint was parted (Victoria and Albert Museum, London).

Animal glues

Animal glues generally appear pale yellowish brown in colour, and dissolve readily in warm or hot water, when they will give off a distinctive odour. Provided the object is not likely to be damaged by water (see following chapter), bonds made with animal glue can be softened by placing the object in warm water. If, after several minutes, submersion in warm water appears to be having no effect, hot water can be slowly added to the warm water to increase its temperature. An object should never be placed directly into hot water, as the rapid expansion caused may result in damage. Boiling water should never be used. The water may be applied on cotton wool swabs when submersion of the object is not desirable.

Bitumen or pitch

Bitumen or pitch is recognizable as a hard, black, fairly brittle substance. It is usually soluble in one of the aromatic hydrocarbons, but it is preferable to remove as much as possible by mechanical means as it dissolves to give a very sticky black liquid. When solvent must be used it is essential to avoid the solution being drawn into porous bodies and, provided water will not cause damage to the object, it should be pre-soaked to reduce its porosity. The solvent should be applied on swabs which are refreshed at frequent intervals.

Shellac

Shellac is one of the easiest adhesives to recognize. It ranges in colour from a light red to dark, treacly brown and is hard and increasingly brittle with age. During its application both the ceramic and the shellac may have been heated. This may have resulted in staining and caused the adhesive to be very difficult to remove. If the shellac was not properly bleached before use this may also have resulted in staining. Koob (1979) reported that pyridine was the most effective solvent found for its removal, best results being achieved by sealing the object, covered in pyridine, in a plastic container for 1–4 hours at 22°C. Pyridine is toxic and a fire hazard and its use is not to be recommended. If it is used the process must be carried out in a fume cupboard, and protective clothing should be worn. Paint strippers containing dichloromethane provide an alternative means of softening shellac (Larney, 1971), but will take longer to break down a joint than pyridine. Industrial methylated spirits (IMS) may have some effect; Williams (1983) writes that it should be heated for use in removing shellac but may result in a violet stain. Great care should be exercised when heating IMS as it is highly flammable. Koob (1979) reports that a 50/50 mixture of IMS and ammonia left a pink stain, but that a 50/50 mixture of ethyl alcohol and acetone will cause shellac to swell sufficiently to allow the joint to be disassembled. Use may be made of the thermoplastic properties of shellac and joints softened by heating in hot water. This should be done by placing the object in warm water and gradually increasing the temperature by the addition of hot water.

Cellulose nitrate adhesives

Cellulose nitrate adhesives range in colour from water white to a light yellow as they age, and although they are initially fairly soft, they become more brittle. They are readily soluble in acetone or amyl acetate. Again, porous bodied ceramics should be pre-soaked in water, provided this will cause no damage. If unfired decoration is present this should be tested for solubility before application of the solvent. The solvent is applied either on swabs of cotton wool, laid along the joints, or by submerging the object in the solvent. As both acetone and amyl acetate are highly volatile, containers should be covered and the object wrapped in polyethylene if swabs are used. Further acetone can be applied to the swabs at frequent intervals using a pipette. An alternative method is to seal the object in a bag or container in an atmosphere of the solvent. Cellulose nitrate adhesives remain thermoplastic for some time and for this reason heating the joints in hot water, in the way described for epoxies, may cause them to part.

After the joints have parted the remaining adhesive is removed mechanically or using solvent. If the joints have been parted using hot water it will often be found that the cellulose nitrate will peel off the break edges.

Rubber adhesives

Rubber cements generally appear yellow to brown in colour and have a rubbery consistency. The cohesive forces within the cement are usually stronger than the adhesive ones to the ceramic and hence on exposed surfaces and parted break edges the rubber cement can often be carefully peeled off. This should not be attempted when the underlying ceramic body is friable or crumbly and the best solvent to use is dichloromethane (this is generally used in the form of a commercial paint stripper, such as water washable Nitromors (USA Zynolyte)). Occasionally joints may be carefully pulled apart after heating in warm water.

The adhesive on many old pressure sensitive tapes is a type of rubber adhesive. Traces of adhesive from old tapes may be removed using ethanol, acetone, 1,1,1-trichloroethane, toluene, or an aliphatic hydrocarbon. Where these fail a mixture of 5ml 1,1,1-trichloroethane, 5 ml acetone, 1 ml 0.88 ammonia solution and 10 ml ethanol may be effective (Horie, 1987).

Silicone adhesives

Silicone adhesives have been used more extensively on glass than on ceramics but may be found on both pottery and high-fired wares. They generally appear transparent to milky white in colour, but have a low glass transition temperature and frequently have picked up dirt. Removal is extremely problematical as they are insoluble (Erhardt, 1983). Removal from high-fired wares can be effected using a mixture of acids with polar organic solvents (Erdhardt, 1983). A solution of 10 ml dodecylbenzenesulphonic acid, 8 ml dichloromethane, 5 ml toluene and 18 ml xylene is applied on cotton wool swabs to the back and front of the joint and left in place for several hours. This process must be carried out in a fume cupboard. The silicone adhesive will swell and degrade. The residue should be rinsed off with organic solvents rather than water to avoid ionization of the acid. The acid content of this solution makes it unsuitable for use on low-fired wares.

Poly(vinyl acetate)

For bonding purposes, poly(vinyl acetates) have generally been used in the form of emulsions, and may appear white, clear or slightly brown in colour. If they appear clear, they will turn cloudy or white when placed in water. They may be slightly rubbery or slightly brittle, depending on their age and original plasticity. Their solubility will depend on their composition and their age; warm water or acetone are often effective solvents, but may take some time to break down the joints. An ethanol and water or industrial methylated spirits and water mixture may also be effective.

Epoxy resins

Epoxy resins may appear light yellow to darkish yellow/brown in colour and are hard but not very brittle. If the resin has been inaccurately mixed it may be softer and may have an orange tint. Epoxy resins are not soluble; however, they will swell and soften in dichloromethane, and commercially available paint strippers containing dichloromethane, are commonly used for their removal (water washable Nitromors (USA Zynolyte)). These must be used with care, and protective gloves and goggles should be worn. Provided porous bodied objects can be pre-soaked in water, and provided there is no unfired decoration or gilding present, the paint stripper is applied by brush along the inside and outside of the joints and then left for some minutes (usually 10 minutes to 1 hour depending on the thickness of the joint) for the epoxy resin to swell. If the joints are very thick the object can be wrapped in polyethylene or placed in a covered container to provide an atmosphere saturated with solvent fumes and enable the paint stripper to be left in place longer without the solvent evaporating off. When the resin swells up out of the joint this is removed using a scalpel, cotton wool swabs, or a brush under running water. Care must be taken to support the object properly whilst this is being done in case the joints part. If the joints do not part after the first application, repeated applications are made until they do. Occasionally, placing the object in warm water and then increasing the temperature to 'hand hot' and leaving it to soak will be sufficient to cause the joints to part, especially if the epoxy resin has been inaccurately mixed. However, care must be taken to ensure that prolonged soaking will not damage the object in any way. Soaking in hot water may also help to part a joint after one or two applications of solvent have been made; however, care should be taken to ensure that the solvent has been removed beforehand or the heating will produce dangerous fumes.

Once the joints have parted the remaining resin is removed either using a scalpel or needle or by further applications of solvent. Where there are very small holes and crevices in the break edge, for example the broken air bubbles in some Chinese glazes, it may be extremely difficult to remove all traces of resin, and this will spoil the appearance of the subsequent restoration. Cleaning with an ultrasonic tool or air abrasive may help.

Polyester adhesives

Polyester adhesives generally appear dark brown in colour and are hard and fairly brittle. They are removed using the same methods as those described for epoxy resins.

Dowels

It is always worth checking for dowels if a joint is proving particularly difficult to part. Where facilities are available X-ray examination will be helpful. Metal dowels can be detected using a small hand-held metal detector, but it should be borne in mind that metal decoration such as gilding or silvering may trigger the detector. Dowels may also be made of non-metallic materials and, unless they are visible to the eye, these are difficult to detect. Often dowels are set into their holes with the same adhesive as that used in the joint and in these cases removal can usually be achieved by continued application of the appropriate solvent. If, however, the joint can be carefully eased apart enough, the dowel may be sawn through using a hacksaw blade or piercing-saw blade. When the joint has been parted the stumps are removed mechanically or by applying solvent.

Where dowels have been set into holes drilled into the break edges, rather than set into hollow limbs, they cause weak spots which will be vulnerable to stresses. If the restorer is unaware of the existence of the dowel, damage can easily be caused and this should always be borne in mind when applying pressure to any joint in an attempt to part it.

Rivets

It is important to appreciate the way in which rivets were inserted into ceramics in order to remove them without causing further damage to the object. In Chapter 5 it is explained that the holes into which they are set were drilled at an angle in towards the joint. For this reason pulling them straight out is likely to result in damage to the surfaces surrounding the holes. In the case of hard-paste porcelain typical shell-like fragments of glaze and body are broken away leaving the rivet hole surrounded by a 'crater'. In the case of glazed earthenwares the glaze surrounding the rivet hole may pull away (Figure 6.7). Even so, some writers do recommend simply softening the packing material around the rivet and pulling or levering them out with pliers or a blade or needle slipped under the rivet. The method does have the advantage of speed but the safest way to remove rivets is to carefully cut them in half and then remove each half separately. Again the packing material (usually plaster or a plaster composition) is first

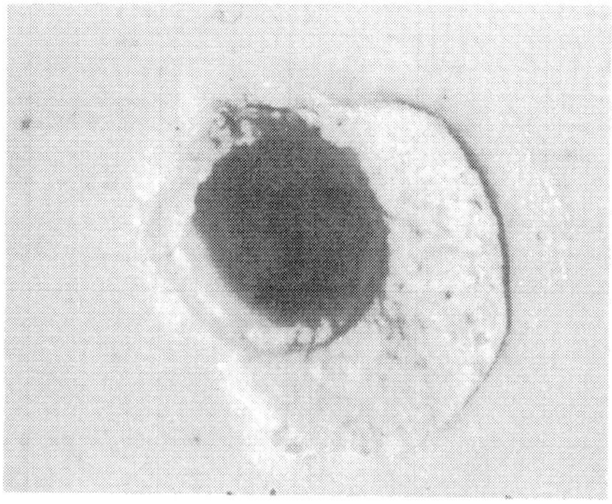

Figure 6.7 Damage to glaze surrounding rivet hole in tin-glazed earthenware object, caused by careless removal of the rivet (Victoria and Albert Museum, London).

softened with warm water applied on cotton wool swabs and then removed mechanically. However, if the ceramic is porous and the rivets show any signs of corrosion it is wise to avoid the application of dampened cotton wool swabs because of the danger of staining. The rivets are then cut in half using a hacksaw blade, a file or a scalpel (Figure 6.8a). There is a danger of damaging the surface of the ceramic during the cutting process, and this can be guarded against by placing strips of adhesive tape on either side of the rivet. If the blade or file comes into contact with these, the angle of sawing is adjusted. It is easier to saw safely through a rivet inserted into a convex surface than one inserted into a concave one. Once the rivet has been sawn through, the two halves can be extracted separately using pliers and pulling at a slight angle away from the break (Figure 6.8b).

Before commencing removal of rivets, it is a wise precaution to tape the joint with pressure sensitive tape to prevent movement of the ceramic and consequent chipping of the break edges. The order in which several rivets in an object are removed is important. Often there is no adhesive in a joint that has been riveted and hence the pieces may start to move after several rivets have been removed, especially if these are removed starting from one end of the break and working along it. The movement of the pieces may then result in the remaining rivets giving way in an uncontrolled manner, or even in breaks occurring around the remaining rivets. It is preferable to remove the rivets in such a way that key rivets, for example one at each end and one in the middle of the joint, are left until last.

When all the rivets have been removed the holes must be thoroughly cleaned of all traces of packing material and of any metal stains (see Chapter 7).

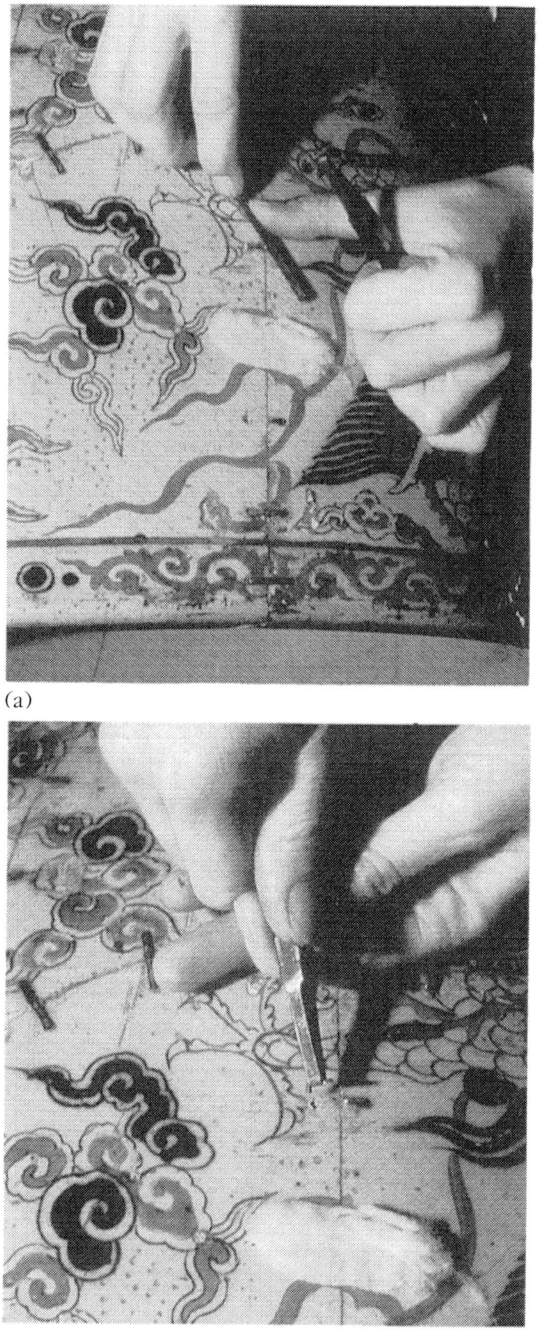

(a)

(b)

Figure 6.8 Removing rivets from a Chinese porcelain jar. In (a) a rivet is being sawn in half using part of a hacksaw blade. Each half is then (b) removed separately with pliers. The cotton wool swab is dampened with water and has been applied to soften the plaster fillings in the holes of another rivet (Victoria and Albert Museum, London).

Tying and lacing

These bindings may be removed by cutting or melting through the lead solder used to join the ends of the wire together. Alternatively it may be easier to cut through the wire itself. Hacksaw blades, files and scalpels may all be useful for cutting and a small soldering iron can be used for melting the solder.

Consolidants

Owing to their deep penetration of the fabric of the ceramic and in many cases to cross-linking of the resins used, removal of material used to consolidate objects is often difficult and total removal impossible. Problems also arise due to the fact that many objects that have been consolidated in the past rely on the consolidant to hold them together. Removal of the consolidant by soaking in solvent is likely to result in the object collapsing. unless the object is supported by some other means. Robson (1988) describes a method of support using rubber latex and plaster of Paris devised at the British Museum for use when removing beeswax and resin mixtures in hot industrial methylated spirits in a Soxhlet extractor. Other methods include using resins with Terylene netting or Eltolene tissue. Alternatively the consolidant can be removed in small sections using solvent in pack form, e.g. mixed with Sepiolite, Laponite RD or carboxymethyl cellulose. The section from which the consolidant has been removed is then reconsolidated with a suitable resin before moving on to the next section.

Display treatments

Removal of most of the materials used to support objects for display has already been covered. The special difficulties that are encountered in their removal often arise because the objects concerned must be treated *in situ*. For example an old method of securing vases on open display was to bond them directly to a marble mantelpiece, a sheet of glass or the top of a display case using poly(vinyl acetate) emulsion. The conservator must use his ingenuity to devise a means of holding solvent around the bond long enough to soften the adhesive. Old mounting treatments for tile panels (see Chapter 15) also rarely employ any material that is intrinsically different from those discussed above but often require special adaptation of the more usual methods to cope with the size and form of the object. Some of the more recent methods of mounting tile panels do, however, employ materials that are not generally used in other conservation treatments: these are polyurethane foam and epoxy resin foam (Urbani and Torraca, 1965; Shorer, 1971; Larney, 1975b). The low-density nature of these foaming systems means that they are relatively easy to remove by mechanical means. Both epoxy resin and polyester foam can be easily cut with a saw, and removal of the bulk of the material from the back of a panel by this method will reduce the amount of solvent that must be used. Care must be taken if aluminium or other mesh has been incorporated in the backing, and safe clearance of the backs of the tiles must be left to allow for irregularities. Removal of the remaining foam can then be achieved using a paint stripper containing dichloromethane (e.g. water washable Nitromors or USA Zynolyte). In the case of the epoxy resin foam system described in Chapter 15, removal is facilitated by the applications of masking tape on the reverse of the tiles. The procedures should be carried out wearing masks with the appropriate filters and using local extraction owing to the hazardous chemicals present in the air spaces in the foams. Polyurethane resins are a particular danger in this respect, as they contain an isocyanate component (Buist and Gudgeon, 1968).

7

Cleaning

Introduction

When referring to the treatment of a ceramic object, the term 'cleaning' is used to describe the removal of any foreign matter that is not part of the original fabric of the object. Foreign matter may be introduced from a variety of sources, as described in Chapter 2. Atmospheric deposits can account for anything from a light coating of dust to a thick, grimy layer; handling may cause greasy or dirty finger marks on the surface or cause dirt to be rubbed into cracks or chips; usage may leave surface encrustations or deposits of food, oils or other material and these may become drawn deep into the body of the ceramic with repeated cycles of warming and cooling; burial, soaking in seawater or freshwater, and exposure to fire can all leave material on the surface or within the body of the ceramic. In some cases the material may even become chemically combined with the original fabric of the object, for example where decoration becomes oxidized. Materials used for previous conservation treatments can also be looked on as 'foreign matter'; the removal of these has been covered in the previous chapter.

Cleaning is probably the most common of the treatment processes used on ceramic objects, not only in the conservation studio but also in a domestic context. It may represent the only treatment of the object or it may be the first step in a series of conservation procedures. There are several reasons why it may be considered desirable. Firstly, surface dirt may be disfiguring, masking the colour, decoration and surface texture. In some cases if such dirt is left in place it can become more deeply ingrained or drawn into the body, producing irreversible staining. Dirt may also serve to emphasize damage such as chips and cracks. Of more serious consequence are deposits such as soluble salts which may actually cause physical damage to an object, pushing off the glaze and fragmenting the body. Removal of dirt may be important in relation to future conservation treatment; for example, grease left along a break edge will prevent an adhesive functioning properly.

However, there are also circumstances when removing dirt or other foreign matter may not be desirable. For example, in the case of some Korean wares staining in the body is looked upon in much the same way as the patina on a bronze object, and will enhance the value of the object (Figure 7.1). In other cases foreign materials may be of intrinsic historical or ethnographic interest. Burial dirt may contain residues of foods, libation oils or other substances that were stored in the object, and fats and oils in the body may have been intentionally applied to cut down the porosity of a low-fired ware. It may be considered important to leave such materials *in situ*. However, when there are also important reasons why this

Figure 7.1 Korean bowl with staining. Staining of this type in Korean ceramics is considered desirable (Victoria and Albert Museum, London).

material should be removed from the object – if for example it would damage the object by shrinking on drying – then the material can be removed and all of it, or a sample of it, kept separately as archival material. Another reason for not removing foreign matter may be that to remove it would be impossible without causing damage to the object, and in such cases the presence of the foreign matter must be accepted. In any cleaning operation great care must be taken to ensure that no damage is done to the object, that removal of original material is kept to an absolute minimum, and that harmful residues are not left behind.

Removal of material that has simply become deposited on the surface of a ceramic is generally not difficult if the object has a sound, continuous glaze. However, removal can become more problematical if the object is unglazed, if there are cracks in the glaze, or if there is unstable surface decoration present, such as flaking enamels or gilding. If dirt has been carried deep into the body of the ceramic, or has become chemically combined, then special techniques must be employed to try to draw it out.

Examination

Examination techniques are covered in depth in Chapter 4. However, it may be helpful to discuss here what it is that must be established from an examination of the object before any cleaning treatment is carried out.

The first thing that should be established is the nature of the ceramic material of which the object is made: whether the body is high fired, low fired or unfired; whether there is a discrete glaze layer and whether there are any other decorative applications such as underglaze or on-glaze enamels, gilding, or unfired painting. Spot tests may be carried out to establish whether there is calcareous material present in the body or decoration as this will have repercussions on the use of acids for removal of insoluble concretions. The presence of any ancillary materials such as metal mounts or paper labels must also be noted and removed before treatment if necessary.

The characteristics of the ceramic will all affect the choice of treatment. Ceramic bodies and glazes which are the product of a high firing tend to be hard and non-porous and much less susceptible to damage through improper use of solvents and other cleaning agents. In contrast, low-fired bodies and glazes are softer and much more porous. They may contain fractions which, owing to a low firing temperature, have remained soluble and would be lost from the body during prolonged soaking in water. Irreversible staining can result from the improper use of cleaning techniques and the harsh use of tools can cause abrasions and scratches.

Secondly, the condition of the object and the extent of any damage must be established and also the presence and condition of any previously applied restoration material. A record should be made of these features and account taken of them when selecting treatments and when handling the object. If the object has been excavated the condition should be especially closely examined and the stability of any deteriorated material such as oxidized surface layers established. It may be necessary to consolidate such areas before treatment (see Chapter 8). An excavated object may contain soluble salts and until desalination treatment can be carried out the object must be maintained in a stable relative humidity in order to prevent damage through the pressure exerted as the salts crystallize.

Thirdly, any foreign matter present must be thoroughly examined to establish its nature and its extent over the surface or within the body of the object. Contents of archaeological vessels may be X-rayed and recorded in detail on scale plans. Where dirt is accessible small spot tests can be made to assess its solubility in a range of solvents, and salt efflorescences and concretions can be investigated to establish their nature. Spot tests should be carried out on an area of the object that is unobtrusive, for example on the base or foot rim, or when possible a small sample of the deposit should be removed and tested separately.

Removal of surface dirt and deposits

The nature of dirt and deposits and the strength of their attachment to the ceramic surface varies widely. Dust and grease may be held loosely to the surface by electrostatic forces or weak chemical bonds (Moncrieff and Weaver, 1983) whereas deposits such as calcium salts may be intimately associated with the surface, especially that of an unglazed object. Removal of surface dirt from high-fired, glazed ceramics does not generally present problems. However, when the surface of the object is matt or textured, or is unstable, or when the object is porous, removal can be more difficult (Figure 7.2).

It is usually desirable to remove surface dirt sooner rather than later in order to avoid the danger of it becoming drawn into the body or into cracks. In the case of wet or damp excavated objects it may be important to remove surface dirt before it dries, both because it is often easier to do so before the dirt has hardened and because the dirt may shrink and cause damage as it dries. The hardening may be due to the reaction of the concretion with atmospheric carbon dioxide to form calcium carbonate. If cleaning cannot

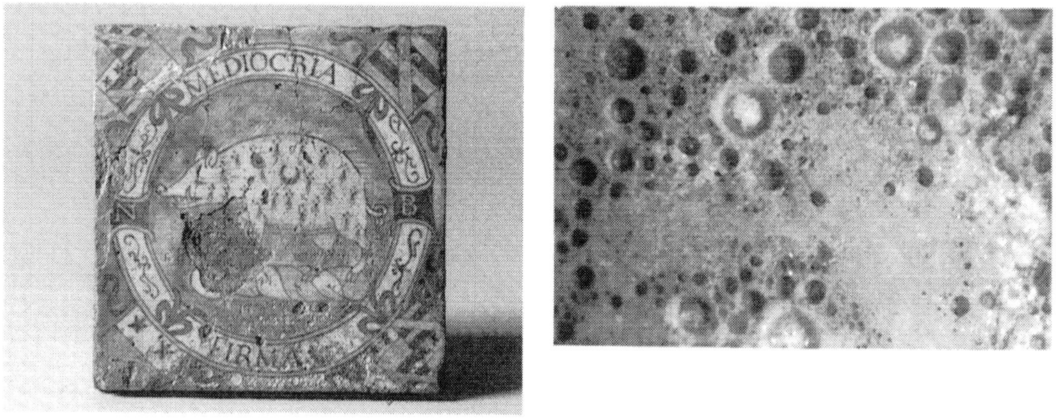

(a) (b)

Figure 7.2 (a) Glazed earthenware tile. In close-up (b) it can be seen that the surface of the glaze contains many small bubbles which trap the dirt (Victoria and Albert Museum, London).

be done on site the object should be kept damp until it can be treated in a laboratory. If the object is very unstable then some form of consolidation may be necessary before treatment (see Chapter 8). Other previous conservation treatments may dictate which type of cleaning method is used.

Methods used to remove surface dirt from ceramics fall mainly into two categories, mechanical methods and chemical methods. However, ultrasonic techniques, lasers and refiring programmes may be considered possible for use under certain circumstances.

Mechanical methods for removal of surface dirt

Mechanical cleaning ranges from light dusting with a hand-held brush, through picking and probing with a scalpel or needle, to the use of sophisticated air abrasive techniques. The advantages of using mechanical methods are that they are, on the whole, more easily controlled than chemical methods and there is no danger of dirt being drawn in solution into the body of the ceramic. This is obviously more of a danger with low-fired, porous bodied ceramics than with high-fired ones. The drawback of mechanical methods is that, used inexpertly or carelessly, there is a danger of scratching, abrading or otherwise physically damaging the fabric of the ceramic. This, again, is more likely to happen in the case of softer, low-fired ceramics. From the point of view of the health and safety of the conservator the use of mechanical techniques may be preferable to the use of toxic solvents; however, adequate precautions must be taken to avoid physical damage to the eyes and hands, and inhalation of fine particles to the lungs.

Dusting

Where the dirt is not strongly adhered to the surface and is not greasy, dusting may be used effectively to remove it. Dusting can be carried out using a brush of a size appropriate to the object, using dry cotton wool swabs or using a soft cloth. In the case of a very large object with no delicate protrusions a vacuum cleaner with a soft, muslin-covered head can be used. The dangers from dusting lie in the possibility of abrading or otherwise damaging the surface of the object and of pushing the dirt into surface irregularities, cracks and chips. A light touch should therefore be used and equipment kept free of large gritty particles. Metal ferrules of brushes should be covered with chamois leather or fabric to avoid inadvertently marking the ceramic (Figure 7.3). If there are any areas of instability on the surface of the object, such as flaking enamels or loosely attached glaze, these should be treated with extreme care or avoided

Figure 7.3 Using a brush for dusting. The ferrule has been covered with foam to prevent damage to the ceramic (Victoria and Albert Museum, London).

altogether. Cotton wool should not be used in such areas as it can snag on loose particles. The use of a rubbing or polishing action should be avoided as this creates static electricity at the surface which will attract further particles of dust.

Picking and cutting

More closely adhered, solid surface deposits, such as hardened burial dirt, encrustations and old restoration materials, will require picking or cutting off the surface with a tool such as a needle or sharp scalpel. Custom made tools formed from other materials, such as Melinex or wood (Smith, in press), can be less damaging, and electric vibrotools with specially modified tips can be useful. In some cases it may be necessary to use a hammer and chisel. There is a danger with the use of all these techniques of causing damage to the object in the form of scratches or gouges, or of cracking or breaking the object if too much pressure is applied in an inappropriate direction. However, if the object is carefully supported, only the minimum pressure necessary is applied and sharp tools are used this can be avoided. Moncrieff and Weaver (1983) describe the physics of picking and flicking off surface deposits.

Abrading

Removal of surface deposits can be carried out using abrasives. The abrasive can have a solid form, such as a glass fibre brush or a rubber burr on a dental drill (Barov, 1988), or it can be dispersed in a cream, or attached to a paper or film. Alternatively an air abrasive system can be used. The abrasive material used must be harder than the deposit in order to be effective, but softer than the ceramic if it is not to cause damage. Difficulties arise when the deposit is as hard, or nearly as hard, as the ceramic itself.

Some of the most commonly used abrasive materials for cleaning ceramic surfaces are the polishing creams, such as Solvol Autosol (a commercially available cream containing kieselguhr, white spirit and methylated soap). Polishing creams are used mainly for removing fairly thin layers of insoluble surface deposits such as light calcium deposits and removing dirt from minor scratches in glazes. They are also useful for removing marks made by tools. Care should be taken in selecting a polishing cream for use. The abrasive quality must not be too harsh and it must not contain any oil or grease. Those sold for polishing chrome or plastic are usually suitable, but household scouring creams and powders should never be used as they are too aggressive and contain bleaches and other additives which may be harmful. Polishing creams should only be used on glazes or high-fired biscuit ware as staining may occur if they are used on unglazed porous bodies. A polishing effect will be caused if they are used on unfired or gilded areas and this should be avoided. Any cracked or flaking areas should also be avoided. The paste is rubbed over the surface deposit with a cotton wool swab or stencil brush, and then polished off with a clean swab, or rinsed off using an appropriate solvent (in the case of Solvol Autosol, white spirits). This must always be done before the cream dries or the cream itself will leave a deposit on the surface of the ceramic which may be difficult to remove later, especially from unglazed biscuit ware.

The use of abrasive papers and films for removal of surface deposits is confined to that of the very finest grades, applied with the minimum of pressure necessary to be effective. They should only be used on hard glazes. Frequent checks should be made using a binocular microscope to ensure that the glaze surface is not becoming scratched. Areas of overglaze decoration should be avoided altogether.

Air abrasive techniques are not commonly used in ceramics conservation. In a lot of instances surface deposits that are difficult to remove in other ways are found on excavated pottery and the use of air abrasive techniques in these cases is dangerous to the object owing to the softness of the pottery. However some experimental work has been carried out by Behrens (1989) which shows that this may be a technique that could be useful for cleaning hard-paste porcelains. At the Victoria and Albert Museum, London, a Cavijet dental tool is used in 'air polishing' mode with sodium bicarbonate as the abrasive for cleaning some earthenware glazes and porcelain. The objects must be very thoroughly rinsed afterwards in order to remove all traces of sodium bicarbonate.

Rubber powders and putties

Rubber powders, e.g. Draft Clean, have been used for many years for removing general surface dirt from the surface of ceramics, in particular unglazed pottery. The powder is lightly rubbed over the surface using a circular motion of the finger. The dirt particles adhere to the rubber and the powder is then brushed off. More recently, a synthetic thermoplastic putty has been used, but there is a danger that the adhesive properties of such a putty may be too strong for some ceramic surfaces, and cause particles of the pottery to be removed (Thomsen and Shashoua, 1991). Alternative rubber materials, such as Kneadable Putty Rubber which consists of a butyl rubber with a pumice and whiting filler, may be more suitable. Care must be taken to discard such materials when they become heavily contaminated to avoid redeposition of residues.

Other techniques

Spyridowicz (in press) reports the use of poly(vinyl acetate) emulsion to clean surfaces. The poly(vinyl acetate) is painted on to the surface to be cleaned, allowed to dry, and then peeled off, bringing the dirt with it. Delicate areas should be avoided.

Chemical methods for removal of surface dirt

Water

Water is often the safest, cheapest, and most effective solvent to use for removing surface dirt and deposits. Burial and other non-greasy dirt can usually be removed by gentle brushing or swabbing with water, and detergents can be added to give the water degreasant properties when greasy dirt is to be removed. Detergents are preferable to soaps as soaps are more likely to form scums and also to attack certain types of decoration. Laboratory detergents should be used rather than commercial household detergents which may contain colouring, perfumes, bleaches, sequestering agents and other additives.

The washing area should be spacious, clean, and clear of clutter, with drainage surfaces nearby. A double sink is useful as the second sink can be used for rinsing. Taps should swivel out of the way, or have rubber nozzles or be wrapped with fabric. When washing large objects directly in the sink, foam padding should be used to stand the object on. Smaller objects should be washed in a plastic bowl to reduce the risk of damage or of losing small fragments down the plughole. A rack, suspended from the top of the sink or bowl, may be useful for containing shards and keeping them protected from the dirt that accumulates in the bottom of the sink. A strainer over the plughole is a wise precaution.

Provided they are sound, high-fired ceramics such as hard-paste porcelains and stonewares can be submerged in warm water to which a few drops of detergent have been added, and washed gently using a soft brush or swabs of cotton wool. Ceramic objects should never be plunged into hot water as the differentials in the thermal expansions of the body, glaze and decoration may result in damage. If the dirt is persistent, provided the object is sound, it may be left to soak for a few minutes before brushing to allow better penetration of the dirt by the water. This may be especially necessary where the dirty area is not a smooth surface, but a rough one, such as a break edge or the surface of an unglazed ware.

Objects should be washed singly, never more than one in a sink or bowl at a time, and when washing several objects the water should be changed frequently as dirty water can become abrasive. It is also preferable to wash fragments one at a time to avoid damage and loss. If more are placed in a bowl of water to soak, the number put in should be carefully noted. It is conceivable that the number taken out may be more than that put in owing to the breakdown of old adhesive bonds, but it should never be less.

If an object is too large to submerge in water, it can be swabbed down with water and detergent using cotton wool or a brush. Opinions are divided as to whether this process should be carried out from the top downwards or from the bottom upwards. Sandwith and Stainton (1985) suggest washing from top to bottom; however, Halahan and Plowden (1987) maintain that washing from bottom upwards is preferable. The latter opinion is based on the idea that some dirt, once wetted and then allowed to dry, may become very difficult to remove. When washing from top to bottom, rivulets of dirty water may run down over the dirt lower down on the surface of the object. If these rivulets are allowed to dry on the surface such a problem may be caused.

After washing, the object or fragments should be thoroughly rinsed in fresh water (ideally distilled water) so that no residues are left behind, and then placed on a perforated tray to drain or blotted dry with a clean cloth or paper towels. A hair dryer on the cold setting may be used to speed up the drying process. Moulded objects that are hollow and have a blow hole should be left to drain supported in such a way that any water inside drains out of the hole.

Again provided they are sound, most glazed earthenwares can also be washed in this way, but they should not be allowed to soak, as the body may contain some soluble fractions which would leach out. Caution should also be exercised when there is any staining in the body of a porous ceramic, particularly any iron staining. Movement of water through the body could cause such stains to spread, and consequently it is safest to use cotton wool swabs in such cases. The cotton wool is wrapped around the end of a swab stick, dipped in the water and then rolled across the surface of the object (Figure 7.4). A rolling action is used rather than a wiping one, and the swabs are kept damp rather than wet, in order that

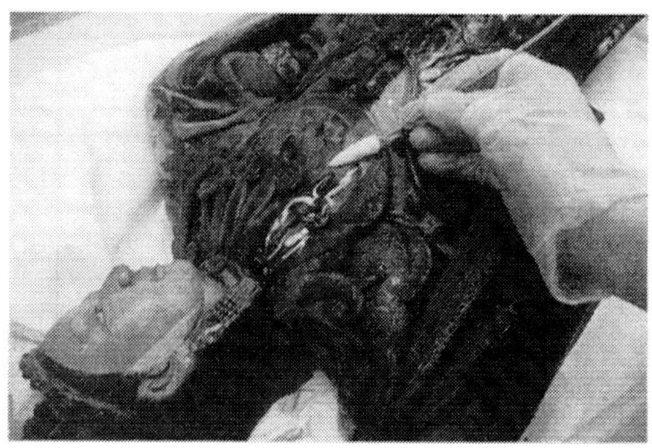

Figure 7.4 The use of a swab for cleaning. The swab is rolled across the surface (Victoria and Albert Museum, London).

the dirt is picked up off the surface rather than being pushed into any surface irregularities, cracks or chips. The swabs should be changed very frequently and the process repeated. Where very fine, accurate cleaning is required a sable brush can be used instead of cotton wool swabs. The danger of the water and dirt being drawn into the body can be further reduced by soaking the object in another solvent first, such as white spirit, in order to cut down its porosity. Obviously the solvent selected for this must be one which is not going to affect the ceramic and in which any dirt and deposits present will not dissolve.

The absorption of water by porous ceramics will mean that the drying time should be extended accordingly; large earthenware objects may take weeks to dry completely. Earthenware is heavier when wet and may be far more fragile than when dry; this should be taken into account when handling.

Unglazed pottery should be treated very cautiously when washing and only washed using the above method if it is well fired and in good condition. It should never be allowed to soak. Any painted decoration or gilding must be spot tested for fastness before washing. This is also true of unfired decoration or gilding on glazed objects. The decoration is dabbed in an inconspicuous area with a small, damp pad of blotting paper or swab of cotton wool. If any pigment or particles lift off, the test should be stopped immediately and on no account should the object be submerged in water. As an alternative, such objects may be washed using water applied on a brush or cotton wool swabs, avoiding the unstable areas. Care should be taken when using swabs to avoid snagging and pulling off loose ceramic particles or leaving fibres on the ceramic surface. Examples of other objects that would be washed in this way would be higher-fired objects with areas of instability such as flaking glaze or enamels, objects with areas of water sensitive restorations, or objects which have ancillary materials which cannot be removed during treatment.

Friable, low-fired pottery should not be cleaned using aqueous methods, but can be cleaned using mechanical methods, or by using alternative solvents. As a compromise, low-fired earthenwares can be cleaned using a 50/50 solution of industrial methylated spirits and water. This will soften burial soil but reduce the amount of water used (Smith, in press).

An alternative way of using water for cleaning is to apply it in the form of steam. Tools are available for this purpose which produce a fine jet of steam from a small nozzle and enable the steam to be localized in a precise area. Steam cleaning is used mainly for the removal of dirt from unglazed earthenware surfaces, but must not be used where there is unfired decoration present. Application of the steam is followed immediately by blotting with absorbent paper, in order to prevent the water and dirt from being drawn into the body of the ceramic.

Other solvents

In cases where water is ineffective as a solvent or where a 'dry' cleaning method is required there is a range of organic solvents that may be used. Information on individual solvents and their uses may be found in Chapter 14. When the exact composition of the deposit to be removed is unknown, tests must be made to determine which solvent will be most effective. Such tests may merely consist of trying a range of solvents on a small area of dirt or, if the sophisticated equipment necessary is available, may involve analysis of the deposit and selection of a known solvent on the basis of the result. When used to clean surface dirt, solvents are usually applied on swabs in the manner described for water, fresh swabs being used until no more dirt appears to be coming off on the swabs. If the object is porous and would be undamaged by water, it can be pre-soaked in water to cut down its porosity and hence avoid absorption of the solvent and dirt.

Many of the solvents that are effective for cleaning ceramics are toxic or harmful and appropriate precautions must be taken during their application (see Chapter 13).

Treatment of some unglazed pottery with certain highly volatile solvents, e.g. acetone, can result in blooming on the surface of porous wares. Amyl acetate can sometimes be effective in the removal of this blooming.

Enzymes

Enzymes may be used on fats, carbohydrates and proteins to enable them to be washed away. The most readily available source of enzymes is human saliva which contains among other components an enzyme called amylase. Romao *et al.* (1990) report that experiments show saliva to be an effective cleaning agent which may be of particular use on pottery decorated with unfired pigments. However, they showed some damage to be caused to vermilion and azurite pigments. Biological washing powders contain certain enzymes that catalyse the breakdown of proteins and can be used in combination with sequestering agents to clean high-fired porcelain. This is discussed below in the section on chelating and sequestering agents.

Acids

Encrustations of calcium carbonate or calcium sulphate formed on the surface of ceramics during burial, or saltwater or freshwater immersion, can be removed using acids. The acids most commonly used are hydrochloric acid and nitric acid and the organic acids oxalic acid, citric acid and acetic acid. Concretions of silicates which may also be found can only be removed using hydrofluoric acid, but the use of this acid is extremely hazardous for both the object and the conservator, and should be avoided. Silicates must therefore be removed by mechanical means. When using any acids protective gloves and goggles should be worn and strict attention should be paid to correct procedures for the preparation and disposal of acids.

There is a danger when using acids on earthenware and pottery that if the ceramic material itself contains calcium compounds, such as chalk or ground shell in the body or chalk in inlaid decoration, these will be attacked. The ceramic must therefore always be tested before treatment with acid and this is done by applying a small drop of dilute nitric acid to an unglazed area or to areas of decoration that are suspected of containing susceptible components. If effervescence is observed there is some form of calcareous filler present and if possible the concretion should be removed mechanically. A second class of objects that are particularly susceptible to damage through acid treatment is those that contain iron oxides in their bodies or glazes. Olive and Pearson (1975), by checking using X-ray diffraction both before and after treatment, showed that hydrochloric and oxalic acid treatments dissolved iron oxides out from the glazes of their experimental pieces and increased their tendency to exfoliation. Ancient lead glazes on pottery may be damaged by the use of nitric acid, the acid reacting with metallic lead exposed by devitrification and resulting in a white carbonate deposit. Hydrochloric acid should be used in these cases.

Acid treatment of carbonates may cause physical damage through the effervescence caused by the evolution of carbon dioxide. This should be borne in mind when treating friable ceramics.

In order to select the appropriate acid treatment the nature of the concretion must first be established. A sample should be removed mechanically and placed on a tile or glass. A drop of dilute nitric acid is applied to the sample and the sample observed for signs of effervescence. If it effervesces strongly carbonates are present. If there is only slight effervescence there may also be sulphates present and this can be confirmed by further adding 2 drops of 1% barium chloride to the sample. If sulphates are present a white precipitate will be formed. Deteriorated glazes may have the appearance of a surface deposit and if the concretion does not react with the acid the possibility that it is, in fact, deteriorated glaze must be considered. A clear glaze that has deteriorated and become opaque will usually regain its transparency if lightly wetted. Hodges (1986), reporting on unpublished work carried out by Leskard, warns that evolution of carbon dioxide during acid treatment of lime encrustations can result in damage to pottery that does not even contain any calcareous filler. The physical effect of the carbon dioxide effervescence causes any clay particles in intimate contact with the encrustation (for example where the encrustation has entered surface pores) to be reduced to a 'sludge'. Hodges suggests that other methods for lime removal, such as the use of sequestering agents or deionizing resins, may provide promising alternative methods, but that research into such methods is necessary.

Treatment for carbonate concretions is carried out using 10% nitric or hydrochloric acid. The ceramic is pre-soaked in deionized or distilled water, and then either it is immersed in the acid, or the acid is applied on cotton wool swabs. Alternatively, the acid may be applied to the concretion drop by drop. The latter method is preferable as it is more controllable, and may be used in the case of a ceramic with calcareous filler if necessary. In such a case the object is rinsed in running water after the application of each drop of acid. In any case as soon as the effervescence at the site of the concretion ceases the acid is rinsed off. If any effervescence is observed anywhere else during treatment the treatment should be immediately halted by rinsing the object thoroughly in water. Checks for damage to the glaze can also be made periodically throughout the treatment by allowing the ceramic to dry out, in which state any damage will be more visible. After treatment the softened concretion is removed using a scalpel and the object then given a final rinse to remove all traces of acid and soluble salts. Rinsing can be followed by soaking and conductivity tests to ensure that all soluble salts have been removed. Thorough rinsing is extremely important as soluble salts left in the body of a ceramic are potentially far more damaging than insoluble concretions.

Sulphate deposits require stronger acid solutions for removal. Some writers recommend concentrated nitric or hydrochloric acid (Gedye, 1968) whilst others suggest 20% nitric acid (Davison and Jackson, 1988,). Treatment of sulphate deposits with nitric acid may result in the formation of sulphuric acid and caution should therefore be exercised with its use in these cases. Objects should not be soaked in more concentrated acids and the acid should be applied in drop form after pre-soaking the object in water. Alternatively, the concretion can be removed mechanically.

Alkalis

Alkalis such as sodium carbonate, sodium bicarbonate and sodium hydroxide can be useful for the removal of grease, animal fats and wax. However, prolonged soaking in strong alkalis can cause damage to glaze and body, and there is a danger of damage through the growth of salt crystals if the alkali is not completely removed. Der Sarkissian and Goodberry (1981) report on the successful use of sodium hydroxide to remove a burnt-on coating of poly(vinyl acetate) from a fire damaged plate. Barov (1988) reports the use of a cleaning agent (AB57) containing ammonium bicarbonate and sodium bicarbonate for removal of plaster residues from the surface of an object. This compound contains carboxymethyl cellulose to give it gel properties.

Sequestering agents

Soaking in solutions containing sequestering agents can be used in some instances to remove surface concretions and dirt. The most commonly used ones are sodium hexametaphosphate, ethylene diamine tetra-acetic acid (EDTA), trisodium phosphate, and sodium citrate. They attack the metal ions in the concretion, and combine with them to form complexes that can then be rinsed away. There is a risk that the underlying ceramic material may be attacked and any metal ions incorporated in body, glaze or decoration removed. This is a particular danger with unfired decoration, deteriorated glazes or lustre ware (Rado, 1975). Different metal ions are more soluble at different pH levels (Olive and Pearson, 1975), calcium at pH 13 and iron at pH 4, and advantage can be taken of this. When using EDTA the pH can be altered by the choice of the disodium salt or the tetrasodium salt of the EDTA. A 5% solution of the tetrasodium salt gives a pH of 11.5 and hence this is used when calcareous concretions are being removed from a ceramic containing iron in the body or decoration. The reaction may proceed at a faster rate if the solution is slightly warm. Gibson (1971) found a temperature of approximately 77°C and the addition of 5% sodium hydroxide significantly speeded up the removal of a chabazite deposit on pottery. However, a caution is given that etching of plain black burnished ware may occur when using sodium hydroxide at this concentration and that the technique should not be used on objects with deteriorated surfaces, unglazed decoration or old restorations. As with the use of acids it is very important to rinse thoroughly after treatment.

Sodium (hexametaphosphate) polyphosphate has been used in combination with commercial detergent powders such as Ariel or Biotex to remove stains. The mixture can be safely and effectively used to clean surface dirt and deposits from some porcelain. Because of the sequestering action of the sodium hexametaphosphate and uncertainty concerning additives present in the detergent powders (e.g. dyes and optical whiteners), caution must be exercised with the use of this combination on anything other than hard-paste porcelain with no coloured decoration or gilding. Hogan (in press) reports problems with the removal of a white bloom on Iznik pottery caused by treatment with Ariel. However, it makes an excellent cleaning solution for surface dirt on biscuit porcelain. Williams (1983) recommended 2–3% Calgon (the formulation of this commercial product has since changed and it no longer contains sodium hexametaphosphate added to warm water and dissolved, followed after two or three minutes by the addition of 2–3% detergent powder, which is again stirred until dissolved. The object or fragments are then placed in the solution and left to soak. After a few minutes, and periodically, the dirty surfaces are gently brushed with a stencil brush to dislodge dirt. The porcelain may be left to soak in the solution overnight, but in many cases the dirt may disappear in a few minutes. The porcelain should be rinsed very well after treatment to remove all traces of the soluble complexes formed and of the detergent.

Ultrasonic methods

Ultrasonic cleaning can be carried out using an ultrasonic bath or a fine ultrasonic tool as used in dentistry for cleaning teeth. The benefit of the second method is that the cleaning can be directed to very specific areas and thus the danger of harming unstable material such as unfired decoration, loose enamel or glaze can be avoided The method can be useful for removing dirt from pitted surfaces such as glazes that were badly fired and contain pinholes, or where a glaze or enamel surface has become worn (Figure 7.5). It may also be useful when cleaning biscuit porcelain and objects with areas inaccessible to tools.

Lasers

Lasers produce a beam of very concentrated light energy which can be directed to extremely precise areas. This energy has been used to vaporize the organic matter in crusts of dirt on stone and light-coloured marble (Amoroso and Fassina, 1983) and stained glass (Asmus, 1975). The authors are not aware of any published work on the use of lasers for cleaning ceramics, but developments may make their use feasible in the future.

Removal of ingrained dirt and stains

When material has become more deeply lodged in surface pores or cracks, ingrained along a break edge or absorbed into the body of the ceramic, simple washing and swabbing is rarely effective. The dirt may indeed be soluble in water or other solvents but the difficulty lies firstly in getting the solvent into the body to the site of the dirt, and secondly in pulling the dirt and solvent mixture out again onto the surface. This is usually achieved by applying the solvent in the form of a pack or poultice. If the material producing the stain is not soluble it may be treated with chemicals such as acids, sequestering agents or enzymes that convert it to a soluble form.

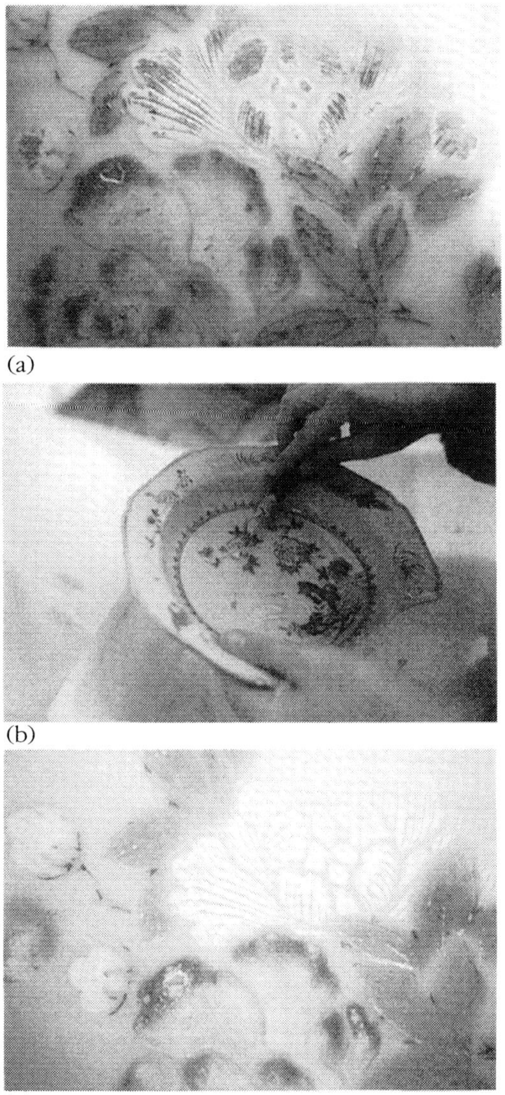

(a)

(b)

(c)

Figure 7.5 The use of an air polishing tool for cleaning worn overglaze enamel: (a) shows the enamels before cleaning; (b) the tool in use; (c) the enamels after cleaning.

Alternatively the stain may be left in place but treated with a bleach to render it colourless.

Organic stains

Many stains in ceramics are organic in origin, often having been caused by food, and hence are soluble in one or more of the organic solvents. Some organic stains, such as those caused by mould growth, are not readily soluble and in these cases removal of the colour of the staining material by bleaching may be an appropriate way of treating the stain. Certain alkalis can be used to remove organic stains of a greasy or waxy nature.

Solvent packs and poultices

When the stain is deep within the body one way of allowing the solvent to penetrate to it is to soak the whole object or fragment in a bath containing solvent. This can be a very extravagant use of solvent and relies on the relatively slow removal of the stain by diffusion and dilution. Instead, the method normally used is to apply the solvent as a pack or poultice. The solvent is mixed with a suitable material and spread over the surface of the object. Some of it becomes absorbed into the body of the ceramic where it dissolves the dirt. As solvent begins to dry off from the outer surface of the pack, the solvent/dirt mixture is drawn back out into the pack. Eventually all the solvent evaporates off the outer surface of the pack, leaving the dirt behind in the pack. If practical, the object or fragment must be completely encased in the pack or the solvent/dirt mixture may simply be moved to another area of the body, and if the solvent being used is very volatile the object and pack should be encased in polythene sheeting or other suitable material to slow down the rate of evaporation of the solvent and allow complete penetration of the body and removal of the stain.

Various poulticing materials can be used, but one of those most commonly used is hydrated magnesium trisilicate, or sepiolite. Hydrated magnesium-aluminium silicate (attapulgite) has also been used, although this clay has been classified as a health hazard, being a possible carcinogen (Marconi, 1989). Recently work has been carried out using a third clay, bentonite (Lazzarini and Lombardi, 1990), for the cleaning of stonework and the desalination of marble, and results comparable to those found with sepiolite have been achieved. Laponite, a synthetic clay has also been used recently, with good results (Ling, 1991; Hogan, in press).

Sepiolite takes the form of a finely divided powder when dry, and is mixed with solvent to a thick paste that is spread over the surface of the object in an even layer 1–2 cm thick. The object should be coated all over in order to ensure that the solvent and dirt is drawn out into the pack. If this is not done, any porous surface that is not coated should be carefully sealed with plastic film to prevent solvent evaporating off from it (Williams, 1987). As the pack dries, cracks appear in it (Figure 7.6) and eventually it reaches a state where it can be simply brushed off the object. This may take two to three days, but will be longer if the pack is covered to slow the process down. If it is felt that owing to the powdery nature of this material there is a risk of leaving deposits of the pack material in cracks, a separating layer of tissue, such as Eltolene

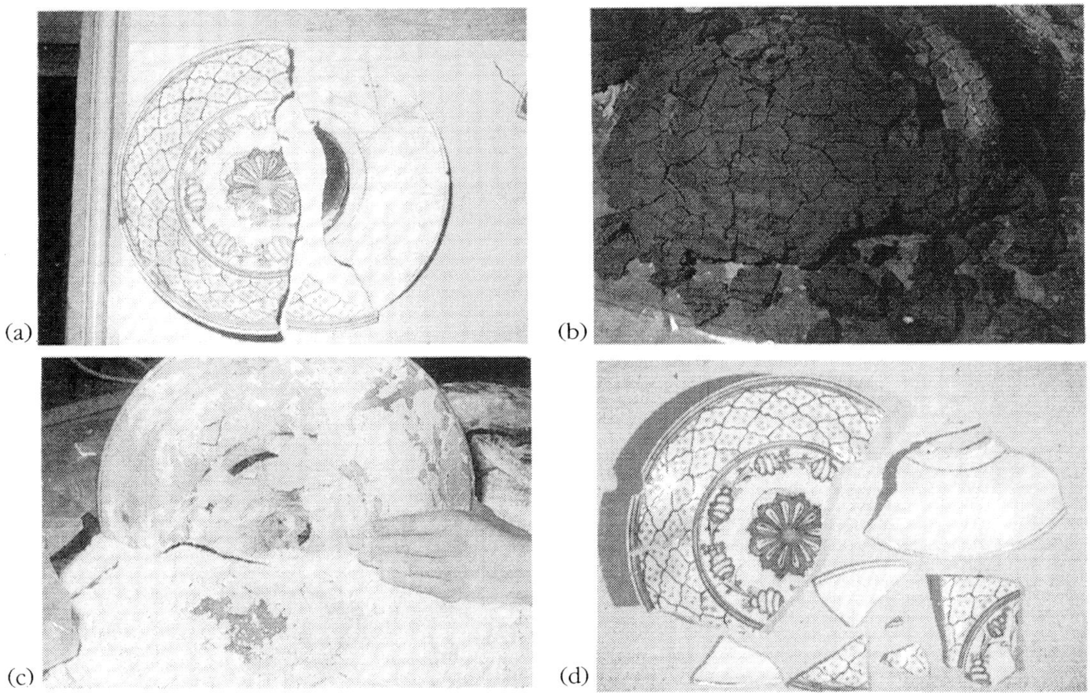

Figure 7.6 The use of a sepiolite pack for stain removal. (a) Shows the dish before application of the pack. The base was stained with a dark brown stain. In (b) the pack, which was made up with white spirits and applied in a thick coating around all the pieces, has begun to dry and crack. In (c) the pack has dried out completely and the sepiolite is being brushed off the surface, and (d) shows the cleaned dish (Victoria and Albert Museum, London).

tissue, can be used between the surface of the object and the pack. New batches of any of the clays used for poulticing should be tested before use as they can occasionally be contaminated with soluble salts.

As an alternative to a clay, paper pulp can be used as a poulticing material. This is prepared by tearing acid-free blotting paper into pieces about 1 cm square and adding them to a small quantity of deionized water or other solvent in a beaker. They are left overnight and stirred to a paste-like consistency in the morning. They can then be applied to the surface of the object in the way described above for clay packs.

Almost any solvent can be used in poultice form, the choice depending on the nature of the dirt, but most success is achieved with the less volatile solvents. If water is used, it must be distilled or deionized water. White spirit is commonly used where the stains originate from greasy food.

Alkalis

Alkalis such as sodium carbonate and bicarbonate and sodium hydroxide can be used for removing wax and grease stains. The object or fragment should be soaked in the solution; however there is the danger that strong alkalis can affect the glaze or body after prolonged soaking. If not completely rinsed away crystals can form, damaging the glaze or body.

Bleaches

Where the stain cannot be removed the alternative is to render it colourless using a bleaching agent. This is a particularly useful method for treating dirty cracks and break edges. Chlorine bleaches should be avoided as they leave chloride ions in the body of the ceramic which are very difficult to rinse out. These may cause severe damage at a later stage by crystallizing out at the surface or under the glaze, and can result in the whole object fragmenting. The safest bleaching agent to use for stains that are of an organic nature is hydrogen peroxide, from which the only residue is water. Hydrogen peroxide releases oxygen atoms which attack the part of the organic molecule that gives it colour. However, the strong oxidizing effect means that hydrogen peroxide should be used with caution on anything other than high-fired ceramic bodies as it may react with uncombined iron in earthenwares and cause iron staining. It may also affect gilding and unfired decoration, and will attack many non-ceramic materials such as human tissues and Formica bench tops. It is wise therefore to place the object on a large sheet of glass or in a polyethylene tray when using hydrogen peroxide, and to wear protective gloves and goggles.

Hydrogen peroxide is used at 20–100 volume strength (see Chapter 14) and combined with a few drops of ammonia. The ammonia catalyses the release of oxygen, hence speeding up the bleaching reaction, and will eventually evaporate off leaving no residue. The ammonia must not be added until the mixture is required for use or otherwise much of the peroxide will already have broken down by the time it is applied to the object. Swabs of cotton wool are soaked in the solution and then applied over the stained area using tweezers (Figure 7.7). Alternatively, small fragments of ceramic may be submerged in the solution in a glass or polyethylene container. The swabs should be renewed, or the solution changed, regularly. It is not recommended to simply pipette further hydrogen peroxide and ammonia onto the swabs as it will be diluted by the water remaining in the swabs as a residue from the initial solution. If the atmosphere is very dry or warm the swabs can be covered with plastic film to cut down evaporation.

When the stain has disappeared, or when repeated applications of hydrogen peroxide appear to be having no further effect, the swabs are removed and the object is soaked in deionized or tap water. Residual hydrogen peroxide and ammonia can affect further treatment and therefore it is important to make sure that they have been completely removed before continuing with treatment. As the ammonia is highly volatile and the hydrogen peroxide breaks down to water on contact with air, provided the object is completely dry there should be no residues. It may take considerably longer for the object to dry than is often allowed, especially if the object is low fired and porous. This is another reason why this treatment should be used with caution on such bodies. Hogan (in press) reports problems with the use of hydrogen peroxide treatment on Iznik pottery. Recent, unpublished work has suggested that peroxide groups may remain, attached to the stain, and these may affect subsequent treatment. Care must also be taken when using peroxide treatment in association with other cleaning treatments such as soaking in biological detergents, and very thorough soaking should be carried out between each stage of treatment.

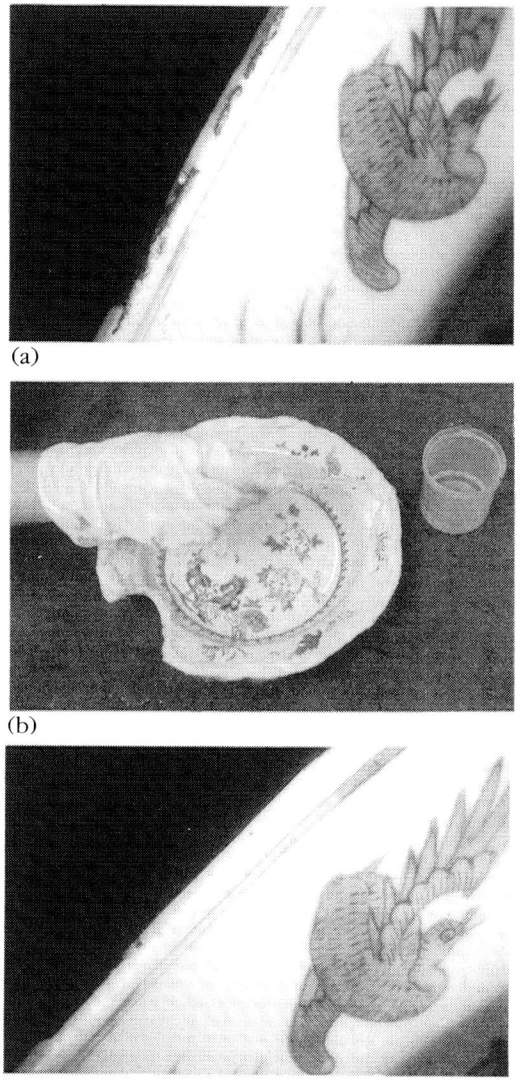

(a) (b) (c)

Figure 7.7 The use of hydrogen peroxide for cleaning chipped edges of a porcelain plate: (a) shows the chipped edge before cleaning; (b) the swabs in place; (c) the cleaned edge.

Metal stains

Metal stains found in ceramic objects may originate from association with metal objects or deposits during burial, or from corroded mounts, rivets or dowels etc. The most commonly found metal stains are iron and copper stains.

Acids

The removal of iron stains from ceramic bodies generally relies on a reduction reaction with one of a number of different acids.

The acids most commonly used are phosphoric, orthophosphoric, oxalic, citric and acetic acids. As emphasized in the discussion of the use of acids in removing calcareous concretions there are inherent dangers in using acid treatments on ceramics. The reader is referred to that section for a discussion of the precautions that should be taken to ensure that no damage is done to the ceramic. Protective gloves and goggles should be worn, and the acids are applied either on cotton wool swabs or paper pulp, or by immersing the ceramic in the acid solution. The effects of phosphoric acid are not fully understood and the possibility of the formation of insoluble calcium phosphate salts in the body is a risk. Proprietary rust removers which contain phosphoric acid such as Jenolite (available as a gel or liquid) can be used. However, these tend to contain not only the acid but other chemicals intended to inhibit future corrosion, and these may interfere with future conservation treatments; for example, they are known to inhibit the curing of epoxies.

Oxalic acid will form insoluble calcium oxalate salts if contact with the ceramic body is prolonged (Figure 7.8).

Removal of dark green copper stains which may arise from dowels or gilt-bronze ornamentation can be achieved using citric acid, which will dissolve the cupric oxide to form a soluble complex.

It is essential to rinse the object very thoroughly after acid treatment to remove the soluble iron complexes formed or these may crystallize out at a later stage and cause damage. A careful watch should be kept during treatment, especially when treating porous types of ceramics, to ensure that the stain is not simply being moved further into the body. If this appears to be happening treatment should be halted immediately.

Electrolytic treatment

Electrolytic treatment can be used in the cleaning and removal of corroded iron rivets. The method relies on the principles of electrolytic reduction, where the corroded object, the iron rivet, acts as a cathode and is connected to the negative terminal of a battery. The current is carried away from the iron by negative ions through an electrolytic solution to the anode, where they are oxidized. For a detailed exposition of the chemical reactions occurring the reader is referred to Lacoudre and Dubus (1988).

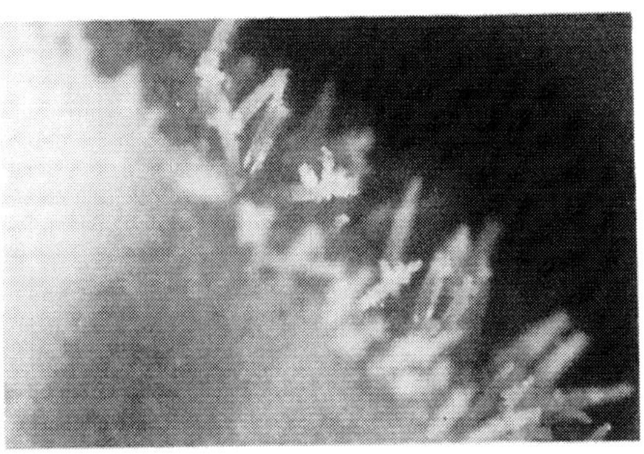

Figure 7.8 Calcium oxalate salts formed on the edge of an earthenware bowl following treatment of iron stains with oxalic acid (Victoria and Albert Museum, London).

Alkalis

A strong solution of ammonia applied on swabs of cotton wool can be used to remove copper stains. Again, very thorough washing after treatment is essential. Williams (1983) suggests that this treatment may be followed by soaking in a biological washing powder and Calgon (see earlier section on the use of chelating and sequestering agents for removal of surface dirt).

Bleaches

The reducing bleaches sodium dithionite (Green *et al.*, 1988) and bisulphite have been used to render iron stains colourless; however the stains may reappear at a later stage owing to natural oxidation or if an oxidizing bleach treatment is subsequently used. Hydrogen peroxide can be used to bleach iron sulphide stains by oxidation.

Sequestering agents

Sequestering agents, such as EDTA (ethylene diamine tetra-acetic acid), sodium hexametaphosphate, trisodium phosphate and sodium citrate, can be used to remove iron stains. Again there may be dangers to the ceramic and the reader is referred to the section on the use of sequestering agents for the removal of surface concretions.

Removal of soluble salts

The ways in which soluble salts are introduced into ceramic objects and the damage that can arise have been discussed in detail in Chapter 2. Soluble salts commonly found in contaminated ceramics include chlorides, nitrates and phosphates. Sulphates and carbonates are also found but these dissolve much more slowly and are sometimes termed insoluble.

If a damp object which has absorbed soluble salts is allowed to dry out the salts will be left behind as crystals. They may remain within the body or they may be drawn to the surface as the water evaporates off and crystallize out at the body/air interface, in pores or under the glaze. If they remain deep in the body initially they may move to the surface during subsequent wetting and drying cycles. The crystallization will almost always cause some degree of damage, ranging from exfoliation of the glaze to complete disintegration of the body. It must be stressed that it is the crystallization that causes the damage, not the presence of the salts in solution, and for this reason wet excavated pottery must always be tested for salt contamination before drying. If being stored wet, pottery may be treated with biocides. In certain circumstances excavated pottery that is salt contaminated may already be dry and may actually be held together by the salt crystals. In such cases consolidation will have to be carried out before the salts can be removed.

Testing for soluble salts

In dry ceramics soluble salts generally appear as fine needle-like crystals on any exposed body surface or growing from cracks in a glaze. In extreme circumstances they can completely coat an object with a furry white layer (Figure 7.9). However they may be less obvious and appear as a fine white powder or even be unnoticeable except under magnification. Their presence may be suspected if, for example, deterioration of the body, glaze or decoration is occurring in the absence of any other obvious cause, and then examination can be made under magnification. In the case of wet objects the soluble salts will not be visible. One method of detecting their presence is to soak the object or fragment in distilled water and then remove a sample of the water and evaporate it off in a watch glass over a bunsen burner. If there are soluble salts present they will remain behind in the watch glass as white crystals.

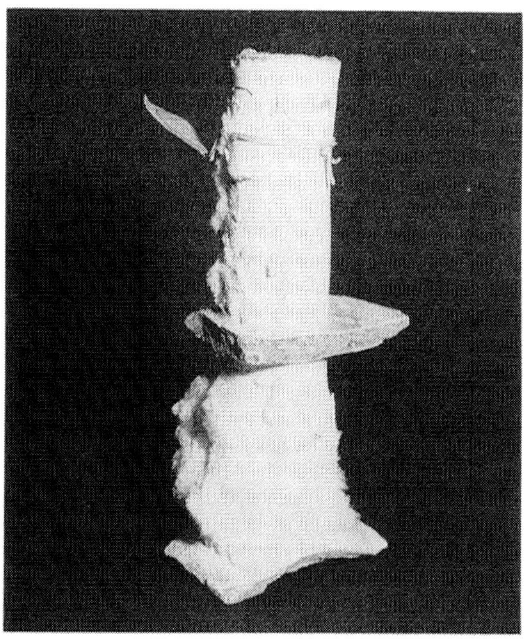

Figure 7.9 Glazed earthenware candlestick with severe salt efflorescence which has pushed off much of the glaze (Victoria and Albert Museum, London).

Alternatively the water can be tested using a conductivity meter. This measures the concentration of any salts present in the water by measuring the amount of electric current that will pass through it between two electrodes as compared with a control. When either of the methods is used it is important to stir the water gently before removing the sample in order to ensure that any pockets of higher concentrations of salts are dispersed.

Although the same basic methods are used to remove soluble salts of all types, it may be of interest to know what type of salt is present. The following simple tests can be used on a solution of the salts dissolved in distilled water. If there is not sufficient salt efflorescence to remove easily from the object to make up a test solution with distilled water, it may be possible to draw out sufficient salts by placing a piece of filter paper, dampened with distilled water, on an affected area of the ceramic. The filter paper is then placed in a container of distilled water in order to produce a solution of the salts in the container.

Chlorides

These form a white precipitate with silver nitrate. To test a solution of the salts made with distilled water, about 10 ml of the solution is placed in a test-tube and 3 drops of dilute nitric acid (10–20%) are added. This will remove any carbonate ions which could otherwise give false results. Three drops of a molar silver nitrate solution are then added. A white precipitate will be observed if chloride ions are present.

Nitrates

The test solution (again made up with distilled water) must first be acidified with a few drops of dilute sulphuric acid. A few fresh crystals of ferrous sulphate are then added and the mixture agitated until these are dissolved. A few millilitres of concentrated sulphuric acid are then poured down the inside of the test-tube, which is held in an inclined position. The sulphuric acid forms a layer in the bottom of the test-tube and a brown ring will be observed at the junction of the two layers if nitrates are present.

Sulphates

Hydrochloric acid is added to the test solution followed by barium chloride. A white precipitate will result if sulphates are present.

X-ray diffraction, neutron activation analysis and various specific ion meters can be used to analyse and measure salt content.

MacLeod and Davies (1987) used a Buchler-Cotlove chloridometer to determine chloride ion concentrations in wash water during desalination of objects from shipwreck sites. Paterakis (1987b) tables the various alternative methods of testing that can be used and in an earlier paper (1987a) discusses comparison of expressions of soluble salt content.

Methods of removal

Removal of salts from within the fabric of an object is usually by diffusion into wash water. MacLeod and Davies (1987) report work to predict required treatment time and release rates. Removal depends on a diffusion gradient between the object and the wash water. There are several methods used, the main ones being: washing in still water; washing in running water; 'agitation-dispersion'; and extraction using a pack. The method used will depend on the type of ceramic and its condition. When the object is in sound condition and the surface decoration is stable it is generally considered reasonable to use normal tap water, unless the tap water is very heavily contaminated with, for example, calcium. However when there is any deterioration of glaze, decoration or body, or when the object is very low fired, deionized or distilled water must be used for the final rinses. Hodges (1986), reporting on unpublished work by Last, suggests that the use of elevated temperatures may improve the effectiveness of some washing techniques.

In the case of low-fired ceramics that are at risk of losing soluble components through prolonged soaking, a preferable alternative may be to brush off any surface salt crystals and store the object in stable conditions of humidity (Moncrieff, 1975). The relative humidity at which the salt is stable varies from salt to salt (Paterakis, 1987b) and this course of action is therefore not recommended when there is more than one type of salt present.

Washing in still water

This method is suitable if the object is in sound condition, but may also be used very carefully with objects which have areas of loose glaze or decoration, or a slightly friable body. If the object is severely deteriorated it may be possible to consolidate the object first (see Chapter 8) and then use this method of desalination. Sufficient drying time for the loss of the solvent from solvent-based consolidants must be allowed in order to avoid blooming and achieve maximum effectiveness of the consolidant. As the method may involve long periods of soaking in water it is not suitable for unfired or very low-fired objects.

The object is placed in a clean container and water very slowly added, allowing time for air in the body to escape gently. If the water is poured in fast, damage can be done by the pressure of the air escaping rapidly. The object is left to soak so that the soluble salts diffuse out of it into the surrounding water. The water is changed regularly, perhaps once a day, to maintain a differential between the salt concentration in the object and in the surrounding water. Obviously the larger the volume of water used, the fewer the number of water changes that will be necessary. The salt content of the water is monitored regularly and the process halted when it remains at the background level of the water being used or when the salt content reaches an acceptable level. Olive and Pearson (1975) quote 150 microsiemens (micromhos) per cubic centimetre ($\mu S/cm^3$) or less for all dissolved salts and Paterakis (1987b) quotes 75–100 ($\mu S/cm^3$) for chloride ions. It is therefore necessary to know the conductivity of the water being used. In most cases it is sufficient for tap water to be used and a final soak given in distilled water if desired. However, objects from marine sites are often given initial treatment in diluted seawater as the diffusion pressure resulting from submersion in freshwater may cause damage (Olive and Pearson, 1975).

The disadvantage of washing in still water is that the salts diffuse relatively slowly through the water and an area of high concentration of salts builds up around the object. The following two methods are used to avoid this problem.

Washing in flowing water

This method employs water running through a sink or bath and hence the object is being continually washed with fresh water. This method is not suitable for objects with any significant degree of deterioration and is also very wasteful of water (Jedrzejewska, 1970; Olive and Pearson, 1975).

Agitation-dispersion

Again this method can only be used with sound objects. It is described by MacLeod and Davies (1987) and employs apparatus that gently agitates the washing water with the result that there is no build-up of salts in the water immediately surrounding the object.

Pack removal

Paper pulp, Laponite RD or sepiolite packs can be used for desalination. They are used in the same way as described for stain removal, using deionized or distilled water as the solvent. Their effect is much slower than the soaking methods as less water is employed; however in some cases, e.g. low-fired or very large objects, their use may be preferable. The pack is changed when partially dry and the salt content tested with a conductivity meter by soaking a sample in deionized or distilled water (Larson, 1980a).

Ultrasonic cleaning

The use of ultrasonic waves combined with soaking in water may provide a more effective form of desalination than simple soaking, but is not suitable for use on friable pottery.

Electrodialysis and electroendosmosis

These methods are used where the pores of the ceramic are very small and prolonged soaking would therefore be required for any of the first three methods. They rely on the passage of an electric current between two stainless steel electrodes placed on either side of the object. In electrodialysis the object is placed in distilled water and a current of 1 A/ dm^2 is passed through the water between the electrodes. The salts from the object dissolve in the water, thus forming an electrolytic solution. Electro-endosmosis is used if there are any fugitive pigments present on the object. One of the electrodes is placed inside the object, this electrode being chosen as the one with the opposite charge to that of the pigments. The other electrode takes the form of a cylinder surrounding the object. The vessel is suspended in a nylon bag in a 0.5% solution of ammonia and a current of 1 A/dm^2 is passed between the electrodes. The salts are attracted to the electrodes (Watkinson, 1975).

Ion exchange resins

The use of ion exchange resins is expensive and involves embedding the object in the resin (Watkinson, 1975). This is not a method that is generally used.

Removal of lead sulphide blackening

Blackening of lead glazes results from the action of sulphate-reducing bacteria during anaerobic burial. Lead sulphide is formed and must be oxidized to lead sulphate in order to restore the original colour. Olive and Pearson (1975) report achieving satisfactory results using applications of 25 volume hydrogen peroxide for up to 36 hours. Acid treatment can be used to remove blackening but may cause damage to the ceramic. An alternative method is to reheat the object under oxidizing conditions (Tennent, in press). This obviously carries risks with it and will rule out future dating using thermoluminescence.

Refiring

Refiring has been successfully used for the removal of carbon deposits on the surface of ceramics that have been subjected to accidental fire. Davison and Harrison (1987) refired Greek pottery shards blackened with carbon to 450°C, a temperature that, owing to knowledge of the original manufacturing temperatures, was deemed to be safe. The carbon was removed in a few hours and the appearance of the original material seemed unaffected. Bogle (in press) found 450°C insufficient to remove carbon from fire blackened porcelain and used a firing temperature of 540°C. At 573°C quartz inversion occurs and therefore temperatures as high as this must not be used. Heating ceramics to these sorts of temperature is generally not advised because of the differentials in the thermal expansions of the materials and the risk of damage occurring due to the release of absorbed moisture. Heating and cooling must therefore be very slow and controlled. Another drawback to heating objects is that potential thermoluminescence evidence is destroyed and dating using this technique becomes impossible. However, in the case of objects that have been subject to fire, this is irrelevant as the information has already been lost.

8

Reinforcement and consolidation

Introduction

As a result of defects in its manufacture, subsequent mechanical damage, or exposure to adverse environmental conditions, a ceramic object may become deteriorated in such a way that any forces exerted on it, either in the process of simple handling or during treatments such as cleaning or desalination, will result in loss of material or even total collapse. In severe cases, excavated objects may be held together only by the surface tension of the water that they have absorbed and simply drying them out will cause their collapse. Where salt efflorescence is causing the body to break up, loss of material may occur without any outside force being exerted. The precise manner in which ceramic objects deteriorate and the causes of such deterioration are covered in detail in Chapter 2. This chapter will look at the ways in which such objects can be treated in order to prevent further loss of material, and allow them to be safely handled.

Temporary reinforcement

Temporary reinforcement is commonly used when lifting excavated objects from the ground and may be used both for severely deteriorated objects and those that are not necessarily in a particularly friable state but which require support to prevent cracks opening or broken pieces shifting or grinding together. Temporary reinforcement can also be used in conjunction with a permanent consolidation treatment and this type of reinforcement will be discussed in the next section. Temporary reinforcement for the lifting of excavated objects may be preferable to consolidation. It is a less invasive method and it may be found that after drying the object regains sufficient strength to make further treatment unnecessary.

Bandaging

Owing to the hollow shape of many ceramic objects it is often possible to use the earth on the inside of an excavated object to help hold it together. Further support can be supplied by wrapping gauze bandages, either dry or coated with a material such as plaster of Paris, around the outside of the object. If the object is merely cracked the earth on the outside of the object can be removed before the bandages are applied. However if the object is broken the bandages may have to be applied gradually as the earth is excavated from the outside. The method of wrapping will depend to a large extent on the idiosyncrasies of the object in question. However as a general rule the bandages should be wrapped in a spiral, lapping each turn over the previous one by one-third of the width of the bandage (Figure 8.1). If more than one layer of bandages is applied they should be wound at an angle to each other (Watkinson, 1987).

When using plaster bandages the object should be covered completely with aluminium foil, plastic film or dry bandages before applying the plaster bandaging. Either ready prepared plaster bandages can be used or they can be made by dipping gauze bandages in a thin plaster of Paris suspension and removing the excess plaster with the fingers before applying them to the object. They are applied in the same way as dry bandages and must be left to dry thoroughly before moving the object. A ready prepared bandaging material, Scotchcast, which contains moisture curing polyurethane can be used in wet situations, even where the object is actually under water (Calver, 1986; Newey *et al.*, 1987).

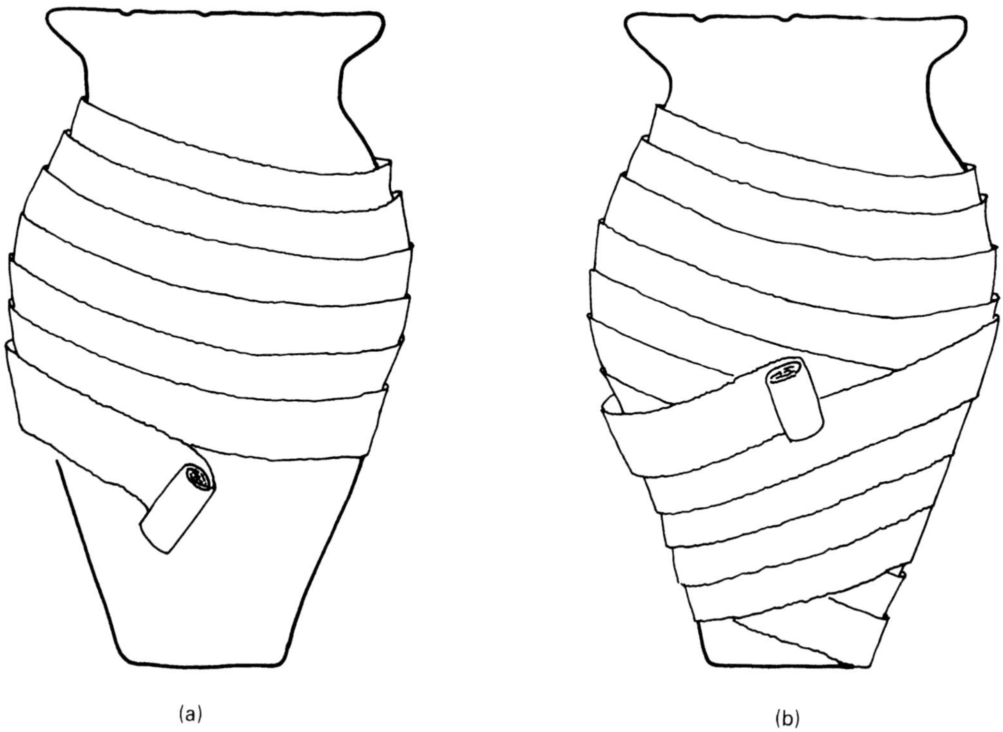

Figure 8.1 Bandaging an object. (a) Successive turns should overlap by one-third of the width of the bandage, and (b) the second layer of bandaging should be applied at an angle to the first.

Block lifting

Block lifting generally involves constructing a frame (usually of wood or cardboard) around the object and lifting the object together with either its surrounding soil block or some other filling in the space between the object and the frame which will support the object. The whole block – frame, support material and object – is then lifted as a single piece. Occasionally a soil block can be lifted without a wooden frame, in which case the soil block may be strengthened by consolidating with resin, or wrapping with gauze bandages dipped in plaster of Paris. In some cases the soil block may need to be kept wet in order to prevent it drying and shrinking and thus damaging the object.

Added support materials for block lifting are commonly plaster of Paris, plaster of Paris mixed with vermiculite, or polyurethane foam. Polyurethane foam has the advantages of being light and easy to remove after curing by cutting with a knife; however it must be used with extreme caution owing to the toxic fumes produced during curing (Moncrieff, 1971; Escritt and Greenacre, 1972; Watkinson and Leigh, 1978). Curing may be adversely affected in cold or damp conditions. The surrounding soil is removed from around the object until it is left sitting on a pedestal of soil, and the frame is constructed around it, allowing at least 2–3 cm gap between the pedestal and frame. Any undercuts should be filled with crumpled tissue, polyether foam, or soil, and the object should be isolated from the support material by a separating layer of aluminium foil or plastic film. The support material may be cast in a single piece (Figure 8.2) or in two halves to facilitate its eventual removal. Further details of these procedures may be found in Sease (1987), Watkinson (1987), and Cronyn (1990).

Consolidation

When the actual fabric of a ceramic object is crumbling or breaking up or when the glaze or other decorative applications are flaking or powdering off the surface a permanent form of strengthening is necessary. Treatment of such an object will usually consist of introducing a material into the fabric of the object that will bind it together: such a material is

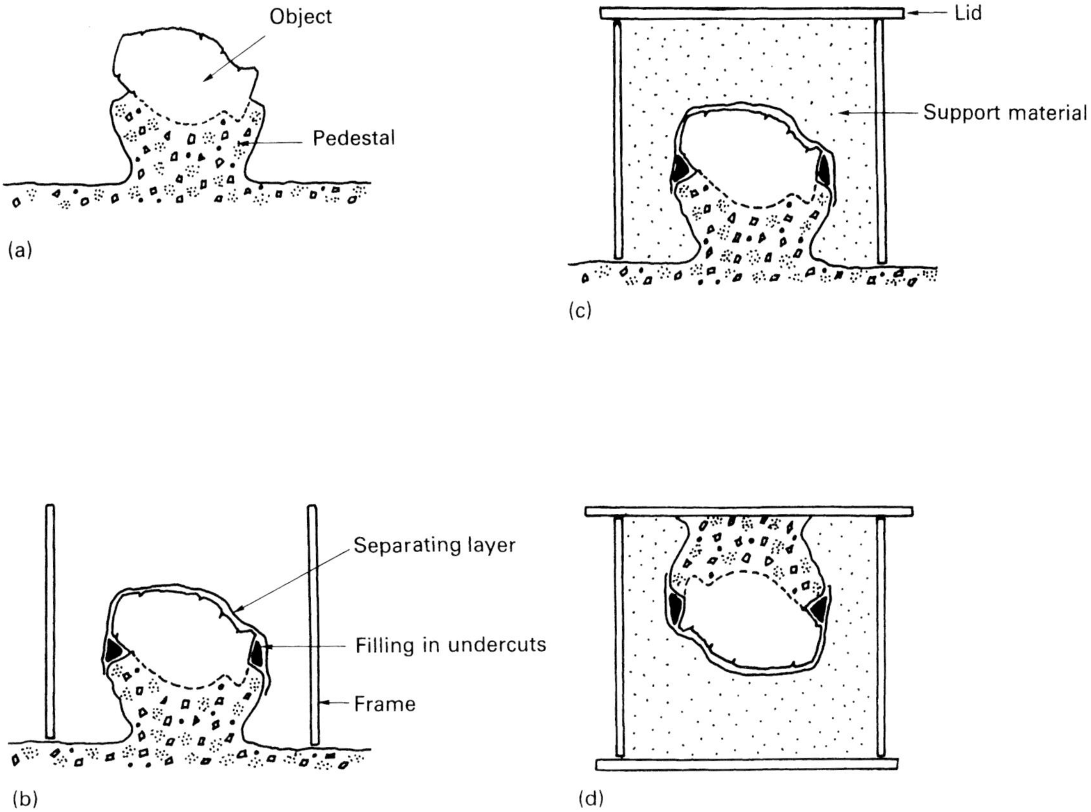

Figure 8.2 Block lifting. (a) Shows the surrounding soil cut away and the object left on a pedestal. In (b) the undercuts have been filled and a separating layer has been applied over the object. A wooden frame has been constructed around the object and pedestal. (c) The space between the object and the frame has been filled with the support material. (d) The pedestal has been undercut and the whole block inverted.

called a consolidant and its application is called consolidation.

Some of the ceramic objects most commonly requiring consolidation are those that have been excavated from the ground and either have lost binding constituents through leaching or have suffered damage through the absorption of soluble salts and subsequent cycles of drying and wetting. Objects can suffer salt damage without having been buried, for example vessels that have been used to contain domestic salt or apothecary jars. When salts are not present it may be possible that some if not all of its strength may be restored to a waterlogged ceramic when it is dry, and if possible a small test piece should be allowed to dry out slowly and then examined. If this test shows that the object does need consolidating it may be possible to consolidate it before drying rather than after.

An alternative method of consolidation of unfired clay objects may be to subject them to a firing. This is only suitable in very special circumstances and is discussed at the end of this chapter.

Choice of materials

Type of consolidant and reversibility

One of the prime requirements of a consolidant is that it should hold the crumbling substrate together. It can do this in one of two ways: either it may link chemically to the particles of the substrate, or it may merely form a mechanical supporting network throughout the substrate without actually reacting with it. Until recently the only consolidants in general use in conservation were of the latter type but now certain isocyanates, silanes, siloxanes and methylmethacrylates which link chemically to the substrate are being developed for use, primarily with stone but also in some cases with ceramics (Paleos and Mavroyannakis, 1981; Hansen and Agnew, 1990). The lack of reversibility of such consolidants must be seen as a drawback, although in practice it is rarely possible to completely remove any type of consolidant from the body of an object, especially from the body of an object that is so friable that it needs consolidation. For this reason consolidants are only used when all other approaches, such as maintaining the object in a controlled environment, are considered to be unsuitable. When considering the different types of 'network' consolidants available, solvent-based systems such as Paraloid B-72 (Acryloid B-72) acrylic resin or poly(vinyl acetate) in toluene or acetone are better from the point of view of reversibility than emulsions, which are more prone to cross-linking. Accepting the fact that at least some of the consolidant will remain in the object indefinitely it is very important that the choice of consolidant is considered carefully.

Penetration

Good penetration of the material is essentia' Extent and speed of penetration will depend on the size of the resin molecule, on the solvent used and on the concentration of resin in the solvent. It will also depend on the physical and chemical state of the object and the method of application of the consolidant. This is discussed below, in the section on application. Thomas (1988) discusses the factors affecting the rate of flow of consolidants into a substrate.

Smith (in press) suggests the use of water-based resins in percentages of 10% or more for temporary on-site consolidation. At these concentrations the consolidant will not penetrate, but will form a surface skin on the ceramic, which will hold the surface in place. The consolidant can be removed by peeling after lifting.

Appearance

The material used as consolidant must not alter the appearance of the object. This is particularly important with unglazed wares or objects with transparent glazes. Many materials when fed into the body of a ceramic will alter the tonal quality, making it appear darker, and the surface appear shiny. Small spot tests can be carried out in an inconspicuous place to find the most suitable consolidant for a particular object. The concentration of resin in solution may be critical in order to achieve the best effect. Poly(vinyl butyral) (Mowital B30H in acetone and IMS) was successfully used to consolidate the Chinese stoneware vase with a transparent green glaze in Figure 8.3 where other consolidants produced shadowing under the glaze. Poly(vinyl butyral) (Mowital B30H) has also been shown to produce minimal colour changes on matt earthenware ceramics (Taylor, 1987).

Condition of object

If the object must be consolidated whilst damp a resin/water emulsion, such as poly(vinyl acetate) emulsion, may be the best form of consolidant to use. If the object is very wet, however, the consolidant may not dry enough to impart any strength to the object and a moisture curing isocyanate system (Hansen and Agnew, 1990) may be the only suitable material to use.

Figure 8.3 Chinese stoneware vase with transparent glaze. Consolidation of the glaze edge was carried out using Mowital B30H (poly(vinyl butyral)) (Victoria and Albert Museum, London).

It may be the case that the object involved has been previously treated in some way, not necessarily to consolidate it but perhaps by the application of adhesive to bond an earlier break, and in such a case the consolidant chosen may be required to be compatible with this previous treatment. For example, if the earlier bond was carried out using cellulose nitrate adhesive an acetone- or toluene- based solvent would be inappropriate. The use of one of the water-based emulsions would be less harmful to the bond.

Environmental conditions

The environmental conditions that the object will be subjected to after treatment will also affect the choice of consolidant. Mould growth can be a problem with some resins, especially where the prevailing conditions may be of high humidity. The glass transition temperature will be an important factor where above average temperatures will be experienced, and stability to UV light must be considered where the object will be exposed to strong lighting conditions.

Further treatment

Successful consolidation will allow the object to be handled safely. However, the consolidation treatment must not prevent other necessary treatments being carried out. Where, for example, a pot is severely contaminated with soluble salts which are causing the body to crumble and the glaze to flake off, it will be desirable to remove these salts. Consolidating the object as a whole with the salts still *in situ* may prevent removal of the salts and any flaking material being laid back down in place. In such a case it may be possible to use a temporary form of reinforcement, such as resin impregnated Terylene net, or Eltolene tissue, to hold the object together and prevent loss of fragments whilst the desalination is carried out. This can then be followed by careful removal of the net or tissue, section by section, as the fragments are laid back down into their correct positions and impregnated with a permanent consolidant. Taylor (1987) describes the treatment of an Egyptian earthenware coilpot which was badly contaminated with salts, was dirty and was laminating. After gentle cleaning and removal of surface salts with a sable brush, the insecure fragments were secured using Eltolene tissue and a 10% solution of Paraloid B-72 (Acryloid B-72) in acetone. Further temporary support was provided by a wrapping of Terylene netting. Desalination was carried out by submerging the object in deionized water. After drying, further consolidation was carried out by injecting Mowital B30H (poly(vinyl butyral)) in acetone and IMS. The Eltolene tissue was then removed using acetone to soften the consolidant. Remaining loose fragments were secured using HMG cellulose nitrate adhesive.

The use of silanes and siloxanes as consolidants may allow subsequent removal of salts by washing.

In most cases surface cleaning and bonding can be carried out after consolidation. The consolidant is cleaned back off the surface with an appropriate solvent and the treatment carried out as normal.

Practical considerations

Depending on the condition of the object it may be desirable to apply the consolidant by brush, airbrush or pipette or by immersion and this should be considered when selecting the appropriate material. The health hazards associated with applying consolidants, especially by airbrush, are usually due to the solvent in the solvent-based consolidants. However, a notable exception is the silanes and siloxanes which are highly toxic and must be used with full protective clothing and in a fume cupboard or with an effective system of local fume extraction.

Application

It is preferable to consolidate the whole of an object in one process, in order to prevent stresses being set up between the consolidated areas and the non-consolidated areas. As mentioned above, the degree of penetration that is achieved will depend not only on the choice of resin but also on the concentration at which it is used. Most resins are used at 5, 10, or 15% concentration as they will not penetrate if used at higher concentrations. Where a choice of solvents may be used a less volatile solvent is usually preferable, allowing greater penetration. Where a solvent-based consolidant is being used on a dry object, the degree of penetration of the consolidant will be improved if the object is initially placed in solvent vapour for 24 hours.

Penetration will also depend on the method of application and the drying procedure. The method of application used will depend on the extent and degree of the deterioration of the object, on its size and shape and on whether the treatment is being carried out in the field, for example before the object is lifted.

Brush application

Application by brush is the simplest method and can be used in the studio or in the field. The consolidant is brushed onto the surface in repeated applications until it no longer sinks in. If the surface is friable and there is danger of disturbing it by brushing, then the consolidant is not applied with a brushing action but merely fed into the surface drop by drop. This method has the benefit of control over the application and can be used for small or large objects. It is useful when consolidating bit by bit as burial earth is removed.

Application by pipette

Controlled application is also possible with a pipette. The consolidant is applied drop by drop until saturation of the area is achieved. This method can be used on very fragile objects, objects of all sizes, and either in the field or in the studio. A precise quantity of consolidant can be applied and if necessary micropipettes can be used (Smith, 1992) (Figure 8.4).

Application by injection

In some circumstances, such as those where a glaze is lifting, it may be advantageous to inject the consolidant into air spaces using a syringe.

Application by spray

Use of a spray to apply consolidant allows large areas to be saturated more quickly. The simplest form of spray is a polyethylene or polypropylene garden spray, which can be useful in the field, but for more detailed applications an airbrush can be used. Care

Figure 8.4 Application of consolidant using a micropipette (Victoria and Albert Museum, London).

must be taken not to use too high an air pressure which could damage a friable surface. Adjustment of the concentration of the consolidant solution will have to be made to allow it to be sprayed through the airbrush without stringing and the choice of solvent may be critical. Usually an airbrush can only be used in the studio where there is access to a compressed air supply and suitable fume extraction equipment.

Application by immersion

Immersion of the object in the consolidant will allow greater penetration of the consolidant. It is generally better to totally immerse the object to prevent stress and the possibility of the consolidated part appearing different from the unconsolidated part; however partial immersion may be used with very large objects if necessary. The object should be stood in a suitable container on a metal or plastic mesh to allow access of the consolidant to the underside. This will also allow the object to be lifted out of the container without direct handling before the consolidant has cured. The consolidant is then poured slowly into the bottom of the container to allow air to escape gradually from the object as the consolidant is absorbed into it. If the consolidant is added too quickly the force of the escaping air may cause damage to friable material. The object should be fully submerged. By adding the consolidant slowly it allows much of it to be taken up by capillary action. Streams of air bubbles may be observed escaping from the object after it has been fully immersed, but provided the consolidant was added slowly these should not cause a problem. The degree of saturation of the object with the consolidant that can be achieved, and the length of time taken for this, will vary depending on the porosity of the object and the consolidant system used. Penetration may be improved by exposing the object for 24 hours before immersion to an atmosphere of the solvent used with the consolidant.

Vacuum impregnation

The method that ensures the greatest penetration of consolidant is vacuum impregnation. However, as in the case of the above method, this method is unsuitable for very fragile objects where submersion in the consolidant could cause fragments to fall off. Neither can it be used for very large objects where the size of tank needed would make it impractical.

The object is placed in the vacuum tank on a wire or plastic mesh, the consolidant added slowly as described above and then the vacuum applied. Streams of bubbles will escape from the object as further consolidant is forced into the object.

Drying

The method of drying plays an important part in achieving good results with consolidation. Too fast drying of solvent-based systems will cause much of the resin to be pulled back out to the surface of the object as the solvent evaporates off. Rapid drying of a solvent/resin system may also result in blooming due to water condensing on the resin through the cooling produced by the evaporation of the solvent. Slowing of the drying can be achieved by placing the consolidated object in an atmosphere of the solvent for at least two days, or, more simply, by covering the object loosely with aluminium foil or polethylene sheeting. Barov (1988) describes the drying of earthenware fragments after consolidation by blotting them, then wrapping them in clean fabric to absorb any excess consolidant and then placing them in plastic bags and drying them for ten weeks. The fragments were turned regularly to ensure even distribution of the consolidant and the plastic bags allowed slow even evaporation of the solvent, thus preventing film formation. The fragments were finally left for two weeks in the open air to complete the drying process. Any consolidant that does dry on the surface of an object should be cleaned back using swabs of cotton wool and solvent.

Subsequent treatment

Care must be taken to ensure that the consolidant has completely cured before undertaking any further handling and treatment such as cleaning. Whilst the consolidant is still wet the object may be even more fragile than it was before treatment started, and submersion in water before the consolidant has completely dried can cause white blooming.

Firing

In certain circumstances, unfired clay objects may be 'consolidated' by firing to relatively low temperatures, in order to allow further treatment such as desalination. Salt contaminated cuneiform tablets at the British Museum, London, are treated in this way to allow subsequent desalination by immersion in water (Organ, 1961). The temperature is raised very slowly, over a period of four days, in stages, to allow free moisture to evaporate and allow chemically combined water to be given off. When a temperature of 710°C is reached this is held for several hours, before allowing the tablets to cool slowly. Firing obviously alters the structure of the body radically, and should only be used as a last resort and where it is felt that the information that will be retained is more important than the information that will be lost. For example, in the case of the cuneiform tablets at the British Museum the value of these objects lies in the inscriptions rather than the ceramic body. Hence firing is felt to be justified as it permanently preserves these inscriptions which would otherwise be lost. However, a sample of untreated material should always be retained in such circumstances in order that study of the body could be made in the future should some unforeseen need arise.

9

Bonding

Introduction

As discussed in Chapter 2, the physical nature of most ceramic objects results in the fact that they are easily broken. The mastery of the procedures involved in bonding fragmented ceramics back together again is thus of utmost importance to the ceramics conservator. Poor workmanship or the use of unsuitable materials at this stage may undermine any further treatment, causing unnecessary work in the later stages of restoration and making it more difficult to achieve a good end result.

Bonding of broken objects may be necessary for several reasons: to allow a functional object to be used again; to restore the form and aesthetic appeal of a decorative object; or to return an object of ethnographic or social history interest to a meaningful condition for display. Bonding broken pieces together also prevents loss of fragments and reduces the risk of staining and further damage to the break edges. However, in certain circumstances, for example where the object is part of a collection used purely for technical study, the object may still retain value in its broken state, and the time spent on bonding would perhaps be time wasted.

The timing of the bonding treatment may also be important. A three-dimensional object may be easier to pack or store in a fragmented state, and thus bonding may be delayed until the object has travelled to a particular location, or until such time as the object is wanted for display. In other cases, certain forms of analysis and examination may be required which will be more easily carried out whilst the object is in pieces, and reconstruction will be delayed until this has been done.

Planning

When a decision has been made to bond together the pieces of a broken object it is important that careful planning and preparation should be carried out before the process is begun. Planning involves not only deciding on the materials and practical procedures to be used in piecing together the damaged object, but also organizing sufficient undisturbed time to allow the unhurried execution of these procedures. In the majority of cases it is preferable that multiple breaks in an object should be reassembled in one process, before the adhesive has had time to cure, and this can take several hours. Interruptions to answer the telephone or attend to clients should be avoided.

Concerning materials and procedures, the following should be considered: the choice of adhesive; the method of application; the order of bonding of the separate pieces; the method of support whilst the adhesive cures.

Choice of adhesive

There are many different adhesives available that are appropriate for use on ceramics. However, an adhesive that is suitable for use on one type of ceramic, e.g. hard-paste porcelain, may not be entirely suitable for use on other types, e.g. tin-glazed earthenware, or unglazed pottery. Before making a choice of adhesive, the conservator must consider carefully the type of ceramic object that is being dealt with, its composition, form and dimensions, and also the condition of the object and the demands in terms of environment and handling that will be made on the repair. The following properties of the adhesive to be used must be considered.

Strength of the adhesive bond

The adhesive bond must be strong enough to hold the broken pieces together and allow the required amount and type of handling. Strength is a rather general term and adhesive joints can be assessed according to their ability to withstand tensile stresses, shear stresses and peeling (Bradley, 1984). Peel strength is really only important when the substrate being bonded is flexible, and so this does not apply to the use of adhesives on ceramics. The strength of the adhesive bond can be seen as having two components: the strength of the adhesive material itself, i.e. its cohesive strength, and the strength of the bond between the adhesive and the ceramic material, i.e. its adhesive strength. The ways in which different types of adhesive bond to the substrate vary, and this is one of the reasons why adhesives tend to be more suitable for use on one type of ceramic than another. The coarser nature of the body of an earthenware and its larger pore size will be suited to an adhesive that achieves most of its bond strength by purely mechanical means. A smoother faced break edge in a hard-paste porcelain will require an adhesive, such as an epoxy resin, that forms strong secondary bonds. Detailed explanations of the way adhesives form bonds can be found in Newey *et al.* (1983) and in Allen (1984).

It is generally suggested that the adhesive bond should be weaker than the ceramic material itself in order to avoid fresh breaks should the object be subjected to stress in the future. However, this will only avoid fresh damage when certain specific types of stress are applied to the object. When an object is dropped, the stresses, and hence the fractures, are concentrated at the point of impact, i.e. the precise point on the surface of the object that came into contact with the floor first. Should the object be dropped again, the point of impact will almost certainly be in a different spot. However weak the adhesive used to bond the object together after the first impact, it is unlikely to fall apart at the old joints during the second. If, however, the original damage was caused by inbuilt, internal stresses (such as when cracks appear apparently spontaneously in objects long after their manufacture), or stresses from some particular form of use, then the argument for using an adhesive weaker than the ceramic material itself holds more validity. In such circumstances, where the object is subjected in the future to the same stresses, acting in the same places, too strong an adhesive would indeed be likely to result in fresh damage. An adhesive that has weaker cohesive forces or weaker adhesive forces than the cohesive forces within the ceramic body itself is preferable.

Ceramics that lack strength or are friable may be unsuitable for bonding however weak the adhesive used. Unless they can be satisfactorily consolidated they should be left in the fragmentary state.

Assessing the strength of the ceramic material and selecting an adhesive of appropriate strength is an inexact process. Most ceramics conservators rely on very broad assessments and 'strong' adhesives, such as epoxy resins and polyesters, tend to be reserved for use on the 'stronger' ceramics, e.g. porcelains and stonewares, or very large, thickly potted earthenwares. Byrne (1984) suggests that the adhesive and cohesive strengths of certain adhesives can be modified by the addition of fumed silica.

Viscosity

The viscosity of the adhesive is important in relation to the porosity of the ceramic substrate. Ideally, an adhesive with a viscosity that is very low would always be used in order to achieve the minimum separation between the two halves of the joint. However, in the case of porous ceramics, a low-viscosity adhesive would be drawn into the body, leaving insufficient adhesive on the surface of the break edge to form a good bond. The absorption of adhesive into the body has three other drawbacks. Firstly, it can cause unsightly shadowing on either side of the break (Figure 9.1); secondly, it can be extremely difficult, if not impossible, to remove from the body if the object is taken apart during future treatment; and thirdly, the consolidant effect of the adhesive that has penetrated the body will mean that any pressure applied to the joints during future dismantling may result in the consolidated strip of body tearing away from the rest of the body, creating fresh damage. For this reason adhesives used on porous bodied ceramics should be of a viscous nature. Higher viscosities can be achieved with solvent systems, e.g. cellulose nitrate adhesives or acrylic adhesives, by using a high solid:solvent ratio, by using a high-molecular-weight polymer, or by creating a thixotropic gel using fumed silica (Byrne, 1984; Selwitz, 1988; Koob, 1986). Epoxy resin adhesives can be allowed to cure partially before applying to porous ceramics.

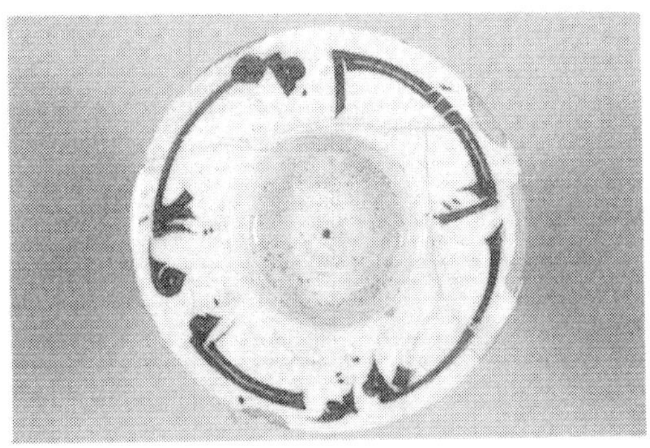

Figure 9.1 Glazed earthenware dish showing shadowing on either side of the joints, caused by the use of an inappropriate adhesive (Victoria and Albert Museum, London).

Reversibility

As with all other conservation treatments, the ideal is that the bonding treatment should be fully reversible without the risk of damage to the object. Where a low-porosity ceramic is involved this ideal is more realistically achievable. However, in the case of porous earthenware and pottery, even when a bulky, viscous adhesive has been used, it is highly unlikely that every trace of adhesive can be removed from the pores and interstices of the break edges. Even some high-fired porcelains can present problems when, for example, the glaze contains microscopic air bubbles which retain the adhesive. The more readily soluble the adhesive remains, the more easily it can be removed. Adhesives that do not cross-link, for example Paraloid B-72 (USA Acryloid B-72), HMG cellulose nitrate (USA Duco Cement), are easier to remove than those that do, e.g. epoxy and polyester resins. The latter cannot be truly dissolved but must be removed by using dichloromethane to swell and soften them. The swelling itself may be a problem and may be a contra-indication for their use in certain situations (Barov, 1986). Poly(vinyl acetate) emulsion can become rather insoluble with age and Byrne (1984) recommends the use of poly(vinyl acetate) dissolved in acetone and bulked up with fumed silica as an alternative adhesive for porous ceramics.

Compatibility

It is important that the adhesive does not shrink significantly during curing or over a period of time. Adhesives that shrink, such as animal glues, can cause physical damage to friable pottery by pulling particles away from the surface. If the object is to be subjected to rapid and severe fluctuations in temperature, for example in the hold of an aeroplane, then the thermal expansion coefficients of the adhesive and the ceramic should be matched to avoid stress.

There must be no risk of damage to the ceramic through chemical interaction with the adhesive or the materials used to reverse it, and compatibility with other treatment materials must be considered. Cellulose nitrate adhesives and HXTAL NYL-1 epoxy resin, for example, cannot be used in situations where they will be in contact with each other as a bright yellow staining results.

Colour and translucency

The colour and translucency of the adhesive may or may not be important. If the object is opaque, and the break edges are badly damaged and the intention is to fill the losses with an opaque filler, then the colour of the adhesive is insignificant. Thus the dark-coloured, thixotropic polyester adhesives such as General and Sebralit (USA Akemi) may be suitable choices for the bonding of badly damaged, heavyweight earthenwares. However, if the adhesive is to be used to bond together an object made of a fine, translucent hard-paste porcelain, then a water white adhesive such as the epoxy resin HXTAL NYL-1 is an appropriate choice. A water white adhesive can be adjusted for colour and translucency by the addition of pigments and fillers such as fumed silica, although care must be taken not to overfill the adhesive and weaken its bonding powers. It is important that the adhesive retains its water whiteness as it ages.

Durability and suitability to environmental conditions

Adhesives used should be durable to avoid possible damage due to failure of joints or the need to re-treat objects frequently. Repeating treatment processes not only wastes conservators' time, but also puts the object at further risk of damage by loss of material, fracture or staining.

The adhesive selected for a particular purpose must be capable of withstanding the prevailing environmental conditions, including temperature, humidity, and light, and be resistant to biological attack. It must be stressed that the durability should be considered in relation to the conditions under which the adhesive is used. So, for example, cellulose nitrate adhesives, which under certain conditions are unstable (Selwitz, 1988; Koob, 1982), may perform acceptably in other circumstances. Barov (1988) points out that their use deep in a joint, covered by opaque filler, will mean that UV light is precluded and oxygen levels are low. In fact, Barov backed up the cellulose nitrate adhesive (Duco Cement) with an additional application of a UV-stable acrylic thermosetting adhesive (Teets Denture Material), and in this way took advantage of the practical properties of the cellulose nitrate adhesive – its fast drying, ease of application, low toxicity and thin film formation – and combined them with the durability of the acrylic. Elston (1990), reporting on the restoration of an Attic kylix, describes the use of cellulose nitrate adhesive (Duco Cement), chosen for its suitable working properties, in combination with the acrylic Acryloid B-72 to give long-term durability.

It may be important that the adhesive functions in particular extreme circumstances, for example on wet objects. Poly(vinyl acetate) emulsion is used for temporary bonding of wet objects (Olive and Pearson, 1975). Another important environmental consideration is that of temperature: adhesives with low glass transition temperatures are not suitable for use in conditions where high temperatures are experienced. The glass transition temperature of Paraloid B-72 is lower than that of HMG cellulose nitrate.

Practical considerations

Ease of use of an adhesive is important and preparation procedures, pot life (i.e. the time that the adhesive remains workable after mixing) and curing time should be considered. Adhesives which require very precisely measured ratios of resin to hardener are more likely to fail through measuring errors than those which only require approximate measurement. The adhesive should generally have a sufficiently long curing time to allow for the slow process of piecing together a severely damaged object. The pot life of some adhesives, e.g. some epoxy resins and methylmethacrylate resins, can be extended by refrigeration (Barov, 1986). However, it is generally preferable that the time taken for a complete cure is not too long in order to minimize the danger of the joints inadvertently slipping out of alignment, and to avoid lengthy delays in the restoration process.

Occasionally, an adhesive with instant tack or one that will cure whilst the joint is hand held is required. In such circumstances, one of the polyester adhesives such as General or Sebralit (USA Akemi) may be used for heavy earthenware objects. For hard-paste porcelain one of the cyanoacrylate adhesives may be used to hand hold a joint whilst curing and this is then followed by impregnation of the joint with a slow curing, low-viscosity epoxy resin to provide long-term strength (Williams, 1989).

Shelf life and minimum quantities available will also be practical considerations, particularly where an adhesive is expensive and infrequently used.

Health and safety

As well as being a health threat, toxic and hazardous adhesives are awkward to use owing to the necessity of working in a fume cupboard and wearing suitable protective clothing. The health and safety considerations of the commonly used adhesives are discussed in Chapter 13.

Order of joining

Where there are more than two fragments to be joined, a decision will have to be made as to the order in which the pieces are bonded together. The order is important for several reasons. The most crucial of these is to avoid locking out a piece. This occurs when it is impossible to fit a particular piece into its correct location after neighbouring pieces have been joined, owing to the shapes of the pieces involved. In Figure 9.2 if A and C are joined first, B cannot then be fitted. A and B should be joined first and then the remaining piece fitted. The second reason why the order of joining is important is that some orders are more likely to achieve a better overall alignment of pieces than others (Figure 9.3). Joining a multitude of small, ill-fitting fragments to each other is usually less successful than using a larger fragment as an anchor piece and joining the smaller pieces on to this piece.

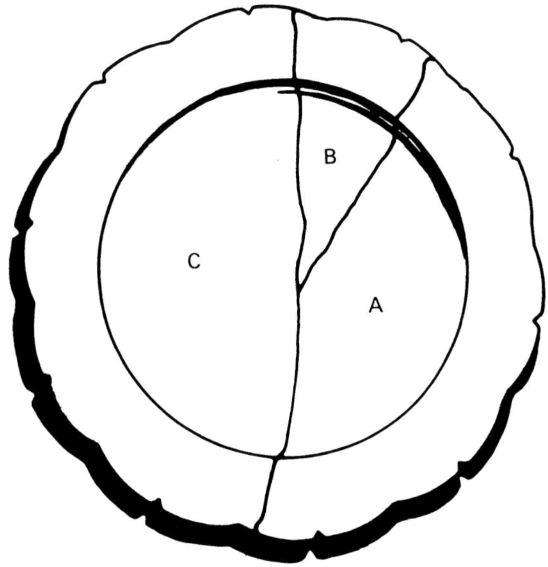

Figure 9.2 Order of joining. If A and C are joined first, B will be locked out.

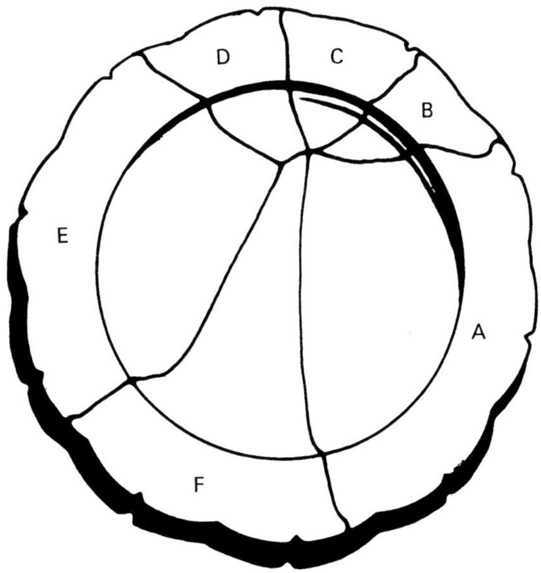

Figure 9.3 Order of joining. Firstly B is joined to A, and then C joined to these two. Then E is joined to F, and D to E and F. Lastly the two groups A + B + C and F + E + D are joined together.

The third reason is that of handling, and again for this reason it is beneficial to have a large piece in each section of joined pieces if possible.

There are a number of different approaches to piecing together an object. Some conservators advocate starting with the base or the rim and building the object up from that (Gedye, 1968; Mibach, 1975; Barov, 1988). Alternatively, pieces are joined together to make a number of larger sections which are then joined together to make up the whole object. The order of joining pieces in the case of enclosed shapes such as vases and teapots generally requires more planning than when joining plates and open dishes where all the joints are visible at once. When deciding on the order all the pieces should be laid out and carefully studied. A trial run of the assembly can be made fitting the pieces together 'dry', with no adhesive, using pressure sensitive tape (bearing in mind the cautions in the section on the methods of support). Various clues can be used to aid with the orientation of the pieces: throwing rings on the inner surface; manufacturing flaws such as impurities and inclusions; and decoration. The pieces can be numbered, either as they are put together, or as they are subsequently taken apart, and the sequence for assembly noted. Numbering is usually done using paper labels or masking tape (Figure 9.4).

When objects previously broken into many pieces are to be re-restored and old bonds taken apart and reassembled it is sometimes helpful to map out the breaks on a diagram before taking apart the old bonds. The easiest way to do this is from a photograph enlarged to life size. The pieces can then be numbered both on the photograph and on the object (Williams, 1989) and a note made of the areas of lost material. Care must be taken to avoid damaging the object if the map is made directly from the object using tracing paper or Melinex.

Figure 9.4 Large Indian dish, supported by retort stands and clamps with the joints strapped with pressure sensitive tape. Before assembly the pieces were labelled with numbers and a diagram was made of the order of assembly (Victoria and Albert Museum, London).

Method of support

The majority of adhesives currently in use do not produce instant tack. The only ones that do this are the so-called 'super-glues', the cyanoacrylate adhesives. Consequently some form of support is necessary to hold the joints in position whilst the adhesive cures.

The simplest way of supporting a joint is by taking advantage of gravity and positioning the object so that the joint lies in a horizontal plane, and the weight of the upper piece acts directly down on the joint. The lower piece may be held in position using props of Plasticine for example or by standing it in a box filled with sand or some other relatively inert material. Sand used should be as clean and pure as possible and builder's sand, which contains lime, and sea sand, which contains chloride ions, should be avoided. Dried peas and rice grains have also been used with success. Great care must be taken to avoid any of the material used coming into contact with the joint and the adhesive. If this does happen it must be very thoroughly cleaned away. The material may be enclosed in small bags in order to avoid this danger, or a separating layer, for example of Clingfilm or other food wrapping film, used. Recently, commercially available systems such as the 'Vari-cushion' have been developed. This is essentially a bean bag with a pneumatic pump for extracting the air. The object is positioned on the cushion, and the cushion formed around it. The air is then extracted and the object is held in place.

When the pieces are simply propped in this way, care must be taken to avoid knocking or jogging them whilst the adhesive is curing. A more secure method, and one that is commonly used when there are several broken pieces to be bonded in one operation, is to strap the joint using pressure sensitive tapes or gummed tapes. This may be combined with propping the object in a suitable position. Tapes can be used simply to hold the broken pieces in position or, with those that have a certain amount of elasticity, to actually apply pressure, forcing the joint tighter. Various different types of pressure sensitive tape are available which have varying characteristics. There are two important areas to consider when using tapes: firstly, the nature of the surface of the ceramic; and secondly, the compatibility of the adhesive on the tape and that to be used in the joint. Using pressure sensitive tapes over areas of gilding, unsound overglaze enamels, or flaking glazes, or on any unfired surface must be done with extreme caution. It is sometimes possible to mask such areas with paper or a coating of a resin such as poly(vinyl alcohol) in order to avoid the tape coming into contact with them. If the tape is used in direct contact with a vulnerable area, when it is removed it should be flooded with an appropriate solvent (e.g. industrial methylated spirits) in order to soften its adhesive and prevent underlying material being pulled off with it. Unglazed, textured or matt surfaces will not usually accept pressure sensitive tapes; masking tape will often work better in such situations, although the use of adhesive tapes on porous surfaces should be avoided as they may cause staining. As far as compatibility of the adhesives is concerned, gummed tapes cannot be used with water sensitive bonding adhesives and certain pressure sensitive tapes will cause discoloration of epoxy resins. Epoxy resins are particularly prone to discoloration, turning purple when in contact with the tape; this discoloration may extend beneath the surface in direct contact with the tape and cannot therefore be cleaned away without dismantling the joint. It may be possible to avoid this problem by using particular tapes e.g. Magitape or Crystal tape. When an object has been consolidated with a solvent-based system it may be preferable to used a gummed paper tape as this can be removed with water rather than any other solvent that may affect the consolidant.

When the pieces to be bonded are such that it is not easy to apply tape or prop the joint horizontally, small supports made from modelling putties such as Plasticine or Aloplast can be used. These are often useful in the case of finely modelled pieces such as fragments of bocage, small limbs etc. Plasticine contains oils and so it must be kept well clear of the joint; however, Aloplast is oil free. Dusting with talc will make removal easier, as will wrapping the putty in a food wrapping film such as Clingfilm. On a larger scale, retort stands and clamps make useful props, although care must be taken to pad the clamps.

Elastic bands are recommended by some restorers (Wissler, 1983) to be used in conjunction with tapes. However, it is more difficult to control and localize the forces applied by elastic bands and distortion of the construction can result. In most cases the correct tape, properly applied, will provide sufficient strength.

Tourniquets of various types, from very basic to refined, purpose made tools, e.g. Multiclips (Figure 9.5), may also be used, but again care must be taken to ensure that the forces so applied act in the appropriate direction only.

If none of the above methods of support are suitable, tacking with a cyanoacrylate may be considered in the case of a non-porous ceramic. This involves using a quick setting cyanoacrylate adhesive applied at key points to hold the pieces in place whilst a slower setting but more durable adhesive such as an epoxy resin cures. More detail on this method will be given in a later section.

Figure 9.5 Multiclips used to hold joints together in neck of large Korean jar (Victoria and Albert Museum, London).

Preparation

Cleanliness is of the utmost importance in any bonding process. Before commencing, the work area should be cleaned and if a renewable surface such as blotting paper or tissue paper is used a fresh surface should be laid. All tools that will be required should be wiped over with solvent and laid out within easy reach. The conservator's hands should also be cleaned. It is beneficial from a health and safety point of view for protective gloves to be worn; however many conservators feel that this robs them of control and sensitivity and prefer to work without gloves. If this is the case great care must be exercised to avoid contact between hands and adhesive.

Object

A last check must be made of the break edges to ensure that they have not become contaminated during the planning stages and that no small fragments of glaze or body have become misplaced. Ideally, this check should be made using some form of optical magnification as even the minutest fragment or particle of dirt can spoil an otherwise good bond. Any particles or dirt can be removed using the methods described in the previous chapter.

At this stage any vulnerable areas that are to be masked off should be painted with resin, or if paper is to be used this should be cut to the required size and shape.

Materials

The adhesive and the support materials must also be prepared in advance. Where the adhesive is a solvent-based one it must be prepared to the correct concentration; an adhesive that cures by reaction with a hardener must be accurately measured out and mixed. If the adhesive is to be tinted or other modifications made, such as the addition of fumed silica, this should again be done in advance of the actual bonding process. Breaking off work to mix up more adhesive should be avoided.

Strips of tape for support should be cut to an appropriate size. In the case of pressure sensitive tapes they can be prepared by sticking uncut strips of tape on a ceramic tile or sheet of glass and using a scalpel to cut them to size. Strips of a variety of sizes will normally be required for any one job. The strips need to be wide enough to have sufficient strength to hold the broken pieces in place without stretching under their weight, but as narrow as possible in order to allow access to the joint for checking alignment. They must not be so long that they cross more than one break. Once prepared the strips can be peeled off the tile or glass and attached by one end only to a convenient surface so that they can be easily removed for use.

Procedure

The procedure for the use of an epoxy resin will be described first. This is a generalized outline for the use of epoxy resin on a low-porosity ceramic. Particular circumstances may require that the general procedure is modified and some of the modifications possible are discussed at the end of the general description. Any differences in the procedure when using alternative adhesives will be discussed below.

Bonding with epoxy resins

The broken pieces of ceramic are given a final swab over with solvent to ensure that they are as free of grease and dirt as possible. This can be done using silk rags or a clean paintbrush in order to avoid leaving cotton wool fibres on the edges.

If pressure sensitive tape is to be used as a method of support this may be applied before or after the adhesive is applied and the two halves of the joint brought together. In the former case the tape strips are attached by one end to the smaller of the two pieces to be joined and at right angles to the line of the break. The unattached end is folded back away from the break edge to avoid the danger of trapping it in the joint when the two halves of the joint are brought together. Strips are positioned like this at intervals along the back and front of the break edge opposing each other. It is important that they are positioned directly opposing each other so that the forces applied when the tapes are stretched across the joint do not tend to twist the joint out of alignment. Positioning strips on one side of a break edge where it is not possible to place a strip on the other side, owing to a foot rim for example, or an area of gilding, should be avoided.

The adhesive is then applied to the second, larger half of the joint only, using a fine tool. Some restorers recommend application with bamboo sticks, others with metal spatulas; with the modern very low-viscosity epoxy resins now available a paintbrush can be used. Whatever tool is used it is important to ensure that the material of the tool is not going to react with the adhesive or leave particles on the break edge. A very thin coating of adhesive only must be applied as too much adhesive, especially over a series of joints, can build up to cause misalignment of pieces. It will also cause excessive adhesive to be squeezed from the joint when the two halves are brought together, making extensive cleaning back necessary. Only in the case of very badly damaged break edges should the application of adhesive be more liberal. In such cases the adhesive can also be applied to both halves of the joint to ensure that small areas of loss are filled with adhesive. Application at either end of a joint should be minimal to prevent a build-up where breaks converge.

Holding a piece in each hand, the two halves of the joint are carefully brought together and gently manoeuvred to lock into position. Occasionally it may be possible to support one half of the joint by

Figure 9.6 Retort stands and clamps used to support large Indian dish during assembly (Victoria and Albert Museum, London).

other means, for example by the use of retort stands and clamps as in Figure 9.6. Correct location can be aided by using such references as surface pattern, surface and edge irregularities, scratches and impurities and can be checked by running the tip of a clean fingernail at right angles back and forth across the joint. It will catch if one edge is proud of the other and adjustment to the joint can be made using gentle pressure. When a satisfactory alignment has been achieved the pieces are pressed firmly together. If pressure is applied before this the break edges may be chipped. A small quantity of excess adhesive will squeeze out along the join. The strips of adhesive tape are then gently smoothed across the join. If the pieces being joined are small, this can be done with the thumb of one hand on the front surface and then the forefinger on the back whilst still maintaining a gentle pressure by forcing the joint together with both hands. If the pieces are large, they can be placed in a position where the joint is in a horizontal plane, with the upper piece balanced on the lower piece which is held with the left hand. The strips of adhesive tape are then very gently smoothed down across the joint using the right hand. After the tape has been smoothed down like this the alignment is again checked; if it is correct, the strips can be lifted in turn and then stretched tightly across the joint as they are smoothed back down again (Figure 9.7). In this way the strips actually apply a positive force, bringing the two halves of the joint together as tightly as possible. This tensioning must be kept very even to avoid pulling the joint out of alignment and the joint should be checked frequently during the procedure. Some tapes are stronger than others and can be stretched to a greater degree without snapping. It is important to be aware of this, as snapping the tape during stretching can cause jarring of the pieces and damage to the break edges.

For multiple joins this process is repeated until all the pieces have been bonded together. For ease of handling, the adhesive is always applied to the larger half of the joint being assembled and the adhesive tape to the smaller piece. When many pieces are being joined care must be taken to avoid a build-up of strips of tape which cross each other. This makes adjustments difficult.

When all the pieces have been assembled a final check is made to ensure that the joints are properly aligned and any discrepancies are corrected by lifting the appropriate tapes and applying pressure. The temptation for the object to be placed in the lap whilst this is done must be resisted as any slip may result in the object falling to the floor. It is always safer to work over a bench.

Perhaps the most common reasons for varying the procedure outlined above are concerned with the shape and structure of the object. Where the shape or surface finish are such that adhesive tape straps cannot be attached, one of the other forms of support for the joint must be used. Sometimes the shape makes it unnecessary to strap on the back and the front of the object, for example when bonding a closed vessel. If the reconstruction of the pieces is particularly complex or delicate, it may be preferable to tape or in some other way assemble the pieces without applying adhesive. Then, when the alignment of all the joints is quite satisfactory, a low-viscosity epoxy resin is fed along the joints. This will be drawn into the joints by capillary action.

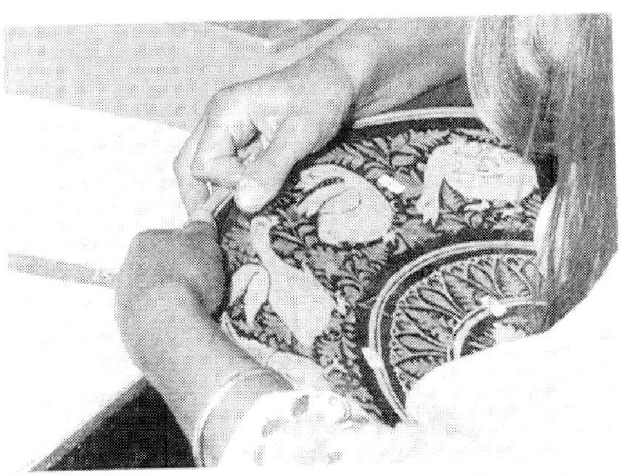

Figure 9.7 Applying tension to pressure sensitive tapes to force join together (Victoria and Albert Museum, London).

Bonding with polyester resins

Polyester resins used for bonding ceramics are of two types: those of a syrupy viscosity which can be treated in most practical ways like epoxy resins, and those that are produced as thixotropic pastes. The latter type are used for bonding heavy earthenwares and cure relatively rapidly. The disadvantage of this is that multiple joins cannot be assembled in one process before the adhesive cures. However, there is one major advantage, and that is that joints can be hand held whilst they cure to a state strong enough to hold the joint together unsupported. Single joints can, of course, be strapped and the procedure used is as described above for epoxy resins. All bonding procedures using polyester resins must be carried out briskly, so that the joint is assembled before the resin becomes too far advanced in its cure and becomes too viscous.

It is not possible to achieve such a thin coating of adhesive on the break edges as, even when freshly mixed, these polyester resins are of a much higher viscosity than the epoxy resins used. However, owing to the nature of the ceramics on which they are used, i.e. large, heavy, generally coarse earthenwares, this is not usually a problem. Some restorers suggest just dotting the resin along the break edge, keeping it to the middle, away from the edges, but care must be taken when doing this as uneven application can result in misalignment of joints.

Greater pressure must be applied to the joints after bringing together the two halves in order to squeeze out the excess adhesive, and this pressure must be maintained if the joint is to be hand held whilst curing. It is not easy to hand hold joints, and if possible, part of the weight of the object should be taken by the bench surface, with the elbows also resting on the bench to steady the grip. The point at which the resin has cured sufficiently to hold the joint can be tested for by checking any residual resin on the mixing tile.

Bonding with poly(vinyl acetate) emulsions

If poly(vinyl acetate) emulsion is applied to a dry, porous surface, water is absorbed from it into the surface thus drying the emulsion and making it much less mobile. For this reason tight joints can only be achieved in porous bodied ceramics with poly(vinyl acetate) emulsion if the break edges are dampened with water before applying the resin. This does increase the movement of the polymer into the body along the break edges, consolidating them and making complete removal of the resin less possible. However, the effect may, in certain situations, be outweighed by the advantages of using this type of adhesive.

The break edges are dampened with deionized or distilled water and the emulsion is mixed to a milky consistency. The emulsion is then applied to one break edge only and the two halves of the break are brought together and firm pressure is applied to squeeze out excess emulsion. Care must be taken when using adhesive tape strapping to avoid wetting it and thus preventing its adhesion to the ceramic. Only minimal manoeuvring of the pieces is possible after the two halves have been brought together, as even when the break edges are dampened the emulsion becomes immobile very quickly. The joint itself takes some time to dry out thoroughly, and delays the curing of the poly(vinyl acetate) emulsion, and therefore handling should preferably be avoided for 2 or 3 days. Cleaning back can be carried out using water before curing or with swabs of acetone or a scalpel after curing.

Bonding with solvent-based adhesives

Adhesives of various different chemical types are solvent based, e.g. cellulose nitrate adhesives, acrylic adhesives such as Paraloid B-72 (Acryloid B-72), and poly(vinyl acetate) solution. These have mainly been used in the past for bonding earthenwares but are used in some circumstances with porcelain if the strength of an epoxy resin bond is not required. A certain amount of instant tack is produced, and adjustment of the joints after initial curing can be made using the appropriate solvent, or in some cases by using gentle heat, e.g. from a hot air blower. This is a valuable property when bonding multiple fractures in an object.

Two methods of bonding with solvent-based adhesives are currently used. In the first, the adhesive is applied to one half of the break only, and the two halves are brought together. In the second, the adhesive is applied to both break edges; the two are brought together for a few seconds, then parted, and finally brought together and strapped or supported in some other way.

Drying time will depend on the ambient temperature, and the thickness and porosity of the ceramic.

Bonding with cyanoacrylates

The almost instant bonds achieved with these adhesives make hand-held joints the only type possible. The pieces must be positioned accurately with very little time for adjustment. The adhesive is applied to one half of the break only, usually as small spots along the break edge. As these adhesives cure partly by means of the pressure applied to the joint it is not possible to pre-strap the joint and then run the adhesive in. Long-term stability and reversibility of many of these adhesives is questionable and their use is usually restricted to simple breaks where little stress acts on the joint and where failure of the joint would not be likely to cause further damage.

Using combinations of adhesives

By using combinations of adhesives the benefits of two different types of adhesives can be gained. A commonly used combination is that of a cyanoacrylate used with a slow setting, low-viscosity epoxy resin. The former type of adhesive is used to achieve instant tack, whilst the latter provides long-term durability and strength. The cyanoacrylate is applied in small spots at key points along the breaks, the joints are assembled and then the epoxy resin is applied along the break edge using a small paintbrush. The epoxy resin will be drawn in by capillary action and the excess is removed after curing. Williams (1989) describes the use of a similar method for bonding glass in his report on the conservation of the Portland Vase (British Museum, London). In this case he used a UV curing methacrylate to tack the pieces together, followed by infiltration of the joints with HXTAL NYL-1 epoxy resin. For bonding porcelain a UV curing acrylic will not be suitable and should be replaced by a cyanoacrylate that polymerizes in the presence of atmospheric moisture. These adhesives are not suitable for use on porous bodied ceramics.

Elston (1990) describes the use of cellulose nitrate adhesive (Duco Cement) and Acryloid B-72 (UK Paraloid B-72) acrylic adhesive in combination for bonding earthenware; again this combination was used to provide the benefits of instant tack from the former adhesive and long-term stability from the latter. The cellulose nitrate adhesive was used at the terminal points of the shards to provide a fast tack and the areas between were coated with the acrylic adhesive. The joints were then assembled.

Caution must be exercised, however, when using combinations of adhesives as reactions may occur between certain different types. For example, cellulose nitrate adhesives cause violent yellowing of some epoxy resins.

Cleaning back and removal of tape

If a large amount of adhesive has been squeezed from the joint during bonding the bulk of it can be lightly cleaned off whilst it is still soft using a brush or a swab lightly dampened with solvent. Care should be taken to use the minimum amount of solvent necessary as too much solvent will flood the joint and weaken the bond. Alternatively, cleaning back can be left until the adhesive has cured; this will avoid the risk of moving the joint out of alignment or introducing dirt, fibres of cotton wool or solvent into the joint. In any event the excess adhesive that has squeezed out of the joint underneath any supporting tapes will need to be removed after the adhesive has cured and the tapes have been removed.

The adhesive should be allowed to cure fully before removing the supporting tapes. Where tape has been applied over an unsound surface it is wise to flood the tape with solvent (e.g. industrial methylated spirits) to soften its adhesive before removal in order to avoid pulling at the unsound surface. One end of the tape is then lifted and it is gently peeled back, using a scalpel to help work solvent underneath as it is peeled. All traces of adhesive must then be removed from the surface using solvent. Often this adhesive will not show immediately, but if left will in time cause disfiguring marks as it picks up dirt and discolours.

The excess adhesive from the joint is then removed using a scalpel. Some restorers recommend removing the excess using abrasive paper owing to a tendency for the adhesive to be pulled out of fine chips along the break edge when removed with a scalpel. If the break edges have been thoroughly cleaned before bonding, if the scalpel blade is very sharp and if it is used with a shaving action rather than to dig at the excess adhesive, this should not be a danger. There is a risk of damaging the surface of the object if the abrasive method is used and hence removal with a scalpel is preferable. Where the adhesive is filling larger chips, final smoothing down can be done with abrasive paper but the bulk of the excess should still be removed with a scalpel.

When the object that has been bonded is unglazed, for example in the case of biscuit porcelain, removal of excess adhesive is often most effectively carried out using a chemical agent to soften it. In the case of epoxy resins this should be done where possible before a full cure has been reached and where the resin can still be removed with acetone or industrial methylated spirits. If the resin has cured completely, dichloromethane (usually in the form of a commercial paint stripper, e.g. water washable Nitromors or USA Zynolyte) must be used. It must be applied extremely carefully in order to avoid contact with the joint and weakening of the bond. The same procedure would be followed if there was any gilding or other unsound area which the excess adhesive had come into contact with, and which would become easily damaged if the scalpel method of removal were used. If the object is porous it is pre-soaked in water in the normal way and then the paint stripper is applied to the area of excess adhesive using a swab or brush and ensuring that none of it comes into contact with the adhesive in the break. The softened adhesive is then removed using a scalpel, needle or other fine instrument or a dampened cotton wool swab. All traces of paint stripper must be completely removed by swabbing with water.

Special situations

Cracks

Cracks vary in the degree of movement they allow. In the case of very tight cracks there is little that can be done to reinforce the crack, and treatment may not even be necessary, other than cleaning as described in the previous chapter. However, with the advent of low-viscosity adhesives such as the epoxy resins HXTAL NYL-1, Ablebond 342-1, it is often possible to introduce adhesive into cracks in porcelains and stonewares by capillary action. The adhesive is applied along the surface of the crack from one side using a fine paintbrush. Warming the adhesive and/or the object with a hot air blower, in a warming oven or over hot water will further reduce the viscosity of the adhesive and can increase the amount that is drawn into the crack. However, care must be taken to ensure that the temperature used will not cause accelerated ageing of the resin. The drawback of applying epoxy resins in this way is that removal is extremely difficult. The same method, but without the warming, can be carried out using solvent-based adhesives, such as the acrylic Paraloid B-72 (USA Acryloid B-72).

An alternative method described by Williams (1983) for use with porcelains is to warm the object slowly to near boiling point in water. This can cause the crack to open up, allowing cyanoacrylate adhesive, which is unaffected by water, to be introduced into the crack. The adhesive will then cure owing to the pressure which is exerted as the crack naturally closes up again when the object cools. However, the high temperatures involved in using this method can result in the crack turning into a break and therefore its use must be questioned.

When the crack is such that it can be moved by hand, the cleaning and introduction of adhesive are both easier. However, care must be taken not to take liberties with this movement and cause the ceramic to break. Several writers suggest introducing a razor blade or spatula into the crack to hold it apart whilst cleaning and applying adhesive. If this method is used, great care must be taken not to chip the edges of the crack or mark them with carbon from the tool. Alternatively the edges of the crack can be carefully displaced out of alignment by hand, first in one direction and then in the other, in order to gain access to the faces of the edges. Again this procedure is not without risk, and should be used only when absolutely necessary. If another restorer is present the second can gently hold open the crack whilst the first works on it.

As mentioned above, in the case of porcelains and stonewares when epoxy resins are used, warming the adhesive and/or object will make introduction of the adhesive easier. The crack should then be taped firmly closed. If this is done with pressure sensitive adhesive tape the object should be allowed to cool first to avoid the adhesive on the tape being softened by the heat and thus slipping.

Feeding low-viscosity epoxy resins into cracks in earthenwares is not advisable owing to the risk of absorption into the body, resulting in poor bonding and disfiguring shadowing. When using poly(vinyl acetate) emulsion or solvent-based adhesives on earthenwares these can be made less viscous by using water in the former case or the appropriate solvent in the latter. The crack can often be further strengthened by making use of chips along the crack and filling these with adhesive reinforced filler as described in the following chapter. Cracks in earthenwares or in high-fired ceramics may be reinforced with a backing of resin impregnated glass fibre ribbon. This method can only be used where the tape will not be seen, for example on closed vessel shapes, or objects such as tiles that are viewed from one side only. The ribbon may be cut into short lengths and applied at right angles to the crack or it may be cut to the length of the crack and laid along it. The width of ribbon used will depend upon the strength of support required; in the case of very large objects ribbon 4–6 cm in width may be used. The resin is applied to the glass fibre ribbon with a paintbrush or spatula, and the ribbon is then laid in place and allowed to cure.

Springing or warping

Springing or warping are the terms used to describe the distortion produced in a crack or break caused by the release of inbuilt tensions. These tensions are built into the object during its manufacture and when a break or crack occurs in such an object the distortion can be such that the edges no longer line up properly. There are two schools of thought on the procedures that should be followed when bonding such cracks and breaks; the first makes use of various methods to apply force to bring the edges back in line (e.g. Williams, 1983 reports the use of a double G-clamp); the second recommends that the object is safer having released the tensions and that the edges should not be forced back together, in case the tensions are released in a fresh break at some point in the future, but should be simply consolidated and filled in the position in which they now lie.

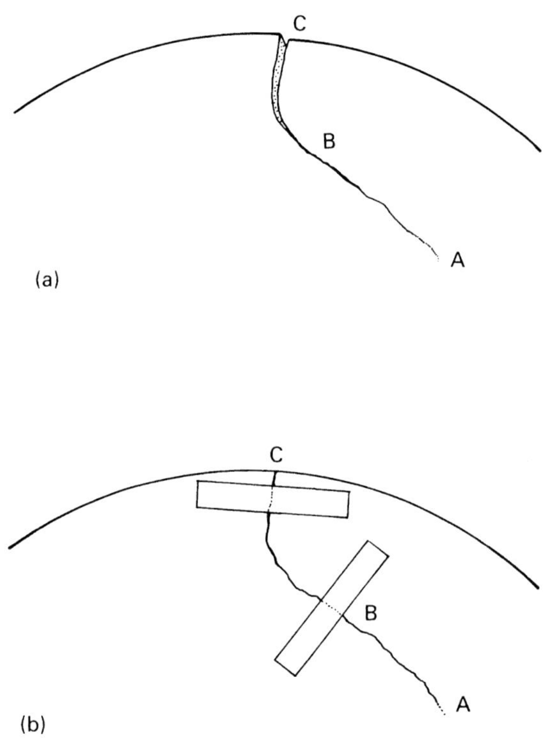

Figure 9.8 Bonding a sprung crack. (a) The length of the crack between A and B which aligns correctly is bonded first. (b) Adhesive is then applied between B and C and pressure sensitive tape used to bring this part of the crack into alignment.

In the former case the break or crack is secured with the appropriate adhesive initially for the extent of its length that does actually line up without a step. Thus in Figure 9.8 the joint is first bonded between A and B. When this has cured adhesive is applied to the remainder of the joint (B–C) and the two edges are brought into line by applying pressure through use of tape, or if necessary a clamp (Navarro, 1989) (Figure 9.9), a tourniquet (Smith, in press), or similar means.

Chips

Often when assembling a broken ceramic there are small chips of glaze or body that must be positioned. Tests will have to be made to determine whether these can only be fitted in position if they are assembled at the same time as the surrounding pieces or whether they can be added after the main pieces have been assembled. Small chips are difficult to hold in position and can throw out the positioning of larger pieces; consequently if they can be left until the rest of the joints have been bonded and have cured this is often preferable. Care must be taken, if this is done, not to get adhesive on the place where the chip is to be positioned when carrying out the main bonding procedure. Once this has cured it may be difficult to remove and hence hinder the good positioning of the chip. The choice of adhesive may be slightly different from that used to bond the rest of the object: for example a glaze chip in a porcelain object may be bonded with a solvent-based adhesive for good colour fastness and easy reversibility, whereas the main bonds may have been made using an epoxy resin to give greater strength.

Figure 9.9 Use of purpose made clamp (Navarro, 1989) to hold sprung break. The bottom of the dish is protected from the sand by food wrapping film (Victoria and Albert Museum, London).

Badly damaged break edges

Aligning joints that have badly damaged break edges and holding them in position whilst the adhesive cures can be difficult. In very bad cases the process may be aided by using a filling material with adhesive properties rather than a simple adhesive, or using a combination of filler and adhesive. On non-porous ceramics epoxy resin putties made by adding an inert filler to the chosen epoxy can be used, and with porous ceramics a plaster or plaster-based material mixed with poly(vinyl acetate) emulsion is often effective. It may be necessary to use small wedges, for example of balsa wood, to help hold the joint in position (Figure 9.10).

Dowelling

Dowelling is not as commonly used now as it was in the past when the choice of suitable adhesives was not as extensive. The drawback of dowelling is that original material must often be drilled away in order to provide a hole in which to insert the dowel. However, there are still circumstances when dowelling may be a wise safety precaution, and often use can be made of old dowel holes or the dowels can be set into hollow areas of the object thus avoiding the removal of fresh material. For example Williams (1987) reused old dowel holes in the restoration of a heavy earthenware sarcophagus, where the added strength given by using this technique meant that the object could be more safely handled. In the case of smaller, lighter objects dowels may also be necessary to give strength, for example where the surface area of the break edges does not allow a large enough area of adhesive to give the necessary strength.

Materials used for making dowels must be stable and of suitable strength: stainless steel is commonly used and has the benefit of being pliable and can therefore be bent to shape if the dowel holes do not lie along a single axis. The diameter of the dowel should be as small as possible whilst still providing sufficient strength, and Parsons and Curl (1963) who cover the technique in great depth recommend that dowel holes should never be such that the margin of ceramic around the hole is less than the diameter of the hole. The dowel is cut to length and may be roughened to provide a better key for the adhesive used to set it into the hole. Parsons and Curl also recommend that a groove should be made down one side, or one side flattened, in order to assist the escape of air from the dowel hole when the dowel is inserted.

Holes must be drilled with a high-speed drill and diamond drill bit when drilling porcelain. They should be such that the dowel fits snugly. It is not necessary that the dowel holes have a single axis; the dowel can

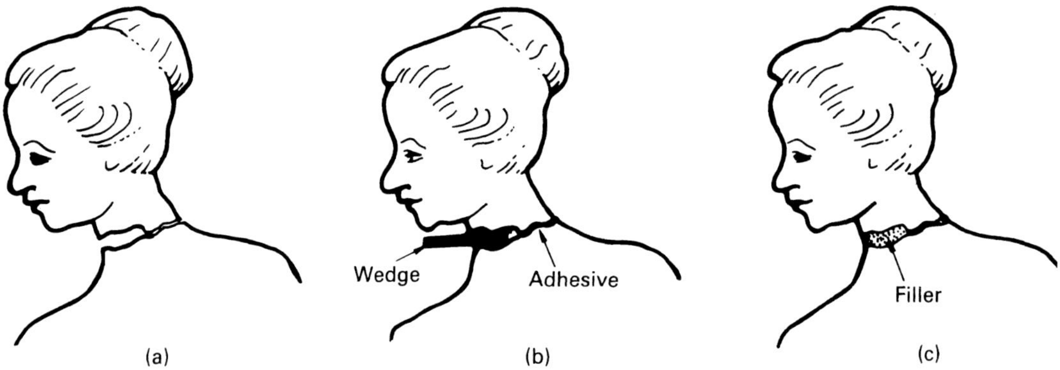

Figure 9.10 Bonding a chipped break (a). In (b) adhesive has been applied to the part of the break that is intact and a wedge has been inserted to support the rest of the joint. (c) Shows the wedge removed and filler applied.

if necessary be bent. Once one half of the break has been drilled the position for the hole on the other half can be determined by coating the rim of the drilled hole with watercolour paint or ink (which can be washed off later), dampening the other half of the break and then bringing the two halves together. The position for the second hole should then be imprinted on the second half of the break.

Once the holes are drilled the dowel is bent into shape with pliers until it allows the two halves of the joint to be brought together when it is in position. A small amount of adhesive is then inserted into each hole, pushing it down well to ensure that no air is trapped in the bottom. One of the break edges is also lightly coated with adhesive and the joint is then assembled with the dowel, strapped if necessary, and left to cure. It is essential that the position of dowels is well documented to allow for future reversal.

10

Replacement of lost material

Introduction

When a ceramic object has been broken there is always loss of material to some degree from the edges of the breaks. This loss may be very minor, especially in the case of hard-paste porcelain, and cleaning the pieces thoroughly and bonding them back together may give a satisfactory result without the need for any further treatment. However, loss of material from break edges may be more extensive in the case of friable ceramic bodies, or where the break edges have been damaged. In such cases filling may be considered important, not only from the point of view of the immediate and long-term appearance of the object, but also from the point of view of the stability of the bonds. Chips left unfilled along a bonded joint may gather dirt and moisture which will make the joints more noticeable and may weaken the bond.

More extensive loss of material such as large chips, holes and missing handles, limbs, etc. can cause the object to be structurally weak and aesthetically displeasing. Where there is no evidence on which to base a reconstruction it may not be ethically acceptable to make up these missing parts; however in many cases evidence can be found from symmetry, extrapolation, other objects in a series, or from documentation such as photographs.

In certain cases, perhaps where the primary importance of the object is not as a decorative piece, it may be considered appropriate to leave losses unfilled, even where these losses are extensive and there is evidence for their reconstruction.

Until recently the approach that was usually taken to replacing missing material was to make fillings using opaque, white materials and to retouch over the top of them with a medium tinted with pigments to match the surrounding ceramic (Figure 10.1a). Although such fillings can in many cases be disguised to a reasonable degree by skilful retouching, if the object has a translucent or semi-translucent body, or a thick transparent glaze, these fillings will always show as shadowed areas when the object is viewed in certain lighting conditions. For this reason, conservators are now making use of the possibilities that some of the modern materials provide of creating fillings that are matched in translucency and colour to the original body and glaze layers. Even reproduction of underglaze painting can be incorporated into the filling in this way and actual retouching can in many instances be dispensed with. This is not a new technique and was described by Parsons and Curl in 1963. The filling process may be carried out in more than one stage, for example where a thick transparent glaze lies over an opaque body. In such a case the first stage would be to apply filler matched to the body up to the level of the body surface, and the second stage to apply filler matched to the glaze (Figure 10.1b). If the glaze layer is less defined, the filling may be executed in one stage, the filling material being matched to the overall appearance of the body/glaze system (Figure 10.1c). Where the glaze is opaque or the object is made from an unglazed opaque material then the old style of opaque, white filler painted with pigments in a medium can be used, or alternatively a single application of filler matched to the glaze can be made (Figure 10.1d).

There are various arguments for and against the use of tinted fillings. Matching the filling very closely to the original fabric of the object makes it far more difficult to distinguish original material from restoration material; however, it does mean that if the filling becomes scratched this is generally not so obvious as it is when a white filling is used in a coloured body. Ageing of the retouching on an unmatched filling can be dealt with by stripping off the old retouching and replacing it, whereas discoloration of

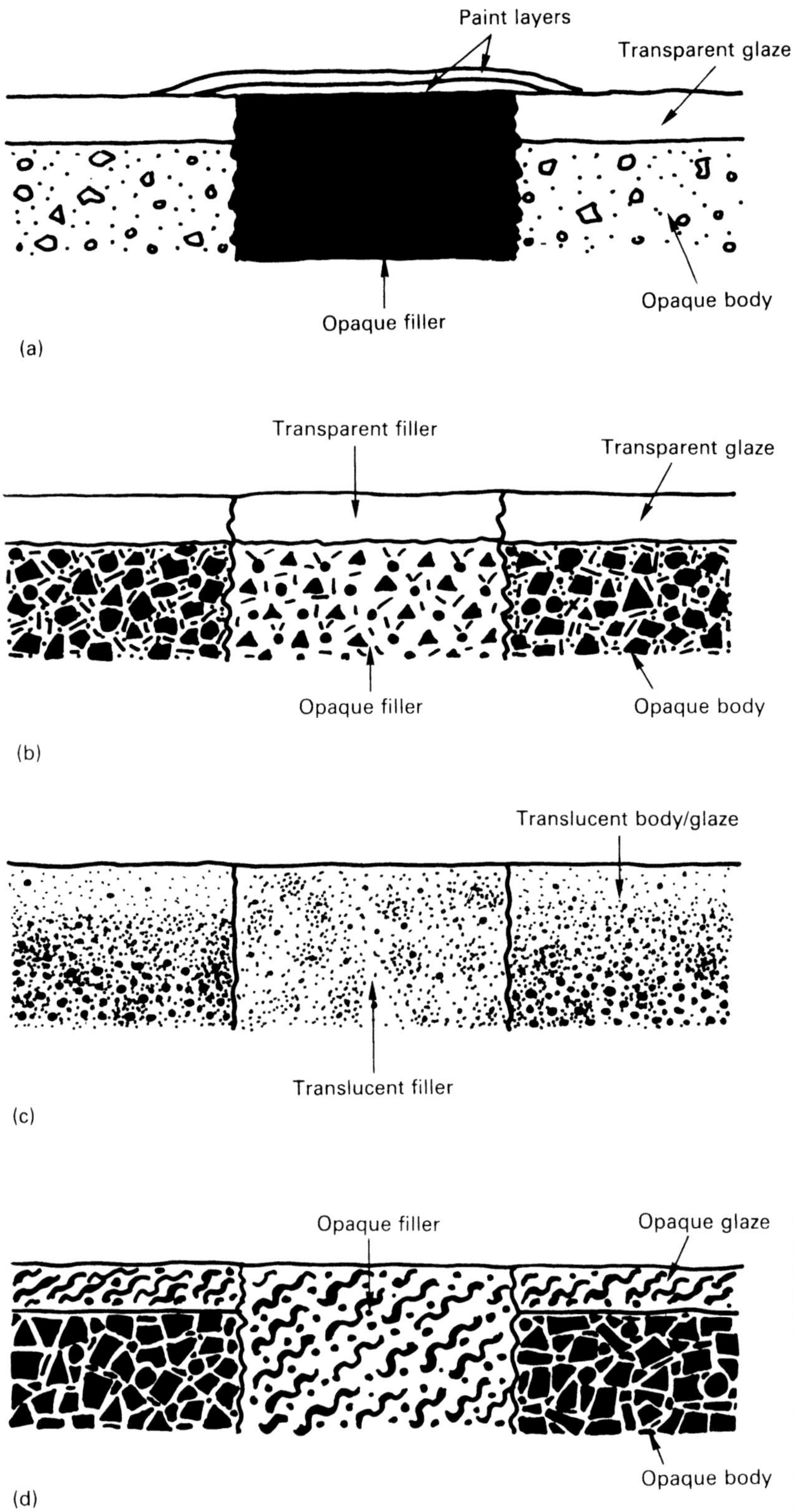

Figure 10.1 Methods of filling: (a) an opaque white filler covered by layers of tinted retouching medium; (b) layer of filler matched to body, covered with a layer of filler matched to glaze; (c) filling in object without defined glaze layer, filler matched to overall appearance of body/glaze; (d) filling matched to opaque glaze.

a matched filling may require replacement of the entire filling.

There are a number of materials in use for filling areas of loss and making up missing pieces, and various techniques are used to shape and apply them to the ceramic. Chapter 14 gives detailed accounts of the properties of the various filling and moulding materials; however, this chapter will discuss the suitability of particular materials for use in particular situations and will describe their practical use.

Materials

Choice of filling materials

In the restoration of ceramic objects today, no attempt is made to use exactly the same material to replace losses as was used to make the original. There are two reasons for this. Firstly, ceramic materials are of a complex composite nature, and analysis and reproduction of ceramic bodies and glazes are extremely costly and difficult exercises. Secondly, the behaviour of clays and glazes during firing, the cycles of expansion and contraction that are involved, and the tendency of the clay to warp would make the accurate reproduction of three-dimensional shapes to fill missing areas virtually impossible. For these reasons, therefore, a range of synthetic materials is used. This does have the benefit of making detection of restorations relatively easy.

The most commonly used fillers are based on epoxy resins, polyester resins, acrylic resins, and calcium compounds, particularly plaster of Paris. The materials used are chosen on the basis of a number of criteria, the fulfilment of which will depend on the type of ceramic object that is being treated and the method used to apply the material. The main criteria are as follows.

The material can be modelled or cast

There are several approaches to shaping filling material: one is to use various modelling techniques whilst the filling material is in a pliable state; alternatively the material may be allowed to harden and is then cut and filed into shape; or thirdly the material may be cast into the required shape using a mould. A combination of these techniques may be used. This provides reasonable scope for the use of a wide variety of materials.

All of the commonly used materials mentioned above can be shaped in all of these ways. Epoxy resins of low viscosity are appropriate for casting although a certain amount of heat may be generated which may affect the mould material. Mould materials are discussed in detail in a later section. For filling small losses and modelling larger ones the working properties of epoxy resins can be modified by the addition of various aggregates such as barium sulphate, fumed colloidal silica, talc etc. The hardness and thus the relative ease of cutting back after curing will vary with the aggregate chosen. Barium sulphate produces a hard filling whilst talc produces a softer filling. Ready prepared epoxy resin putties are available commercially but there may be drawbacks to the use of some of these owing to certain of the added materials (Bradley and Green, 1987).

Polyester resins are also suitable for casting but are more inclined than epoxy resins to produce heat during curing. They also have a tendency to shrink by up to 15% which will mean that the cast is smaller than the original from which the mould is taken. Ready prepared polyester resin pastes are available and can be used with or without a mould.

White acrylic modelling pastes, composed of acrylic emulsion filled with calcium carbonate, are available and have good colour stability. They are easily cut back after curing, and can be sanded and polished.

The use of plaster of Paris requires some practice owing to its relatively fast setting time, but it can be cast and to a certain extent modelled. Mibach (1975) gives some helpful details concerning its use. Various proprietary fillers based on calcium sulphate or calcium carbonate, such as the Polyfilla range of fillers, are available and these tend to be slower setting and allow more detailed modelling in the uncured state. On the whole they are softer than plaster of Paris when cured, and are consequently easier to cut back.

The material can be adjusted by the addition of dyes, pigments and/or fillers to reproduce the appearance of the ceramic body/glaze

When a filling is to be matched in colour, translucency, gloss and texture to the surrounding ceramic it is important that the filling material can be easily adjusted in all these ways. Epoxy resins and polyester resins are the most commonly used materials when any degree of translucency is required, for example for matching a translucent porcelain body or a transparent glaze. They will tend to have a gloss finish which is useful when matching glaze finishes, but when desired, material can be added to give them a matt appearance. Fumed colloidal silica can be used for this purpose with minimal loss of translucency. Plaster of Paris and Polyfilla will not give any transparency or gloss and can only be used for opaque fillings, for example in earthenwares and pottery.

Different textures can be achieved with most of the commonly used fillers by adding a variety of materials. Any inert material can be used; however, care should be taken not to adversely affect the strength or adhesive properties of the filler. When necessary, texture can be reproduced by modelling rather than by the addition of material to the filler. Smith (in press) reports recent attempts to produce a filling material for losses in Bronze Age urns using materials such as paper and wood pulp.

Epoxy and polyester resins can be tinted using dry ground pigments or specially formulated dyes. Fillers based on acrylic emulsions can be tinted using acrylic colours, water colours or dry ground pigments. Large quantities of dry ground pigments are required to tint plaster of Paris and calcium-based fillers, but special cement dyes (Mibach, 1975) can be used. Tinted plaster of Paris and Polyfilla lighten in colour when they dry, although the colour will darken again if certain surface coatings are applied. The final colour with plaster of Paris and Polyfilla can be tested by spreading a small amount of the mixed filler on a tile or absorbent paper and drying it rapidly over a radiator or in an oven. It is difficult to mix a second batch of filler to exactly match the first, and it is therefore important to mix a sufficient quantity to start with. Epoxy resin mixtures can be stored in the icebox of a fridge for some time which allows them to be used for more than one application. When dry pigments are added to plaster of Paris or Polyfilla before the addition of water this allows the storage of some of the dry material for use in a second application.

The material must allow the application of surface coatings

Even when the filling material is such that it can be matched in all the above ways to the original ceramic it may still be important that it will accept the application of other materials on its surface, for example to reproduce over glaze enamelling or gilding. Where the filling is not matched to the ceramic the surface coating must serve to adjust its appearance appropriately. Polymer surface coatings must generally be used when coating resin-based fillings. Acrylic paints are commonly used for coating plaster of Paris and Polyfilla fillings, although shellac is also used on plaster of Paris. Owing to their absorbent natures, plaster of Paris and Polyfilla should be sealed before coating. Depending on the nature of any subsequent surface coating to be applied, this can be done using, for example, bleached shellac such as Rustins White Polish (Williams, 1987) or an initial sealing coat of the surface coating to be used.

Care must be taken to ensure that the filling material and the surface coating are compatible. Bradley and Green (1987) report yellowing of a urea-formaldehyde-based lacquer, Rustins Plastic Coating, when used over a commercially prepared epoxy putty, Milliput. This occurred in the dark and was due to antioxidant contained in the Milliput.

The following chapter gives further details on choice of a retouching medium.

The material must adhere to the ceramic

Although recent work by Koob (1987) has demonstrated that there are some benefits to making removable fillings that are adhered to the object in a secondary procedure, it is most usual to apply the filling directly to the break edge and rely on the adhesive powers of the filling material to keep it in place. This requires materials with stronger adhesive powers in the case of fillings in high-fired wares as opposed to those in low-fired wares as the coarser nature of the break edges in most lower-fired wares allows a certain amount of mechanical locking in place. This is one of the reasons why materials such as epoxy resins and polyesters are commonly used for fillings in high-fired wares. Plaster of Paris and Polyfilla, which do not adhere very well to high-fired wares, can be used perfectly satisfactorily with low-fired wares. It is good practice to seal the edges of low-fired wares, especially when applying plaster of Paris fillings, as otherwise water is absorbed into the break edge and the cohesion within the filling itself is reduced. Poly(vinyl acetate) emulsion or Paraloid B-72 (USA Acryloid B-72) can be used for this purpose (Koob, 1987; Hogan, in press).

The material must be of appropriate strength and density

Fillings may be required to give structural support to the object and must therefore be of appropriate strength. If a large proportion of an object must be reconstructed with filler the appropriate density may be important to balance the weight of the object. Plaster of Paris and Polyfilla can be modified by the addition of resins such as poly(vinyl acetate) emulsion and carboxymethyl cellulose (Mibach, 1975) to make them stronger, and are appropriate for use with a range of ceramics including many archaeological ceramics and earthenwares. Epoxy putties are very strong and dense and more suitable for use with stonewares and hard-paste porcelains. Lightweight fillers can be created by adding ceramic microspheres to various resins, for example the acrylic Paraloid B-72 (Acryloid B-72), or to low-viscosity epoxy resins.

The material must be durable

Filling materials must remain unaltered with ageing and be resistant to biological attack. Stability of colour and translucency are most important in the case of filling materials that are to be used without an opaque surface coating.

The material must not contaminate the ceramic

When treating porous bodied ceramics there is a danger that mobile material from the filler may be carried into the body of the ceramic and cause staining or other damage. Fillers containing oils such as linseed oil putties are obvious dangers, but Bradley and Green (1987) found unexpected staining occurring with use of a proprietary epoxy putty filler, Milliput, when used on soft-paste porcelain, and suspected that this was due to butylated hydroxy toluene in the filler, which became mobilized by water used for smoothing down the filling. The use of liquid epoxy and polyester resins for casting directly onto the ceramic is not appropriate when the ceramic body is porous as these materials penetrate the body and consolidate the areas surrounding the filling. This may not only cause shadowing around the filling but create a danger of fresh damage occurring if the object was placed under strain in the future, with the consolidated areas tearing away from the unconsolidated areas. The use of plaster of Paris as a filling material must take account of the possibility of contamination of the ceramic with soluble salts. Break edges of porous bodied ceramics should thus be sealed before application of plaster of Paris. Koob (1987) suggests the use of Paraloid B-72 (Acryloid B-72) for this purpose.

The material must be reversible

The removal of the major bulk of a filling is generally not a problem. It is the removal of the filling material in contact with the ceramic break edge that can be difficult to achieve without damaging the ceramic. This is one of the reasons why Koob (1987) developed a procedure for making detachable plaster of Paris fillings. Difficulties can also be minimized when creating fillings in porous bodied ceramics by sealing the break edges before applying the filler. Appropriate sealants include Paraloid B-72 (Acryloid B-72), poly(vinyl acetate), and poly(vinyl alcohol) (Barov, 1988). It is also wise to seal the surface surrounding a loss before applying the filling material, if the surface is unglazed or textured, in order to avoid filling material lodging in it and causing ghosting. The excess filling material around the filling, together with the separating layer, is removed after completion of the filling. If any ghosting has occurred attempts should be made to remove this using a poultice containing a suitable solvent. In practice it may be impossible to completely remove ghosting.

Epoxy-resin- or polyester-based fillers which must be softened with dichloromethane for removal are also difficult to remove from small irregularities, for example the minute air bubbles which occur in some oriental glazes.

The material must not shrink on curing or with age

Shrinkage can be a purely practical problem from the point of view of achieving a satisfactory filling but it can also be a problem in that it can harm the object. When filling materials that are bonded to the ceramic shrink they can damage friable break edges by pulling particles of the ceramic material away. Epoxy resins and putties do not shrink or swell significantly on curing; however polyester resins may shrink by up to 15%. Plaster of Paris tends to swell slightly on curing (approximately 0.15–0.5%), but Polyfilla shows slight shrinkage.

The thermal expansion of the material must be compatible with that of the ceramic

When a filling material is to be used on objects that will be subject to large fluctuations in ambient temperature, for example during air transport, its coefficient of thermal expansion must be similar to that of the ceramic material. Barov and Lambert (1984) found that in the case of filling materials with very different coefficients of thermal expansion to that of a ceramic test mould fired to 926°C, the filling material could actually cause the ceramic to crack and break. In other cases the filler pulled away from the edge of the ceramic. They found that adding inert material such as glass microspheres or mica to a resin filler improved its compatibility with the ceramic. Plaster of Paris showed good compatibility as did an acrylic paste and Ablebond 342-1 epoxy filled with glass microspheres.

The material must be safe to use

Materials that give off toxic fumes during use or which produce hazardous dusts when abraded should be avoided. In the case of polyester- or epoxy-resin-based fillers it is wise to use local fume extraction and to wear protective gloves during use and protective face masks when abrading and cutting back. Although the dust produced when plaster of Paris or Polyfilla fillings are abraded is not hazardous it can be very drying to the skin and encourage dermatitis. The wearing of protective gloves is therefore recommended as is the use of goggles, particularly for wearers of contact lenses.

Plaster of Paris and other calcium-based fillers

Plaster of Paris is currently, and has been in the past, one of the most commonly used materials for fillings, especially in low-fired ceramics. A variety of different grades of plaster of Paris is available and the choice of plaster for particular circumstances is discussed by Chase and Zycherman (1981). Different grades show variations in hardness, durability, colour, setting time, and expansion on setting. Proprietary calcium-carbonate- and calcium-sulphate-based fillers such as Polyfilla are used in preference to plaster of Paris by many conservators as they are easier to shape, remaining workable for longer and thus allowing the filling to be wet modelled to a greater extent, and being softer when cured and thus more easily cut back and carved. Such proprietary fillers, unlike straight plaster of Paris, adhere reasonably well to earthenwares and allow further filler to be added once the first application has cured.

The densities, strengths and thermal expansions of plaster of Paris and plaster-based fillers are compatible with most earthenwares, although adjustments can be made by mixing various additives such as poly(vinyl acetate) emulsion into the uncured filler or consolidating the cured filler with resin, such as an epoxy resin or an acrylic resin. The relatively rough texture of an earthenware break edge allows these fillers to key in well, which compensates for their lack of adhesive power. They will not adhere well to break edges of higher-fired wares and where greater adhesive power is required poly(vinyl acetate) emulsion can be added.

The linear expansion on curing of plaster of Paris varies from grade to grade. All grades expand slightly on curing (commonly up to about 0.5%), although some specially designed casting plasters show a linear expansion as low as 0.15%. Polyfilla, however, shrinks to some degree and allowance must be made for this. Polyfilla (interior grade), the grade used for the bulk of most fillings, is somewhat coarse, but where necessary this can be overcome by applying a thin layer of Fine Surface Polyfilla on top of it. Fine Surface Polyfilla cannot be used alone except for very small fillings (i.e. in layers no thicker than 1–2 mm) as it shrinks quite considerably on drying. Plaster of Paris is not generally suitable for filling very small chips.

Fillers of this type can be used tinted, if required, and their textures modified by the addition of a variety of materials. Surface decoration may be applied using a range of retouching media after the fillings have cured (see following chapter).

Plaster of Paris and Polyfilla are reasonably stable, the resin additives in the proprietary fillers tending to make them more durable than most plaster of Paris. Neither Polyfilla nor plaster of Paris is easy to remove completely from the ceramic body once cured, although sealing the surface of the ceramic (e.g. with Paraloid B-72 or poly(vinyl acetate) emulsion) will greatly improve reversibility. Sealing is also a wise precaution when using plaster of Paris in order to prevent contamination of the ceramic with soluble salts.

Resin-based fillers

Plaster-of-Paris-based fillers can be used for fillings in some stoneware or porcelain objects but on the whole they are not appropriate as they do not have the adhesive properties necessary to bond to the smoother break edges. They are not suitable for the finer modelling and moulding that is often necessary with porcelains, nor do they have the translucency and gloss needed when making matched fillings in porcelains.

The materials that are most commonly used for fillings in stonewares and porcelains are epoxy, acrylic and polyester resins. When employed as modelling materials they are used in a putty form, produced by the addition of various fillers, together with dyes or pigments. They are either purchased ready bound as proprietary commercial fillers or they may be mixed at the bench. The latter is generally preferable as the properties of the putty can be tailored to the requirements of the job in hand, and the precise composition of the putty will be known. The choice of filler will depend on the texture and translucency required, e.g. fumed colloidal silica or glass microspheres give a high degree of translucency but materials such as powdered pumice or sand may be used to give a coarser texture when translucency is not a priority. An alternative approach is to use the resin mixed with a white aggregate such as kaolin, barium sulphate or talc (French chalk), making no attempt to match the translucency or colour of the ceramic, and then to apply a surface coating which carries the pigment or dye. Various media can be used to apply surface coatings to adjust the colour and texture and this will be discussed in the next chapter.

Putties made with resins tend to produce hard, dense, durable fillings. Because they are so hard when cured it is preferable that most of the shaping is done prior to curing; however they can be cut back with scalpels, files, abrasive papers or drills after curing. Protective gloves should be worn when working with epoxy or polyester putties and dust masks should be worn when cutting back the cured resins. Casting the shape either *in situ* on the object or off the object avoids the need for as much working after the filling has cured. Both epoxy and polyester resins can be used as casting materials with moulds and for these techniques are generally used without the addition of filler in order to maintain their fluid nature and give a smoother, glossier finish.

Epoxy resins and putties, in particular, adhere strongly to the ceramic. On the whole little of the resin penetrates the body of the ceramic as neither stonewares nor porcelains are porous to a significant degree. Both epoxy and polyester resins soften in dichloromethane, and paint strippers containing dichloromethane are generally used to remove fillings made from these materials. Acrylic fillers are more readily reversible and will soften in a range of solvents including ketones, esters and aromatic hydrocarbons.

In cases where a matched filling is not being made, a fine calcium-based filler such as Fine Surface Polyfilla or cellulose stopper may be used in conjunction with resin-based putties to fill minor holes and discrepancies after the main filling has cured. The benefit of doing this is that the calcium-based filler cures much faster than the resin-based putty and is easier to cut back.

Support materials

Filling materials can be applied to small chips and cracks without using any form of support. Larger fillings will often require some form of support for the filling material until it has cured. This is usually a temporary external support but in certain circumstances the permanent support of an internal armature or core may be used. Such permanent supports will be discussed under the section on modelling.

The amount of support required will depend on the shape and position of the filling and the type of filling material used. In some cases only a very simple prop is necessary, whereas in others an intricate mould of several parts may be required. However, the basic requirements of a support material are that it must not interact with the ceramic or the filling material, it must be easily shaped, and it will hold this shape. There are various materials that may be used.

Non-setting modelling putties

Simple props may be made using non-setting modelling materials such as Plasticine, Aloplast or Klean Klay. Plasticine has the drawback that it contains oil which can stain porous ceramics and affect the resin used for the filling. If it is used it should be dusted well with talc, barium sulphate, fumed silica, etc. where it will come into contact with the ceramic or the resin. Alternatively a separating layer of food wrapping film may be used. Koob (1987) recommends warming the Plasticine under hot water and using it warm and wet.

Pressure sensitive tapes

Pressure sensitive tapes can be used for supporting small fillings, such as those made in lacing or tying holes, or in small chips in the rims of plates. They will not, however, hold a shape, and stretched across a chip in the rim of a bowl will give a flat backing to the filling rather than a curved one. They are best therefore used only for supporting very small or flat fillings. Again they should be dusted with talc, barium sulphate, fumed silica etc. where they will come into contact with the filling material as they can otherwise be difficult to remove once the filling material has cured. Caution should be exercised when using pressure sensitive tapes on archaeological ceramics or any ceramics with deteriorated surfaces, and a test should be made in an unobtrusive area first to ensure that the tape does not damage the surface by pulling away fragments when it is removed. Care must be taken to ensure that the adhesive on the pressure sensitive tape is compatible with the filling material. This problem is discussed in relation to adhesives in Chapter 9.

Sheet dental wax

This is available in the form of sheets of toughened wax which may be softened by warming in hot water or with a hot air blower. When warm the wax can be used to make shallow press moulds. It will not pick up fine details and as it is rigid when cooled it is not suitable for moulding undercuts. However, it is ideal for moulding the curved edges of bowls and plates and is therefore predominantly used as a support for fillings made in these situations. Dental wax is suitable for use with all the fillers mentioned above, although its use with large quantities of epoxy resin or polyester resin should be avoided owing to the heat generated during curing. Poly(vinyl alcohol) may be used as a separating agent between dental wax and cast resin. A drop of detergent, e.g. Synperonic, should be added to the poly(vinyl alcohol) to enable it to flow on the surface of the wax and not pull back into pools. It is applied to the wax with a soft paintbrush.

Dental impression compound

Dental impression compounds are hard rigid materials that soften in hot water. They produce rigid moulds which will take greater detail than sheet wax. However, they cannot be removed from undercuts so care should be taken not to trap the compound onto the ceramic object. They do not require a separating medium from the object or from the filling material, and may be used with any of the filling materials mentioned above. They may be reused by softening in hot water again.

Unfired clay

Unfired clay is occasionally used on archaeological sites where it may be readily available, but should not be used directly on the surface of low-fired, porous or coarse ceramics as it would be difficult to remove. A separating layer of a food wrap such as Clingfilm can be used to prevent contamination of the object.

Silicone rubber putties

Silicone rubber putties are two-part materials that are mixed by kneading together the putty and hardener in the hands until the hardener has been dispersed. The important difference between these and the dental impression compounds is that they remain flexible when cured. They can therefore be used for taking press moulds of areas with moderate undercuts, with no fear of damaging the ceramic when the mould is removed. They cure rapidly, so mixing and application must be carried out without delay. No separating medium is required between the putty and the ceramic or the putty and the casting material; however, silicone rubbers contain oils and for this reason they should not be used on porous bodied ceramics. Any of the fillers mentioned above may be used as casting materials, although one of the putties in use, Coposil, which is a pink colour, will stain many materials pink when they are cast into it.

Silicone rubber pastes and liquids
Silicone rubbers are expensive but can be used to make very accurate, detailed moulds. Most are not as flexible as latex rubber moulds (see below) and cannot therefore be used to mould such deep undercuts; however, they do have a certain degree of flexibility and can be used where moderate undercuts are present. They are often used to make multi-part moulds.

Silicone rubbers are available in liquid form, in which case retaining walls must be built around the area to be moulded, or they may be obtained in butter-on formulations that can be applied with a spatula. A combination of the two types may be used in one mould. Liquid silicone rubbers can also be modified by the addition of fumed silica to form a putty-like consistency. A plaster of Paris or resin mother mould can be used with silicone rubber moulds and these may be reinforced by the addition of glass fibre.

Silicone rubbers are available that are compatible with epoxy or polyester resins. However, with repeated casting of epoxies, absorption of elements of the resin hardener into the silicone rubber results in adhesion between the epoxy resin and the rubber. This can be avoided by heating the mould in a ventilated oven at 100–150°C for eight hours between castings. If silicone rubbers are used for taking moulds from porous ceramics, care should be taken to ensure that staining does not occur due to the oil content in the silicone rubber.

Rubber latex
Rubber latex is relatively cheap compared with silicone rubber and easier to use. It is an opaque white liquid which dries to give a very flexible mould. The flexibility is a great advantage when taking moulds of areas with deep undercuts or parts such as whole hands or heads, but it can be a problem in that the mould is easily distorted. Special latex thickeners are available that allow the mould to be built up more quickly, and materials such as cotton flock or wood flour are commonly added to make the mould more rigid. Large latex moulds are generally used with a plaster mother mould to prevent distortion. Rubber latex moulds have a tendency to shrink, distort and embrittle quite quickly, sometimes in as little as two months (Horie, 1987) and so should be used to make the cast as soon as possible after completion.

Rubber latex is suitable for use with most sound ceramics, including earthenwares and terracottas, as it will not stain. However, owing to its ammonia content it may affect gilding and a small spot test should be made or an alternative material used when gilding is present. Rubber latex is incompatible with polyester resins and should not be used with these. Its use with large quantities of epoxy resins that generate heat on curing should also be avoided as the rubber latex mould can become burnt.

Filling minor losses

Before commencing to fill any area of loss it is essential that the broken surface is thoroughly clean, especially in the case of porcelain where the translucency of the body and the filling material will allow any dirt to show through and draw attention to the repair. The restorer's hands and all tools to be used should also be scrupulously clean.

Small chips and losses along break edges

Porcelain and stoneware
If one of the epoxy resins has been used for bonding a break, many of the minor chips can be filled in the bonding process by making use of the adhesive that squeezes out from the joint. If this is to be done the resin used for bonding the joint can be tinted to match the colour and translucency of the ceramic. Ablebond 342-1 or HXTAL NYL-1 can be used in this way with the addition of fumed silica and pigments or dyes. However, it must be borne in mind that the addition of such materials to the adhesive will weaken its bonding power and should therefore be kept to a minimum. The excess resin that squeezes out from the joint during assembly is allowed to cure, and then cut back as required after curing, using a sharp scalpel or abrasive papers. The filling is then polished as required (see sections on cutting back and polishing). No further filling may be necessary.

If the chips are too large to be dealt with in this way, or if the adhesive used is not suitable, then filling must be carried out as a separate operation after the adhesive has cured (Figure 10.2). The appropriate filling material is pressed thoroughly down into the chips using a spatula or modelling tool, the bulk of any excess removed, and then the filling smoothed over using a tool dipped in solvent (IMS when working with epoxy putties, acetone for polyester putties). Care must be taken not to wet the filling too much or it may not cure properly. Very shallow chips may not hold the filler well, and when using epoxy putties in such cases it is beneficial to coat the surface of the chip with a thin layer of epoxy resin first to improve adhesion. Where distinct glaze and body layers are being reproduced separate applications of resin may be needed.

Epoxy putties are hard when cured and cutting them back with a scalpel or abrasives is a time consuming job. It is also during the process of cutting back that there is the greatest risk of damaging the

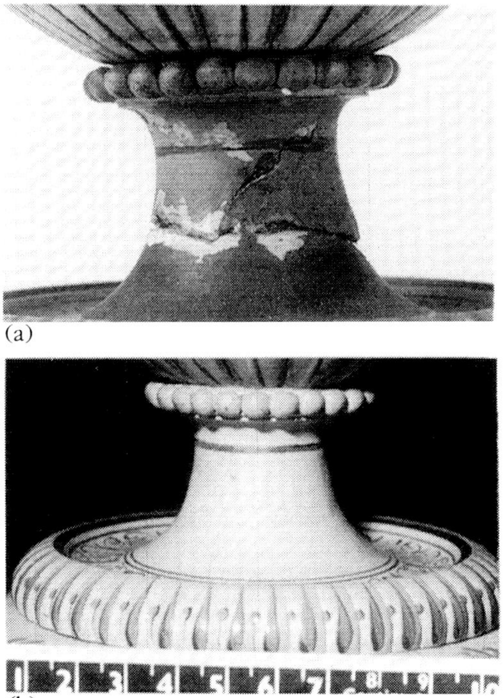

(a)

(b)

Figure 10.2 (a) Breaks and chips in stoneware object, (b) bonded and filled with epoxy resin matched to body (Victoria and Albert Museum, London).

ceramic, as all but the finest abrasives used will scratch most glazes, enamels or gilding. It is therefore preferable not to overfill to a large degree, but to work back the excess whilst it is still mobile. On the other hand, underfilling will mean that a further application of putty must be applied after the first has cured. Again, this is time consuming, and it is not always easy to match subsequent batches of filling material to the first. If it is likely that more than one application will have to be made it is useful to mix enough filler in one batch for all the applications and store it in the freezer.

When used in large quantities the shrinkage that occurs in polyester putties on curing can result in cracks appearing in the filling. In such cases it is therefore better to build up larger fillings in several layers, allowing each to cure before the next is applied.

Earthenwares

Fillings of losses along joints in earthenwares are rarely made with the adhesive used to bond the joint, as the adhesives used are not on the whole suitable. Polyester resins used for bonding very large earthenware objects are the exception. No attempt is made to match these in colour or texture to the ceramic and they will normally be overpainted.

Unglazed earthenwares will generally be filled using a calcium-based filler such as Polyfilla or plaster of Paris (Figure 10.3). The break edges are dampened first to avoid the rapid absorption of water from the filler and consequent weakening of the filler. Alternatively the edges can be sealed using poly(vinyl acetate) emulsion or an acrylic such as Paraloid B-72 (Acryloid B-72). This will also make the filling easier to reverse. The filling material is applied using a spatula and smoothed into shape. Care must be taken to avoid forming air pockets in the bottom of the cavity and the filler should be added bit by bit and pressed down well. If further additions of Polyfilla or plaster of Paris must be made after the first application has cured, the cured filler should be dampened in the area to which the addition is to be made. Fine Surface Polyfilla can be used to fill small blemishes in a filling made with Interior Grade Polyfilla.

Glazed earthenwares may be filled using Polyfilla or plaster of Paris alone, or by using a Polyfilla or plaster of Paris filling covered with a layer of resin tinted to match the glaze. In the first case the filling is usually used untinted and then overpainted. In the second the underlying filling must be tinted to match the body of the ceramic as the resin 'glaze' layer may be partially translucent. Great care should be taken when cutting back the resin as earthenware glazes are soft and more liable to scratching and abrasion.

Rivet and lacing holes

Care must be taken to ensure that the rivet holes are as free as possible of old packing material, and, especially in porcelains where the filling may be

Figure 10.3 Opaque white filler (Polyfilla) used to fill losses along break edges in large Indian dish (Victoria and Albert Museum, London).

translucent, that any metal stains have been removed (Figure 10.4).

If the hole goes right through the ceramic one side should be blocked off using a small strip of adhesive tape or a small piece of dental wax. When filling with epoxy putties the sides of the rivet hole may be coated with a thin layer of epoxy resin. This will improve adhesion of the putty which may pull away from the ceramic slightly while the filling is being shaped. The epoxy putty is then introduced and pressed in well using a wooden swab stick. Care must be taken to ensure that there is no air trapped at the bottom of the hole. Excess is removed. If body and glaze are being reproduced by two separate layers of filler the body filler must be very carefully applied and excess on the glaze edges should be removed before it cures. The surface of the body filler is flattened with the square end of a swab stick and it is then allowed to cure. The filler matched to the glaze is then applied.

Filling rivet and lacing holes with plaster of Paris or Polyfilla is carried out in much the same way as filling with resins. The sides of the holes are not coated with adhesive as there is generally no adhesion problem. The shrinkage of Polyfilla will usually necessitate a second application of filler after the first is dry. It is very difficult to apply plaster of Paris or Polyfilla to fill the hole in the body without getting it on the edges of a glaze, and it is difficult to clean the filler back off the glaze edges. Filling rivet and lacing holes in glazed earthenwares in separate body and glaze layers is consequently difficult but with care it can be done satisfactorily.

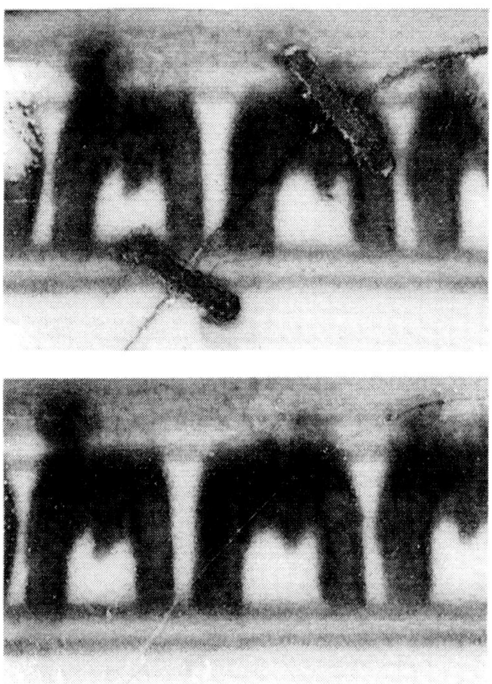

(a)

(b)

Figure 10.4 (a) Blue and white porcelain object with riveted joint. (b) Rivets removed, break edges and rivet holes cleaned and filled with matched filler (epoxy resin with pigments and fumed silica) (Victoria and Albert Museum, London).

Rim chips

Rim chips, ranging in size from a few millimetres to large 'bites' of several centimetres, are very common losses in plates and bowls. The restoration of these generally requires the material used to be supported during curing. Small fillings of this type can be supported by strips of adhesive tape but, as mentioned above, the tape will not accurately take on a curve and if it is used for supporting anything other than very small edge chips of a few millimetres in size the filling will have to be done in two stages. If the adhesive tape is used to support the inside of the curve, a certain amount of cutting back of the inside of the filling will be necessary after curing; if it is used on the outside of the curve, the outside of the filling will have to be built up with the addition of further filling material after the first application has cured.

One way of achieving the correct shape in a curved filling is to use an intact area of the object over which to form the filler. Elston (1990) writes of the use of this technique for shaping a filling for the restoration of an eye-cup. Thin plastic film is laid over the appropriate area of the object as a separating layer and the filling material is applied on top of this. The filling material can be left in place until it has cured sufficiently to hold its shape, and it is then moved into position and fixed in place with further filling material.

Alternatively, one of the support materials may be used to create a mould of the shape, and either dental impression compound or sheet dental wax are commonly used when filling simple losses from rims (Figure 10.5). An open mould is usually used, i.e. the support material is used on one side only. This enables a putty to be pressed into place. If a liquid filler is to be used a more enclosed mould may be made. The compound or wax is softened by immersing in hot water or gently heating with a hot air blower and then placed over an intact area of the rim that corresponds to the missing area in order to shape it. It is allowed to cool in position and then removed, carefully wiped dry and repositioned over the damaged area. Enough compound or wax should be used to ensure that the support will overlap the intact area well on either side of the damaged area. The support is then taped in place using adhesive tape, or attached using poly(vinyl alcohol). Alternatively, in the case of a dental wax support, the edges

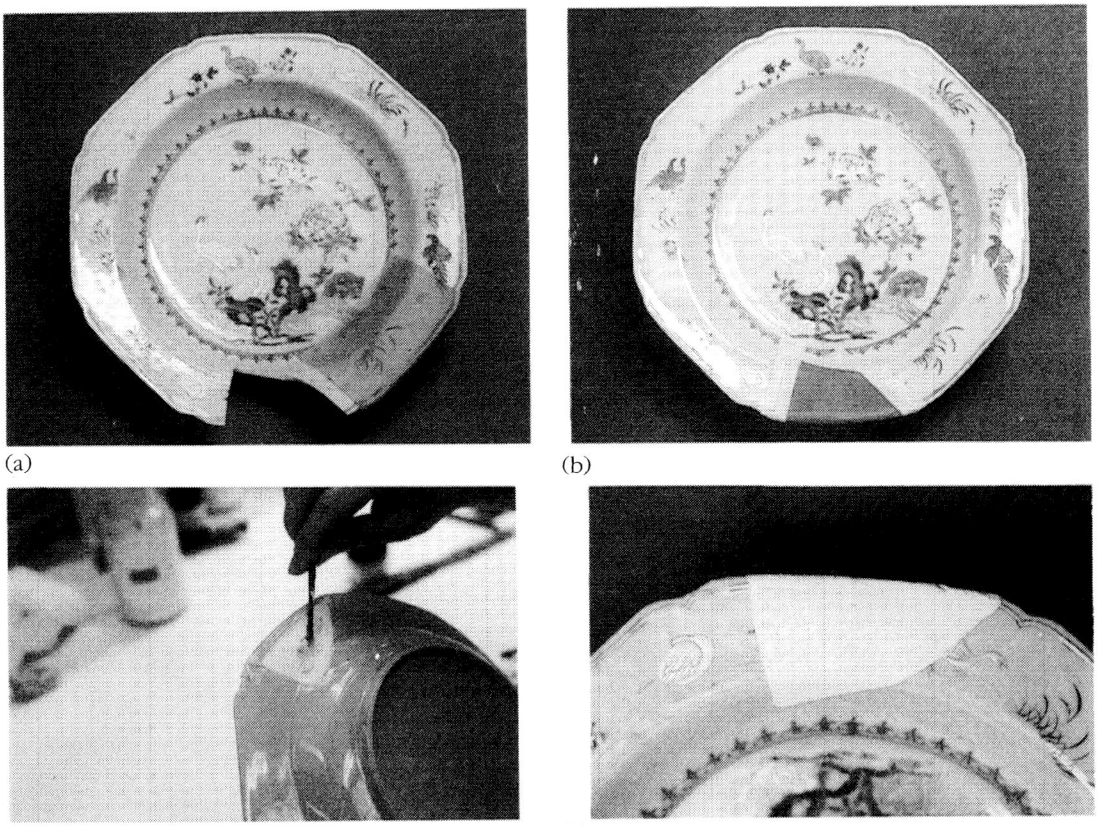

(a) (b) (c) (d)

Figure 10.5 Dental wax support used for filling in rim of Chinese plate: (a) wax sheet pressed onto intact area of rim; (b) wax sheet moved into position across area to be filled; (c) filling material applied with spatula from back of plate; (d) filling cured and wax support removed.

may be sealed to a non-porous ceramic surface using a heated spatula. The filling material is then carefully pressed into the support and shaped using a spatula. The filling material should be of a consistency that allows it to be easily pressed into position but should not be too soft or it may slump during curing. If an epoxy putty is used as the filling material the break edges may be pre-coated with a little epoxy resin to which no pigment or filler has been added in order to improve the adhesion of the putty. The object is then placed to cure in an attitude that encourages the filling material to remain in position. Once the filling material has cured the tape securing the support is carefully removed (using solvent if necessary) and then the support itself is removed. If the support has been carefully shaped and positioned there may be very little further filling or shaping necessary on the side of the support. For this reason when using a support it is generally preferable to use the support on the side of the area to be filled that is less accessible or less easy to shape. For example it would be used on the inner surface of a chip in the neck of a vase, as the inner surface would be difficult to gain access to. It would also be placed on the inner surface of a chip in the rim of a bowl, as the convex shape of the outer surface of the filling would be easier to achieve free-hand.

Holes

Holes in objects often occur at the point of impact of a blow or fall, where the body has shattered into minute fragments that cannot be replaced. They may also occur due to loss of larger fragments. Some form of support is required on one side of the hole when filling, and the procedure is much the same as for filling losses in rims. Again, the use of adhesive tape will be limited to rather small holes, and it may be necessary to add further filler to reproduce a curved surface after the first application has cured and the tape been removed. If the hole is in a very awkward place such as in the shoulder of a flask or bottle, adhesive tape may be the only form of support practical to use. Dental wax or impression compound are suitable supports for many holes, and as with edge 'bites' are positioned over a similar area that is intact to take up the shape before moving them over the hole. Again the support should be used on the side that would be more difficult to work on after filling.

Making up larger losses

Larger losses can be made up by either modelling or using moulds. Wherever possible it is preferable to use a mould as this is a more accurate way of reproducing a missing part and is also generally quicker. However, moulding depends upon the availability of a part identical to that which is missing from which to take the mould. This may be on the same object, for example a second handle on a vase with one handle missing, or on another identical object, for example when figures have been made from the same original factory moulds. These identical parts must be in a fit condition to withstand the moulding process. Modelling may be used where only a photograph is available as a guide or where the shape of the missing part can be relatively accurately assumed from interpolation. It can also be used when the identical piece is not in good enough condition to take a mould from.

Moulding techniques

The process of moulding ranges in complexity from very simple one-piece moulds, such as the supports discussed in the previous section, to intricate moulds made up of several pieces. The simple supports mentioned above are used when there is little detail and no undercut involved. Where the mould is to be taken from a more intricately modelled area with a moderate degree of undercut, simple press moulds can sometimes be taken using the silicone rubber putties. However, if the shape is highly three-dimensional with deep undercuts different materials and techniques must be used. In the past materials that set hard, such as wax and plaster of Paris, were used, the mould being formed in several pieces, but today flexible moulding materials are available that make the process simpler. These flexible materials can cope with a certain degree of undercut and thus cut down the number of pieces that the mould must be made from; liquid latex, which has the greatest degree of flexibility of the materials used, can be used to make a mould of a simple knop, for example, in a single piece. However, pieces with more intricate modelling or deeper undercuts will still require moulds of several pieces, and for these silicone rubber is generally used.

Once the mould has been made the missing pieces are reproduced by casting a suitable material in the mould. The missing piece is either cast directly onto the damaged object by positioning the mould carefully over the missing area and then casting, or it is cast separately and then joined onto the damaged object.

Press moulds using silicone rubber putties

The surface of the pattern piece from which the mould is to be taken should be carefully checked for dust, dirt and grease and cleaned if necessary. If there is any doubt that the surface will withstand the moulding process without sustaining damage, it should not be carried out.

A quantity of the silicone rubber putty sufficient to cover the area to be moulded to a depth of about 1.5 cm should be mixed up, rolled into a ball and then pressed onto the area (Figure 10.6a). If the mould is made too thin it will not hold its shape well. Care should be taken to ensure that the mould will overlap the area to be filled by at least 1 cm and sometimes it is helpful to overlap to a greater degree in order to include reference points for the positioning of the

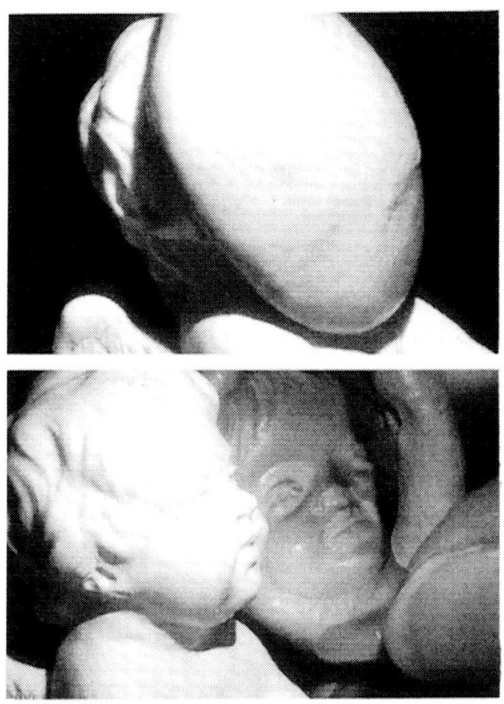

(a)

(b)

Figure 10.6 Silicone rubber putty (Copol-sil) used to take impression of face: (a) pressed into position over face; (b) peeled off, after curing, to show impression (Victoria and Albert Museum, London).

mould if the missing area is to be cast directly onto the damaged piece. After a few minutes the mould may be removed by carefully easing it off at one edge and peeling it back (Figure 10.6b).

The missing piece may be cast separately or *in situ* on the damaged object; in the latter case the mould is held in position using pressure sensitive tape.

Rubber latex moulds

Whether or not a filler or thickener is to be combined with the liquid latex in subsequent layers, the first layer of latex is applied to the pattern piece neat (Figure 10.7). It can be applied with a cotton wool swab on a stick, or with a brush that has been dipped in soft soap in order to make it easier to clean off the latex. The latex should be dabbed on, rather then painted on, to avoid pulling at the latex as it starts to set. For this reason each area should only be covered once; further thickness will be built up in subsequent layers. Care should be taken to avoid incorporating air bubbles into the latex, especially in small crevices such as between the fingers of a hand, and any that do appear should be burst with a needle. If this is not done they will spoil the surface of the mould and appear as blemishes on the cast piece which will have to be removed. This first layer is then allowed to vulcanize by evaporation of the solvent, and when cured will appear transparent and brown in colour. Curing can be speeded up by the use of gentle heat, such as the warmth from standing the object near a radiator or desk lamp or placing it in a warm oven, but a very gentle heat only should be used as overheating will cause distortion of the mould.

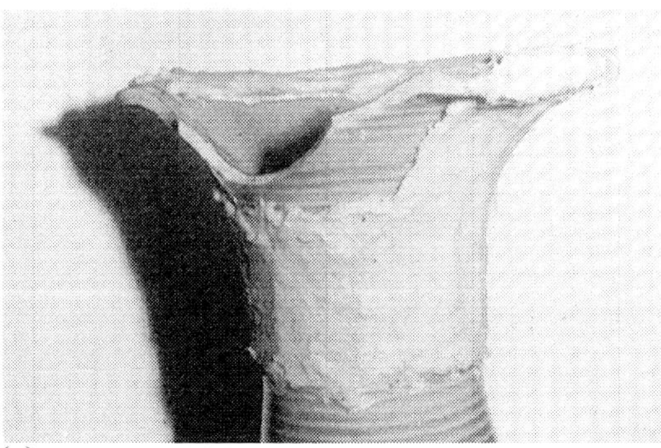

(a)

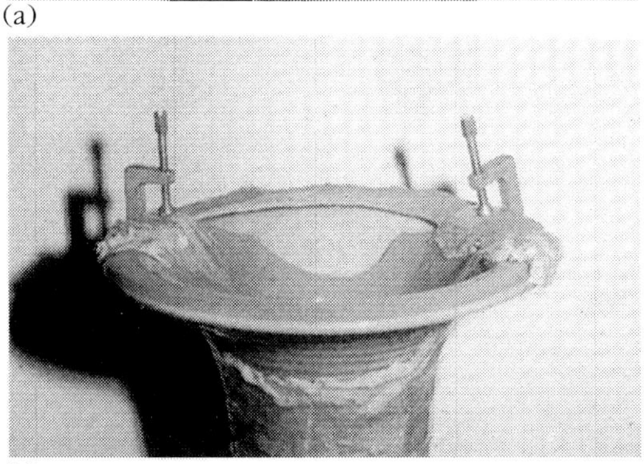

(b)

Figure 10.7 Latex mould used as a support for filling in rim of vase. (a) Latex has been applied to the intact portion of the rim. Cotton flock has been used as a thickener. (b) The mould has been repositioned over the area of loss and clamped in place with pressure sensitive tapes and G-clamps (Victoria and Albert Museum, London).

Subsequent coats are applied in the same way, allowing each coat to cure before applying the next. The number of coats will depend upon how thick a mould is required. The thicker the mould, the stronger it becomes and the less prone to distortion, but for greatest flexibility the number should be kept to a minimum. If a very small but intricate area such as a small foot or flower is being moulded, maximum flexibility will be required in order to be able to peel the mould back off the pattern piece, and little strength will be necessary as the weight of the casting material will not be enough to distort the mould. Three or four coats of latex will probably be sufficient in such a case. If, however, the piece is bigger the mould will be more liable to distortion and seven or eight coats may be necessary. When completed the latex mould should be removed from the object with care to avoid damaging delicate parts. If a long thin mould has been made, for example a mould of an arm or a leg, the outer surface of the latex should be dusted with talc and then the mould removed by rolling it back off the pattern piece.

If latex thickener is added to the latex it will allow thicker coats of latex to be applied and hence cut down the number of applications that must be made. This thickener does not significantly alter the flexibility of the latex. Where a high degree of flexibility is not essential a filler can be added to the rubber latex to make it more rigid so that it holds its shape better when cured. Cotton flock, sawdust, bandages or glass fibre matting are all used for this purpose. The first two or three coats, however, are always applied neat to give a good smooth surface to the mould. When cotton flock or sawdust are mixed with the latex, enough is added to give a paste-like consistency, and it is then laid over the coats of neat latex, using a palette knife or a wooden spatula. A layer of about 0.5–1 cm will be sufficient, depending on the size of the mould. This is then left to cure for about 24 hours until the latex has turned pale brown and translucent. If bandages or glass fibre matting are used these are first cut into small pieces and then dipped into the latex and laid on top of the initial neat layer. The bandages should be well saturated with latex and should overlap slightly. They are left to cure naturally and then a second coat with bandages is applied with the bandages in this coat aligned at right angles to those in the first coat.

An alternative to using a filler mixed in with the latex in order to make the mould more rigid is to make a mother mould using plaster of Paris. The latex mould is made using neat latex in several coats and allowed to cure completely. It is left in position on the pattern object and the outside coated with a release agent such as butcher's wax, soft soap or petroleum jelly. A layer of plaster of Paris 1–2 cm thick is then applied over the mould and allowed to harden. This layer will obviously have no flexibility and may need to be made in more pieces than the latex mould in order to be safely removable. The plaster is allowed to set and then removed from the latex and the latex mould is removed separately from the pattern. The latex mould is then placed back into the mother mould for casting.

Silicone rubber moulds

One-piece moulds

Simple one-piece moulds can be made using liquid silicone rubber, where the piece to be cast is of a suitable shape (Figure 10.8). The pattern piece is secured onto a piece of glass using a drop of wax or Plasticine and the surrounding glass is painted with a release agent. If there are any undercuts or if the base of the pattern piece, in contact with the glass, is not completely flat, Plasticine should be used to fill them. The pattern piece is then painted with a coat of silicone rubber which is left to cure for at least one hour. This is done, as with liquid latex, in order to ensure that the inner surface of the mould is smooth and free from air bubbles. Any air bubbles present are burst with a needle. A wall is then built around the piece, allowing 1–2 cm gap around it on all sides and extending 1–2 cm higher than the piece. The wall may be built using Plasticine, tin foil or children's plastic building bricks, such as Lego. The latter are useful as they can be quickly assembled and can be reused. If foil or bricks are used they should be sealed to the glass with a coil of Plasticine. Silicone rubber is then poured to fill the space between the pattern piece and the wall and to cover the piece to a depth of 1–2 cm. It should be poured slowly to avoid air being trapped, and should not be poured directly onto the pattern piece. The mould is then left to cure completely, the time varying with different types of silicone rubber, and then the walls are removed and the pattern piece is carefully eased out of the mould.

Piece-moulds

Where the undercuts do not allow a simple one-piece mould to be made it is necessary to make a piece-mould. This is often the case when, for example, moulds of handles of cups or vases are being taken. The mould may be of only two pieces or of more, depending on the shape of the piece to be cast, and the object must be carefully examined to work out how many pieces will be necessary and where it will be best to make the joins between the pieces. Sometimes it may be expedient to fill some of the undercuts with modelling putty (Plasticine) in order to reduce the number of mould pieces necessary.

Figure 10.9a–c shows the processes involved in preparing a two-piece mould. The procedures are basically the same when preparing piece-moulds of more parts. The object to be moulded is a lid and the seam between the two halves of the mould is to lie around the rim of the lid. In Figure 10.9a the lid has been placed on a sheet of non-setting modelling putty and indentations have been made around the circumference to form keys in the silicone rubber. The lid has been coated with a layer of silicone rubber with the rubber extending well beyond the edge of the lid and over the impressions made to form the keys. When forming a mould of silicone rubber, an

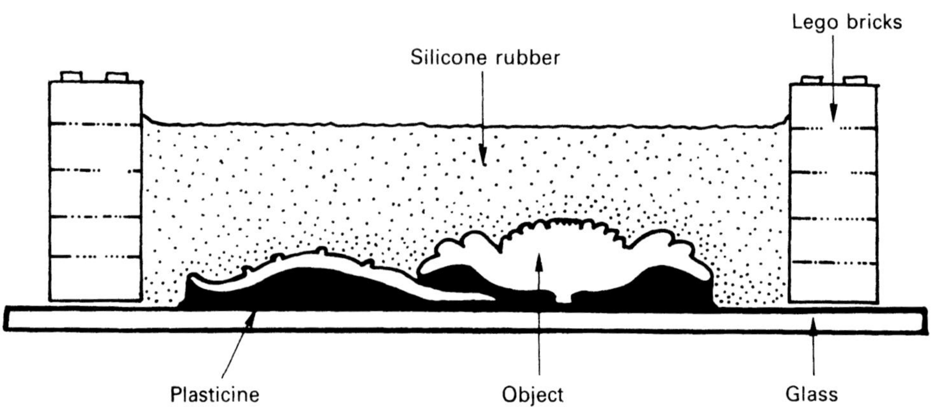

Figure 10.8 Section through one-part silicone rubber mould.

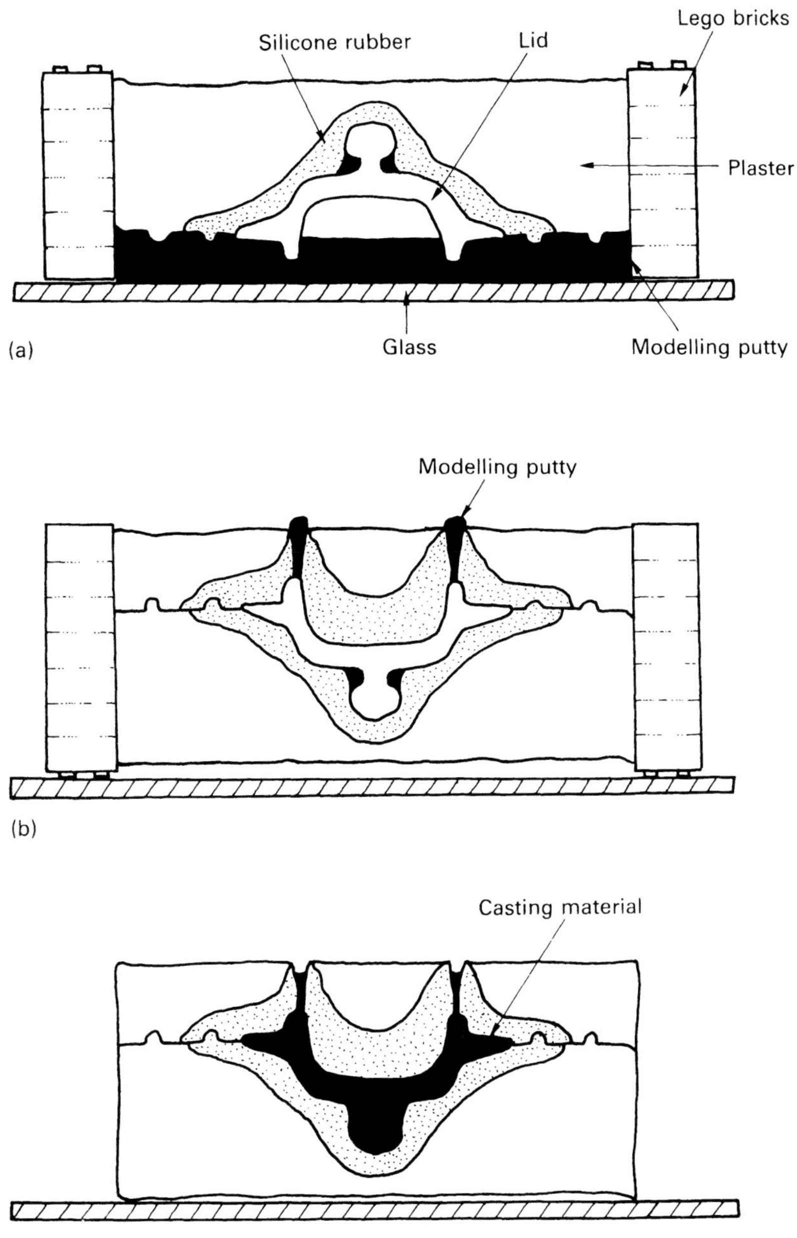

Figure 10.9 Formation of a two-part silicone rubber mould with mother mould. (a) First half of silicone rubber mould and of mother mould have been formed. (b) Second half of silicone rubber mould and of mother mould have been formed. (c) Original lid removed, mould reassembled and filled with casting material.

initial layer is painted on, any air bubbles are removed by pricking with a needle and the silicone rubber is left to set. A further coat of silicone rubber is then made using a rubber with the consistency of a paste. This is allowed to cure. A supporting mother mould may or may not be used, depending on the size and shape of the mould, and the likelihood of its warping. In Figure 10.9a a supporting mother mould, either of filled epoxy resin or of plaster of Paris, has been used. Dovetails can be cut in the edge of the silicone rubber in order to provide keys for the mother mould. A plaster of Paris or epoxy resin mother mould will require retaining walls to be built around the lid. If no mother mould is to be used, further layers of silicone rubber can be applied to give sufficient rigidity to the mould.

In Figure 10.9b the lid has been inverted and the strip of modelling putty removed from the rim. Any remnants of modelling putty have been cleaned off using solvent. Modelling putty has been attached to form runners to allow the casting material to be poured in, and air and excess casting material to escape. Releasing agent has been applied to the exposed edge of the silicone rubber and mother mould. The interior of the lid has been coated with silicone rubber and the second half of the mother mould created. Once these have cured the two halves of the mould are gently prised apart and the original lid and the modelling putty in the runners removed. Figure 10.9c shows the mould reassembled and filled with the casting material. Once this has cured the mould is removed and the excess casting material in the runners and around the knop is cut away.

Variations on this procedure can be made: for example a silicone rubber of a pouring consistency can be used throughout, in which case retaining walls must be made around the object or part to be moulded (Figure 10.10). Alternatively silicone rubber of a paste-like or 'butter-on' consistency may be used throughout, the initial layer of liquid rubber being dispensed with. In this case great care must be taken to apply the rubber without trapping any air on the surface of the original. Refinements in the way that the keys and runners are made and situated also exist and the reader is referred to Larsen (1981) for further details.

Casting techniques

In general, pieces are cast in a mould and then, after curing, the cast piece is bonded onto the object. In certain circumstances it is possible to cast a piece directly onto an object and if this is done a casting material with sufficient adhesive properties must be used. This will normally be an epoxy resin.

When the cast is being made off the object, the mould is first propped or held at a suitable angle with the air vents at the highest point. Care must be taken that if there is no protective mother mould the mould is not distorted in any way, and in some cases, for example with a small rubber latex mould, it may be easiest to suspend the mould using a pin or needle passed through the end of the mould.

In order to ensure that there are no air bubbles in the casting material before pouring, the resin should be left to stand for several minutes after mixing. If epoxy resin or polyester resin are being used for the cast a thin coat can be painted on to the inner surface of the mould first, and the mould can be stretched as this is done in order to achieve the best possible coating. This first coat can also contain colouring materials or, if required, dry pigments can be brushed

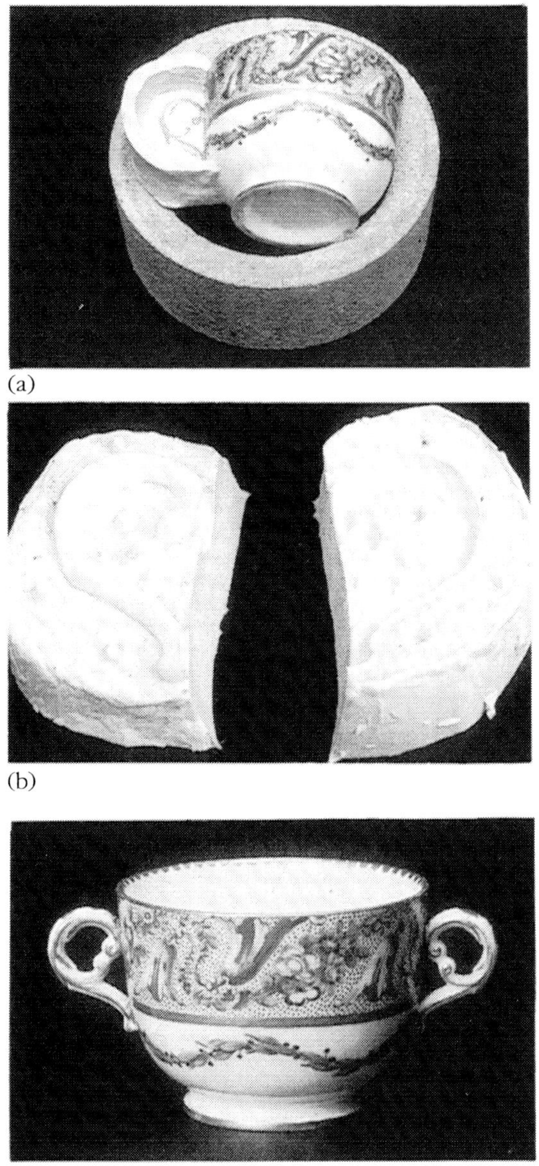

(a) (b) (c)

Figure 10.10 Formation of silicone rubber two-part mould of a cup handle, using liquid silicone rubber. (a) Cup, supported in a cork ring, ready for the first half of the mould to be poured. Plasticine retaining walls have been built around the handle. (b) Finished mould, parted, following casting of the handle. (c) Cast handle (right) attached to cup and retouched (Victoria and Albert Museum, London).

onto the surface of the mould first. If necessary the first coat of resin can be applied to the individual pieces of the mould before they are assembled. In cases of very small moulds, enough resin can be painted on in this way to fill the mould, so that when the pieces of the mould are brought together, excess casting material is squeezed out of the pour hole. A mother mould is generally necessary and the pieces are clamped tightly together until the casting material has cured.

More usually, the bulk of the casting material is poured into the assembled mould, paying special attention to introduce the resin carefully where there is fine detail, such as small fingers or toes, so that air bubbles do not form in them. Pouring is done very slowly, down one side of the aperture of a single-piece mould or through the special pour holes of a multiple-piece mould. The mould may be gently tapped at intervals throughout the pouring to help dislodge any air bubbles that may have formed. A slight excess should be poured to allow for air bubbles that may escape after pouring is finished, or alternatively the resin level should be observed during curing and topped up if necessary. After casting the filled mould may be placed in a vacuum chamber to extract air bubbles.

The cast mould should be left for adequate time for the casting material to thoroughly cure, and then the mould is peeled off or taken apart and removed. Any seam lines on the cast, or flaws due to air bubbles, can then be abraded and filled as necessary. Fillings may be made using Fine Surface Polyfilla, unless the cast is a matched resin one, in which case it can be patched with resin from the original batch that has been set aside for this purpose in a sealed container in an icebox.

Modelling

Modelling up of missing pieces can be carried out in two ways: either the piece is modelled directly in the final material; or it is modelled in a preferred modelling medium such as Plasticine or modelling wax, a mould is taken and the piece is then cast. If the modelling is being carried out in the final material, for example an epoxy putty, a combination of modelling whilst the material is still malleable and carving after it has cured is used. In either case the modelling may be done in position on the object or off the object on a board or a support such as a metal or wooden pin. The joint between the original and the modelled piece is one of the most important areas to model correctly. The profile must show a smooth join between the two with no lumps or changes of angle at the joint.

Callipers may be helpful in achieving the correct proportions when matching the modelled piece to an existing one, but allowances must be made for any surface coating that will be applied after modelling. Layers of glaze medium will soften detail and increase the dimensions of the modelled piece.

Use of internal supports

It is probably easier to attain the correct proportions and shape when working directly on the object, but care must be taken, when carving and abrading the modelled piece after it has cured, not to dislodge it by overforceful working. This is especially easy to do when working on a piece with a very small area of attachment to the object, for example a finger. Some restorers recommend modelling such pieces on a wire armature made from fuse wire or stainless steel dowelling and inserted into a hole drilled in the ceramic and bonded in place. The hole must be drilled with a diamond drill bit. There are two reasons why this method is undesirable. Firstly, it involves removing original material from the object, and secondly there is a danger of accidentally causing further damage to the object. It is preferable to build up such pieces gradually, using several layers of modelling material. Each layer is allowed to cure before adding the next, so that the final shape is achieved with very little cutting back and the danger of breaking off the modelled piece is avoided. If the piece does get broken despite these precautions, it can be bonded back in place using an appropriate adhesive.

If it is felt desirable to use an armature, this can be done by simply bonding the wire onto the broken surface of the object, using for example epoxy putty, rather than setting it into a hole drilled in the object (Figure 10.11). If the putty is applied to the broken surface and then allowed to cure to a firm consistency before inserting the wire or wires they will hold their position better. A thixotropic polyester adhesive such as General or Sebralit (USA Akemi) can also be used and has the advantage that the wire can be hand held in position whilst the adhesive sets. However, the brown colour will make it unsuitable for use in some cases. When the adhesive or putty has cured the wire or dowel should be roughly coated with soft epoxy putty to provide a better key for the next, stiffer and more bulky application of epoxy putty.

When modelling up large missing portions of earthenware vessels AJK dough, formed from poly(vinyl acetal), solvents, jute or cellulose flock and kaolin, has been used in the past. This was subsequently replaced by BJK dough, in which the poly(vinyl acetal) was replaced with poly(vinyl butyral). A lattice framework of strips of dough was formed (Figure 10.12a) and then, when this had cured, a further coating of the dough was applied on top (Figure 10.12b). However, the use of BJK dough is becoming less widespread as it has a tendency to shrink and is also costly and time consuming to

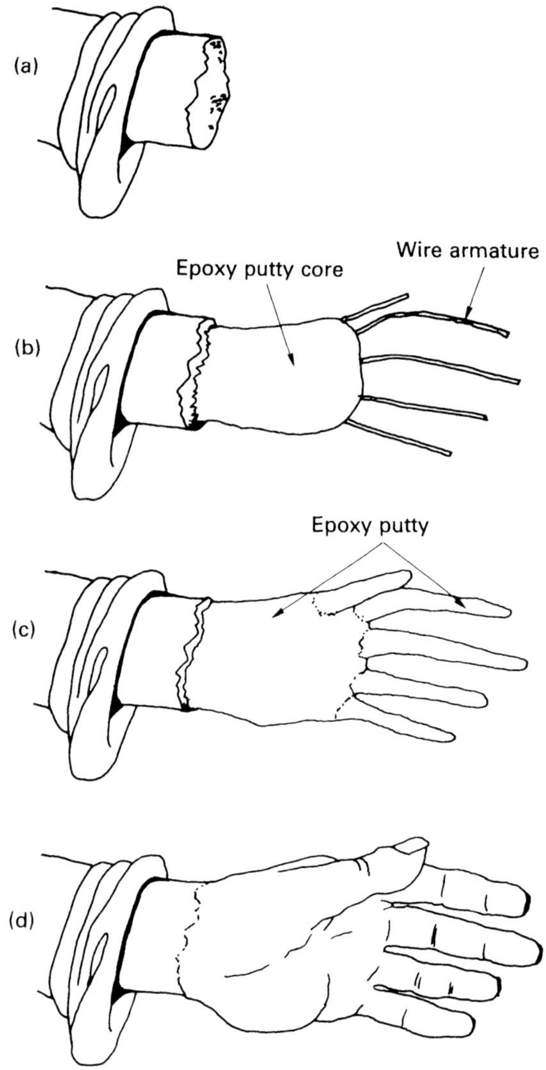

Figure 10.11 Building up a replacement hand on a wire armature. In (b) a core of epoxy putty has been pressed onto the broken wrist and wires have been inserted to form armatures on which to model the fingers. (c) The fingers and hand are gradually built up with more epoxy putty, until (d) the final dimmensions are achieved.

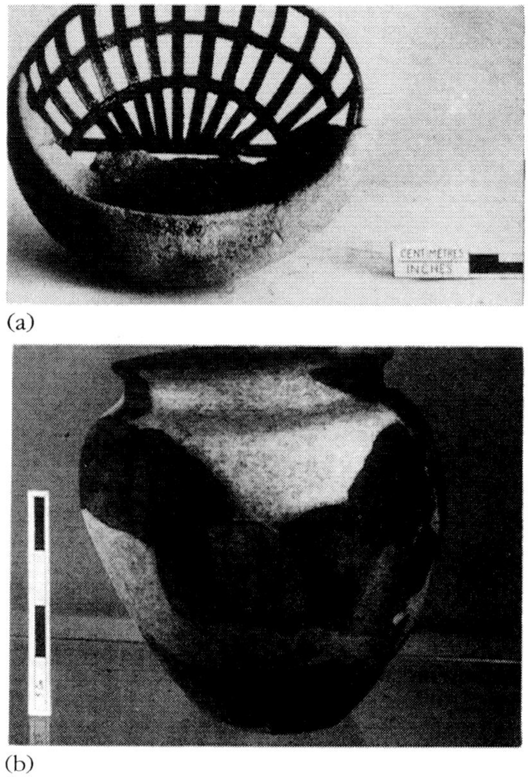

Figure 10.12 BJK dough used to fill a large loss: (a) a lattice is created using strips of BJK dough, which is then (b) used to locate the floating pieces and provide a base for further filling (Patricia Jackson).

prepare and use. Details of its preparation and use can be found in Gedye (1968). A possible replacement material for forming a latticework support is described by Brown (1989). This material, Hexcelite, is used in the medical field for supporting fractured limbs.

Even very careful building up of a piece will result in some bumps and surface imperfections that must be cut back. A very sharp scalpel can be used to remove the lumps by cutting or scraping, but more usually needle files and abrasive papers are used to abrade these away.

Reconstruction from a few remaining shards

Even when only a few fragments of an object remain it may be desirable to display them in such a way that gives some indication of the shape and dimensions of the original object of which they were a part. The ethics of such reconstructions are touched on in Chapter 5. There are various techniques that may be used but all of them require that sufficient material remains of the original from which to deduce the diameters and the profile of the object. Provided this is the case an object can be built up from a very small amount of original material.

The fragments that do remain are first bonded together where possible in order to ascertain the internal and external profiles. These can be taken using a contour gauge, or alternatively by casting strips of epoxy putty covered in plastic film against the fragments. The profiles should be taken at right angles to any throwing rings or bands of decoration. Next the necessary diameters must be established, and to do this the curve of the circumference in the relevant places is taken, again using a contour gauge or cast strips of resin. By comparing these circumferences with complete circles drawn on paper the diameters can be deduced.

There are several ways in which these various measurements may be used to fabricate a reconstruction of the objects. Mibach (1975) describes a method using polystyrene sheeting, in which circles are cut from the polystyrene to diameters taken from the sectional drawing of the object. These circles are bonded together and the steps between them filled with plaster of Paris to give the interior shape of the object. The shards are then attached to this core and the spaces between them filled with reinforcement and polyester paste with a final coating of plaster of Paris. The core is finally removed by cutting with a hot spatula or dissolving it with acetone.

A technique that is more commonly used is that of 'spinning'. The profiles and diameters are taken as above and used to cut templates of the inner and outer surfaces of the object. The templates can be cut in sheet acrylic (Perspex, or USA Plexiglas), wood or sheet metal. The internal template is mounted on the spinning machine (Figure 10.13) and used to shape a core out of Plasticine, clay or other suitable material. This is allowed to harden if necessary and is then coated with the material from which the reconstruction is to be formed. The internal surface template is replaced with the external surface template and the machine spun again to give an even layer. After this has cured the core is removed. There are various refinements and variations to this technique and the reconstruction layer can be made up of several layers of different materials in order to give the required properties. Further details can be read in Mibach (1975), Williams (1980), Barov (1988) and Elston (1990).

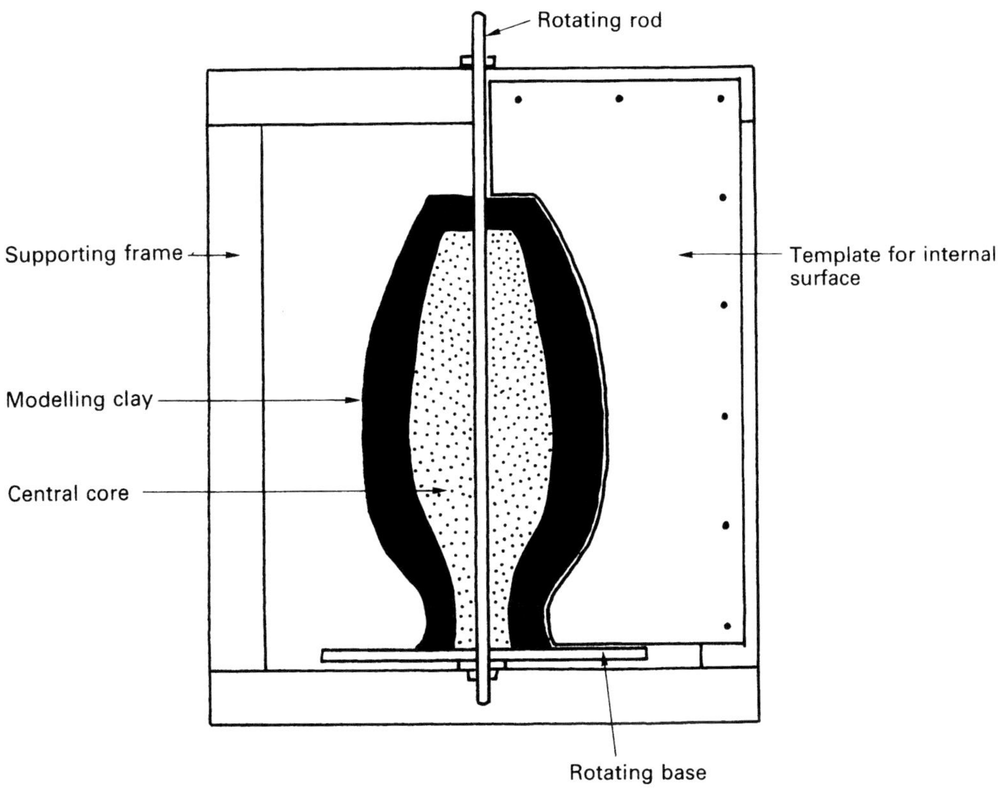

Figure 10.13 Using a spinning machine and templates to reconstruct an object. A central core of approximate dimensions is formed around a central rotating rod. This core is coated with modelling clay and then spun against the template to give an accurate reproduction of the form and dimensions of the inner surface of the object. This will then be coated with a suitable resin, the template for the inner surface replaced with the template for the outer surface, and the machine spun again.

Cutting back and polishing

The cutting back and polishing of fillings and areas of restoration is a vital part of their formation. Fillings produced using any of the materials and techniques discussed above will require some work after curing to make the joint with the original ceramic smooth or to even out minor flaws or more major irregularities. This stage is important when the restored area is subsequently to be painted with a surface coating as the surface coating will highlight any irregularities in the filler. It is also very important when the filling is a tinted epoxy filling that is to remain uncoated as the correct surface reflectance is achieved by the polishing.

The amount of working of the filling that is carried out before curing and the amount that is left until after curing will depend on the filling material chosen and the situation and type of ceramic. The materials that cure to a very hard finish, e.g. epoxy and polyester resins, are best shaped as far as possible before curing, leaving only the smoothing of minor flaws and surface irregularities to be done in the cured state. However, the working of materials that cure to a softer, more easily worked finish, such as Polyfilla, can be left until after curing.

A range of cutting and abrading techniques can be used, including the use of scalpels; rifflers and files; abrasive papers, cloths and films; and abrasive pastes. The technique chosen will depend on the filling material to be worked, on the type of ceramic in which the filling has been made and the position and accessibility of the filling. However, extreme care must be taken when using any abrasive techniques in order to avoid damaging the surface of the ceramic.

Scalpels

Scalpels can be used to cut away large quantities of excess filling material or to shave or scrape off lesser amounts. The benefits of using scalpels are that material can be cut away relatively quickly and no dust is generated. However, care must be taken when cutting away parts of a filling, especially one that is not very well adhered to the ceramic, to avoid lifting out more than intended. This is easily done, for example when removing excess epoxy resin filling from along a joint. Unless the excess is shaved off in very fine layers, and this requires a very sharp scalpel, lifting forces can unintentionally be applied to the filling which will pull it out from the joint. A slight slip with a scalpel can also result in removal of more material than intended. Great care must be taken not to damage soft ceramic bodies, decoration and glazes.

Rifflers and files

Rifflers and files are available in a range of shapes, sizes and grades. The coarser ones can, like scalpels, be used to remove relatively large amounts of filler rapidly, but without the danger of lifting the filling and without such a risk of removing more than intended. Care must still be taken to avoid damaging the surrounding ceramic, and on no account should a file or riffler be allowed to come into contact with any part of any type of ceramic during its use to abrade fillings.

Abrasive papers, films and cloths

An enormous range of abrasive papers is available, produced using different types and grades of abrasive material bound to a paper backing. The abrasives on the types most commonly used in ceramics restoration are glass, silicon carbide, and aluminium oxide. For shaping fillings, silicone carbide papers in a range of grits are probably the most useful. Flexible films and cloths coated with aluminium oxide are also available and these tend to be of very fine grades, and are used for final polishing of tinted fillings and paint layers rather than shaping fillings.

Papers and films should be cut into small squares (1–2 cm square) or strips (1–2 cm wide) for use. The square or strip is held between the thumb and forefinger and used in such a way that only a very small area of one corner of the paper or film comes into contact with the surface of the filling, with pressure being applied by the very tip of the forefinger. A corner produced by folding a paper is most suitable as it has a rounded edge. The paper or film can be moved in strokes or with a circular action, which is more common when carrying out final polishing. When working on the edge of a filling, at its joint with the ceramic, the paper or film should be moved in strokes, placing it down on the filling and moving out over the edge towards the ceramic. Great care should be taken not to continue the abrasive action onto the ceramic surface, as even with most of the finest abrasives used on the harder ceramics damage can occur. This type of damage is one of the commonest forms of damage caused by careless or ill-informed working. It is irreparable and should be guarded against at all cost.

Abrasive pastes

These are used for final polishing of tinted resin fillings or of paint layers. There are a variety of proprietary pastes available and they can be used applied with cotton wool, white tissue or cloth. They may also be applied using a polishing bit on a drill, although this is more difficult to control. As with all polishing actions, static charges produced at the surface are inclined to attract dust.

11

Retouching: the theory

Introduction

If the term 'conservation' is taken to mean the slowing down or prevention of deterioration of an object, then cleaning, bonding and building up missing parts can all be regarded as 'conservation' procedures. For example, cleaning may remove damaging salts or grease that could spread or prevent other procedures being carried out; bonding prevents loss of pieces and damage to the break edges; consolidation and building up of missing parts restore structural strength to the object. The process of retouching, however, cannot truly be considered a conservation technique. Except in so far as it seals the filling material (something that can be done separately anyway), retouching does not prevent or slow down any deterioration of the object. What it can do, however, is allow the object to be appreciated for its aesthetic qualities, when otherwise it might be disfigured by unsightly damage. It restores aesthetic value to the object. It is a 'restoration' technique.

The aim of retouching is to disguise fillings that have been made in a damaged object and allow them to blend in, to a greater or lesser degree, with the surrounding ceramic. In doing so, the retouching should be limited as far as possible to the surface of the filling and should not be allowed to extend over its edges more than is necessary in order to make it blend into the surrounding, undamaged surface. Retouching should not be used to hide stains and dirt that have not been removed by cleaning or to cover poorly executed fillings; indeed it is more likely to highlight the latter.

The surface of most ceramic artifacts is much more three-dimensional than most casual observers would suppose. The body may be coarse or smooth, matt or burnished to a gloss; it may be dark and optically dense, or it may even have a certain degree of translucency. There may be decoration painted onto or incised into its surface. Any glaze may be relatively thick and may be transparent, semi-transparent or opaque. It may be glossy or matt and be of a smooth or rough texture. If it is to any degree transparent the underlying body will show through. There may be stains within the glaze, and there may be enamel decoration or gilding on the surface of the glaze. It may be no easy task to replicate the appearance that all these individual elements combine to present.

Until recently the approach that was widely taken to restoration of missing material was to make fillings using opaque white material and to retouch over the top with a medium coloured with pigments. The retouching may have been intended simply to make the filling less distracting, without totally disguising it, or indeed to make it as 'invisible' as possible. As discussed in the introduction to the previous chapter, this can be successful in some circumstances but less so in others. There is a danger when applying retouching medium that in an attempt to fade out the edges of the retouching so that they blend unnoticeably into the surrounding surface, the retouching medium is spread unnecessarily far over the undamaged ceramic surface. This is especially likely to happen when retouching an opaque filling in a ceramic that is to some degree translucent. The conservator may be tempted to spread the retouching medium further and further to try to make the shadowing around its edges less noticeable, or even to bring the retouching up to a convenient cut-off point, such as the edge of a pattern or the point of attachment of a handle or spout, where the edge will not be so noticeable. In these circumstances a filling which is matched in colour and translucency to the ceramic (see Chapter 10) is likely to be visually more successful and ethically more satisfactory: there is no need for any overlap at all.

Despite the recent development of techniques for creating matched fillings, retouching remains a skill that is vitally important to the ceramics restorer. Even when matched fillings are used, it may be necessary to carry out some retouching in order to replicate overglaze enamels or to shade or modify the filling in some way. There are advantages to the method of having a layer of retouching over an opaque filling. When the retouching medium discolours, as most of them will in time, it can be easily removed and replaced. Replacing a discoloured filling (and most of the materials used for tinted fillings will also discolour in time) is generally a much bigger job. When reversing an unmatched filling it is easier to distinguish filling material from original material.

This chapter will describe the retouching techniques used to cover opaque fillings, to make them less obtrusive or to match them to the surrounding ceramic surface, as well as those used to replicate the various decorative techniques.

Invisible?

The conservator may not necessarily aim to make the retouched area visually indiscernible from the original, or as it is termed 'invisible', but may simply aim to make it less distracting to the observer viewing the object as a whole. Several factors may govern the approach that is taken.

Firstly, in some collections it may be policy to make areas of restoration obvious. The restored area may simply be toned to a colour sympathetic with the general background colour of the object (Figures 5.10, 5.11, and 5.12) with no attempt made to fill in any pattern or shading. When this is done the tone is generally kept lighter rather than darker than the background colour of the object in order to avoid the retouched areas appearing as lacunae. Alternatively, any pattern may also be filled in, but painted a tone lighter than the original in order to make the restoration clearly distinguishable (Elston, 1990). Even when more closely matched, detailed inpainting is carried out, a widely held rule is that the retouched areas should be unobtrusive when viewed from the sort of distance that is usual when an object is on display in a showcase, but easily discernible on closer inspection. This is referred to as the 6 inch/6 foot rule.

Secondly, in some cases there may not be sufficient evidence of the original appearance of the object on which to base an invisible restoration. For example a restored area in a bowl decorated with a random pattern may simply be retouched to match the background colour and gloss, whereas a similar restoration in a bowl decorated with a regular pattern, the missing parts of which could be interpolated, could be retouched to appear 'invisible'. The type of evidence that is generally held to be acceptable as a basis for detailed restoration is interpolation of a regular pattern, photographs of the object before damage, or evidence from other objects in a set, e.g. plates in a dinner service printed with the same design.

Thirdly, achieving an 'invisible' retouch can be very time consuming, and in situations where conservators' time is limited and objects with acute conservation problems are in need of treatment, it may be felt that spending the time necessary to achieve an invisible retouch is not justifiable. The amount of money the owner is prepared to spend on the restoration may limit the amount of time that can be spent on the retouching.

Further discussion of the ethics of restoration is made in Chapter 5.

Materials

The materials that are used for retouching can be divided into three groups: the dyes or pigments that are used to match the colour of the ceramic; the medium which is used to carry the colourants, impart gloss, and give an appearance of depth to the 'glaze'; and finally various additives that are used to adjust the surface texture or finish, such as matting agents. Paints, where the pigments are already combined with a medium, are sometimes used for retouching ceramics. Those based on acrylic emulsions are commonly used for retouching earthenwares. The benefit of using a clear medium and pigments is that a chosen intensity and density of colour can be achieved.

Colourants

Basically all colouring materials can be divided into either dyes or pigments. Dyes or pigments may be used in their pure form to tint the retouching medium or they may be used ready combined in a medium. For example pigments may be added in the form of oil paints. The important point is that if pigments or dyes, ready combined with a medium, are to be used as colourants, it must be established that this medium is compatible with the retouching medium.

Pigments

The benefit of using pure pigments is that there is an enormous range available. Provided care is taken to select only those pigments that are shown to be light fast they can be stored indefinitely and, owing to the extremely small quantities in which they are used, are an economical choice despite the initial expense of purchasing a wide range. Artist's quality pigments should always be selected, being finer ground and of more reliable light fastness, and they should be stored in sealed jars to prevent contamination with dust and atmospheric particles.

Pigments vary in their hardness, the fineness to which they are ground, and the readiness with which they will disperse in a retouching medium. Some can merely be stirred into a spot of retouching medium on a palette or tile whilst others must be thoroughly ground into the medium using a spatula. If this is not done, coarse lumps will remain which will spoil the smooth surface of the retouching, and if the surface is rubbed down with abrasive film they will show up as streaks or spots of colour. Some pigments have a tendency to flocculate in the retouching medium, especially if too much thinners has been added. Ultramarine is one such pigment and a very commonly used one. The problem only manifests itself when the paint mixture is lying in thick spots or pools. When using these pigments they should be ground well into the retouching medium and the mixture applied in thin films only.

Although there is a very wide range of pigments that may be used with most of the retouching media mentioned below, some pigments may react with one or other of the media and discoloration of the mixture will result either immediately or after a period of time. Work on compatibility of pigments and media has been carried out (Tennent, 1982) and recommendations made of safe ranges of pigments for certain media. Such work suggests that the light fastness of the whole system to be used, the colourant together with the medium and any additives, should be considered rather than that of the colourant or medium alone (Tennent and Townsend, 1984b; Bradley, 1990b).

Most conservators find that they have particular 'favourites' among the pigments and most colours can be mixed in very different ways. However the following range of pigments is a good basic one that should be sufficient for most colour matching:

titanium white, ivory black
burnt sienna, light red, alizarin crimson, cadmium red
yellow ochre, chrome yellow, lemon yellow, raw sienna
French ultramarine blue, cobalt blue, Prussian blue
viridian green, terre-verte,
cobalt violet
burnt umber, raw umber.

Pigment dispersions

The benefit of using these over dry ground pigments is that the pigment, being already dispersed, will disperse in the retouching medium more readily and without further grinding. However, the medium used in the dispersion may not be compatible with the retouching medium and tests must be made. The dispersion medium may also cause discoloration of the mixture. The most frequently used dispersions are oil paints which are used by many restorers to tint a variety of media including polyurethane-based lacquers (e.g. Torlife) and urea-formaldehyde-based lacquers (e.g. Rustins Plastic Coating). Oil paints are essentially ground pigments mixed with oil and a filler. However, the oil is not compatible with all the media used for retouching and in these cases the paints will not mix in well and may cause discoloration. Before mixing into the retouching medium it is advisable to remove as much oil as possible from the paints. This is done by squeezing a small quantity out onto acid-free blotting paper several hours before use. Pigments dispersed in dioctylphthalate (DOP) can also be used with several retouching media (Tennent, 1982) but are more difficult to obtain.

Barov (1988) describes the use of inks to replicate the decoration on a Greek vase. These were chosen because of the density of colour they gave and their fluidity. Water-based ink was used which allowed for corrections and it was sealed using an acrylic emulsion.

Dyes

Unlike pigments, dyes become dissolved in the polymer medium and produce transparent colours. There are ranges of dyes available commercially for tinting epoxy resins and polyester resins but unfortunately there are a limited number of dyes available that are sufficiently light stable for use in retouching ceramics.

Retouching media

There are several requirements of a material that will make it a good retouching medium for use in ceramics conservation, and there is no one material in use at present that meets all of them totally satisfactorily. The materials in use today are, however, much more satisfactory than most of those discussed in Chapter 5, and as continuous research and development are carried out, it is worth testing new materials as they become available. The major criteria that should be fulfilled are as follows.

It should not damage or affect the ceramic in any way and and should be completely reversible without damaging the ceramic

In theory the retouching medium should not come into contact with the ceramic, but should only coat the surface of the filling. However, in practice there is often some minimal overlap in order to soften the edge of the restoration.

Overlap of medium onto the surface of the porcelain is likely to be unacceptable, and where this is permissible future removal of the paint is less likely to be a problem than in the case of archaeological wares.

It should cure at room temperature
The reason for this is that even the low heats (100°C) that stoving enamels require may be dangerous to some ceramics (Horlock-Stringer, 1991). This may seem anomalous with the fact that they have been fired to much higher temperatures during manufacture. However, absorption of moisture into the body and general deterioration of the structure do occur in certain circumstances (see Chapter 2) and can mean that damage including cracking of the glaze and loss of enamel can occur at even these low temperatures. Heating may also cause any subsequent thermoluminescence tests to be invalid.

It should adhere well to the underlying filling
Some materials, such as acrylic emulsions, have a tendency to peel off the surface of the filling, especially when they are abraded. The adhesion of the surface coating will obviously depend on the nature of the filling material as well as the properties of the surface coating itself.

It should not react with the filling material
Bradley and Green (1987) cite the example of the ureaformaldehyde-based lacquer Rustins Plastic Coating discolouring as a consequence of a reaction with a component of the filling material Milliput.

It should be water white and have good resistance to ageing
A very slight coloration in the fresh resin is usually acceptable as this will not generally be evident in the very thin films in which a surface coating is applied. However, it is desirable that the resin will not discolour over a period of time, either through exposure to ultraviolet radiation or owing to chemical processes that occur in the dark.

It should be capable of carrying pigments without affecting their colourant properties
Most of the pigments used in ceramics conservation are inorganic and generally remain unaffected by most media used for retouching (Tennent, 1982). However, Williams (1983) points out that retouching media with an acid component, such as the urea-formaldehyde-based lacquers Rustins Plastic Coating and China Glaze, will react with ultramarine pigments, causing hydrogen sulphide to be given off. Despite this fact, ultramarine pigments are used with reasonable success with such media.

It should be applicable by brush or airbrush and coat the ceramic surface evenly
If the resin cures too quickly it will clog the brush or airbrush and will not flow evenly onto the surface; nor will it settle into a smooth coating. Its behaviour in these respects depends not only upon the formulation of the resin itself but upon the solvent it is used with. Flow promoters can be used with various resins. Navarro (1990) suggests the use of two flow promoters to allow a low-viscosity epoxy resin to be used as a retouching medium.

It should cure to give a hard gloss finish that can be abraded and polished
Most applications of retouching medium will require some smoothing with abrasives to remove brush strokes and other irregularities. These may then require polishing back up to a high gloss. The hardness of a medium may be affected by additions of solvent. Should a matt finish be required, this can be achieved by the addition of matting agents to the retouching medium.

Once cured it should be undisturbed by subsequent applications of uncured medium
It is very rare that a single coat of retouching medium will achieve the match of colour and texture that is required. Several coats are normally necessary and any painted decoration and overglaze enamels will generally be applied as separate coats. Most solvent curing systems are therefore difficult to use as media for retouching fillings in ceramics, as the solvent content of a subsequent coat will redissolve and disturb an underlying one.

It should not pose a health hazard to the user
Owing to the ways in which retouching is carried out, that is at close range, over prolonged periods of time and often by means of an airbrush which projects a fine dispersion of the resin and solvent into the air, attention must be paid to the toxicity of materials used. It is impractical to expect a conservator to carry out intricate retouching in a fume cupboard or wearing an air-fed helmet and consequently toxic materials with low TLVs (see Chapter 13) cannot be used. Local extraction or the use of respirators with appropriate cartridges can be useful and are important when using an airbrush to spray media dissolved in toxic solvents.

Unfortunately it seems at present that there is no resin available that fulfils all of these criteria. There are resins in use, mainly those based on polyurethane or urea formaldehyde, that fulfil all the criteria except that of being colour fast. There are others commonly used, amongst them several acrylic emulsions and resins, and vinyl paints, that are colour fast but which present more difficulties in application (Barov, 1988; Elston, 1990). Research continues to be carried out into the development of surface coatings, but at present there is no perfect retouching medium available. A compromise must therefore be made and a medium chosen with the requirements of the particular job in hand in mind. For example, shellac is still commonly used as a retouching medium for fillings in ancient Egyptian, Greek and Roman wares

(Figure 11.1). In such situations the lack of water whiteness is not a problem, and the lack of ready reversibility is compensated for by keeping the retouching strictly to the surface of the filling. It is quick drying and the surface reflectance is generally sympathetic with that of the wares, minor adjustments being made using abrasive papers, cloths and creams. The solvent used is industrial methylated spirits, which has the benefit of having a relatively high TLV. In contrast, the fillings in the early British food vessel in Figure 11.2 were retouched using Cryla Colour acrylic paints. These have no translucency and the very flat appearance they give was more suited to the object. On the other hand a medium such as Rustins Plastic Coating is more generally used for porcelains where the water whiteness and high gloss is important.

Matting Agents

Some retouching media are available in a matt finish, but on the whole a matt finish is achieved by the addition of a matting agent to a gloss medium. In this way the finish can be adjusted to have the precise degree of reflectance required. Fumed silica is commonly used. There are various types available and they differ in the way in which they alter the appearance and behaviour of the retouching medium. They affect not only the reflectance but also the transparency and colour of the resin and its viscosity and hence ease of application. Elston (1990) carried out tests to investigate the effect of the addition of a silica matting agent on the bonding strength of an acrylic paint. She concluded that additions up to 40% of matting agent had no appreciable effect on the bond strength of the paint.

Polishes

Many of the hard curing retouching media such as the polyurethanes, ureaformaldehydes, and acrylic solvent systems can be given a higher degree of gloss by polishing with fine abrasives. This can be done using various different paste or liquid polishes provided they do not contain materials that could be absorbed by the ceramic and cause staining. Dry abrasives such

(a)

(b)

Figure 11.1 Restoration of Greek amphora dating from 500 BC. (a) Losses in amphora filled with plaster of Paris. (b) Plaster of Paris has been sealed and retouched using shellac with the addition of dry pigments and matting agent. The final surface appearance was achieved by polishing with Solvol Autosol (British Museum, London).

(a)

(b)

Figure 11.2 Middle Bronze Age food vessel from Goodmanham Barrow. (a) Losses filled with plaster of Paris. (b) Plaster of Paris has been sealed with shellac and then retouched using Cryla Colour acrylic paints (British Museum, London).

as Ultrafine polishing cloth, Micro-mesh cushioned abrasive cloth or the finest grades of aluminium oxide film can also be used, as can glass fibre brushes. Microcrystalline wax can also heighten gloss and obliterate minor scratches. Barov (1988) writes of achieving a desired finish for restorations in a Greek vase by the use of an application of microcrystalline wax over a vinyl paint which was then burnished with an agate burnisher.

Colour matching

When considering the topic of colour matching it is important to appreciate the way in which colour is perceived by people. Colour depends on four things: the quality of light which strikes the perceived surface; the way in which that surface absorbs and reflects this incident light; the way in which the reflected light excites the light receptors in the eye; and lastly the way in which the brain interprets the signals from the eye. Obviously the restorer only has control over the first two factors but it is important to be aware of the second two. People's powers of colour discrimination vary widely and anyone who has any doubts about their own abilities is advised to have their colour vision tested before embarking on a career in conservation. In some training establishments performance on such tests may be taken into consideration during selection procedures (Buys and Murrel, 1990).

Varying the spectral quality of the light that strikes the surface will vary the spectrum of light reflected to the eye. One might feel that this is not an issue as far as colour matching is concerned as long as the same light is striking the two surfaces to be matched. However, it is an important factor owing to the phenomenon of metamerism, which allows two different mixtures of light of different wavelengths to be perceived by the brain as matching colours when viewed under certain lighting conditions, but not under others (Staniforth, 1985). This phenomenon becomes very obvious if, for example, a retouch is carried out in daylight conditions and the object then exhibited under fluorescent strip lighting. Blues, in particular, are prone to this effect and consequently all retouching should ideally be carried out under the same lighting conditions as those pertaining in the display area. This is not always possible and the display conditions may be changed in the future. An alternative is for the restorer to decide on a reasonable standard of lighting and to carry out retouching under these conditions. Lighting is discussed further in Chapter 13.

The ways in which the eye and brain can play 'tricks' with colour are well documented: it is very easy to make assumptions about colour (Gregory, 1979). It is important therefore to observe an object to be retouched very carefully in order to appreciate the subtleties of its colour. No 'white' plate can ever be matched purely with a white pigment, and instances when any other single colour from the restorer's palette can be used to reproduce ceramic decoration are very rare. Familiarity with the ways in which colours relate on a colour wheel can help with colour matching, as can the concept of 'warm' and 'cool' colours (Graham, 1966; Padgham and Saunders, 1975; Varley, 1980). The use of instruments to measure colour has been investigated (Tennent, in press) but is not generally practical.

Method of application

Hand-held paintbrush

Skill with use of a hand held paintbrush is essential even if much of the retouching is carried out using an airbrush. Although the type of blurred effect that is found on underglaze painted objects can be very successfully reproduced using an airbrush, much painted decoration is best reproduced using a hand-held paintbrush. Many restorers use only hand-held paintbrushes for all their retouching, even for reproducing a background glaze, finding it easier to control precisely where the retouching medium is applied.

Best quality sable, or sable and synthetic mixture, brushes should be used for all retouching. These, if properly looked after, will not shed hairs, and have good strength and spring to the bristles. Brushes made from most synthetic materials are not appropriate as they are affected by the retouching media and solvents and become misshapen. Retouching media are denser and more viscous than water colour paints and many restorers find that brushes with shorter bristles, such as those used by miniaturists, give more control than a standard water colour sable brush. However, Chinese brushes can be useful for reproducing the paint strokes used in the decoration of some oriental wares. For applying background coats large-sized brushes may be used – even a 7 or 8 brush for very large areas, although a 2, 3 or 4 is more generally used. For reproducing very fine decoration some restorers use the smallest-sized brushes (0 or 00 size) but these hold very little retouching medium and dry quickly and hence a slightly larger brush (no. 1 size) with a good, fine tip may be preferable.

The restorer must work quickly when applying retouching media with a hand-held paintbrush, or the medium will start to cure and clog the brush. For this reason the pigments must be ground in rapidly and the colour matched without delay. When using two-part media, a freshly mixed batch should always be used as this will give the greatest working time. Some restorers use a separate brush, sound but of lesser quality, for preparing the mixture, and keep the best quality brushes solely for applying the medium to the object. There is a temptation to keep adding solvent to maintain the workability of the medium; however, this must be avoided or the strength and gloss of the cured medium will be adversely affected.

The difficulty when retouching using a hand-held paintbrush is to achieve a smooth finish without unwanted brush marks. This is especially hard to do when retouching large plain areas. The retouching medium must be applied using smooth even strokes that slightly overlap. Correct loading of the brush is important: too much paint will cause heavy lines or blobs of paint, whilst insufficient paint will result in a patchy, 'dry' looking coverage. The paint should not be reworked once applied. When the first coat of paint has cured it should be very lightly abraded to smooth out any irregularities before applying the next coat. The way in which the layers are built up to achieve an integrated retouch is described in the next section. When retouching painted decoration it may actually be desirable to achieve the appearance of a brush stroke. The size of the brush used and the direction of the stroke will be important in achieving the correct effect.

If the application of the paint is not successful for any reason there are two possible courses of action open. The first is to try to wipe off as much as possible of the paint, using solvent, and the second is to leave the application to cure and then remove as much as necessary using abrasive paper. The latter method is more time consuming, but safer, as there is not the danger of disturbing any underlying, or surrounding paint.

Immediately after use all brushes should be cleaned well in solvent, making certain that the paint has been completely removed from the stock of the brush. Brushes should not be left to stand in solvent unless a brush holder is used to hold the tip off the bottom of the container, otherwise the tip will become permanently bent. Ideally brushes should be kept stored in a covered box or in a jar protected by plastic hair protectors. Brushes that are not kept properly clean will cause problems by shedding particles of cured retouching medium or dust etc. during use.

Airbrushes

Airbrushes, when used carefully, provide the ideal way of coating large surface areas very evenly and relatively quickly. They also can be useful for painting patterns, especially where a blurred appearance is required, and can be invaluable for retouching awkwardly shaped areas, such as handles and knops, where it is difficult to smooth down a hand retouch. The use of an airbrush makes it much easier to merge the edge of the retouched area into the surrounding surface so that the line between the two is unnoticeable. However, one of their biggest drawbacks is that in doing so it is all too easy to spread the retouching medium over a much wider area than necessary. Their use for retouching areas of restoration in objects where any overlap of the paint medium onto the original ceramic surface is unacceptable is obviously limited. An airbrush requires a supply of compressed air and must only be used to spray the type of hazardous substances used for retouching ceramics where there is suitable ventilation (see Chapter 13).

There is a large number of different types of small airbrush available, mainly developed for use by commercial artists spraying low-viscosity inks. The types of material sprayed by ceramics restorers are much more viscous, may contain particles of pigment or matting agent, and are not easy to clean out of the brush thoroughly. For these reasons airbrushes are inclined to clog when used in ceramics restoration and great care must be exercised in their maintenance.

The basic principles of the functioning of an airbrush are that a stream of compressed air or other gas is forced through the brush and draws with it paint from a reservoir. As it is forced out through the nozzle the speed is such that the paint atomizes and forms a fine spray. The amount of paint that mixes with the compressed air is controlled by the needle which fits into a fine nozzle. The nature of the spray that is produced is varied also by the air pressure and the flow of air. The precise mechanisms for allowing these adjustments vary from airbrush to airbrush, but the choice of airbrush is in many cases a matter for personal preference and it is worth the ceramics restorer's time to try out several models before settling on a particular one to use. Further details of airbrush design can be found in Williams (1983) and Dell (1986).

The compressed air supply may either be produced by a compressor or be taken from an aerosol can, in which case it is more frequently freon or butane rather than air. A canned supply can be useful for working on location out of the studio but generally has the drawback that the pressure is not controllable and will gradually diminish as the can is used. More sophisticated cans can be fitted with a regulator to maintain a constant pressure.

For general use a compressor is preferable. Many different types and sizes are available and a model must be chosen with the following factors in mind: the number of airbrushes to be run off the compressor at any one time; the pressure required; the length of time for which the compressor will be operated; noise; bulk; mode of operation. The most suitable types incorporate a storage tank which eliminates any unevenness in the output. A regulator to adjust the pressure output and a moisture trap are both essential.

Achieving an even, controlled coat of paint with an airbrush requires considerable practice. As mentioned previously it is only too easy to overspray and cover an unnecessarily large area of the original ceramic surface as well as the filling that is to be concealed. Table 11.1 outlines the causes of some of the problems encountered during spraying, but in general terms the desired effect is achieved by the precise control of the following variables.

Air pressure
Adjusted by: regulator on the compressor, usual range 15–60 psi.
Effect: increasing the air pressure increases the amount of air whilst the amount of paint taken up remains the same. If the air pressure is too high 'starfish' will appear; if it is too low spitting will occur.

Volume of air
Adjusted by: pressing button or lever on airbrush.
Effect: increasing the volume of air also increases the amount of paint drawn out of the reservoir. If the volume is too high pooling of the paint will occur; if it is too low a hazy, diffused spray will result.

Flow of paint
Adjusted by: positioning of needle. Whether or not this can be done during operation or has to be pre-set will be determined by the type of airbrush.
Effect: increases paint flow without increasing volume of air. A dry, spotty effect results if the flow is too low; if it is too high the paint will run and flood.

Viscosity of paint
Adjusted by: adding appropriate thinners to the paint. Paint should always be used freshly mixed.
Effect: too thin a paint mixture results in running and pooling; too thick a mixture will result in splattering of the paint and blocking of the nozzle.

Distance of the nozzle from the ceramic surface
Adjusted by: moving closer or further away.
Effect: moving the nozzle further away from the surface results in a broader, more diffuse spray, whilst moving it closer will give a more defined, narrower line. The flow of paint and air must be adjusted in accordance with the distance of the nozzle from the surface to avoid pooling and running when spraying close.

Movement of brush
Adjusted by: not only is the speed of the movement important but the type of movement also. The movement should come from the whole arm and not from the wrist in order to get a smooth, steady spray.
Effect: failure to move the brush continuously will result in blobs and pooling. Erratic movements will result in uneven spray. The spray should be started and stopped off the ceramic surface and not over the area to be sprayed. The speed of movement necessary to prevent pooling will depend on the air pressure used.

Cleaning

Proper cleaning and maintenance of an airbrush is vital for its good functioning. Many of the problems listed above are caused by poor cleaning, which is especially important when spraying the type of media used for retouching ceramics. Basic cleaning should be carried out every time there is a pause in spraying even for just a few minutes, and more thorough cleaning at the end of a spraying session is essential.

For short breaks in spraying the colour cup should be removed if the model allows this and replaced with a cup containing solvent. The solvent should be sprayed through the pen until the spray is completely clear, with the position of the needle being altered several times during the process. Where the model

Table 11.1 Spraying faults

Problem	*Possible causes*
Lack of air flow	Compressor malfunctioning
	Blocked or damaged air feed
	Damaged air valve
	Damaged nozzle washer or spray head washer
Lack of paint flow	Dried paint or other blockage in nozzle or other area of paint flow
	Needle stuck in nozzle
	Loose needle locking nut
	Paint too viscous
Bubbles in reservoir	Loose nozzle cap
	Damaged nozzle
	Nozzle washer damaged, possibly by over-tightening
Paint leaking from nozzle	Loose nozzle cap
Needle not returning after being pulled back	Loose locking nut
	Dirty needle
Uneven spray	Nozzle dirty
	Nozzle washer damaged
Spray coming out at an angle	Bent needle
	Split nozzle
Spattering	Air pressure too low
	Impurities in paint
	Pigment insufficiently ground
	Paint too viscous
	Damaged nozzle or needle
	Moisture in air supply
	Air valve clogged
Paint running	Nozzle too close to surface
	Paint flow too high
	Paint too thin
	Airbrush moved too slowly
Starfish	Air pressure too high
Paint surface textured	Insufficient thinners
Hazy edge to spray	Brush held at incorrect angle to surface
	Brush held too far from surface
	Pressure too high

has a fixed cup the remaining paint must be tipped out or the needle opened to its widest setting and the paint sprayed out. The cup is then flushed through with solvent.

For longer breaks, more thorough flushing is advised, followed by removal and cleaning of the needle and of the spray head. Great care must be exercised when cleaning both of these parts in order to avoid damage. The needle is very easily bent during removal and cleaning and the nozzle of the spray head can be easily split. Gentle cleaning with solvent and a paintbrush or twist of tissue will avoid damage and the spray head assembly can be stored soaking in the appropriate solvent. When cleaning more than one airbrush at a time, care should be taken not to mix component parts even of brushes of the same model as they are very finely matched during manufacture and replacement.

If paint has been allowed to harden in the brush more drastic stripping down and cleaning is necessary. In some instances this can be carried out by the user but most manufacturers would advise returning the brush for professional cleaning and servicing.

Some models require regular oiling.

Rubbing down and polishing

Rubbing down is a very important part of the retouching process and also requires skill. Most applications of retouching medium will require a certain amount of smoothing down to remove unevenness caused by brush strokes or imperfect spraying. Final coats may require polishing to produce the desired degree of gloss. A range of abrasive papers is used as discussed in the section on abrading fillings in Chapter 10. These are generally cut into 1–2 cm squares for ease of use and economy. The corners of the squares only are used for fine

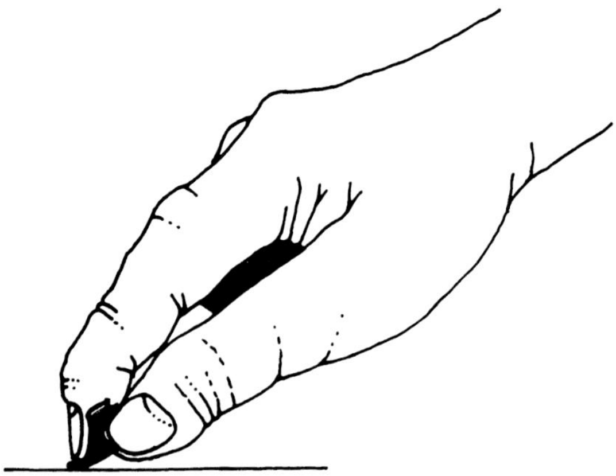

Figure 11.3 Only the very tip of the index finger should be used to apply pressure to the abrasive paper.

abrasive work and pressure is applied with the very tip of the forefinger (Figure 11.3). In this way the abrasive action can be directed very accurately. Care must be taken to ensure that the remainder of the paper behind the finger is not resting on the painted surface or on the surface of the object. This is very important as even very fine abrasives can cause damage to unglazed bodies, glazes and enamels, and especially to gilded decoration.

Where a feathered or sprayed edge of an area of retouching is being smoothed down, the paper or film should be drawn across the surface in strokes at right angles to the edge. The paper or film is placed down on the retouched area, drawn out towards the edge and lifted as the edge is reached. Great care should be taken to avoid abrading the surface of the ceramic itself. Other areas of retouching can be smoothed down by moving the paper or film in strokes or using a circular motion. When the surface is completely smooth it will be uniformly matt in appearance with no areas of gloss remaining, and no visible scratches. It may be necessary to work through a range of abrasives, starting with for example 800 grade wet or dry paper and finishing with a fine grade film, such as Flex-i-grit 4000. Abrasive papers and films are the most commonly used form of abrasive for rubbing down retouching medium; however, polishing cloths are also used when a very gentle action is required, or when the purpose is to heighten surface reflectance. Glass fibre brushes may also be used.

Polishing creams can be used for final polishing, and a bright gloss can be restored to many surface coatings by polishing after rubbing down with abrasive papers and films. Care should be taken when using on the edge of sprayed areas as the abrasive action of the polish may result in the edge of the spray being rubbed away, leaving a hard edge to the retouching. It may be preferable in the case of a sprayed retouch to achieve the correct gloss with an unabraded coating of medium. Increased gloss can also be achieved by applying microcrystalline wax and this can be useful for polishing the haze which is sometimes present at the edge of a sprayed retouch. Care must be taken, however, not to spread the wax over the surface of the ceramic, thus altering its visual properties.

12

Retouching: the practice

Introduction

The many subtleties of appearance of ceramic objects are achieved through the use of a wide range of raw materials and a great diversity of manufacturing techniques. Before starting any restoration that is intended to reproduce the appearance of the original, it is important to examine the object very carefully in order to establish how the particular effects have been achieved. The appearance of the body and any slip, glaze, stains, enamels, gilding or other decoration present must be noted. Some ceramics have a transparent glaze which may be tinted with colour but which allows the colour and texture of the body to show through. Others may have an opaque, coloured slip under a transparent or semi-transparent glaze, and still others, for example those coated with a tin glaze, have almost no surface transparency at all. Decoration may be over, in, or under the glaze, and may have been printed or painted. There may be gilding, silvering, or lustre effects.

A decision will have been made right at the beginning of the conservation process as to how completely the fillings should be disguised and the manner in which this is to be achieved, i.e. whether it is more appropriate to use tinted fillings, or fillings with a tinted surface coating (see Chapter 10). If the latter technique is used, a more detailed consideration must be made of the painting procedure once the fillings have been made.

When the fillings are to be not disguised but merely made less obtrusive, they are generally retouched to a colour approximating that of the general background colour of the surface of the object. The colour is generally kept lighter rather than darker to avoid giving the fillings the appearance of holes. The procedure used will generally follow that outlined below for retouching fillings in an unglazed object.

When the appearance of the fillings is to be matched more closely to that of the surrounding ceramic, again it must first be established which is the 'background colour' of the object. This is the colour to which the filling must now be matched and on top of which (except in the case of underglaze painting) any separate decoration will be laid. In fact, the surface coating must not only be tinted but must be adjusted to create the appropriate translucency, depth and gloss. In the case of an unglazed object the background colour is that of the body, unless it is completely encased in a slip, in which case it is the colour of the slip. In the case of an object with a distinctly separate clear or tinted transparent glaze, the background colour is again the colour of the body or any overlying slip. The fillings must initially be matched to this background colour and the glaze layers will be added later. In an object with an opaque glaze the background colour is the colour of the glaze. The degree of opacity of the glaze must be taken into consideration in preparing the surface coating and a separate gloss coat may or may not be necessary to achieve the correct surface reflectance. The colour of the body is only a consideration if there are areas where the glaze layer is very thin and the body colour shows through. If this is the case the filling may first be colour matched to the body and then subsequently coated with layers to match the glaze. In the case of hard-paste porcelains where the body and glaze have merged and there is a high degree of translucency, the background 'colour' must take this translucency into consideration and the appropriate appearance of depth must be achieved, together with the correct colouring, in the background coats. This is generally done by applying initial layers of quite heavily pigmented surface coating, followed by layers with decreasing quantities of pigment and hence of greater transparency.

The basic procedures for retouching fillings in the four different types of ceramics discussed above can be summarized as follows.

Unglazed objects

1 Test and sealing coats: clear gloss medium with or without pigment.
2 Background colour (possibly several coats): clear gloss medium + pigment + additives to give texture if necessary.
3 Polishing or burnishing to give correct surface finish.

Objects with a clear or tinted transparent glaze overlying the body or a slip

1 Test and sealing coats: clear gloss medium with or without pigment.
2 Background colour (possibly several coats): clear gloss medium + pigment.
3 Glaze (possibly several coats): clear gloss medium + pigment where necessary.
4 Polishing where necessary to give correct surface finish.

Objects with an opaque glaze

1 Test and sealing coats: clear gloss medium with or without pigment.
2 Background colour (possibly several coats): clear gloss medium + pigment.
3 Optional gloss coat: clear gloss medium.
4 Polishing where necessary to give correct surface finish.

Objects with semi-transparent glaze

1 Test and sealing coats: clear gloss medium with or without pigment.
2 Background colour: several coats of clear gloss medium + pigment with the proportion of pigment, especially white pigment, decreasing with each layer.
3 Optional gloss coat: clear gloss medium.
4 Polishing where necessary to give correct surface finish.

These procedures are based on the use of a clear gloss medium as opposed to a premixed paint. Additives to provide texture can be included when applying background or glaze coats.

Preparation

The importance of cleanliness throughout the retouching process cannot be too strongly emphasized. Amongst other things, dust and dirt can prevent proper adhesion of the paint, clog brushes and airbrushes, and disrupt an otherwise smooth finish. Some restorers like to use a separate room for all retouching, so that dust and dirt generated by procedures such as cleaning, removal of old restorations and rubbing down fillings are kept well away. If an airbrush is to be used, a separate room or booth is highly desirable so that adequate fume extraction and ventilation can be provided. The conditions of temperature and humidity should be within the ranges specified by the manufacturer for use of the medium.

Before commencing, hands should be cleaned and the brushes or the airbrush checked for dust or particles of cured medium. Any equipment such as palette knives, spatulas and mixing surfaces should be degreased with acetone or industrial methylated spirits. All equipment and materials to be used should be placed so that they are easily accessible.

The medium that is to be used may also need preparation. If it is a two-part medium the two parts must be weighed or measured out and carefully mixed. Small glass vials with closures are useful for mixing and storing small quantities of medium. Even if the medium does not need mixing, a small quantity, sufficient for the job in hand, should be decanted from the main supply and the medium used from here rather than direct from the can or bottle, in order to avoid unnecessary contamination or exposure to the air of the main supply.

Sealing and testing the filling

Generally the first stage in retouching is to seal the filling if it is at all porous and to make sure that the surface is absolutely smooth and that there are no lumps or ridges at the joint between the filler and the surrounding surface. Plaster of Paris fillings may be sealed with shellac or Paraloid B-72 (Acryloid B-72). When a clear gloss retouching medium plus pigments is to be used to cover fillings, the fillings are sealed with an initial coat of gloss medium to which a high proportion of white pigment is commonly added. There are two reasons for adding the white pigment. Firstly it gives bulk to the coat and enables it to be used to fill minor discrepancies in the filling. Secondly it helps even out the colour of the filling if it appears patchy; for example where Fine Surface Polyfilla has been used to fill small flaws in an epoxy putty or Polyfilla (interior grade).

The series of Figures 12.1 a–e shows the sequence for applying these coats in cases where it is acceptable to overlap the surrounding ceramic by a small amount. When an 'invisible' retouch is not being aimed for, and in cases where even a slight overlap is not acceptable, the procedure is the same but each coat must finish at the edge of the filling. It is much more difficult to achieve an 'invisible' retouch without

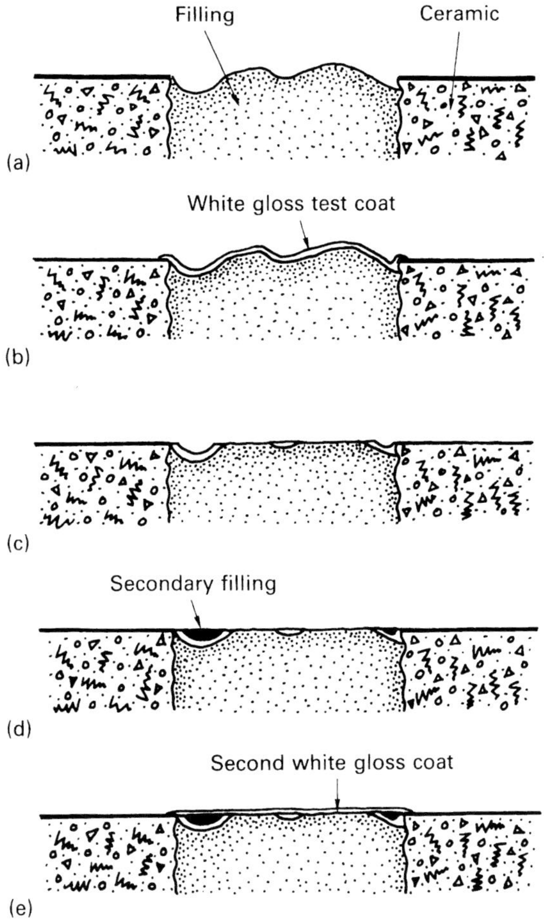

Figure 12.1 Preparation of a filling for retouching. (a) Cross-section through filling. Although the surface may appear to be smooth after cutting back, there will usually be a certain amount of unevenness. (b) First coat of gloss white paint has been applied. (c) Gloss white coat has been smoothed with fine abrasive paper, and has been rubbed through on the high points of the filling, but remains unabraded and glossy on the low spots. (d) Further filler has been applied to the low spots and smoothed with abrasive paper. (e) A second coat of gloss white paint has been applied.

having some overlap. Figure 12.1 a shows how the medium is brushed or sprayed evenly over the surface of the filling so that it just overlaps the joints between the filling and the surrounding surface. When working around the edges of a filling using a hand-held paint-brush it is best to use strokes at an angle to the edge of the filling rather than parallel to it in order to avoid producing a ridge accentuating the edge. The medium is allowed to cure and then the painted surface is carefully observed. The smooth glossy coating will highlight any unevenness in the filling and these will become even more apparent if the surface of the medium is very gently abraded using a fine silicon carbide or aluminium oxide paper. The white coating will be rubbed through on high spots and low spots will stand out as remaining glossy (Figure 12.1c). If they are small, any such flaws can be smoothed out using abrasive papers or filled using blobs of heavily pigmented retouching medium or retouching medium mixed with pigment and talc. A suitable filler such as Fine Surface Polyfilla may be used if they are larger (Figure 12.1d). If much rubbing down or filling has to be done it is then followed by a second white coat to again check the finish and even up the colour (Figures 12.1e, 12.2).

Background colours

As stated in the introduction, the background colour in the case of an unglazed ceramic is that of the body, as it is in the case of an object with a transparent or semi-transparent glaze. If the object has a slip over the body it is the colour of this slip. If the object has an opaque glaze it is the colour of this glaze. When an area has been filled with a non-colour-matched opaque filler the first stage in retouching is to match its surface colour to that of the background colour (Figure 12.3). Reproduction of overglaze enamel decoration, gilding or in-glaze stains will be carried out on top of this layer. Even underglaze painting is usually reproduced by first creating a smooth background colour and then painting over it, although in this case further application of background colour may be applied after the decoration has been painted in order to achieve a blurred effect.

Applying a well matched background colour which fades imperceptibly into the surrounding surface is

Figure 12.2 Filling in rim of Chinese plate: the final coat of gloss white paint has been applied to create an even base on which to apply the background colour.

Figure 12.3 Filling in rim of Chinese plate: background colour applied.

the essence of a good 'invisible' retouch. It may be carried out using either a hand-held paintbrush or an airbrush, but either way it is one of the most difficult things to do well and it is during this process that there is the greatest danger of spreading the paint over a wider area than necessary.

Mixing the colour

The colourants and medium are mixed together on a palette. The requirements of a good mixing palette are that it is chemically unaffected by the media used, it is physically hard enough to allow proper grinding of the pigments, and its colour is such that it will not influence judgement of the colours mixed on it. White ceramic tiles and white formica are all suitable: oil painter's disposable paper palettes may also be used but these are not generally hard enough for grinding down some of the coarser pigments.

A small quantity of a range of appropriate dry ground pigments or ready bound colours should be laid out along one edge of the palette using a spatula. If they are coarse, dry pigments may each be separately ground into a small amount of medium before adding to the main mixture in order to make mixing easier, but the feasibility of this will depend on the medium to be used and the speed with which it cures. A small quantity of the clear or pigmented medium is then placed in the middle of the tile and pigments or colours are gradually added with the spatula or a small palette knife until the required colour is achieved. Pigments that are coarse should be ground in well until there are no visible particles left. Care should be taken only to add very little of each colour to the mixture at a time to avoid getting the colour too strong. If too much of one colour is added and other colours have to be added to compensate for this, not only may the colour become very strong and the mixture very opaque, but when using dry ground pigments the medium will become overladen with pigment and may remain soft when cured. With most media it is important to work quickly and to keep the mixture well gathered in a pool rather than spread across the palette to avoid it starting to cure before the colour match is achieved. More of the medium can be added to the mixture to make it workable but it is not advisable, except in the case of solvent-based media, to add solvent as this will impair the eventual curing. If the ambient temperature in the studio is high it may be possible to extend the working life of the paint mixture by standing the palette over ice.

Once a near match has been achieved the colour can be compared with the original either by placing a small blob actually on the object or by placing a blob on the edge of the palette and holding it next to the object. It is best, however, to test the colour on top of the same coloured background that it will be painted onto. This is especially true with semi-transparent or transparent colours where the colour of the background will contribute substantially to their appearance. Thus a clear glaze mixture that is only slightly tinted should be tested over the background colour that has already been applied. If it is tested over an area of original glaze the effect will not be the same and the required colour and density cannot be properly judged. When using some media, in particular acrylic paints, the colour will dry to a slightly different tone from the appearance when wet. Allowance may have to be made for this. The mixture is adjusted if necessary by the addition of further colour or medium. It is always best, however, to err on the side of the mixture being too light, rather than too dark, as a lighter colour is easier to darken with subsequent coats than a darker one is to lighten.

Background colours are often rather subtle shades, and especial care must be taken to assess them, and the mixture, carefully and critically. The proportion of pigment to medium is important, more pigment obviously giving a denser look to the paint and enabling it to cover better. The initial background coat is almost always a highly pigmented one so that the filling can be well covered and its edges softened.

Application by brush

To a certain extent with most processes, but particularly with retouching, individual conservators develop their own techniques. However, there are some general principles which must be observed. The important things to aim for when applying a background coat are that the application must be as even as possible and the edges should fade as imperceptibly as possible into the surrounding surface. Rubbing down with fine abrasive papers between coats will help maintain an even paint layer and can be used to remove excess paint around the edges, but time is saved, and the results are often better, if the paint is applied carefully in the beginning.

It is usual to work around the edges of the filling first, always using strokes at an angle to the line of the edge in order to avoid accentuating it. If the retouch is to overlap the ceramic surface, before the paint has dried too much its outer edge may be feathered out using a brush dipped in clear, unpigmented medium, or alternatively in solvent. Care must be taken, however, not to draw the paint out unnecessarily far over the ceramic surface. When the edges of the filling have been covered the centre is painted using smooth, even, overlapping strokes. Once an area has been covered it should not be reworked or the even finish will be destroyed.

If the density of the paint is not sufficient to conceal the underlying filling there is a temptation to apply the paint more thickly. In certain circumstances this may be acceptable, for example when retouching an object with a very coarse, uneven surface, or heavily glazed areas of modelling, but generally it will only serve to emphasize the filling. It is almost always preferable to build up the necessary coverage in several layers of paint, allowing each layer to cure and then rubbing it down before applying the next. Only in this way can a sufficiently smooth, even coverage be achieved. If there are any dust particles or brush hairs in the paint these can be either removed very carefully whilst the paint is still wet using, for example, an old airbrush needle, or left until the paint has cured and then dislodged by rubbing with abrasive paper. This may mar an otherwise perfect finish and it is obviously better to try to avoid such contamination in the first place. If the application is not successful, it may be necessary to remove it as described in the previous chapter.

Once a satisfactory coating has been achieved it is left to cure fully. It is then carefully abraded to remove any unevenness caused by brush strokes. This must be done very lightly in order to avoid rubbing through the paint layer and exposing the white sealing layer. A very fine grade of abrasive paper, for example 1000 wet or dry silicon carbide paper or 400 Flexigrit aluminium oxide paper, is used, or alternatively a fine polishing cloth (e.g. Ultrafine). When working over a feathered edge area, straight strokes should be used with each stroke starting with the paper being placed down on the painted surface and then drawn out to the edge of the paint. The stroke should finish with the paper being lifted as the edge of the paint is reached. In effect the stroke of the abrasive paper is following that of the paintbrush in applying the retouching medium. This process of abrading the paint along the edge of the retouched area must be carried out with extreme care; it is during this process that irreversible damage to the ceramic can commonly occur. If the abrasive paper is allowed to drag across the surface of ceramic body or glaze as it is drawn off the paint surface, depending on the type of abrasive paper in use and on the hardness of the body, glaze or decoration, scratching can result. Low-fired, unglazed pottery and enamels and gilded decoration on higher-fired wares are particularly susceptible, but even hard-paste porcelains can be easily damaged by quite fine grades of abrasive papers. The important rule to follow at all times, therefore, is that the abrasive paper should only come into contact with the retouching medium and never with the surface of the object itself.

Rubbing down this first background coat will cause it to appear lighter; however were it to be polished or coated with clear gloss medium it would return to its original colour (Eastaugh, 1984).

Subsequent coats are applied according to the sequence decided on at the outset (see above). Each coat should be rubbed down before application of the next one. Application of more coats than necessary should be avoided, especially when retouching very small areas, to avoid the paint building up into a hump.

Application by airbrush

Application of background colours using an airbrush follows essentially the same procedures as those used for applying them with a hand-held brush. Once the use of the airbrush has been mastered it makes the even application of the paint, and the fading out of the paint at the edges, much easier. However, it also makes it easier to apply an unnecessarily large amount of retouching medium over an unnecessarily wide area. It may be beneficial to mask off certain areas before spraying, to protect the original material. This can be done using a simple paper shield (Williams, 1983) or rubber latex (Barov, 1988; Elston, 1990).

Where it is deemed unacceptable to overlap the surface of the ceramic around the edges of the filling, either the surrounding area must be masked off or the airbrush should only be used for coating the central areas of the filling. The latter approach can be useful when very large fillings must be painted, the airbrush providing a quick way of covering the bulk of the filling evenly, whilst a hand held brush is used to cover the area around the edges of the filling adjacent to the ceramic. More generally, however, an airbrush is used in situations where some minimal overlap onto the surface of the ceramic is acceptable. As with the use of hand held paint brushes, individual restorers will develop their own methods of applying the retouching medium but it is usual to spray around the edges of the filling first and then to cover the middle. The spray around the edges can either be applied by spraying a line along the line of the edge, controlling the spray so that it falls mainly within, but just slightly over, the edge to blur it, or alternatively the spray can be applied at right angles to the edge in the same way that the brush strokes are applied when retouching by hand. In order to control the spray more closely the air pressure should be reduced and the nozzle of the airbrush held closer to the surface. The airbrush is held so that it lies parallel to the edge of the filling and short straight lines sprayed at right angles to the edge. In order to do this the airbrush is really moved in a circular path. As it is drawn up off the surface the spray fades away and provided a smooth, continuous motion is maintained, a blurred edge to the filling can be achieved without the danger of a ridge building up which is found with the previous method of application. The inner area of the filling is covered by again using straight lines or a circular motion. If straight lines are used these are applied parallel to each other and slightly overlapping. A small area is covered at a time, rather than trying to spray lines right across the filling. A second series of overlapping lines is then sprayed in between the first ones in order to even out the application. When a circular motion is used the surface is worked over using small overlapping circles. Personal preference will dictate which methods are used.

Once an even coat has been applied the retouching medium is left to cure and then rubbed down in the same way as described for hand retouching. However, there is more danger with a sprayed edge of rubbing right through the retouching as it fades out to a much thinner layer. It is important not to do this as the effect of the fading edge will be lost. A very light touch and very fine abrasive film or cloth should therefore be used in these areas. If the angle of the spray and the pressure and volume of paint have been such that excessive misting is produced around the edges, this can be polished off using a fine abrasive paste.

Subsequent coats are applied in the same way, with the composition of the paint being made up according to the chosen spraying sequence.

Washing back

When the piece being retouched has painted decoration adjacent to the filling that has not been masked off, it is important to remove any background colour that may have been sprayed over the decoration before it cures. It is much easier to remove it whilst it is still wet and a softer edge to the paint can be achieved in this way. A brush is dipped into solvent and then wiped almost dry with tissue or blotted on blotting paper. The encroaching spray is then removed with the brush by drawing it along the lines of the decoration, rinsing frequently in solvent and then redrying it. The brush must be kept dry as if it is used wet the retouching medium will run into ridges around the edges of the decoration. By using the brush dry and only drawing the brush in one direction, the medium is effectively pulled off the surface rather than pushed back to the edges of the decoration. If hard edges are formed these can be softened by rubbing with fine abrasive film once the retouching medium has cured.

Special effects in background coats

A ceramic glaze is seldom smooth and even in colour. Variations occur due to impurities in the glaze, uneven kiln atmosphere, pooling of the glaze and a host of other manufacturing defects. Some effects may be intentional. Most simply require the conservator to use common sense and imagination in order to reproduce them; however, there are some which occur more often than others and which deserve discussion.

Shading

Frequently it will be found that the colour is not constant over the surface of the object. For example the glaze may pool slightly around the attachments of handles or knops, or in ridges caused by uneven pressure during the throwing of a pot. It is important that account is taken of this or the repair will stand out. Careful observation will reveal the cause of the effect and adjustment is made to the colour, or intensity of colour, in the appropriate coat or coats. It is usually easiest to achieve these effects with an airbrush.

Crazing

Crazing is found in the glaze of many ceramics. It can be an intentional effect produced during the manufacture of the object, or it can be the result of later deterioration. There are various different ways of imitating crazing and it may be necessary to try several of them in order to discover which reproduces the effect most closely in a particular case. Whichever method is used the pattern of the crazing must be carefully studied. Firstly, crazing may be reproduced by painting very fine lines on the surface of the retouched area. These may be in a dark colour or in a light colour depending on the appearance of the crazing. Occasionally the effect may be most closely matched by painting dark lines highlighted with lighter lines. The paint mixture can have a high proportion of solvent in it to help achieve a thin, flat line and a further coat of clear glaze may or may not be painted over the top. If the appearance of the crazing is appropriate crazing may be drawn in with a fine pencil and then coated with clear glaze.

An alternative method of reproducing the crazing is to actually incise lines in the retouched area using a needle held in a pin vice or the tip of a scalpel. Pigment can be washed or rubbed into these lines if necessary. Again a coat of clear glaze may be applied over the top.

If the crazing is very light and fine it may be more effective simply to apply a wash of tinted medium over the area rather than to try to reproduce the crazing.

Spots and inclusions

Spotting may be fairly regular, in both the size of the spots and their distribution, or it may be totally irregular. The spatter cup of the airbrush may be useful for the former type, but irregular spots are best reproduced by hand with a brush. Raised inclusions can be imitated using a coarse powder such as pumice, sand or crushed charcoal applied with a little retouching medium.

Surface finishing

It may be found on completion of the background coats that the surface reflectance does not match that of the original ceramic. It is sometimes preferable that this should be the case, in order to further distinguish areas of restoration from the original ceramic. However, where it is not desirable, there are various ways in which the reflectance can be altered. Heightened gloss can be achieved either by application of a further coat of clear gloss medium or by polishing with an abrasive cloth, a glass fibre brush or an abrasive cream or liquid, e.g. Solvol Autosol or Prelim. A burnished appearance is generally achieved by polishing in this way. A lower reflectance is achieved by careful use of abrasive papers or by application of medium containing a matting agent.

Decoration

The decision to restore any painted decoration to a filled area will have to be based on a consideration of the evidence that exists of the original appearance of the piece. Often the retouching may simply involve interpolation of a border pattern or joining up lines across a small filling. However, when large fillings occur in the middle of extensive painted decoration, retouching of the decoration cannot ethically be carried out unless there is some firm evidence as to the appearance of the original. The type of evidence that may be acceptable was discussed in Chapter 5 in relation to replacing missing parts.

Decoration may have originally been applied before the glaze or on top of it. It may have migrated during firing and give the appearance of actually lying within the glaze. The point in the retouching sequence at which the painted decoration is applied will vary accordingly. Overglaze enamels, such as those on *famille rose* Chinese porcelain or on Meissen figurines, will be painted last of all, over the final clear coat of retouching medium. Some are bulky, standing proud of the surface, whilst others lie very smooth and flat on the surface. Underglaze painting will be painted under the final clear coats and may even be painted underneath one or more of the pigmented coats in order to achieve the correct appearance. The same will apply to in-glaze stains. It is vital, however, that the background coats that have been applied are completely smooth and free from brush strokes. If this is not the case, when the painted decoration is smoothed down with abrasive papers it will appear patchy.

Marking out the pattern

It is often helpful to mark out the pattern, or at least guidelines or dots, using either a pencil or little spots of retouching medium. For guidelines a pair of callipers can be useful for taking measurements from an area of the original, although it must be borne in mind that repeating patterns are frequently slightly irregular in size.

For marking out a whole pattern the easiest thing to do is to take a tracing from an intact area. The reverse of the tracing is then coated by rubbing a pencil over it. An H or HB pencil is probably best as very soft pencils can leave too much graphite on the tracing paper which will then cause smudges on the paint surface. The pattern is then transferred to the paint surface by placing it in position, graphite side down, and drawing over the traced lines again. Pressing too hard should be avoided as this may damage the paint surface. Any smudges on the paint surface should be removed using cotton wool on a swab stick.

Mixing and applying the paint

The paint is mixed in the same way as described for background colours. The process of application when painting large areas of decoration usually takes longer than when applying coats of background colour and it can be more difficult to keep the paint workable. It is generally preferable to mix fresh batches of paint rather than to add solvent to revive a two-part medium, as the medium will not cure properly. If a solvent is added to painted decoration that is to be coated with further layers of retouching medium it is best to apply these further layers using an airbrush to avoid disturbing the decoration.

The type of paintbrush used, the loading of the paint and the direction of the brush stroke will all contribute to the effect achieved. It is important to experiment with these in order to be able to imitate the range of decorative painting found on ceramic objects.

With certain types of decoration the correct effect can be achieved with one application of paint but with others it will be necessary to apply several coats of paint and smooth down each one with abrasive paper in between.

With very complex patterns it is often best to paint part of the pattern or perhaps one colour of a polychrome pattern first, and allow this to cure before painting further areas or colours. This allows corrections or alterations to be made to the parts painted later in the sequence without disturbing those painted first. When colours lie over each other without merging, as for example in the case where the outline of a pattern is printed and the colour has been filled in with transparent washes, these will also be painted separately, allowing curing in between.

Some methods of approaching the main types of decoration are discussed below.

Underglaze decoration

Underglaze decoration is simulated by applying paint over the correctly matched background coats but before any clear glaze coats are applied. The difficulty in reproducing underglaze decoration is in achieving a blurred edge to the paint to imitate the way that the original colour merges into the glaze. Applying one or more further tinted coats of background colour over the painted decoration can help to achieve the correct effect but will not be sufficient to soften hard edges to the painting. With skilful control the best effects are often achieved by applying the painted decoration with an airbrush, or by combining hand painting with some airbrush application. If an airbrush is not used the edges of the paint must be blurred by applying a small quantity of clear medium over the paint, before it has cured, and working the edges of the paint with the brush to cause them to merge into the clear medium. This must be done by painting only a small area of decoration at a time so that the clear medium can be applied before the paint has hardened. Applying a further coat or coats of lightly pigmented medium on top of the painted decoration may help soften the effect, and where the stronger colour of the painted decoration is required this can be achieved by carefully abrading through the coat with a fine abrasive paper.

Underglaze decoration, unlike overglaze enamels, does not disrupt the smooth surface of the glaze. The paintwork must therefore be kept as flat as possible and then layers of clear or lightly pigmented glaze built up over it until a sufficient thickness has been achieved to allow the surface to be smoothed flat with abrasive paper without removing any of the paint from the decoration.

Hand-painted on-glaze enamels

Hand-painted on-glaze enamels were originally applied to the surface of the glaze using a brush, and fired just sufficiently to fuse them to the surface. For this reason they are easier to reproduce with a hand-held brush and paint than some other forms of decoration, e.g. where the decoration was pounced or printed onto the surface. They may be smooth and lie relatively flat on the surface of the glaze or they may be thick and lumpy and stand proud of it. The consistency of the medium used to retouch the two types must be altered accordingly. For decoration of the former type, the effect is achieved with a thin coating of paint, and hence the paint must be used speedily before the medium has started to cure. If necessary, solvent is added to the paint to thin it. However, the desired effect will not be achieved by adding solvent to a two-part medium that has already started to go tacky. The effect must be achieved as far as possible in a single layer of paint to avoid building up a thickness of paint.

With the second type of on-glaze enamel decoration the opposite is true and the paint is used thicker and may be built up in several applications. An alternative to doing this is to actually thicken the retouching medium with a bulking agent such as fumed silica. If necessary the decoration can be painted with gloss medium after it has cured to counteract the matting effect of the fumed silica; however, these types of enamel are generally slightly dull in appearance.

Close observation of the original decoration is essential in order to appreciate any effects such as shading or spotting within a single colour. These can then be reproduced as necessary. Shading may be most easily reproduced by applying an even coat of colour, leaving it to cure, and then using fine grade abrasive paper to thin down the paint in the appropriate areas and allow more background colour to show through and give a lighter effect. An airbrush can be used to apply thin washes of colour that have no discernible brush marks, and where hard edges are required these can be achieved with the use of masking fluid, such as rubber latex, or a paper shield (Figure 12.4), or by wiping back the edges with a brush dipped in solvent and blotted almost dry.

Transfer printing

This type of decoration is difficult to reproduce, owing mainly to its very fine, even nature. The colour was not originally applied with a brush (see Chapter 1) and this makes it difficult to imitate using a brush. Any obvious brush strokes must be avoided and, where the printing resulted in fine dots rather than washes of colour, the paint must be applied accordingly. At the same time the paint must be kept very smooth and flat. An airbrush can be used for some types of printed decoration, for example for reproducing shading and stippled backgrounds, but usually the scale of the decoration is such that sufficient control cannot be achieved with an airbrush. One way of imitating the speckled appearance produced by printing is to use a brush to dab dry pigment onto a surface that has been painted with

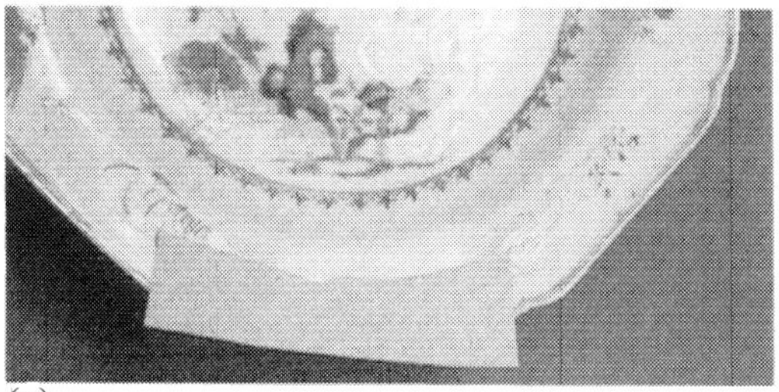
(a)

(b)

(c)

Figure 12.4 Retouching on-glaze decoration on restored area of rim of Chinese plate. (a) Part of the decoration lends itself to retouching with an airbrush. It is very smooth and even, fading off on the inner side, but with a hard edge on the outer side. A paper shield is used to give the hard outer edge. (b) Shield removed. When this part of the decoration is dry the other on-glaze enamels will be painted on using a hand-held brush. (c) Retouching complete.

medium and allowed to almost dry. For doing this it is best to use a brush that has had the tip cut off it to produce a kind of miniature stencil brush. The same type of brush can be used to remove part of the paint from a solid wash of colour to give a more 'printed' effect, or to smudge on paint that has been thinned with solvent. The paintbrush can be substituted with a piece of silk cloth (which will not leave fibres in the paint), a small sponge, or a fingertip if these will achieve the appropriate effect. In most cases it is best to use the paint slightly thinned with solvent in order to keep the painting flat on the surface.

In some cases the original decoration is formed of unpainted areas in a speckled background. This can be reproduced by first laying down a speckled background and then removing the paint from the appropriate areas using a brush dipped in solvent and blotted almost dry. If the brush is too wet a ridge of paint will form around the edges.

Gilding

Gilding is applied at the end of the manufacturing process and many different forms of gilding are found on ceramic objects. Early gilding, prior to the mid eighteenth century, in both China and Europe was applied in the form of gold leaf laid on an oil or size. This type of gilding wears off easily and has often been lost completely. Later gilding was applied as a powder, in honey and other substances, or as an amalgam with mercury and painted on with a brush. Both these types of gilding were fired on to the glaze surface using a gentle heat and then burnished after firing. They survive better than unfired gilding but are still prone to abrasion and wear. The gold may have been applied so thickly that it is raised, it may have been tooled with a pattern, or the design may have been acid etched into the surface of the porcelain underneath the gilding.

Gold, in the form of either leaf or powder, is extremely expensive; it is also difficult to work with. For these reasons conservators have tried to reproduce the effects of gilding using materials other than gold. It is extremely difficult to do this. Bronze powders have been commonly used, either mixed with a chosen retouching medium or in the form of commercially prepared bronze paints such as Liquid Leaf. These can give quite a satisfactory look when imitating the type of coarse gilding found on some Satsuma and other wares; however, they are not a satisfactory finish for imitating fine, highly burnished gold decoration. Bronze also has the drawback that it will oxidize in time when in contact with the atmosphere and become dull and dark in appearance. If bronze paints are used they must therefore be protected by a sealing coat.

Gold, applied either as powder or as leaf, gives the best results. The techniques used will depend on the original techniques used to apply the gold to the object. In cases where the gold leaf was originally applied using a size and left unfired, the original techniques can be closely followed to achieve a good match. However, when the original gilding was fired onto the object, it is more difficult to imitate, owing to the fact that the firing and subsequent burnishing give a very deep, rich appearance to the gilding that is not matched by unfired leaf. Applying the gold in the form of powder gold can sometimes give a more sympathetic finish, especially when reproducing slightly worn gilding, and it allows the edge of the restoration to be blended better into the original.

Gold leaf

The handling and application of gold leaf are part of a skill that takes many years to perfect. The gold in gold leaf is beaten out to a thickness of only 0.001 mm, which means it is barely more than one molecule in thickness. A loose leaf is therefore very difficult to handle and will crumple at the slightest breath of wind. Leaf can be obtained in the form of 'transfer gold leaf', where it has been attached to sheets of tissue paper, and this makes handling easier. However, it is not an appropriate form of leaf to use with some of the techniques for application. Gold leaf varies in shade from reddish tinges to a yellow-green gold, according to the amount of copper or silver mixed with it. The more pure the gold, i.e. the higher the carat, the better it tends to match fired gilding on ceramics. The highest-carat gold leaf generally available is 23.5 carat.

Gold leaf will pick up and highlight any unevenness in the surface over which it is applied. Great care must therefore be taken in finishing the surface of the restoration when gold leaf is to be applied over it. The degree of reflectance that can be achieved in the gilding will depend largely on the gloss of the underlying filled area.

In order to attach the leaf to the surface of the restoration some form of binding medium must be used. Two media commonly used in other areas of gilding, oil size and gelatin, can also be used in ceramics restoration. Various of the retouching media are also suitable. The important criterion is that the medium can be applied in a very thin, smooth layer or the effect of the gloss finish to the restoration will be lost.

Oil size

Gold leaf is often applied to metal work or to furniture using oil sizes that dry very slowly and flatten out into a perfectly smooth layer. The point at which the gold leaf is applied to the oil is crucial, in order that the oil has had enough time to dry uncovered but still retains enough tack to hold the gold leaf. A range of oil sizes is available, taking between 10 minutes and 24 hours to dry, although the drying time will depend on the ambient temperature. The chosen size is painted onto the area to be gilded, allowed to dry for the appropriate number of minutes and then, when it is just still tacky, the leaf is applied.

Gelatin

Gelatin dissolved in water is also used by gilders as a medium to attach the gold leaf to furniture and picture frames. It can be used for applying gold leaf to ceramics, and like oil size will form only a very thin layer between the leaf and the ceramic surface. The use of gelatin has the advantage that it is not necessary to wait for a certain period of time before attaching the leaf. The solution is applied by brush and then the leaf laid straight on top. However, owing to the surface tension of the water, the solution beads up when applied and therefore the gold cannot be applied with any precision; more gold than necessary must be applied and then worked back using a scalpel after the water and gelatin have dried. The water dries very slowly, and as it does the leaf flattens out. As there is no bulky medium between the paint surface and the leaf, provided the paint surface is quite smooth the leaf will appear bright and shiny. This method is not suitable for use with transfer gold as the attachment of the gold leaf to the gelatin-painted surface is not initially strong enough to pull the leaf off the backing sheet.

The easiest way to handle and measure gelatin is to use it in the form of gelatin capsules used by chemists for pills. One capsule dissolved in 250 ml of hot water will give an appropriate strength of solution. This is painted on the area where the leaf is to be applied using a very clean sable brush. The gold leaf is cut roughly to size and shape. If enough water and gelatin have been applied and the positioning is not correct first time, the gold can be very gently coaxed into position by pulling at the edges with a brush. Minor wrinkles will flatten out as the water dries, and large creases can be brushed off when the drying is complete. Drying will take a long time as it depends on the evaporation of the water and the leaf is best left undisturbed for at least two days. A soft, loose brush is then taken and brushed across the surface to remove any unattached gold, and then a scalpel is used to carefully scrape away unwanted areas of leaf. This must be done very carefully in order to avoid damaging the paint surface; a curved scalpel blade will be more satisfactory than a straight one.

Retouching medium

Retouching medium can be used as a size on which to apply gold leaf but it is not always easy to apply a coat that is sufficiently smooth. Applied by hand the retouching medium may retain brush strokes, and spraying it through an airbrush is not generally appropriate as the excess applied may cause problems unless the surrounding areas have been masked off. However, retouching medium has the benefit of being readily available in the ceramics conservator's studio. Either loose leaf or transfer leaf can be used with retouching media.

The loose gold leaf is cut to the correct size and shape on a gilder's cushion. If transfer leaf is used this is easier to cut to a more precise shape, as the leaf will not tear in the same way as it will when it is loose. However, if the leaf is cut a little too large the excess may be brushed off after the retouching medium has cured.

The retouching medium should be used thinned in order to reduce the risk of brush strokes or too thick an application, and is tinted very slightly to make it easier to see where it has been applied. It is painted onto the surface of the restoration as accurately as possible. If a mistake is made during the application of the retouching medium it is best to leave it to cure completely, remove it using abrasive and then start again. If solvent is used to remove mistakes a sticky patch may remain which will hold the leaf. When the retouching medium has dried to a stage at which it is just tacky, but no longer wet, the leaf is applied; if transfer leaf is used it can be placed in position with forceps and gentle pressure is applied using either the tip of a finger or an agate burnisher to smooth it down onto the surface. The backing tissue is then peeled away leaving the gold leaf in place. Whether or not the application has been successful it is then left until the retouching medium has completely cured. A soft brush is then used to remove any unattached leaf and if there are patches that have not taken the leaf these are repainted with medium and leaf reapplied. If this is attempted before the first application has cured there is a risk of disturbing it. Minor adjustments to the gilding can be made after the retouching medium has cured using a very sharp scalpel to gently scrape away leaf along the edges of the application.

Tablet gold

Tablet gold is very finely powdered gold bound with a medium, usually a gum. This form of gold is best suited to reproducing narrow lines, dots and flourishes, not for wide smooth areas or bands. It is used as a paint by dipping the brush in water and then working it against the tablet until it is fully loaded with gold. Too much water will result in a granular appearance as the particles of gold will be too dispersed. The action used in applying the gold should be one of dabbing it onto the surface rather than brushing it on. The brush used should not be rinsed after use, but should be allowed to dry and kept solely for the purpose of applying tablet gold. In this way the gold particles that have worked into it will not be wasted.

Powder gold

Powder gold is very finely divided gold and, like the leaf, is available in a range of shades created by mixing it with copper and silver. Again the highest purity, the 23.5 carat powder, is generally the best match for fired gold decoration on ceramics. Powder gold gives a softer finish than leaf and its use enables the edges of the restoration to be blended into the original more smoothly. It is also possible to achieve a greater range of effects, from thin, worn gilding, to a deep, rich finish.

Either an oil size or a retouching medium is used to attach the powder to the surface of the restoration. As with the application of leaf, the brilliance of the result depends upon the perfection of the underlying surface and the smoothness of the size layer.

The chosen medium is painted onto the surface where the gold is to be applied. The medium used can be tinted to make it easier to see where it has been applied. As when applying leaf, if an error is made it is best to leave the medium to cure rather than to try to wipe it away. The medium is left to cure until it is only just still tacky and the powder gold is then dusted on very lightly using a soft, loose brush (Figure 12.5). It is best to carry out this operation on top of a sheet of clean paper so that any excess can be saved and returned to the jar. The gilding is then left to dry completely and if desired a further application can be made on top of the first. The gold can be burnished carefully using an agate burnisher applied over a sheet of Melinex, and finally polished with a pad of velvet or silk.

Bronze paints and powders

Bronze paints can either be obtained as commercial preparations or be mixed using bronze powders and a retouching medium. When mixing powders with retouching media the finest available grade of powder should be used, and the ratio of powder to medium should be kept high, in order to avoid a

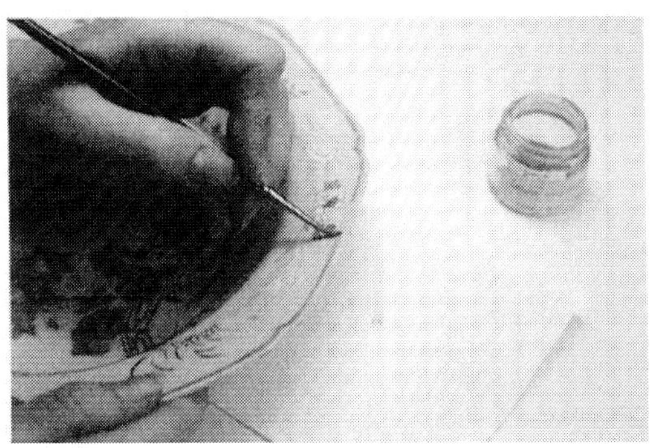

Figure 12.5 Powder gold being applied with a brush to the restored rim of Chinese plate.

grainy appearance. The brush should be well loaded and the paint not brushed out too much. Great care must be exercised when painting with bronze paints as trying to rectify mistakes can leave disfiguring smears on the surface of the restoration that are difficult to remove. A sealing coat of retouching medium should be applied once the bronze paint has cured, to insulate the bronze from the oxidizing effects of the atmosphere.

Bronze powders can also be used in exactly the same way as powder gold. Their advantage is that they are much cheaper than gold. However, it is not possible to achieve such a good match to original gilding using bronze powders. Again, bronze powders should be coated to seal them from the atmosphere.

Silvering

Silver decoration can be reproduced using silver leaf or platinum leaf. Both are applied in the same way as gold leaf; however, silver leaf will require sealing against the effects of the atmosphere. This is best done with a cellulose nitrate lacquer such as Frigiline as many of the retouching media used in ceramics restoration are acid and will tarnish silver. Aluminium powders may also be used to reproduce silver decoration and are applied in the same way as powder gold. The best effects are achieved with the more finely divided powders.

Lustres

The satisfactory reproduction of lustre decoration is difficult to achieve. Each lustre has different characteristics and generally a great deal of experimentation is needed to achieve a reasonable result. Various materials and combinations of materials are used.

Bronze, gold and aluminium powders can be used and in certain circumstances will give good results. They are applied, mixed with retouching medium, either on top of a coat of medium tinted with pigments, or together with the pigments in the same coat. Alternatively, pigments in medium can be applied over the top of gold leaf.

Commercially produced lustre pigments, composed of mica mixed with pigment, are available and can be effective when applied mixed with retouching medium. These have the advantage over bronze powders that they do not tarnish on exposure to the atmosphere.

Part Three

13

Planning and equipping the studio

Unlike other conservation disciplines, such as furniture or textiles, the treatment of ceramics can be pursued with minimal facilities and equipment. Indeed, it is partly due to this, combined with the increasing interest in collecting pottery and porcelain, that ceramics conservation has recently enjoyed a rapid growth in popularity as a hobby interest, quite often being practised at home with negligible overheads. Such a situation may suit those who carry out restoration work on an informal, infrequent basis. However, for professional restorers and conservators in private business, museums, or archaeological sites, it will be extremely important that their studios are well designed and suitably equipped.

The considerations involved in the initial planning of a studio, although numerous, are commonly influenced by the constraints of two powerful elements: money and space. By examining the stages in designing a studio, and looking at how to maximize use of the available space, this chapter aims to help those individuals involved with running and maintaining an existing studio, as well as offering some guidance to those who are either reassessing their space, or just setting up. The basic requirements for the work space will be considered, as well as the equipment and tools commonly used in the course of restoring ceramics. Finally, the importance of observing all aspects of health and safety, as a duty and obligation both to ourselves and colleagues, forms the last section in this chapter.

The bare shell

Deciding on a location for the studio is usually determined by several factors. For conservators working in museums or on archaeological sites, the decision will have already been made. Those who are in private practice may be able to choose premises readily accessible to clients, or to their homes. Although the option to set up at home may seem the most convenient and economical choice, the lack of space and restrictions enforced by planning controls may cause problems later. Conservators attached to an archaeological site may face completely different problems related to the resources of their surroundings.

The requirements for the studio are dictated by three criteria: the safety of the objects, the comfort and safety of the conservator, and the demands made by practical conservation procedures. The amount of space available will determine how many people can comfortably work together and consequently the planning of individual work areas. The location of the space may also inflict limitations on the type of objects that may be worked on, especially where access is restricted.

Architects may not necessarily provide the answers when it comes to designing specialist areas. Their expertise is more valuable for determining structural details such as floor loading, and for giving guidance on installation of electrical, gas, water and drainage services. They may also give help on general aesthetic features of the building. Consultants will help with individual aspects such as fume extraction, lighting or furniture, though it is worth bearing in mind that they could have a vested interest in certain products.

Other restorers already working in their own studios, whether well designed or otherwise, can be one of the most valuable sources of advice. Hearing at first hand the positive and negative aspects of a work area can often be much more enlightening and inspiring than hours of studying catalogues.

Primary considerations

Assuming the studio is not to be purpose-built, the conversion of an existing bare shell into the perfect conservation or restoration studio will initially involve a thorough assessment of the elected space. There may be structural and integral features that, although inconvenient, would be too costly to alter. The space could also have other faults that might have a direct effect on its use. The main considerations at this stage include: access, floor loading, the strength of the walls, the quality of the light, security, services (electricity, water and drainage supplies), other activities in the building, and health and safety. Further details on these will not be given here and advice on each of these should be sought from a specialist.

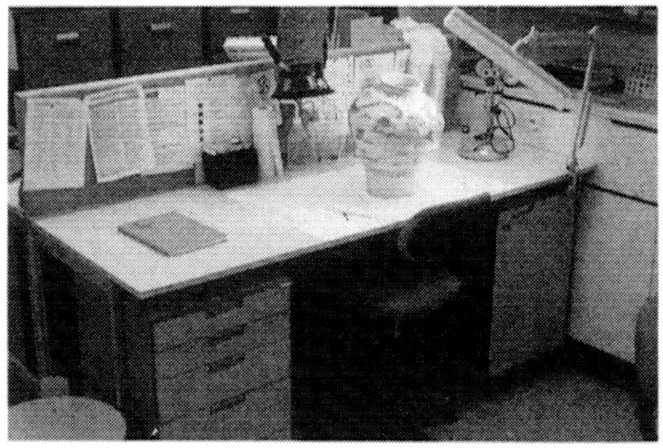

Figure 13.2 The personal work space (Victoria and Albert Museum, London).

Division of space

The layout of the space will depend on its size and shape, the exits, and the number of people who will work in it (Figure 13.1). The nature of the various processes involved in restoring ceramics calls for division of the studio into specific areas:

Reception area A spacious uncluttered area with a table near the point of entry where clients or curators can be received and their objects unpacked.
Wet area An area for treatments that involve water. It should be in a separate part of the studio, away from other activities. There should also be a separate wash-hand basin for staff use.
Main work area Each individual should have a personal workplace (Figure 13.2). This will be the space where they will probably spend most of the working day. Benches should have a well lit situation, preferably with a window view, positioned away from the main gangway. They should include storage for the conservator's tools, materials, documentation, books and personal items, as well as a cupboard for objects not presently being treated. Each work station should provide enough space for the individual and her possessions without being cluttered or cramped (Deasy and Lasswell, 1985). Adjacent to the individual work areas there should also be a communal space for general use. This area should accommodate equipment such as a fridge, an oven, and cupboards for storage of objects and smaller tools. It might also include a multi-purpose table area separate from the work benches, and a bench for microscope work.
Retouching area A dust-free area, preferably a separate room, should be allocated for retouching and airbrush work. The space should also have powerful ventilation in the form of either a spray booth or an extractor, so that airborne solvent may be quickly dispersed elsewhere. In museums and other large institutions it may be possible to install an airline for compressed air.
Office area There should be a separate room for administration, containing desks, filing cabinets, computer and telephone.
Staff room It is important that there should be a separate area where people can go during their breaks, to eat, drink and smoke. This should reduce the temptation to break health and safety rules by consuming food or drink in the work area.

Figure 13.1 A ceramics conservation studio that has been specially designed as a work space for four conservators (Victoria and Albert Museum, London).

Detailed requirements

Once the main areas have been determined, attention can then be focused on the finer details within the space. In aiming to keep the space as efficient and streamlined as possible, a careful consideration of the layout of each area will be necessary, avoiding the wastage of space and using furnishings that are practical and easily maintained. Dust generating materials, such as carpets, upholstery and curtains, should be kept to a minimum, and all surfaces including floors, walls, bench tops, tables and cupboards should be easy to keep clean.

It may be more economical for the private restorer to buy carefully designed kitchen furniture and fittings, bearing in mind the following basic requirements.

Benches

Benches should ideally be the same height as all other work surfaces, including sink units, trolleys and side benches, so that the space can be flexible allowing the possibility of rearrangement. They should have a firm work top, with adequate space to accommodate objects, tools and equipment. Organ (1968) has recommended a width of 80 cm and a height of 70 cm, though this would make for an unsatisfactory arrangement if bench heights are to be kept uniform throughout, especially for tall workers or those with back problems. The uniform height of the surfaces should make allowance for equipment such as fridges and ovens. Thought should be given to comfort, with adequate space below the work top for people's legs. It may also be worth considering the shape of the work top: an L or U shape may be preferred, in order to separate paperwork or examination processes. The surface of the bench should be an easily washable laminate that is durable and resistant to solvents. It should be in a light neutral colour, especially avoiding blue colours that would interfere with colour matching. Portable benches on castors, of the same height as the main bench, can also be useful when an extra surface is needed.

Chairs

A chair, though often mistakenly dismissed as a less important item, will play a crucial role in ensuring the long-term comfort of the sedentary restorer. It should have a well padded back and seat that can be adjusted to various heights so as to allow the worker to rearrange position in relation to the object. Feet should also be supported for added comfort and better posture. It should be possible to rotate or swivel around on the seat.

Floors

Floors should be non-slip, solvent resistant and easily cleaned.

Doors

Entrance doors should be wide and preferably double. A reinforced glass window in the door can help avoid accidents. Hooks are useful to temporarily pin back the door while an object is manoeuvred through the gap, but fire doors should always be closed again afterwards.

Walls

Walls should be coated in a washable paint in a light neutral colour. Brilliant white walls tend to produce glare that can be distracting and tiring to work with.

Storage

Storage space, such as cupboards and drawers, will avoid cluttering work surfaces with objects, equipment, tools and personal belongings. It is important to have solid secure cupboards with adjustable shelves where objects can be stored prior to or after treatment. Shelves may be padded with a thin layer of a dense closed-cell polyethylene foam to prevent damage from vibration or impact. During the various stages of treatment, it may be more convenient to keep the object on open shelving or spare bench surfaces, covering the objects with tissue or polyethylene to prevent dust settling on surfaces.

Resins, solvents and other materials should be stored in the correct environment. For most materials, ordinary cupboards will suffice, though others such as hydrogen peroxide, epoxy adhesives, polyesters and silicone rubbers may require cooler temperatures and should be stored in a fridge. Chemicals should be stored in an approved, lockable, flameproof cupboard made of mild steel, preferably well away from the main working area. Current UK legislation allows a maximum of 50 litres of flammable solvents to be stored in suitable fire resistant cupboards.

Wet area

The wet area should ideally consist of two large stainless steel sinks with a draining area and adjacent work surface (Figure 13.3). The space below can be used for the storage of basins, buckets and trays. There should be enough room next to the sink to rest objects undergoing treatment. An extractor over the draining area is useful to remove unwanted fumes

Figure 13.3 Wet area, with a pair of large sinks and a draining area served by local exhaust ventilation. There is also a water heater and a water deionizer (Victoria and Albert Museum, London).

from the objects receiving solvent treatment. Swivel taps should be fitted so that they can be turned out of the way of large objects if necessary. The taps can also be padded with rubber tubing to cut down the risk of damage arising from accidental collisions between the taps and objects. In archaeological workshops the wet area may also include large tanks for desalinating objects. A water deionizer, or still, should be located at this point, and a water heater if necessary.

Electricity

Electrical points should be plentiful and conveniently situated at bench level for use in the working area. The needs of the left and right handed individuals should be considered when deciding where to locate them. Regulations concerning the protection of power supply sources in situations where solvents are in use should also be observed.

Lighting

Lighting can be supplemented by desk lamps, and general overhead light produced by fluorescent tubes. For detailed colour work the type of electrical light source becomes very important to achieve a near perfect colour match. Metameric problems can arise when a perfect colour match in one light appears altered in another light (Staniforth, 1985). This is due to the difference between the spectral reflectance of the pigment in the retouching medium and that of the ceramic glaze. Staniforth describes how the metameric differences are apparent when an object is retouched in natural light and then viewed in tungsten lighting. The appearance of the colour of an object relates to the *colour rendering* ability of the type of light in which it is viewed. Lights can be rated according to their closeness to natural light. Natural light has a *colour rendering index* (CRI) of 100, under which colours will appear *true*. Electric lights with a CRI near 100 will give colour rendering close to that of natural light. Another consideration is the *colour temperature* of electric light sources, measured in kelvins and generally determined by the power of the lamp. It should be around 3500 to 6000 K for colour matching, using a source that has a CRI of near 100. Ideal daylight simulation, or north light, is approximately 5000 to 5500 K. Light with a low colour temperature tends to produce a yellow light that reduces the contrasts in the colour and requires greater concentration to detect differences, leading to eye strain. A further factor in the simulation of north facing daylight for colour matching work involves producing an emission of uniform amounts of light of all the different wavelengths in the visible spectrum (Jaqueline and Money, 1991). Unfortunately an artificial light source tends to give out variable light in which some wavelengths are more dominant than others. Normal household tungsten light gives off a warm light because it produces more light at the red end of the spectrum (Figure 13.4). However, there are lights available which have been specially designed to simulate daylight. The simplest of these is the tungsten light bulb which incorporates a blue filter to give a colder light that imitates natural north light. It can be fitted into domestic light appliances that have bayonet fittings. A combination of an ordinary tungsten light with a cool fluorescent light can give a good colour matching light. In the Conservation Department at the Victoria and Albert Museum the main overhead light is provided by double fluorescent strip lights, each pair being composed of a warm and a cool tube with an ultraviolet filter. Lighting technology is constantly being updated; for current information on the best options available, experts or manufacturers should be consulted. At the time of writing, the Philips TLD 95 fluorescent tube (that recently superseded the GraphicA 47 model) has proved successful, consisting of a fluorescent lamp incorporating a double coating. However, it should be

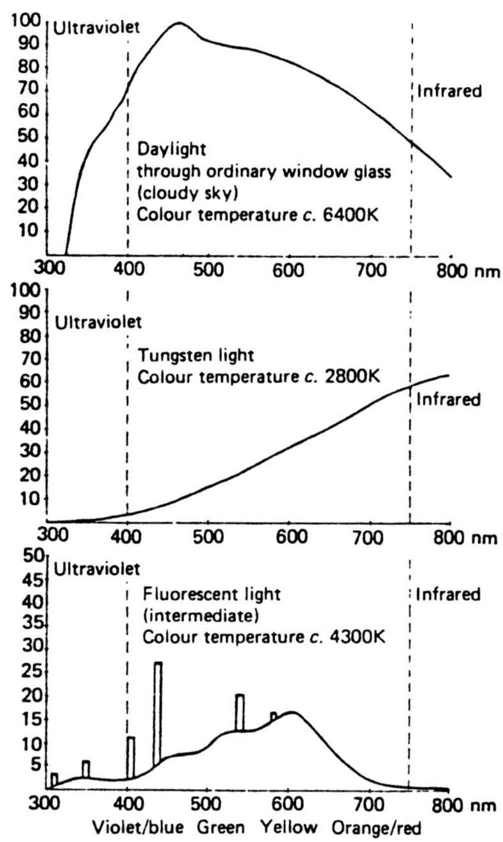

Figure 13.4 Comparison of spectral distribution of radiant energy for daylight, tungsten light and fluorescent light (Kuhn, 1986).

remembered that the only sure way to ensure that areas of retouching remain perfectly colour matched later, when on display, is to carry out the retouching in lighting conditions identical to those in the display area.

Fume extraction

Fume extraction will be required for many of the processes involved in the treatment of ceramics where vapours and fumes produced by the use of certain materials will be hazardous to health (Center for Occupational Hazards, 1985b). The types of ventilation system divide into two categories:

Dilution or *general ventilation* which works by *diluting* the contaminated air, mixing it with clean air, before extracting the mixture out of the studio.
Local exhaust ventilation (LEV) removes all vapours at their source before they have a chance to circulate into the studio. LEV is the most suitable type for ceramic conservators.

LEV normally consists of a movable duct system which terminates in a hood through which the contaminated air is pulled by a fan out of the studio (Figure 13.5). If effective, the system should eliminate all the toxic fumes and vapours, before the user inhales them. To make this possible, the hood of the system has to be as close as possible to the process, so that vapours from the solvents do not have a chance to escape elsewhere. The ventilation should pull the fumes away from the breathing zone of the individual. For airborne solvents lighter than air, the extraction should be above the source, but those with heavier fumes should be extracted from below. There are a number of extractors currently available and models are continuously being improved. Consultants and health and safety advisers should always be approached to gain information on the best currently available systems. Her Majesty's Stationery Office publishes helpful guides to the subject (HSE, 1988, 1993).

The most important criterion in choosing an extraction system for a studio will be the flow rate which governs its ability to extract volumes of air, usually measured in cubic metres per second or hour (m^3/s, m^3/h). In general more powerful extractors will be noisier, though some may be fitted with silencers, making them more expensive. The system can be either entirely free-standing and portable, incorporating a disposable filter system, or built into the studio with ducts to transfer the fumes to the exterior of the building, in which case it should be installed by an expert. Where unpleasant fumes are being expelled into the outside atmosphere it should be remembered that warm air will also be extracted; consequently, during cold weather, use of an over-powerful extractor may reduce temperatures in the studio considerably. Other factors to consider are the ease of use of the extractor and moving the trunking and hood. Maintenance demands must be seriously weighed up against the cost and requirements. Ideally, contaminated air should be removed well away from the studio, though not directed to an outlet that might be a hazard for other individuals. The extracted air should be replaced with an input supply of clean air. For general retouching on a work bench, an extraction system capable of removing toxic vapours at a speed of approximately 0.5 m/s at the source should give adequate protection (Hughes, 1987; Center for Occupational Hazards, 1985b); other processes may demand a higher air speed.

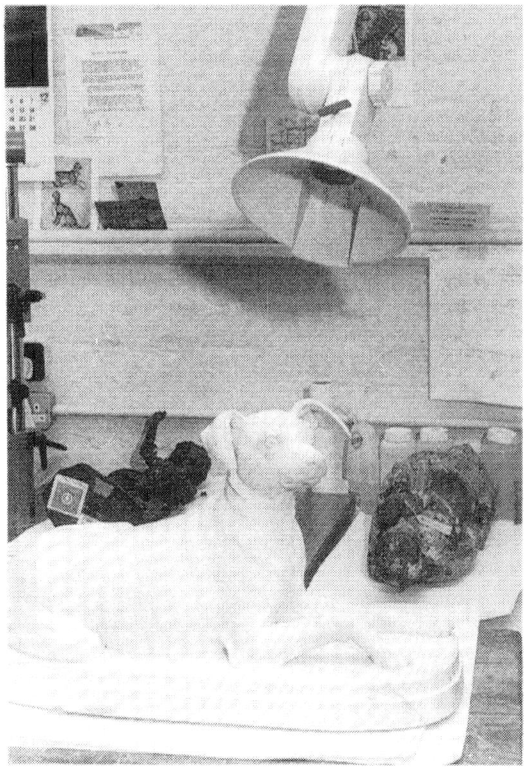

Figure 13.5 Local exhaust ventilation in use, to extract fumes emitted whilst the polyester resin filling at the dog's ear cures (Victoria and Albert Museum, London).

When using an airbrush a larger, more powerful system will be necessary to take the greater quantities of solvent away from the worker. Air speeds of 0.6 to 1 m/s at the mouth of the hood have been recommended (Center for Occupational Hazards, 1985b). In such a situation a spray booth should be used. This is another form of local exhaust system where the hood is large enough to accommodate the object and with room to spare for the action of the airbrush.

Fume cupboards are also effective for extracting noxious airborne substances. They consist of a cupboard area with vertically sliding doors. Objects undergoing treatments which demand the use of toxic solvents may be placed in the cupboard for the duration of the treatment. Such a cupboard might also be used for retouching and airbrush work, though LEV or specially designed spray booths are a better option. Fume cupboards should comply with BS 7258.

Heating

Heating will be a necessary service that should be considered early during the planning stages. Safety should be paramount when making the choice: the system must be hazard free when operated in the presence of volatile flammable chemicals. Systems that involve naked flames such as gas fires, paraffin heaters, or pilot lights would be a serious risk. Convection heaters should also be avoided, as they will stir up solvents and airborne particles within the immediate area. A normal domestic heating system should be adequate provided the boiler is not in the main working area.

Equipment

The next stage in setting up the studio will involve acquiring equipment. Some of the items are not essential to the running of the studio, but they could prove a worthwhile investment, by reducing time and labour and achieving better results than cheap improvised alternatives.

Water heater

If there is not a reliable supply of hot water in the building it will be worth installing a small electric hot water heater above the sink.

Water deionizer or still

Because of the impure nature of most water supplies, deionized or distilled water should ideally be substituted for many processes involving cleaning, soaking or desalination. It is important to have some idea of the quantities which might be required before buying a unit, as they vary in their output rate.

Fridge

The shelf life of most synthetic resins and silicone rubbers will usually be extended by storing them at low temperatures in a fridge. Hydrogen peroxide should also be stored in the cool darkness of a fridge. If the fridge has a freezing compartment, this will also be useful in extending the pot life of epoxy resins. Under no circumstances, however, should the same fridge be used for the storage of food and drink.

Oven

Porous ceramics can take several weeks or even months to dry completely. The gentle warmth of an oven on a low setting will greatly reduce the time by speeding up evaporation of the retained moisture. The curing time of epoxy adhesives can be cut down by warming, though this may alter the ageing properties of the adhesive and is not recommended. In order to cure, *stoving enamels* will require heating in an oven.

A convection oven provides an even circulating heat which is effective for drying damp objects. In choosing an oven, a number of points should be considered, including: its weight; the internal capacity; the external dimensions in relation to the existing work surfaces; the noise output (some convection ovens have noisy internal fans); the rate at which it heats up; and also the sensitivity of the thermostat. Being able to pre-set the oven so that it switches off after a certain length of time may also be a useful feature, and a glass panel in the door allows the objects to be observed undisturbed. Finally, some ovens can be run on domestic supplies, while others will require three-phase electricity and hence special wiring.

Binocular microscope

This has already been considered in Chapter 4. Basic binocular microscopes for bench work, with built-in light sources, are useful for observing the object in detail during the course of treatment. For example, when cleaning or consolidating an area, there is a need to be extra sure that there is no risk of damage occurring to the surface. Powerful magnification is not necessary under such circumstances: $\times 10$ to $\times 35$ is usually adequate. A long focal length will allow room to work between the lens and the object. For detailed examination a more sophisticated microscope with powerful magnification may be necessary. Added extras worth considering include a zoom lens that alters the level of magnification without having to refocus, an adjustable lighting system with a dimming control, and an attachment for a camera.

Compressed air supply

This will be necessary if the restorer intends to use an airbrush, or air abrasive equipment. Though it is possible to have a compressed air supply built into the studio, portable compressors are the cheaper option. There is a wide choice of compressors available that offer various useful features. The essential requirements to look for when deciding which model to opt for include:

Capacity Should be capable of producing 40 psi (pounds per square inch).

Size and weight For convenience it should be easy to move and carry and small enough to store away if necessary.
Noise Some compressors can be extremely noisy and consequently unpleasant to work with.
Pressure gauge To give a visible indication of the pressure of the air being supplied.
Regulator For airbrush work it should be possible to alter the air pressure in order to achieve different effects.
Air filter and water trap The surrounding air being supplied to the compressor will inevitably contain dust particles and moisture. A filter will remove the former, while the water trap will cut down the build-up of moisture and avoid water droplets being passed through the airbrush.
Reserve tank Allows air to be stored, ensuring a constant flow of air to the airbrush. It also allows more than one airbrush to be used at a time.

Other less desirable alternatives to a compressor include foot pumps, or aerosol cans of air. The inexpensive foot pump compressor is basically a set of bellows, mounted to the floor, operated by foot action. It produces air at intermittent rates. Canned air is a simple, though expensive alternative, where the airbrush is connected to the top of a can which provides an even supply of air for a limited period of time. The use of the compressor in conjunction with the airbrush is discussed in Chapter 12.

Instruments and hand tools

During the treatment of ceramics each process will involve a range of hand tools and instruments. Some of the simplest tools, such as the scalpel and spatula, are the most versatile and indispensable. Others have very specialist applications. Some tools may be *borrowed* from other professions such as dental instruments and sculptor's modelling tools. Sometimes a certain task may require a tool to be specially made, and after it has served its purpose it may become redundant. The following summary is intended to serve as a check list, and the tools have been set out in sequence according to the process for which they are most generally used.

General

Some tools may be appropriate to a number of tasks (Figure 13.6).

Pin vices consisting of a small hand piece that grips fine needles are helpful for probing and picking during examination. They can also be used to remove pockets of unwanted material.

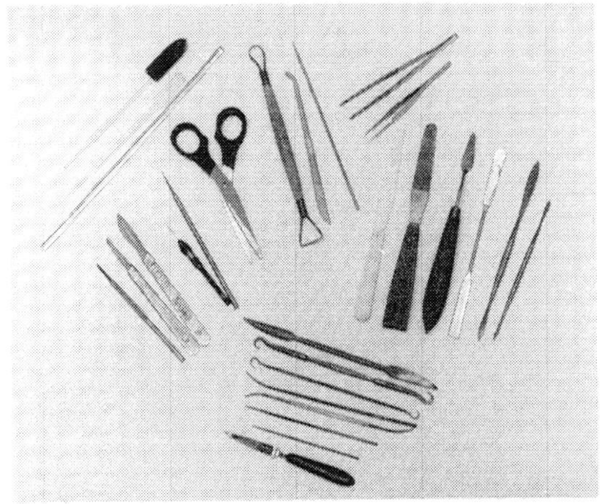

Figure 13.6 General tools that are used for various purposes in several stages during treatment.

Brushes of various qualities and sizes should be reserved especially for cleaning purposes (Figure 13.7). These might include a selection of cheap decorator's brushes, toothbrushes, and sable brushes. Sable brushes, which are dust and dirt free, can be used for gentle cleaning and for removal of dirt from awkward inaccessible places. Their tips can also be modified by trimming the hairs if necessary. Hog's hair brushes, in various shapes and sizes, are useful for dusting and cleaning intricate delicate surfaces. The metal ferrules can be padded with chamois or adhesive fabric tape, to prevent them damaging or scratching vulnerable surfaces. Stencil brushes, with their short wooden handles and stiff hog's bristles, are available in different sizes and grades of stiffness. They can be useful for removing ingrained dirt from

Figure 13.7 Brushes for cleaning. Some have had padding wrapped round their ferrules in order to avoid the potential risk of damaging an object whilst in use.

objects, usually in combination with a warm solution of water and non-ionic detergent. Glass bristle brushes, which consist of a tightly bound bundle of glass fibres, are sometimes used for mechanical removal of stubborn deposits such as salt encrustations, old mortar on the reverse of tiles, or old adhesives. They are abrasive, and care should be taken to carefully monitor progress and ensure no damage is occurring. With use, the bristles gradually break, and the brush slowly wears down.

Swab sticks consisting of wooden cocktail sticks, toothpicks or bamboo satay sticks, can be used with small amounts of cotton wool twisted onto their tips for delicate cleaning work. The swabs are saturated with solvent for application to a surface and the sticks may be reused a number of times.

Dental tools are available in various forms, and suitable for reaching into small inaccessible areas. They can be modified by bending or sharpening their tips if necessary, and used, for example, to pick out old rivet holes or for fine modelling.

Files and rifflers will be useful, not only in the dismantling stage, but also later on for removing the excess from cured resin fillings. Needle files are available with round, triangular, square or flattened shafts in coarse, medium or fine grades. After use they should be carefully cleaned with a soft brush. Sculptor's rifflers can be used for cutting away old or new fillings. They come in a range of shapes, sizes and grades, with both curved and flat tips. They should be cleaned with a wire brush.

Surgical scalpels and blades are useful for cutting and scraping. The large handle (number 3) used with the curved number 23 blade, and the small handle (number 4) with the number 15 blade tend to be the most popular. Eye surgeons use even finer scalpels, which can provide an excellent level of precision for detailed microscope work. The small fine blades are, however, very expensive. It is possible to sharpen blades with a carborundum stone, though replacement number 15 and 23 blades are easily obtained. Care and caution should be exercised when handling both old and new blades. Old blades should be disposed of in a special *sharps* bin.

Tweezers are useful for picking up solvent saturated swabs, and other applications where fingers cannot be used. Tweezers with fine tips will give greater precision when lifting unwanted particles or hairs out of the way, or positioning small fragments into inaccessible corners.

Scissors have numerous uses. An old pair can be kept for cutting abrasive paper into strips since it will rapidly blunt good sharp scissors.

Spatulas and palette knives are used for mixing, scooping, and scraping jobs. The small double-ended sculptor's spatulas are especially suited to blending and applying small amounts of adhesive, while larger ones and palette knives are better for mixing up greater quantities of viscous resins. They should be cleaned immediately after use. Plastic palette knives are a cheap disposable alternative that avoids the potential risk of contamination by metal.

Solvent containers should be solvent resistant vessels which can be easily cleaned for reuse. They should be of an appropriate size that will contain small quantities of a reasonable depth, and not spill or overturn when in use. There are specially designed dispensing containers which will release small quantities of solvent at a time into a reservoir in the cap.

Pipettes are used for transferring measured volumes of liquids. Disposable polyethylene pipettes are an accurate and safe means of measuring volumes of less viscous resins into containers. Micropipettes made from glass can be used to direct small quantities of consolidant into cracks and fissures in a more precise manner than would be possible with a brush (Figure 8.4).

Examination

For initial routine examination in the studio, the following tools and equipment can be invaluable. The more complex analytical instruments are not considered here.

Metal detectors such as those used by electricians to locate hidden cables can be used to detect concealed dowels in objects (Figure 4.3).

Ultraviolet inspection lamps may aid the detection of invisible restorations (Figure 4.7).

Magnifiers such as basic hand-held magnifying glasses (Figure 4.4), illuminated hand magnifiers, head band magnifiers (Optivisors), tripod magnifiers and binocular microscopes are invaluable for examination. Any magnifying aid is better than none at all, and if expense is no object then a trinocular microscope which has an attachment for a camera will prove an extremely useful item for both examination and recording purposes.

Cleaning

Ultrasonic cleaning and air polishing dental instruments, although prohibitively expensive for the smaller conservation studio, have applications for the ceramics conservator which are worth mentioning (Figure 7.5). The tip of the ultrasonic hand piece generates high-frequency waves that are transmitted through the water as microscopically pulsating small bubbles, capable of loosening dirt and deposits. The metal tip of the instrument is allowed to glide above the surface, discharging a jet of water. It should not be allowed to come directly in contact with the ceramic, as the vibration can abrade even hard surfaces. The ultrasonic mode should not be used on soft friable bodies. The air polishing mode uses an extremely fine grade abrasive powder, such as sodium bicarbonate, delivered by way of a compressed air stream through a fine nozzle simultaneously with a jet of water. The abrasive action is extremely gentle, though sufficient to remove ingrained accretions from inaccessible areas such as pits, cracks and rivet holes. However, the process has the potential to cause salt contamination of low-fired porous wares, unless immediately followed by washing.

Steam cleaners have been successfully used to remove ingrained dirt from terracotta surfaces, and almost certainly have potential applications for the treatment of other ceramics. Low-pressure steam has the ability to remove greasy dirt from the surface without saturating the body with water (Larson, 1990). It is possible to improvise with less sophisticated equipment such as a specially constructed steam kettle (Larson, 1980b, 1986).

Conductivity meters will assess the concentration of soluble salts in water by the measurement of the related ability of the water solution to conduct electricity. The ion concentration determines the ability of the water to allow the passage of an electric current, and as the amount of salts in the wash water decreases, so will the conductivity. The instrument usually consists of a sensitive probe attached to a meter, which, depending on its age, may be battery operated with a digital display.

Vacuum cleaners will be useful in removing unwanted particles. Small, rechargeable, cordless models are more portable and useful for work on site. For removing dust particles from objects, the nozzle should be well padded. Nylon mesh may be placed over the end of the nozzle as an extra precaution to avoid the possibility of sucking up any loose or detached parts of the object.

Dismantling

Dental drills offer greater control and consequently greater sensitivity than standard drills. Some of the more sophisticated models offer variable speeds controlled by a foot pedal, with a lightweight hand piece capable of taking a wide range of chuck sizes. Silicon carbide coated abrasives can greatly reduce time when cutting back large hard fillings. Diamond tipped points will cut into ceramics and can be obtained in a range of sizes and shapes allowing very precise and controlled drilling (Figure 13.8). Grinding and drilling with diamond tipped points are best achieved with the tips that are ball, tube, cone or needle shaped, while, for slicing and cutting the discs are most appropriate. Although diamond tipped points are expensive, they will last a long time provided they are properly cared for, and not abused by excessive heating during use. They should be kept cool during drilling by supplying a small fine jet of cold water to the area, or by immersing the object and drill tip in water, whilst avoiding water contact with any other parts of the drill. Alternatively, if the drill tip is dipped into a beaker of cold water at regular intervals, this should be sufficient to keep it cool.

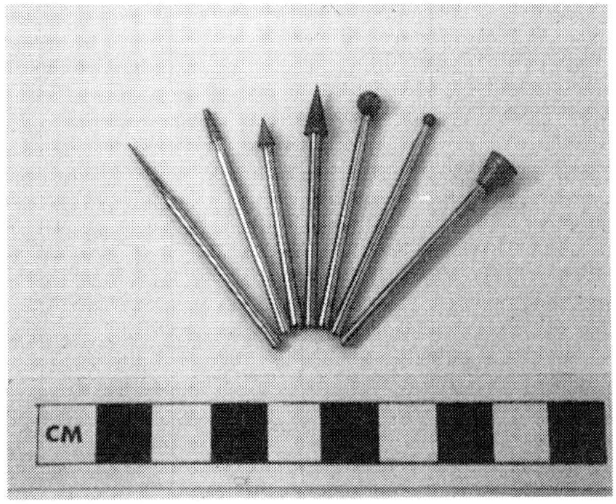

Figure 13.8 Diamond tipped points for use in a dental drill.

Hacksaw blades aid quick removal of large fillings. Old rivets can be sliced in half using blades that have been cut into small lengths; each half rivet may then be easily removed.

Pliers with long-nosed tips can be used for loosening tight nuts in awkward places (Figure 13.9).

Wire cutters can be useful for cutting through wire attachments on the back of plates or tiles.

Screwdrivers will undo screws on mounts, frames, and backing systems.

Hammers and chisels are invaluable for removal of large areas of plaster from the reverse of tiles.

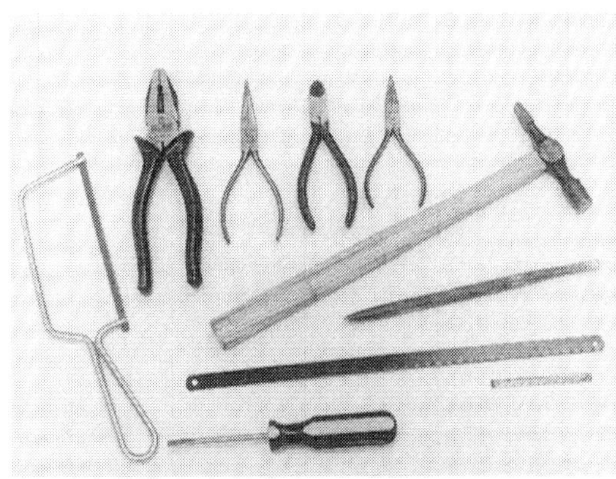

Figure 13.9 Tools for dismantling.

Bonding, filling and consolidation

Modelling tools such as those used by artists, made from boxwood, are available in a range of shapes and sizes and are useful for modelling.

Tweezers (vacuum type), although an expensive luxury, can be handy for lifting very small fragments by a suction action.

Heated spatulas in their simplest form consist of a flat tipped metal tool warmed over a spirit lamp. They are useful for sealing the edges of dental wax supports or moulds onto the surface of an object so as to avoid leakage of resin casts. They may also be used for levelling thermoplastic resins (separated by silicone release paper). Thermostatically controlled electrically heated spatulas will offer a safer controllable alternative.

Scales (beam balance or electronic scales) will be helpful for the precise measurement required by some two-part resin systems. They should be capable of weighing quite small quantities from 0.1 g upwards. Digital electronic scales are probably the simplest and most convenient to use, though a more expensive option.

Glass rods for stirring and mixing resins should be cleaned immediately following use.

Vacuum pump tanks are used in the consolidation of fragile porous archaeological materials. The vacuum extracts air from the pores of the object, allowing the consolidant to then pass into the fabric of the object.

Hot air blower (or hair drier) will assist softening of dental wax for moulding. It can also be used to warm adhesives, in order to lower their viscosity and facilitate their movement into a tight joint by capillary action.

Clamps (e.g. metal G-clamps) will be useful for holding things rigidly in position (Figure 13.10). Special clamps and jacks can be made for specific purposes, for example to coax a sprung join back into correct alignment (Williams, 1983; Navarro, 1989).

Vices provide a means of gripping materials securely whilst cutting or drilling. They can be temporarily clamped to the bench top as necessary.

Tape dispensers help to simplify the action of removing lengths of adhesive tape from a roll.

Props are helpful for supporting objects while adhesive cures. Science laboratory retort stands, special vacuum cushions (e.g. Vari-cushion: Jessop) and sand-filled containers can be used.

Callipers or dividers are essential for taking accurate measurements from an object while modelling or making detailed condition reports.

Retouching

Airbrushes of various designs are available; the choice is usually a matter of personal preference. To ensure trouble-free performance, the airbrush should be cleaned thoroughly after each session, and serviced regularly. They are useful for covering large areas in instances where hand retouching would be unsatisfactory.

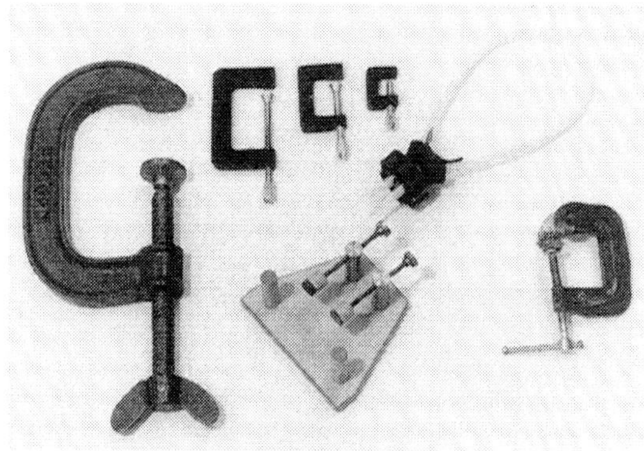

Figure 13.10 Various clamps.

Paintbrushes especially good quality artist's ones will perform better for hand retouching and last a longer period of time. Sable haired brushes give the best results, although some of the better quality synthetic and natural blends also achieve good standards. Those with shorter hairs used for miniature painting give greater control than the general water colour brushes with longer hairs. The most useful sizes are in the finer end of the range: (00 to 3); the larger brushes (7 or 8) will occasionally be useful for filling in greater areas. If properly looked after, brushes will last for several weeks. Such care involves meticulous cleaning routines, removing all traces of pigment and resin immediately after use, by gentle but thorough rinsing in a clean pot of the appropriate thinners, followed by rinsing in clean warm soapy water. They should then be dried by blotting on a clean paper towel, gently easing the hairs into a point. Both during use and cleaning, it is advisable to avoid bending the hairs too severely, since the pressure of the edge of the metal ferrule against the individual hairs will damage and weaken them. Brushes should not be left resting on their tips, either in thinners or otherwise. They should be stored in clean, dry, dust-free boxes or trays. Damage by moths during storage is best prevented by inclusion of mothballs or naphthalene.

Palettes such as white glazed tiles provide an easily cleaned shiny surface on which to mix pigments with retouching medium, and also for mixing aggregates or pigments into adhesives. On occasions, it may be preferable to attach a piece of acetate to the tile on which to mix quantities of adhesive; this can then be disposed of easily, avoiding the need to spend time cleaning up the tile. Tiles with black glaze can be used for airbrush trials, the dark background making it easier to see the quality of the sprayed line. While retouching media can usually be soaked off the tile by leaving it in water overnight, adhesives will have to be cleaned off immediately, to avoid them hardening on the tile. Adhesive tape is often cut up into smaller strips on a tile, since it provides a clean hard surface that is usually resistant to the normal pressure of a scalpel. Plain white glazed saucers or plates can also be used as a mixing surface. Other specially designed ceramic palettes consist of glazed oblongs with a series of depressions in the surface for mixing in.

Pigment containers will be necessary for small amounts of pigments to keep them free of dust or draughts. These can be glass vials, obtainable from laboratory suppliers, or plastic micro-test-tubes. Other containers can be made by improvising (e.g. using empty make-up compacts, or by backing a section of egg-crate light diffuser with wood or Perspex), so that each small cell can be filled with pigment (Figure 13.11).

Gilding tools such as a gilder's pad, knife and tip (brush) should be acquired if gold leaf is used frequently.

Agate burnishers will give a high shine when used to burnish fillings gilded with gold leaf or powder.

Health and safety in the conservation studio

Recent years have seen a marked change in the formerly relaxed attitude of the conservator towards health and safety. This has been provoked by changes in the law over the past 20 years, including the Health and Safety at Work Act of 1974 in the UK, and the Occupational Safety and Health Act 1970 in the USA. Documents have been published detailing aspects of the legislation. More recently in the UK, the Control of Substances Hazardous to Health (COSHH) Regulations 1989 have made the employer legally responsible for ensuring that potentially harmful substances are used safely in the workplace. This section aims to highlight the more relevant areas.

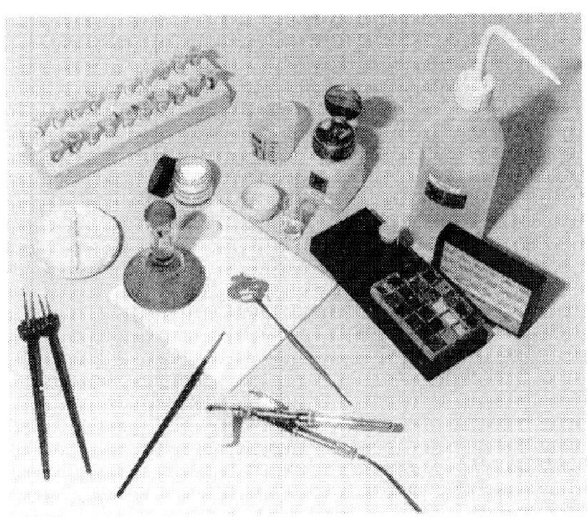

Figure 13.11 Some of the tools and equipment that are used during the retouching stage.

The health and safety of the individuals is of paramount importance when planning and designing a conservation studio. This should take into consideration the use of both potentially hazardous materials, and equipment. A well planned and efficient studio will not only be a pleasure to work in, but also help reduce problems of health and safety.

Neglecting potential areas of risk may eventually cause an accident and or ill health. By their very nature, accidents are difficult to predict or control, but their incidence can have far reaching, and often disastrous effects. In addition, the accumulative effects of neglecting some aspect of health and safety can, in time, lead to a deterioration in health or the onset of an allergic response (Howie, 1987).

Even in the most carefully designed studio, the human element is capable of initiating disaster for a number of reasons including: complacency, ignorance, negligence, laziness and stress.

All potential risks can be reduced by increasing our own awareness and that of our colleagues and students. For those working on their own, in a small studio, the risks are similar but reduced. In a large studio, the potential for accidents will be proportionally greater; larger quantities of hazardous materials are available, and more elaborate machinery may be in use. There may also be a tendency for an individual to regard the issue of health and safety as the employer's responsibility.

In ceramics conservation and restoration the number of potential hazards is large, the main areas being the risk of fires, the misuse of chemicals, and dangers from tools and machinery.

Fire

Studios in public buildings such as museums or colleges will be governed by strict regulations laid down by the Fire Precautions Act 1971 (UK), which state that a competent fire officer should be appointed with responsibility to implement the required standards. He should carry out regular checks on fire extinguishers and fire exit routes.

In a smaller studio it will be the owner's responsibility to make sure that there are adequate extinguishers, which should be checked regularly, and also to ensure that members of staff are aware of their existence and how to use them. Guidance should be sought from the local fire authority. Insurance policies for studios in private premises such as the home should take into account the use of flammable liquids, as this may not be covered by a domestic policy.

Understanding the conditions which can give rise to a fire will help in preventing their occurrence. Fire consists of a chemical reaction where heat is evolved as a result of oxygen combining with another substance (the fuel), initiated by an input of energy, usually as heat. Once the energy level of the reaction has been raised, combustion can occur. Such combustion usually occurs between vapours or gases present in a suitable concentration in the air and oxygen. For example, a small spark generated by electrical equipment such as a compressor or a drill may be enough to ignite flammable vapours or liquids at ambient temperatures.

Prevention of fire

In the event of a serious fire, fire fighting experts should be summoned immediately. For a small fire of a containable size there are five main types of fire extinguisher available, their individual use being determined by the nature of the fire. Adequate protection for a studio will be provided by a water extinguisher for general purposes; a dry powder extinguisher for both general purposes and flammable liquid; and a carbon dioxide extinguisher for flammable liquid and electrical fires. Fire buckets containing sand may be used on all small fires. A choice of too many different extinguishers can cause confusion in a crisis. The most important rules to remember with respect to extinguishers is not to use water or foam on electrical equipment and not to use water on flammable liquids.

Employees should also be reminded about the importance of observing simple precautions. Since electrical fires are probably the most common type of fire, both at home and in the studio, all equipment should be checked regularly to ensure that the wiring is in good order, and that plugs have the correct fuse as instructed by the manufacturers. Avoid the temptation to overload sockets by using adaptors. The maximum output from the plug should be 13 amperes.

The storage of flammable liquids and materials should be carefully controlled. Only small quantities (around 250 millilitres) of the most frequently used solvents such as acetone, thinners, methylated spirit and white spirit should be kept on the work bench. These small amounts should be kept in narrow necked solvent resistant plastic dispenser bottles. Other reserves, of up to 50 litres, should be kept in specially designed fire resistant steel cabinets which can be locked. Larger quantities should be put in a store, away from the main building. The store should be well ventilated, and with adequate provision for decanting smaller amounts for the work room.

Within the main work area, flammable materials and solvents should be separated from any potential ignition sources. Even small amounts of solvents such as acetone, IMS and thinners will produce enough vapour at room temperature to easily be ignited by a stray spark. The use of adjustable extraction should reduce the concentration of the vapour. Swabs or paper towels impregnated with solvents should be disposed of in metal safety bins, which should be emptied at regular intervals. Any spillage should be wiped up quickly with paper towels and then disposed of similarly.

Flammable liquid waste can also be stored in special canisters before finally being removed for disposal. The local authority should be contacted for advice on disposal of waste solvents. Under no circumstances should naked flames be used anywhere near flammable substances. Smoking must be strictly prohibited in the studio and *No Smoking* signs should be prominently displayed. A stray cigarette disposed of in a volatile environment could have devastating consequences (Slade, 1987).

Health risks from solvents and materials

All materials within the studio whether potentially harmful or otherwise should be clearly labelled with the chemical name, common name and recognized hazard-warning pictograms (Figure 13.12). Although some solvents may not look or smell particularly dangerous, the fact that in application, the small molecules are expected to dissolve or swell materials, implies that they are also capable of causing some disruption within human bodies. Some solvents may be less hazardous to health than others, though all, with the exception of water, can be toxic if abused. Those substances which are described as *toxic* or *poisonous* have the potential to cause fatal or serious illness if consumed, inhaled or absorbed into the body. The effect can be cumulative, and repeated exposures can build up to cause a severe health condition or death. Other substances such as acids and bleaches are *corrosive* and capable of destroying living tissue upon contact, causing severe burns. *Irritant* substances are those solids, liquids, dusts or vapours which can produce illness through skin contact, inhalation or swallowing, giving rise to an inflammation of skin or membranes of digestive or respiratory systems. All organic solvents (containing carbon) are toxic to a certain degree and can damage the nervous system, respiratory system, skin, eyes and internal organs (Pascoe, 1980; Center for Occupational Hazards, 1985a; Smith, 1991). Evidence suggests that simultaneous exposure to two or more chemicals can be especially damaging. Smoking and

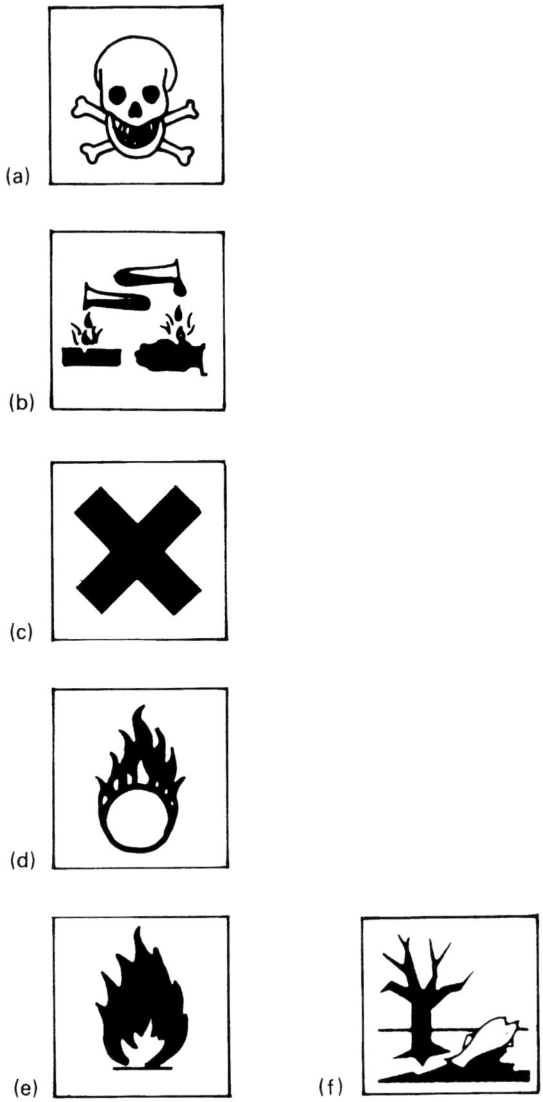

Figure 13.12 Hazard warning symbols. (a) *Toxic* (poisonous) substances: exposure through swallowing, inhalation or skin contact can cause death or serious illness. (b) *Corrosive* materials that can destroy living tissues by contact. (c) *Harmful* substances which can cause illness as a result of accidental consumption by inhalation, swallowing or contact with the skin; also *irritant* materials that may cause an inflammatory reaction of the skin, mucous membranes or respiratory system. (d) *Oxidizing* agents that can cause fire on contact with combustible substances. (e) *Highly flammable* gas or liquid with flashpoint below 21°C, or *extremely flammable* substance with flashpoint below 0°C and boiling point 35°C or less. (f) Dangerous to the environment.

consumption of alcoholic drinks will also increase the toxic effect of certain chemicals, either before or after exposure (Clydesdale, 1990).

Harmful materials may enter the body in various ways; they can be ingested through the mouth, or inhaled as a vapour through the lungs, or the skin can provide an entry route (Waldron, 1987). Entry into the digestive system may occur when eating or drinking at the work bench, transferring dust or chemicals from the hands onto food and into the mouth. On no account should eating or drinking take place in the studio. The combined use of utensils such as cups, plates, knives and towels for both domestic and conservation treatment purposes should never occur. Using pipettes without safety bulbs, or storing harmful materials in old food cartons or bottles, especially if former labels are still visible, are unwise practices.

Prevention of inhalation and absorption of volatile toxins through the lungs and the skin is made difficult by the possibility of rapid transfer over a large surface area directly into the bloodstream. The practice of using adequate extraction (or respiratory protection), and protective clothing such as gloves, eye shields and overalls should be taken when handling solvents. The use of swab sticks, tweezers and long-handled brushes should avoid solvents coming into contact with skin where gloves are not being worn. When using an airbrush, powerful fume extraction, and respiratory protection should be used to safeguard against airborne resin and thinners, and any exposed skin should ideally be covered or protected by barrier cream. Although the skin may not absorb all chemicals, solvents can remove natural oils from the skin, drying and exposing it to the action of other substances that can act as irritants. Gloves need not necessarily inhibit work, when one considers the precise work which surgeons are able to perform wearing similar protection (Hamilton-Eddy, 1984).

Since the majority of ceramic conservators are female, it is worth emphasizing their greater vulnerability to the adverse effects of certain chemicals. The composition of the female body has proportionally less muscle but 5–15% more fat than men, leading to a greater susceptibility to the damaging effects of organic solvents. Individuals with higher ratios of fat to body weight are more vulnerable to the toxic effects of chemicals. Prolonged exposure to some chemicals can affect the reproductive organs. The menstrual cycle and fertility may be disrupted. In particular, pregnant women working with toxic chemicals risk damaging the foetus through the transfer of harmful toxins via the placenta. It is extremely important that the advice of the family doctor is sought prior to the onset of pregnancy, in order to discuss potential risks from the working environment. If necessary, the local doctor will be able to refer the patient to more specialist sources of information.

In the UK the Health and Safety Executive publishes current information related to the use of potentially harmful substances. Safe levels are constantly being reviewed as more information becomes available. In the US the *threshold limit value* (TLV) is used as a measure of the concentration of vapour that can be tolerated without detectable harm by the average worker during a 40 hour week. It is usually given as parts per million (ppm), or as milligrams per cubic metre (mg/m^3). The lower the TLV number, the more toxic is the chemical. As an approximate guide, a TLV below 100 ppm is considered highly toxic compared with a value between 100 and 500 ppm which is moderately toxic (e.g. the TLV of dichloromethane is 50 ppm, toluene is 100 ppm, white spirit is 300 ppm, acetone is 750 ppm). The *time weighted average* (TWA) takes the average value of the exposure over an 8 hour, 5 day working week. The *maximum exposure limit* (MEL) has been applicable in the UK since 1989 and is legally enforceable under the Control of Substances Hazardous to Health (COSHH) Regulations. It is the 'maximum concentration of an airborne substance, averaged over a reference period, to which employees may be exposed by inhalation under any circumstances'. COSHH requires employers and managers to keep MEL assigned substances to as low a level as reasonably practicable, it is a criminal offence to go over the limit. The MELs are divided into *short-term exposure limits* (STELs) for highly toxic or irritating substances, and *long-term exposure limits* (LTELs). The former are the maximum concentrations allowed for any worker averaged over a 15 minute period of exposure, with no more than four such exposures being permitted during any one day, any exposure being separated from the next by an hour. The latter are the concentrations averaged over an 8 hour period. Also in the UK since 1989 the *occupational exposure standards* (OESs) have been laid down by the COSHH Regulations and must be complied with by law. These are defined as 'the concentration of an airborne substance, averaged over a reference period, at which according to current knowledge there is no evidence that it is likely to be injurious to employees, if they are exposed by inhalation day after day at that concentration' Employers and managers are required to keep levels of exposure to such substances at, or below, the limit set. OESs may also be quoted as LTELs and STELs. Helpful and concise information on occupational exposure limits is available from the Health and Safety Executive in guidance note EH40.

A serious risk for the ceramics conservator will be that from irritant materials. Though anyone is potentially at risk, some people will be more susceptible than others, particularly those who suffer from dermatitis, eczema, asthma or hay fever. Even apparently innocuous substances such as soaps and detergents can cause dermatitis, especially if the skin has become dry through prolonged contact with solvents. Other examples include *biological washing powders* and nickel (present in spatulas, scalpel handles, and other metal tools) which may also cause a non-allergic reaction in the skin. As a result of prolonged contact, the body's defence mechanism may respond to a potential invasion of unwanted materials by activating its immune system and displaying the symptoms of an allergy. Some materials tend to be particularly common allergy initiators, though any foreign substance can spark off the allergic response causing serious irritation of the sensitive membranes of the nose, throat and eyes, or dermatological reactions.

The main routes of entry into the body will be through the lungs, by inhaling noxious vapours, or through the skin. Consequently, there should always be adequate ventilation to draw away any vapours when mixing epoxies or polyesters, as both the resin and the curing agent can cause serious problems. The precaution of wearing gloves and goggles should always be taken when handling such resins. Once a person has become sensitized, the only way to ensure that further attacks do not occur is to avoid any further exposure. Such a situation might prove devastating to the career of a professional restorer (Bailey, 1987). The cured resin will only present a health risk when reduced to fine dust during rubbing down or abrasion. Dust masks must be worn at this stage to avoid any inhalation of particles of the cured resin.

Some general safety reminders

1 Protective clothing such as a laboratory coat should be worn to avoid damaging other clothing unnecessarily. Long hair should be tied back, and any jewellery removed, as these can snag and catch on objects or machinery with sometimes disastrous results.
2 Respiratory protection with filters specifically designed to protect against inhalation of dust, fibrous materials, organic solvent vapours, and acid vapours, should be worn as appropriate. These usually consist of a rigid mask that may also include a protective eye shield. There are a number of different types of *respiratory protective equipment* (RPE) to be worn to avoid exposure to airborne contaminants. Some of the more sophisticated equipment incorporates an air supply, to aid breathing for use in situations where the correct levels of oxygen are not available. The type of RPE used is dependent on the nature and concentration of the contaminant. Disposable dust masks which cover just the nose and mouth provide protection against small amounts of particulate materials. High-efficiency dust respirators provide greater protection, and usually

consist of rubber or plastic face protection covering eyes, nose and mouth. They are fitted with cartridges or canisters that remove specific types of airborne contaminant. Those with twin cartridges and twin exhaust valves offer good comfortable protection over long periods of time in extreme conditions. Advice on the most suitable apparatus for specific applications should be sought from the local Health and Safety Executive, as well as manufacturers and suppliers (Bartlett and Rowles, 1987; Clydesdale, 1990; HSE, 1990; Jackson, 1992).

3 Eyes should be protected from the possibility of impact and chemical splashes by glasses or goggles with side guards. These should be worn when using solvents, acids, scalpels, drills and other machinery. British Standards specify requirements for particular types of work. Contact lenses should not be worn when handling solvents or in a dusty environment; soft lenses can absorb and react with solvents, and fine dust and grit can also get trapped behind lenses. The correct type of eye protection must be used when working with ultraviolet light sources.

4 Gloves should be worn when handling chemicals, for example, disposable vinyl or latex gloves when mixing resins, and solvent resistant gloves when handling solvents. Again there are British standards for these.

5 The studio should have adequate first-aid supplies, including an eye-wash bottle, plasters, dressings, disinfectants and creams.

6 All equipment and fire extinguishers should be maintained regularly.

7 Work benches should be tidy and well organized with no unnecessary equipment cluttering the surface.

8 All materials must be correctly labelled with appropriate hazard warning pictograms and safety phrases.

9 Flexes and furniture should not cause obstruction.

10. Sharp implements such as needles, scalpel blades and glass must be disposed of in special containers which are clearly labelled.

11. When moving Winchester bottles (2.5 litres) from one space to another, a carrier should be used. The temptation to carry them by their neck which is their weakest part should be avoided.

12. For decanting corrosive chemicals from large containers to smaller bottles, hand siphons and funnels must be used in a well ventilated area. Any spillage should be wiped up immediately, and solvent saturated rags disposed of in appropriate fireproof metal bins.

13. When lifting heavy objects, care should be taken not to strain the back; this applies particularly to women as they are generally more susceptible to strains of the lower back region between the spine and the pelvic girdle. Back injuries have been shown to develop over a period of time amongst those who regularly lift loads (Sherman, 1987).

14. Stress and boredom can be avoided by taking regular breaks from processes requiring prolonged concentration.

Useful sources of information for setting up a studio

As well as the usual specialist professional sources of conservation related information (UKIC, AIC, ICOM, IIC etc.: see Appendix I), probably some of the most useful advice can be gained from existing local contacts. Bank managers, accountants, independent insurance brokers and solicitors will be able to help with some of the major financial and legal formalities and technicalities. Other advice can be gained from government-based organizations, which will be listed in the local phone book. Some of these produce a number of helpful booklets and information sheets:

Department of Trade and Industry: give advice on running a business
Inland Revenue Inspector of taxes: booklet IR28 *Starting in Business*
Department of Employment: information for employers and employees
Advisory, Conciliation, and Arbitration Service (ACAS): guidance on a wide range of employment issues
Health and Safety Executive
Department of Health and Social Security
Fire Protection Association
Small Businesses Advisory Service
National Federation of Self-Employed and Small Businesses
Small Firms Service
Local Enterprise Agencies.

14

Materials for ceramics conservation

The practical aspects of restoring ceramics have already been discussed in earlier chapters, and the importance of a wide range of materials that fulfil very specific demands has been made apparent. An understanding of the physical and chemical properties of those materials helps the conservator to understand how a particular material interacts with the ceramic substrate. It should also assist in the selection of the most appropriate materials to use in the treatment of an object.

This chapter will consider the properties of the materials most frequently used in ceramics conservation and restoration. They are discussed in sequence according to the stage of treatment to which they relate and can be easily cross-referred with the corresponding section in the earlier chapters.

Cleaning materials

There are many different materials that can be used in a variety of ways for the removal of unwanted substances. The choice will depend on the precise circumstances. The conservator should understand how the cleaning material achieves its effect. More importantly, the conservator should be fully aware of the risks that may be involved both to the object, and to his or her own health.

Water

Water is one of the few materials in ceramics conservation that is not hazardous to health. It is without doubt the most useful and important cleaning agent for ceramics, whether used on its own or modified by other substances. It has the additional advantage of being readily available and inexpensive.

Pure water does not exist in a natural state; as falling rain it will become contaminated by gases in the air, then as it percolates through the ground it will dissolve mineral substances. By the time it reaches the tap it will have been further deliberately contaminated by the addition of chemicals to make it more palatable and safe for human consumption. The amount of dissolved substances in the water will vary, depending on the geology of the area. In *hard water* areas, calcium and magnesium, as well as sulphates, chlorides, carbonates and bicarbonates, may be present in significant amounts. This can be demonstrated to a certain extent by allowing a sample of hard water to dry on a glazed surface; the resulting residue of insoluble, inorganic material left behind represents the impurities responsible for the *hardness* of the water. Such residues can only be removed from the surface either mechanically or chemically. The insoluble scum that hard water forms with soap is another indication of the presence of salts in the water. *Temporary hardness*, which is due to the presence of calcium bicarbonate (i.e. hydrogen carbonate) ($Ca(HCO_3)_2$) can be removed by boiling the water for a few minutes. The heat decomposes the calcium bicarbonate into calcium carbonate (chalk) ($CaCO_3$), and carbon dioxide (CO_2) is expelled. In areas where the water is of this nature, the insides of kettles become coated with a layer of calcium carbonate caused by the decomposition of the bicarbonate. *Permanent hardness* is mainly due to the presence of dissolved calcium sulphate ($CaSO_4$) and cannot be removed by boiling.

For conservation purposes, the ideal would be almost always to use water which has been purified. However, this is an unrealistic and costly goal, and for many processes tap water will be acceptable. In the initial stages of salt removal from porous pottery by soaking, tap water can be used since it is unlikely to have any detrimental effects; despite containing salts, it will still have the capacity to dissolve more material than it already contains. The final rinses, however, may be carried out using purified water. Similarly, objects can be washed quite satisfactorily in tap water, provided any remaining water is removed immediately by blotting dry with absorbent paper towels or a cloth. Ideally though, purified water should be used for the final rinse.

Water can be purified by several methods including distillation and deionization. Distillation involves boiling the water and collecting the steam which is then condensed to form pure water. Deionization involves passing the water through insoluble ion exchange resins, which remove the unwanted impurities as positive or negative ions, and replace them with other ions from the resin. Of the two methods, deionization is probably the more economical, though the product is less pure and in hard water areas the resins may get exhausted quickly.

It is possible to soften small amounts of permanently hard water by adding compounds such as sodium carbonate (washing soda) ($Na_2CO_3.10H_2O$), which can replace the calcium ions responsible for causing the hardness with sodium ions. On a larger scale, the Permutit process is used, where a complex of natural clay minerals (hydrated sodium aluminium silicates) brings about an exchange of calcium and magnesium ions for sodium ions. Such treatments are suitable for domestic purposes, but not for conservation, since the water will still contain salts that will be deposited as the water dries.

Soaps and detergents

Unfortunately, water used on its own is not effective for removing grease from objects. The addition of a surfactant such as a soap or detergent will, in simple terms, make the water *wetter* and capable of removing more dirt. Soap in its most basic form is the salt of an organic acid, produced by the process of saponification, where vegetable oils or animal fats are heated with an alkali. Detergents, though similar to soaps, owe their origin to mineral acids. On a molecular level, the surfactants consist of a polar and non-polar part, compatible with water and unwanted greasy dirt respectively. The polar, hydrophilic part may be anionic, cationic or non-ionic depending on its molecular structure (Moncrieff and Weaver, 1983).

Detergents are used in preference to soap in the treatment of ceramic objects as soaps tend to react with the salts in hard water forming a scum that can be difficult to remove. Even if purified water is used, soluble calcium in the ceramic body may also react with the soap. Soft soap used to be favoured for cleaning marble; however, it will leave behind a yellowish grey layer of insoluble scum that can be difficult to remove later.

Commercial detergents are usually mixtures of a number of chemicals such as surface-active ingredients (wetting agents), bleach, water-softening chemicals, alkalis, fluorescent whiteners, dyes, cellulose derivatives (suspension and thickening agents), sequestering agents (for removing stains) and perfumes. It is therefore preferable to use a purer detergent with a known composition, such as Synperonic N (ICI) (previously Metapol and Lissapol) which consists of a nonylphenol ethoxylate non-ionic surfactant in liquid form, or Triton X-100 (Rohm and Haas, USA), an octylphenol ethoxylate non-ionic surfactant. Such detergents will avoid the risk of introducing any unknown and unnecessary chemicals into the body of ceramic objects. These tend to be more concentrated and consequently should be used sparingly (around 1% in water). It has been shown that dishwasher detergents and soaps can attack colours on modern ceramics with on-glaze enamelled decoration (Rado, 1975).

Biological washing powders

The use of so-called *biological* detergent washing powders has been recommended for cleaning porcelain. Williams (1983) suggests using a solution of such detergents, mixed with Calgon (Albright and Wilson), a sequestering agent formerly composed of sodium hexametaphosphate, but recently altered to a more environmentally friendly composition containing zeolite products. Impressive results can be achieved using the mixture in solution for cleaning porcelain and Parian ware. The products suggested include Biotex (Blumøller) and Ariel (Proctor and Gamble) which can be purchased at supermarkets in the UK. General details of the composition of such clothes washing powders are sometimes described on the packaging. They contain a cocktail of numerous chemicals, some of which may be potentially damaging to some ceramics (Table 14.1). The addition of Calgon, a water softener, would seem unnecessary, as the washing powder contains water softeners, and the solution appears to work effectively on its own. Such washing solutions should never be used on porous bodies or unstable surfaces. They should be reserved for high-fired vitrified bodies from which they can be successfully removed by rinsing and soaking.

In simple terms the main difference between these and other types of detergent is that they contain enzymes. Enzymes are biological catalysts that help to speed up the complex reactions involved in dissolving dirt. They occur naturally as protein molecules in living organisms and are responsible for catalysing the numerous chemical reactions taking place in living

Table 14.1 General components of a clothes washing powder and their potential effects on a ceramic body (courtesy L. Green, British Museum, London)

Chemical	*Properties*	*Potential effect on ceramics*
Surfactant	Reduces surface tension	May absorb to ceramic – not easily removed. Could discolour with time
Builder (e.g. sodium tripolyphosphate)	Co-ordinates with Ca^{2+}, Mg^{2+} ions. Acts as pH buffer	May strip structural Ca^{2+}, Mg^{2+} ions from body
Chelating agents (e.g. EDTA)	Chelate: stabilization of transition metal ions in solution by formation of complexes	Potentially harmful to overpainted glazes
Polycarboxylate (e.g. carboxymethyl cellulose)	May chelate with transition metal ions, and Ca^{2+}, Mg^{2+}. Suspends small particles	May remove transition metals from overpainted glaze and strip structural Ca^{2+}; Mg^{2+} may be affected
Peroxygen bleaches (e.g. perborate)	Low-temperature bleach produces peroxide above 10°C in presence of water	Oxidation of organic materials (peroxide 0_2^{2-} can be stable for months, peroxyacids for only a few hours)
Enzymes (e.g. protease, amylase, lipase)	Break down proteins, starches or fats	Could be absorbed into clay, possibly causing discoloration
Waterglass (sodium silicate)	Builder acts as a corrosion inhibitor and keeps soil in suspension (alkaline)	May react with vitreous materials e.g. glaze, particularly if degraded (but only in very aggressive conditions, e.g. boiling for several days)
Optical brighteners	Fluoresce, giving out 'white light'. Designed to 'stick to' surfaces	May interact with other materials or degrade with time producing other molecules, with potential to discolour
Perfume	Designed to 'stick'. Complex organic molecules	Unknown long-term effects
Sodium sulphate	Bulking agent: helps to keep other ingredients free-flowing	May crystallize in ceramics, causing structural decay
Silicone/wax/calcium soap	Sud suppressor	May deposit

tissue. There are many different kinds of enzymes, that will, under the right conditions, bring about specific reactions between particular substances. They usually have an optimum temperature at which they perform best, but they are destroyed at high temperatures. Commercial products are designed to clean clothing by catalysing the breakdown of the particular protein-based substances that constitute the *dirt*, resulting in soluble products which can be rinsed away. Although the inorganic vitrified ceramic surface is unlikely to be at any risk from short-term contact with enzymes, the main concerns of using these products are the other constituents within the washing powder and the potential problems that might arise later should they remain on the glaze surface, or trapped in surface flaws due to insufficient rinsing.

Such familiar domestic products as biological washing powder are easily dismissed as harmless to health, but there is a risk of developing allergies to them as a result of inhalation of the dry powder, or skin contact. Dust masks should be worn when preparing solutions and hands should be protected by gloves to avoid skin contact.

Chelating agents

Chelating or sequestering is the process where complexes are formed around particular ions, making them soluble and enabling them to be removed (Richey, 1975). Such a reaction can be very useful in removing unwanted metal ions. In commercial products, such as shampoos and detergents, they are added to soften the water by *locking-up* the iron, calcium and magnesium ions. In ceramics conservation they can be used to remove insoluble salt deposits, concretions, and metal stains, by converting the metal into a soluble form which can be rinsed away. Unfortunately, with ceramics, there are potential risks in the use of chelating agents, as the unwanted material is often chemically very similar to some of the constituents in ceramic bodies. Where contaminants are in close association with the surface of the object, it may be almost impossible to contain the reaction between the deposit and the chelating agent without risk of some activity between adjacent metal ions in the decoration, glaze or body. Unfired decoration can be completely destroyed by such treatment; enamels, gilding and lustre may be attacked, resulting in their disintegration; previously unstable or weathered glazes may be further attacked, leading to flaking and exposure of vulnerable underlying areas.

Three groups of chelating agents of particular interest in ceramics conservation will be considered: polyphosphates, aminocarboxylic acids and hydroxycarboxylic acids.

Polyphosphates

These complex-builders are a common ingredient in commercial detergent formulations where they act as water softeners. They dissolve and form complexes with the calcium, magnesium and other unwanted metal compounds in hard water. Sodium hexametaphosphate, $Na(PO_3)_6$, formerly a constituent of Calgon, is an example of such a sequestering agent which has been used with biological detergents (Williams, 1983) supposedly to increase their cleaning power by acting as a water softener. It has also been successfully used during the later stages of removal of concretions from abraded glaze on marine archaeological stoneware objects (Olive and Pearson, 1975). It is not recommended, however, that polyphosphates be used on earthenwares as the body is susceptible to chemical attack. It should be noted that Calgon no longer contains polyphosphates, but is now composed of zeolite compounds: types of hydrated aluminosilicates which act as insoluble sequestering agents, capable of forming complexes with magnesium and calcium.

Since polyphosphates have been shown to damage stained glass surfaces, it seems advisable to be wary about their use on glazed surfaces (Moncrieff, 1975; Newton and Davison, 1989).

Aminocarboxylic acids

An example of this group of chelating agents which has an application in ceramics conservation is ethylene diamine tetra-acetic acid (EDTA) ($(HOOCCH_2)_2NCH_2CH_2N(CH_2COOH)_2$), a weak acid which readily forms complexes with metals. The ability of EDTA to chelate different metal ions can be varied by altering the pH of the solution.

Although EDTA has been successfully used for the removal of calcareous concretions on marine archaeological ceramics (Gibson, 1971; Olive and Pearson, 1975; Moncrieff, 1975), without any apparent damage to the iron content of the ceramic object, it should be used with caution. All health and safety instructions should be carefully observed during use.

Hydroxycarboxylic acids

These include citric acid ($C_3H_5O(COOH)_3$) and tartaric acid ($COOH.(CH.OH)_2.COOH$). The type of reaction that occurs depends on the acidity of the solution. At pH 11 and above they are more effective at chelating calcium than the aminocarboxylic acids or polyphosphates. Below pH 11 they form only weak complexes with the alkaline earth metals (magnesium and calcium). They are, however, capable of chelating iron and other multivalent ions at all pHs. Again, the risk of damage occurring to an object should be considered, as chelating agents are not selective in their reactions.

Bleaches

Bleaching involves the removal of unwanted colour, such as staining caused by dirt. A bleach will chemically change the material responsible for the stain into a colourless substance. The effect is brought about by either oxidation or reduction reactions (Moncrieff and Weaver, 1983).

Bleaching by oxidation is the most common of the two types in ceramics conservation. The chemicals used release active oxygen atoms (O), which are much less stable than the ordinary oxygen atoms (O_2), and these react with the colour-giving chemicals, oxidizing them to a colourless state.

Sunlight

The cheapest, most readily available bleaching agent is sunlight. The light disrupts the naturally occurring oxygen in the air exciting it and altering it into an active state: $O_2 \rightarrow 2O$.

Examples of the effect are readily available in our own homes: faded curtains and furnishings. However, although this particular category of bleaching may have uses in textiles conservation, the effects are too slow and weak for bleaching stains in ceramics.

Hydrogen peroxide

Hydrogen peroxide solution can be used on vitrified non-porous bodies to bleach organic residues and black iron sulphide stains (Olive and Pearson, 1975). It has the advantage of breaking down during the reaction to produce water and the active oxygen, the latter of which oxidizes and removes the colour from the dirt: $H_2O_2 \rightarrow H_2O + O$.

Hydrogen peroxide may be bought at chemist shops as a solution of varying strengths in water. The concentration is usually indicated by the volume of oxygen gas which would be produced by one unit volume of the solution. The weaker 30 volume and 20 volume solutions are readily available, while the full strength hydrogen peroxide at 100 volumes (30% solution) will have to be obtained from specialist suppliers. For bleaching ceramics a 20 volume solution (that is a 6% solution) will usually give the required effect. Acid stabilizers are often added to commercial solutions, so a few drops of ammonia will counteract this and act as a catalyst, speeding up the release of oxygen.

Caution should be taken when handling peroxide solutions (OES: LTEL 8-hour TWA 1 ppm, STEL 15-minutes 2 ppm). Goggles, gloves, and protective clothing must be worn to avoid accidental skin contact as it will attack skin and clothing.

If hydrogen peroxide is to be applied to low-fired porous bodies, it is essential that preliminary tests are made. There is a significant risk of absorption into the body and consequential staining due to oxidation of any metallic components. In certain cases, treatment of earthenwares can be very successful, for example on creamware objects and frit bodies; however, conversely a staining problem might easily be exacerbated by the application of hydrogen peroxide. It has also been reported that the residual by-products from hydrogen peroxide can remain active within the ceramics for up to two years. Some gilded objects can also be damaged by contact with hydrogen peroxide (Williams, 1983).

The strength of hydrogen peroxide tends to diminish with prolonged storage. Owing to the combustible oxygen which it is capable of evolving it should not be stored near flammable solvents. Ideal storage conditions are a cool dark place such as a fridge.

Domestic bleaches

As a general rule, those domestic bleaches that are sold in supermarkets for household application should not be used to clean ceramics. Despite their apparent effectiveness, they can cause serious problems later. Absorption into the body through glaze or body defects results in the gradual formation of crystals under the glaze, in cracks, or along a repaired break. Repeated cycles of wetting and drying cause the disruption of the glaze as the crystals slowly develop and enlarge.

Sodium hypochlorite (NaOCl) is a common domestic bleach which breaks down into sodium chloride, oxygen, and also unused bleach. The residual bleach dries to form a solid. This bleach can be very dangerous when mixed with other cleaners, sometimes giving rise to the release of poisonous chlorine gas (Moncrieff and Weaver, 1983).

Reducing bleaches

Other bleaches achieve their cleaning effect by reduction reactions and are particularly useful in the conversion of metals from their corroded state into the metal form. Sodium hydrosulphite ($Na_2S_2O_4.2H_2O$), also known as sodium dithionite or bisulphite, is sometimes used to bleach iron stains. *Colour-run* removers available in supermarkets intended for removing dye stains from textiles often contain sodium hydrosulphite as the main ingredient; such products (e.g. Dygon) have been used to remove iron stains from marble (Moncrieff, 1975). The staining may however return if some of the metal remains and reoxidation occurs. Treatment should always be followed by thorough rinsing in order to remove any remaining traces of the bleach or its by-products.

Sodium hydrosulphite should be used under extraction or in a fume cupboard to avoid inhalation of the poisonous sulphur gases. When handling the powder, dust masks should be worn for the same reason, and skin contact prevented by wearing gloves.

Acids

Different acids display a wide range of properties, but all these owe their origin to a single characteristic, whereby hydrogen ions (H+) are produced when an acid is dissolved in water. The degree of ionization of an acid in water determines the strength of the acid. If the ionization is almost complete the acid is said to be a strong acid; if the ionization is slight, the acid is said to be weak. These terms should not be confused with the words 'concentrated' and 'dilute' (Moncrieff and Weaver, 1983). Acids by definition have a pH below 7.

Inorganic acids

The inorganic acids, or mineral acids as they are more commonly known, are those that do not contain carbon. They include examples such as hydrochloric acid (HCl), nitric acid (HNO_3), and hydrofluoric acid (HF). The former two can be used to remove concrete, as well as calcareous concretions and carbonate deposits, converting the insoluble material to a soluble salt that can then be rinsed away. Hydrofluoric acid can remove iron stains; however it will also readily etch glass and glazes (Olive and Pearson, 1975).

The inorganic acids are usually supplied as concentrated solutions. They should be handled with great caution as acids can cause serious burns. When making up solutions, always add the acid to water and never the other way around. The intense heat generated by the acid's reaction with the water can cause it to boil and spit in a violent manner. Acid resistant gloves, eye protection and aprons (or overalls) should always be worn when handling acids. Any spillage should be wiped away and rinsed immediately to avoid accidents later. Use of hydrofluoric acid should be avoided owing to the particularly serious and painful nature of the burns it can cause.

Organic acids

Those acids that contain carbon, such as acetic acid (CH_3COOH), citric acid ($HO_2CC(OH)(CH_2CO_2H)_2$), and oxalic acid ($HOOC.COOH.2H_2O$), will also remove carbonates. As mentioned earlier, some will remove metal stains by forming complex compounds with the unwanted metal which can be rinsed away. Caution should always be observed when considering application to bodies or glazes which contain iron oxide.

The common orange-brown staining of ceramic glaze and body, associated with the corrosion of rivets, results from the hydrolysis of iron (III) oxide (ferric oxide). Cleaning such a stain relies on its removal. However, during the course of time iron III hydroxide loses water and converts to the insoluble mineral iron III oxide hydrate. The stains therefore have to be reduced with acids to iron II salts, and then oxidized again to fresh iron III salts which can be more easily removed (Stambolov, 1968). Dilute solutions of orthophosphoric acid (H_3PO_4), and oxalic acid ($COOH_2.2H_2O$), will act as reducing agents, in the latter case dissolving rust as iron II oxalate.

The effects of phosphoric acid are not fully understood, and the possibility of the formation of insoluble calcium phosphate salts in the body could be harmful. Phosphoric acid is one of the ingredients of the commercial rust remover, Jenolite (Duckhams), which is available as a liquid or gel. In the majority of cases it will remove the stain with no problems. Contact with the acid should be brief as the acid can etch glazes. Williams (1983) warns of the unforeseen spread of the staining and advises halting the process and not washing the object for at least three days to avoid the stain enlarging any further. Jenolite is intended to remove rust from corroded metal, and to prevent further corrosion by protecting the metal surface with a coating. Any application on ceramics should be followed by thorough rinsing. The product should not be used on edges which are intended to be bonded with epoxy, since the rust inhibitor will impede curing of the resin.

Oxalic acid, a mild, though poisonous acid present in some vegetation, will also form insoluble calcium oxalate salts if acid contact with the body is prolonged. Citric acid can be used to remove the dark green copper stains which may arise from dowels or gilt-bronze ornamentation, dissolving the cupric oxide to form a soluble complex.

Any acid treatment of ceramics should always be followed by thorough soaking, washing and rinsing to remove absolutely all traces of the acid.

Alkalis

Alkalis (or bases) characteristically produce OH^- ions in solution. By definition they are substances which have pHs above 7. They include the basic hydroxides and oxides of metals and ammonia that are soluble in water. The common ones are sodium hydroxide, potassium hydroxide, calcium hydroxide and ammonia solution. They share the property of being able to neutralize an acid by reacting with it to form a salt and water only.

Ammonia

Ammonia gas (NH_3) readily dissolves in water to produce ammonia solution which consists of ammonium hydroxide (NH_4OH), a strong alkali. The saturated solution, which has a specific gravity of 0.880, is sometimes referred to as *eight eighty ammonia*. It is usually applied as a 35% solution in water. The odour associated with ammonia is a powerful irritant to the nose, eyes and lungs; if direct contact with the skin occurs, it will burn (OES: LTEL 8-hour TWA 25 ppm, STEL 15 minutes 35 ppm). It has already been mentioned in the role of a catalyst with hydrogen peroxide for bleaching organic dirt. In its concentrated form, ammonia has been used to successfully remove stains caused by the copper. Williams (1983) suggests leaving the swabs in place on copper stains for at least 12 hours, and following this by washing in Ariel and Calgon solution.

Ammonia can also be used with alcohol to remove shellac, though it is advisable to make tests first, as pink staining can sometimes occur, and adverse reactions with gilded areas have been observed (Koob, 1979).

Animal fats, which are normally insoluble, can sometimes be saponified by ammonia solution. This has little application in treating ceramics except in the case of residues associated with domestic vessels.

Sodium hydroxide (NaOH)

Sodium hydroxide, otherwise known as *caustic soda*, has been used to remove grease, wax and fat deposits from ceramics by saponification. It can also restore lead glazes back to their original colour after they have become blackened from burial by sulphurous organic material. However, the treatment should be avoided owing to the potential risks to the object. Any applications of the alkali must be followed by very thorough rinsing, to remove all traces and to avoid any residues crystallizing and disrupting glaze and body. In describing treatments for removing white and black deposits from ancient pottery, Gibson (1971) mentions the use of sodium hydroxide combined in a solution with the chelating agent ethylene diamine tetra-acetic acid (EDTA).

Sodium hydroxide in a solid form is sold as pellets. The pellets and any solutions made from them should be handled with care to avoid burning the skin. (OES: STEL 15 minutes 2 mgm^{-3}). It also attacks wool and silk. The solid is strongly hygroscopic and readily deliquesces even in the air, with considerable evolution of heat on contact with water. Consequently, when making up solutions, pellets should be added carefully to the water to avoid violent reactions (Plenderleith and Werner, 1974). Gloves and eye protection should be worn.

Sodium carbonate (Na_2CO_3) and sodium bicarbonate ($NaHCO_3$)

Commonly known as *washing soda*, sodium carbonate can be used to destroy the cohesion of fats by forming soaps. As with caustic soda it should be handled carefully and all traces should be rinsed away from the ceramic after treatment. Sodium bicarbonate (also known as *baking soda*) is sometimes used as a mild airborne abrasive in conjunction with dental equipment.

Organic solvents

A solvent is defined as being a substance that has the power to dissolve other substances (solutes) in it. The dissolution reaction may or may not be reversible. The organic solvents are used in ceramics conservation for two main functions: firstly, to remove unwanted material including dirt, grease and old restoration materials, and secondly, to apply polymer systems such as adhesives, consolidants and coatings.

Solutions

The conservation of objects made from materials other than ceramics is often complicated by the necessity to avoid the risk of a solvent dissolving part of the object. With ceramics this is not usually a concern, unless the object has received unfired decorative treatments, or the body has been fired to a very low temperature. Normally the main requirements for the ceramics conservator will be to find a solvent with a suitable evaporation rate, which will effectively dissolve the solute and allow time for the solute to be manipulated into the desired situation. In practice this means that for a cleaning application a solvent is required that will not only readily dissolve the dirt or the resin, but also allow sufficient time for the dirt to be mopped up without pushing it any further into the fabric of the object. Similarly, when joining pieces of ceramic with adhesive, it is necessary for the adhesive in solution to remain tacky long enough for the two substrates to be precisely aligned and united.

The degree to which a solid dissolves in a liquid is dependent on the chemical compositions of the ingredients involved. The maxim *like dissolves like* is commonly quoted when considering the action of a solvent, and is best illustrated by examples. Grease will normally dissolve in petroleum spirits, both being composed of hydrocarbon molecules, while alcohols will readily dissolve in water since their molecules both contain hydroxyl groups. On the other hand, grease will not dissolve in water because of their differing compositions. A third solvent may sometimes be added to bring about the solution of one material in another; e.g. white spirit will dissolve in alcohol when a small amount of butan-1-ol is added.

When a solvent acts on a solute, the solvent molecules are able to move into the molecules of the solute and disrupt the bonds, forcing them apart. The speed at which this occurs is affected by the temperature and the intermolecular forces of both the substances. If the solvent fails to break the bonds in the molecules of the solute the solid will just swell, as in the case of epoxy adhesives, or go into colloidal solution.

The most important criteria in selecting a solvent for a particular purpose, as described by Horie (1987), include: chemical type, purity, solubility, evaporation rate, toxicity and flammability. Other detailed explanations of the properties of solvents can be sought in various texts (Marsden, 1963; Mellan, 1970; Burrel, 1975; Torraca, 1975). Outlined below, however, are some of the organic solvents which are more commonly used in ceramics conservation.

Aspects of health and safety have been covered towards the end of Chapter 13, and so will only have brief mention here. All organic solvents are potentially dangerous in use. Hazard warnings should be closely observed and precautions taken. Where possible those solvents that are less dangerous should be used in preference to those with more hazardous properties.

Types of solvent

The molecular structure that determines the behaviour of different solvents also allows them to be grouped into classes which have distinct characteristics in common. All organic solvents by definition contain carbon which, owing to its chemical nature, is capable of forming chains and rings of atoms. Chains and rings may occur in the same molecule. There are three basic subdivisions of organic solvents:

Aliphatic (alkyl), which have open chains of atoms sometimes with branches. They are the least toxic group of the hydrocarbons.
Aromatic (aryl), where benzene (C_6H_6), or its derivatives are incorporated in the structure.
Alicyclic, consisting of closed chains of molecules with ends joined to form a saturated ring structure of carbon atoms.

Hydrocarbons

These include solvents containing only hydrogen and carbon molecules, which interact by very weak Van der Waals forces. The size of the molecule varies depending on the number of carbon atoms involved. Because of their low polarity, hydrocarbons with small molecules tend to be gases at room temperature (i.e. methane, butane and propane), while those with longer larger molecules range from liquids such as white spirit and petroleum, to solids like paraffin wax.

Since the pure hydrocarbons tend to be costly to manufacture, most of those used in conservation are mixtures. Manufacturers' data will give information on flashpoints and boiling points, but details about precise composition are rarely available owing to the variable nature of the constituents.

Of the many hydrocarbon solvents, white spirit (USA mineral spirit), xylene, and toluene are probably most commonly used in ceramics conservation. None are miscible with water, and all are highly inflammable and narcotic. They should be used in well ventilated conditions or with fume extraction.

White spirit

This is sold commercially as a paint thinner and as a milder substitute for turpentine. Various synonyms include mineral spirit, solvent naphtha, and petroleum spirits. White spirit is probably the most commonly used of the hydrocarbon solvents, having applications as a good solvent for oils, grease, fat, wax, tar and some resins. It is also used to remove old retouching (Williams, 1983) and as a thinners for polyurethane (Larney, 1975b), alkyd and oil paints. White spirit can also be mixed with non-ionic detergent and water to make a cleaning emulsion that can be used to clean greasy surfaces; Larney (1975b) suggests making a 50:50 emulsion of white spirit with water and a teaspoon of non-ionic detergent (one pint total).

It is composed mainly of aliphatic hydrocarbon molecules (with straight chains) and also some aromatic and alicyclic hydrocarbons which are added to enhance the solvent properties. It has a boiling range between 130°C and 220°C, and OES with LTEL 8-hour TWA of 100 ppm and STEL 15-minutes of 125 ppm. Adequate ventilation should be available for the solvent's use and it is also advisable to wear goggles and gloves if there is a danger of splashes and skin contact. Stoddart solvent, which is very similar to white spirit, and has similar applications, consists of approximately 85% nonane (C_9H_{20}) and trimethyl benzene ($(CH_3)_3C_6H_3$).

Toluene ($C_6H_5CH_3$) and xylene ($C_6H_4(CH_3)_2$)

These are both aromatic hydrocarbons belonging to the same group as benzene, and derived mainly from coal tar. Toluene is more volatile and inflammable than xylene (toluene BP 111°C, OES: LTEL 8-hour TWA 50 ppm, STEL 15-minutes 150 ppm; xylene BP 139°'C, OES: LTEL 8-hour TWA 100 ppm, STEL 15 minutes 150 ppm), and also more effective as a solvent. Both solvents will dissolve substances that are soluble in white spirit. They are used for removal of grease, fats, oils, wax, and tar. They will also break down PVA, PVAL, rubber, and some natural resins and cellulose derivatives. They are common constituents as diluents for resins such as urea formaldehyde and polyurethane-based lacquers. Both solvents are toxic and their use should be avoided where possible unless adequate ventilation is available. Benzene, to which they are both closely related, should never be used as a substitute owing to its carcinogenic properties.

Chlorinated hydrocarbons

Where a hydrogen atom in a hydrocarbon is replaced by chlorine, the resulting compound is known as a chlorinated hydrocarbon. The products formed are less flammable than the non-polar hydrocarbons, though they are very volatile owing to their low polarity. They dry rapidly giving off dense vapours, which are heavier than air. They are not miscible with water. Although some are extremely effective in removing dirt, grease, fat and wax, their use is generally limited owing to their toxic nature. Examples include chloroform, carbon tetrachloride, dichloromethane and trichloroethane. Some are used as *paint strippers* and to break down old adhesives because of the rate at which they are able to swell old polymer systems. Strong fume extraction is necessary for their application, since the fumes are toxic and have a narcotic effect. Most chlorinated hydrocarbons will decompose when heated; some break down in the presence of moisture or metals to form hydrochloric acid. Of the chlorinated hydrocarbons the two most likely to be used by the ceramics conservator are dichloromethane and 1,1,1-trichloroethane.

Dichloromethane ($CH_2.Cl_2$)

This is also referred to as methylene dichloride (BP 40°C, MEL: LTEL 8-hour TWA 100 ppm, STEL 15-minutes 300 ppm). It is a major component in many commercial water washable paint stripper gels, such as Nitromors (Henkel) or Zynolyte (USA). In this form it is frequently used by ceramics conservators for removing old areas of retouching and to break down old bonds made with adhesives such as epoxies, shellac, rubber, polyesters, acrylics, pressure sensitive tapes, and occasionally PVA or PVAL. Dichloromethane is a suspected carcinogen, and possible irreversible effects may occur, pregnant and nursing mothers must not use, or be exposed to its vapours, consequently exposure should be reduced to the lowest level. The correct grade of gloves should always be worn when using the solvent and eyes should be protected from accidental splashes.

When applying dichloromethane-based paint strippers, a long-handled paintbrush should be used under local fume extraction. The gel should always be rinsed off thoroughly with cold water, never hot, as this will generate poisonous phosgene gas ($COCl_2$). To avoid the possibility of shadowing or *tide marks*, especially on unglazed or matt finishes, all traces of the paint stripper must be completely removed.

In certain situations, when breaking down old repairs, an atmosphere of dichloromethane can be more effective than the application of a paint stripper. The object is placed in a sealed container with the solvent; evaporation of the solvent creates an atmosphere that will swell old adhesives such as epoxy and polyester.

Chlorinated solvents should be kept separate from others to avoid the potential risks of accumulation of explosive mixtures with solvents (Pascoe, 1980).

Alcohols

The alcohol group is characterized by having the hydroxyl group (OH) present. The simple alcohols, which include methanol and ethanol, have the general formula $C_nH_{2n+1}OH$. They are of low molecular weight, with the polar hydroxyl group being attached to a small hydrocarbon chain. Consequently they are liquids at room temperature, volatile, colourless and miscible with water. However, higher up the alcohol series, the increased molecule size reduces the effect of the hydroxyl group, making them less polar. As a group, the alcohols do not have the same degreasing properties as the hydrocarbons, but they can be useful for dissolving certain resins.

Ethanol (C_2H_5OH)

This is commonly referred to as *alcohol* and is probably the best known of the group. It is also sometimes called ethyl alcohol, and is a highly flammable chemical (flashpoint 12.2°C, BP 78°C, OES: LTEL 8-hour TWA 100 ppm, STEL 15-minutes none). Ethanol can be highly reactive with certain substances, in particular peroxides (hydrogen peroxide, especially with ammonia added) and dichloromethane, and should be kept away from potentially incompatible substances (Clydesdale, 1990). It should be used only with good fume extraction, wearing goggles and gloves, and with contact lenses removed. The purchase of ethanol requires a special license from HM Customs and Excise in the UK, and proof of safe storage in lockable metal cupboards together with information on its intended use.

Industrial methylated spirits

Industrial methylated spirits (IMS) consists mainly of ethanol with a small amount (usually around 9.5%) of methanol, and water, with quantities varying according to the grade. It tends to be used in preference to the more expensive pure ethanol. In the UK it can only be supplied under special licence from HM Customs and Excise. The freely available form of methylated spirits which contains a purple dye, as well as the solvent pyridine, should be avoided for conservation purposes as it may stain the object.

IMS (flashpoint 12°C) may reverse shellac bonds which have not responded to other solvents. Williams (1983) describes heating the alcohol for maximum effect; such treatments should only be used as a last resort and with extreme caution. IMS can be used as an agent for surface cleaning and will remove grease caused by handling. It can aid drying when added to the final rinse after washing.

Isopropanol ($(CH_3)_2CHOH$)

Also known as isopropyl alcohol and propan-2-ol (OES: LTEL 8-hour TWA 400 ppm, STEL 15-minutes 500 ppm), it is highly flammable (flashpoint 12°C, BP 82.4°C), though less volatile than IMS or ethanol. Isopropanol is also incompatible with strong oxidizing agents. It can be used as an effective solvent for poly(vinyl butyral). Eyes and skin should be protected during use.

Ketones

The ketone group of solvents shares the characteristic of having a carbonyl group (a double-bonded oxygen atom (C=O) bonded to two hydrocarbon groups). The group includes acetone and butanone among others. Their polarity tends to vary, depending on the structure of the molecule and the relationship of the atoms to the carbon atom. Only acetone is sufficiently polar to be miscible with water.

Acetone (CH_3COCH_3)

Acetone, the most commonly known member of the ketone group, is also known as dimethyl ketone or as propanone (OES: LTEL 8-hour TWA 750 ppm, STEL 15-minutes 1500 ppm, highly flammable with a flashpoint of -20°C, BP 56°C). Acetone has a distinctive, not unpleasant smell. It is miscible with water and has several applications. Owing to its dissolving power acetone can be used to remove oils, grease, some types of wax, cellulose derivatives (including cellulose nitrate adhesives), some paints, acrylics, poly(vinyl acetate) and shellac. It is consequently useful as a cleaning solvent for swabbing ceramic surfaces to remove greasy dirt and to soften certain types of old restorations. Some adhesives and consolidants are applied as a solution in acetone (e.g. acrylic resin Paraloid/Acryloid B-72). When added to water, acetone will speed up drying, as it evaporates quickly. The rapid evaporation can be a disadvantage and, in certain applications on porous or matt surfaces, can contribute to a blooming effect that may be difficult to remove later. The rate of evaporation can be controlled by the ratio of acetone to water. The vapour is slightly toxic so inhalation should be avoided and gloves and goggles should be worn when handling large quantities.

Ethers

The ethers are a group of organic solvents formed by the condensation of two alcohol molecules. They have a characteristic molecular structure R-O-R, where a hydrocarbon group (R) is linked to another (not necessarily the same) by an oxygen bridge (-O-). Ethers tend to have a low polarity, and are consequently volatile and not miscible with water. They are effective solvents for fats, oils, wax, grease and some resins.

Cellosolve (2-ethoxyethanol or ethylene monoethyl ether $C_2H_5OCH_2CH_2OH$) is an example of an ether used in conservation (BP 135°C, MEL: LTEL 8-hour TWA 10 ppm). It is miscible with water, and may be used either on its own or in combination with other solvents to dissolve oils, waxes, fats and a variety of resins including PVA, the methacrylate acrylic resins and rubbery adhesives (such as the sticky residue of pressure sensitive tapes). Its vapours are toxic, and it is easily absorbed through the skin. Pregnant and nursing mothers must avoid the use of 2-ethoxyethanol.

Esters

Esters are produced by the action of an alcohol on an organic acid, where the hydrogen of the acid is replaced by an organic radical group from the alcohol. Esters generally have a pleasant fruity smell, and in addition to their use as solvents are also used as flavourings and essences. They are usually polar and miscible with water. The ester group includes solvents such as methyl acetate and amyl acetate (the latter has a greater molecular weight and consequently lower volatility). They will effectively dissolve cellulose nitrate, and those of higher molecular mass will also dissolve poly(vinyl acetate). Amyl acetate ($CH_3COOC_5H_{11}$) has been used to remove the white bloom which can sometimes occur as a result of solvent cleaning on matt porous surface. The fumes of esters can be narcotic in high concentrations.

Materials for poulticing

Poulticing has been successfully used as a technique to remove stains and salts from ceramics and sculpture (Larney, 1971; Larson, 1990). The method relies on applying an inert material, saturated with solvent, to the surface of the stained object. The poultice holds the solvent in close contact with the surface, enabling it to dissolve the substance causing the stain. As the solvent evaporates, the dirt is drawn from the pores of the ceramic into the poultice and ultimately to the surface. The range of materials which have successfully been used include: sepiolite, attapulgite, laponite, methyl cellulose, paper pulp and cotton wool.

Sepiolite

Sepiolite is a fine grey-white naturally occurring clay containing hydrated magnesium silicate. It consists of extremely small laths, or needle-shaped particles, each with twenty-four to twenty-seven channels running lengthwise which help to create a system of pores. The pores are responsible for the exceptional ability of the material to absorb quantities of solvents to form a thick paste. There are, however, some drawbacks to its use: complete removal of particles from craggy and irregular surfaces is sometimes difficult; the impurities present in the clay can cause additional problems.

Dust masks should be worn when handling the material owing to the risks of inhaling the fine particles. Skin should be protected as sepiolite has been shown to act as an irritant.

Attapulgite clays

Attapulgite is another naturally occurring clay mainly composed of a hydrated magnesium aluminium silicate (Amoroso and Fassina, 1983). Its molecular structure, in the form of three-dimensional chains, prevents it from swelling like common clays and makes it capable of absorbing large quantities of liquid; 1000 g of attapulgite can absorb 1500 g of water whilst maintaining the same volume (Heuman and Garland, 1987). Clydesdale (1990) suggests that attapulgite may be safer in use than sepiolite, though equally effective.

Laponite RD

Laponite RD (Laporte) is a synthetic, inorganic, fine, white, clay colloid which has been successfully used as a poulticing material for removal of stains from pre-soaked ceramics. The free-flowing powder forms a thixotropic gel when mixed with liquids, and stays in place when applied. The large surface area and surface activity of the platelet-shaped particles make it a particularly effective medium for drawing out stains, and its semi-transparent nature makes it possible to monitor the stain removal visibly (Ling, 1991).

Laponite has also been used for the localized removal of corrosion products from metals (Dove, 1984), and for the removal of glue paste from the back of glue lined paintings. Suppliers suggest there is a slight risk of skin irritation after prolonged contact and recommend the use of gloves.

Other poulticing materials

Paper pulp may be used as a poulticing material. It can be made by tearing acid-free blotting paper into small pieces and mixing it with liquid to make a pulp. Cotton wool saturated with solvent makes a convenient pack, though tends to be less successful in drawing out stains than other materials so far discussed. Bentonite, another clay product with similar properties to Sepiolite and attapulgite, has been used for cleaning and desalinating stone in Italy, where the material is readily available (Lazzarini and Lombardi, 1990). Wood or cellulose pulps (e.g. Arbocel (Rettenmaier)) have also been used as poulticing material mixed with water or IMS or acetone.

Dry cleaning materials

There may be occasions when it is undesirable to wet an object, as in the case of unglazed highly porous bodies or those with water soluble decoration. In such a situation there are products available that can be applied to the surface and worked over it.

Draft Clean powder (Smith) is a finely divided powder consisting of particles of gum eraser normally used for cleaning paper. The particles are rubbed over the dirty surface in a circular motion using a short bristled stencil brush or a fingertip. Similarly, a clean gum eraser can also be useful. However, care should be taken to avoid abrading the surface.

Kneadable Putty Rubber (Daler Rowney) has also proved useful for cleaning matt glazed and unglazed ceramic surfaces. The putty consists of a butyl rubber mixed with ground pumice, which acts as a mild abrasive, and calcium carbonate (whiting) as a filler. Unwanted dirt is removed from the surface by a gentle rolling action without risk of deposition of any detrimental residues (Thomsen and Shashoua, 1991).

Synthetic putty materials, e.g. Groom/Stick, (Picreator Enterprises), have been used for the removal of dust and dirt from matt glazed or unglazed surfaces. Under gentle pressure the putty achieves its effect by temporarily adhering to both the surface of the object and the dirt. When the putty is lifted away the loosely attached dirt is pulled away on the putty, the bond between the dirt and the putty being stronger than that between the dirt and the surface of the object. However, the putty can also remove ceramic material from unstable friable surfaces, and may after prolonged use start to deposit greasy residues (Thomsen and Shashoua, 1991).

Adhesives, consolidants, gap fillers and coatings

The manufacture of synthetic resins forms a major area in the developing field of commercial and industrial polymer chemistry. However, of the numerous products available, only a few meet the requirements necessary for conserving ceramics, and of these, only a very small number have been made specifically for conservation. By close assessment of the different types of polymer systems and evaluation of their performance, a range of different resins has been adopted which have been found suitable for use on ceramics. The synthetic polymers currently in use represent those which have been shown to perform most satisfactorily (Blackshaw and Ward, 1983).

The following sections consider the main groups of resins used to conserve ceramics, and give a brief summary of aspects of their physical and chemical characteristics in relation to their use. The majority of the materials discussed can be harmful to health and the protective precautions recommended by the manufacturers' technical data should be complied with during preparation and application.

The complexities of polymer chemistry will not be considered here, since the subject has been covered in detail elsewhere (Newey *et al.*, 1983; Horie, 1987). However, it is worth briefly clarifying some of the recurring terms which will appear in the following accounts of the resins.

Almost all the resins used by ceramics conservators are made of synthetic polymers, a polymer being an organic molecule composed of a very long chain of hundreds or thousands of smaller units or *monomers*.

The molecular structures of polymers are responsible for their enormous range of properties. Chemists are able to engineer the molecular structure of polymers, altering their properties and behaviour, to fit specific requirements for application. Polymers which have no branches or cross-links in their chains are known as linear, and tend to be flexible and *thermoplastic*. Thermoplastic resins are those which can be softened and melted by repeated heating without changing their properties. They can also display properties of crystallinity where the molecule chains are aligned in a regular manner with the possibility of some weak bonds between them. Such structures tend to be harder and less flexible than when the polymer chains are mixed randomly together. Thermoplastic adhesives are usually soluble in solvents (e.g. acrylics, PVAs, and wax).

Polymers made from very long-chained molecules tend to be less flexible; the molecules may be very tangled, so when stretched the molecules slide past each other and are unable to return to their original position. Side branches on the molecules also reduce the flexibility of the polymer, inhibiting the potential for the molecules to move freely side by side. Heating will supply enough energy for the molecules to move and expand, so that they become mobile and capable of flowing. The temperature at which this change from a solid brittle state to a soft plastic state occurs is known as the *glass transition temperature* (T_g).

Thermosetting polymers are three-dimensional molecular structures with cross-links between the chains. Thermosets are typically two-part resins, where the long-chained polymer or resin is mixed with a *cross-linking* agent or hardener. The hardener reacts with special sites on the long molecules, cross-linking them, and producing a three-dimensional structure. The slower the polymerization, the more thorough the cross-linking and therefore the stronger the resulting adhesive. The type of chains and the number and length of cross-links determine the hardness (e.g. epoxy resins) or the softness (e.g. silicone rubbers). The cross-linking agent may take other forms, such as atmospheric moisture in the case of cyanoacrylates; or it may be already mixed with the polymer, but require energy in the form of heat or ultraviolet light to initiate the reaction.

For conservation purposes we require durable non-yellowing polymers which remain reversible with age. Double-bonded polymer molecules should be avoided as they are more reactive than polymer molecules with single bonds. In conditions with high light levels they are susceptible to breakdown and will produce groups of molecules called *chromaphores*, responsible for unwanted colours in polymers.

Polymers are often modified by additives such as plasticizers, antioxidants and fungicides, designed to improve various physical and chemical properties. Plasticizers may be added to make thermoplastic polymers more flexible. They are usually solvents with high boiling points, and achieve their effect by holding the polymer chains apart, allowing more movement of the individual molecules. However, they tend to reduce the strength of the adhesive, and as the plasticizer gradually evaporates the polymer becomes more brittle. Antioxidants slow down the atmospheric oxidation of polymers; they achieve their effect by being oxidized in preference to the polymer. The addition of fungicides may prevent attack by microbes. Two polymers are sometimes reacted together to form a *copolymer*, which shares the modified properties of the two contributing polymers.

Many of the resins used in treating ceramics have more than one use. Some may be used as both an adhesive and a consolidant. Others may have three functions: as an adhesive, a filler and a coating. For this reason the various synthetic resins will be considered here as a group.

Types of resin

The synthetic resins which are used as adhesives, consolidants, gap fillers and coatings may be grouped according to their chemical and physical behaviour during application and setting or curing (Allen, 1984):

Temperature cured resins These are thermoplastic materials which are applied to the joint in their melted liquid state, and on cooling they *freeze* to a solid. The glass transition temperature of such adhesives is critical, especially in hot environments. Many *natural* resins such as shellac and beeswax have been traditionally used as so-called *melt–freeze* adhesives for centuries. Some adhesives within this group also fall into the following category of thermoplastic soluble adhesives (e.g. shellac, PVA and the acrylic resin Paraloid/Acryloid B-72).

Solvent resins These consist of thermoplastic materials that have been dissolved in a solvent for ease of application. As the solvent evaporates, the material reverts to its solid form, held to the object by secondary bonds. The advantage of this kind of resin is that it may be diluted to the desired viscosity for application, and is usually easily reversed by solvent action, should the need arise. Unfortunately, because of their nature, they are prone to shrinkage and embrittlement. There is also a class of solvent adhesive where heat may be applied to cure the resin (e.g. animal glues, soluble nylon, and again, shellac); these can be cross-linked by heat.

Reaction curing resins These thermosetting network polymers are formed as a result of a chemical reaction between an initiator and a cross-linking monomer. Some reactions may result in loss of volatile substances, causing some slight shrinkage (e.g. phenol, urea and melamine formaldehydes, and also silicone rubber), while others react to give network polymers without the loss of volatile matter (e.g. epoxies and polyesters).

The following sections consider a number of the more common types of resins used by the ceramics conservator. It should be remembered that some may have dual or triple functions, as adhesives, consolidants and gap fillers.

Natural resins

Although natural resins are less frequently used in ceramics conservation, they were used extensively in the past before the advent of the synthetic adhesives. It is therefore likely that some treatments may involve the removal of such adhesives from objects that have been restored many years previously. The natural resins most frequently used for bonding ceramics included animal glue and shellac. However, despite the emergence of a constantly widening spectrum of synthetic polymers, such resins should not be totally dismissed, as they have some applications, for example as consolidants or coatings.

Shellac

Shellac has been widely used in Europe and the Far East as an adhesive for mending broken ceramics until relatively recently. It is still used as a coating for retouching fillings on archaeological ceramics. The resin is derived from a secretion of lac insects such as *Laccifer lacca* which inhabits certain trees of South Asia. Mills and White (1987) describe the raw lac as a complex mixture of esters of various polyhydroxy carboxylic organic acids (70–80%), some wax (6–7%) and dyes (4–8%). The dyes consist of an insoluble yellow dye and a water soluble red dye which is partially removed during processing. Shellac was generally prepared as a solution in hot alcohol, or heated up on its own for application onto a hot object. Other methods included fusing the resin with hot sulphur (Thiacourt, 1868). In time it will cross-link, becoming brittle to such a degree that the bond fails (Koob, 1979; 1984). The resin is usually recognizable by its distinct dark brown toffee-like colour.

Reversibility
With age, shellac becomes increasingly insoluble, though it still retains thermoplastic properties, softening when heated. It may be possible to remove the adhesive mechanically with a scalpel. Larney (1971) and Evetts (1983) suggest breaking down old bonds with a 50/50 mixture of ammonia and industrial methylated spirits, though Koob (1984) notes the risk of a pink stain. Dichloromethane (applied as a proprietary paint stripper) will slowly remove the adhesive, though again there seems to be a risk of a purple stain (Larney, 1975b). Koob (1979) has had success breaking down the adhesive using the organic solvent pyridine (C_5H_5N) (BP 115°C, OES: LTEL 8-hour TWA 5 ppm, STEL 15-minutes 10 ppm), a colourless, highly flammable liquid, extracted from bone oil and coal tar, with an unpleasant toxic vapour.

Soluble nylon

Soluble nylon has been used in the past, mainly by archaeological conservators, as a consolidant for friable pottery surfaces prior to the removal of salts by soaking (Plenderleith and Werner, 1974; Gedye, 1968). At the time it was regarded as appropriate owing to its low viscosity and the ease with which it could be applied. It gave good penetration and had low shrinkage on drying; the resulting consolidant, matt in appearance though not water soluble, was permeable to the vapours of water and solvents. Later, the popularity of soluble nylon diminished (Sease, 1981) when attention was focused on its undesirable ageing properties. It has a tendency to cross-link, becoming brittle, insoluble and subject to shrinkage accompanied by an associated lack of strength. In addition to this, the low T_g (room temperature) makes surface dirt almost impossible to remove. There are various forms of soluble nylon, N-methoxymethyl nylon which dissolves in methanol and ethanol being the most commonly adopted for conservation purposes. Porous surfaces which have been treated with soluble nylon have a darkened appearance as a result of the wetting nature of the consolidant and also because of its tendency to attract dirt.

Reversibility
Aged soluble nylon is not reversible, particularly where it has penetrated deeply into the surface. Any attempt to remove it from an already friable disrupted surface by the use of solvents may result in further damage.

Vinyl polymers

Poly(vinyl acetate) (PVAC)

Poly(vinyl acetate) is usually referred to as PVA. However, to avoid confusion with poly(vinyl alcohol), PVAC is more correct for the acetate, while the alcohol is better referred to as PVAL. It is widely used either as an aqueous emulsion or as a solution in organic solvents. This versatile resin has been adopted for a range of applications including bonding, filling, consolidation and coating. It has a low T_g of around room temperature, causing it to be susceptible to dirt pick-up and *cold flow* where bonded joints gradually lose their alignment under the stress of the object's weight. As an emulsion in water, poly(vinyl acetate) has a white milky appearance, but becomes clear on drying. Poly(vinyl acetate) is one of the most resistant polymers to the effects of light. It will cross-link to a limited extent with time, and will suffer only minor oxidation (Horie, 1987).

There are many different grades of poly(vinyl acetate) available which differ in their compositions. Commonly used examples include: Mowlith DMC2 (Hoechst), Rhodopas (Rhône-Poulenc), Jade (Aabitt), Vinamul (Clearway Plastics), PVA AYAF (Union Carbide) and Evostick Resin W (Evode). Poly(vinyl acetate) is also soluble in alcohol, toluene, acetone and ethyl acetate. The viscosity varies according to the molecular weight of the particular grade (Moore and Murphy, 1962). This allows the degree of penetration into the pores of the body to be controlled by selection of a poly(vinyl acetate) with the required molecular weight.

Poly(vinyl acetate) has proved useful as a consolidant (Dowman, 1970) and for bonding pottery (Larney, 1971; 1975a; 1975b; Plenderleith and Werner, 1974), though for objects with multiple and complex breaks, assembly using the emulsion can be difficult. It is usually necessary to pre-wet each break edge to ensure good adhesive contact, and this can cause difficulties in supporting the pieces with tape during drying. Larney (1975b) describes the use of solid poly(vinyl acetate) for making small fillings. The resin, dissolved in acetone or alcohol, has also been used as a medium for retouching paintings on canvas (Berger, 1990), though a similar application for ceramics is unlikely to be successful. Conservators working in hot climates will find little use for poly(vinyl acetate) as an adhesive owing to its low T_g. Initially it has a clear glassy appearance when cured; later, after ageing and dirt pick-up, it becomes yellow to pink or brown. Mibach (1975) suggests applications of the resin to prime the surface of a porous body, adjacent to the area being filled, to prevent ghosting.

Reversibility
It softens in warm water. It is also soluble in acetone, ethanol, toluene, and occasionally paint removers that contain dichloromethane.

Poly(vinyl alcohol) (PVAL)
Poly(vinyl alcohol) has been used to adhere glaze flakes in preference to the acetate emulsion in situations where minimal tonal colour changes are important (Larney, 1975b). It is also sometimes used as a protective separating layer between vulnerable surfaces and other adhesives or moulding materials. It is derived from poly(vinyl acetate), the acetate groups being replaced by a molecule with hydroxyl groups. It usually retains some of the acetate groups within the molecule and is technically a copolymer of vinyl alcohol and vinyl acetate. Examples include: Gelvatol (Monsanto), Rhodoviol (Rhône-Poulenc), Mowiol (Hoechst) and Polyviol (Wacker). In its purest form poly(vinyl alcohol) has good light ageing properties and is comparatively resistant to oxidation, but will cross-link becoming insoluble in acid or alkaline conditions. Under normal circumstances it will undergo slow chain scission, breaking the very long polymer chains. Since poly(vinyl alcohol) dissolves readily in water and is soluble in only very few organic solvents, it can be used for applications where resistance to organic solvents is desirable, though it is not a very strong adhesive.

The resin is a suspected carcinogen, and should be handled using necessary protection: gloves, protective clothing and fume extraction (Clydesdale, 1990).

Reversibility
It is soluble in water, but very resistant to organic solvents, oils and grease.

Poly(vinyl butyral) (PVB)
Poly(vinyl butyral) is a form of poly(vinyl acetal) which is made by reacting poly(vinyl alcohol) with an aldehyde. The molecular weight and the number of hydroxyl groups can be varied according to the precise nature of the manufacturing process. The hydroxyl content determines the solubility of the PVB (Horie, 1987). Examples include Butvar (Monsato), Mowital B30H (Hoechst) and Rhovinal (Rhône-Poulenc). In solution (with 55% ethanol and 45% toluene), it can be applied as a consolidant to unstable surfaces and has the advantage of causing less shadowing than other consolidants.

However, there are concerns about the ageing properties of poly(vinyl butyral) (Kuhn, 1986); it is known to cross-link under acid conditions and at elevated temperatures (Horie, 1987). When severely cross-linked and degraded it becomes increasingly insoluble (Ciabach, 1983).

PVB has also found a use as an ingredient in the gap-filling and modelling material BJK dough, which was developed at the Institute of Archaeology, London, originally using Alvar, a form of poly(vinyl acetal). The fibrous dough which is made of a mixture of jute, flock, acetone, IMS, amyl acetate, toluene and Butvar, can be kneaded into a paste and formed into the required shape. It is a light thermoplastic material, although it is prone to shrinkage due to solvent evaporation, and is also difficult to work.

Dust masks should be worn to avoid inhaling airborne particles from the resin. It is also advisable to wear goggles (Clydesdale, 1990).

Reversibility
PVB is soluble in ethyl alcohol, toluene, ethyl acetate, Cellosolve, acetone, isopropyl alcohol, methyl alcohol and the chlorinated hydrocarbons.

Acrylic polymers

Members of the family of acrylic polymers are usually made up of a combination of methacrylate and acrylate monomers derived from esters of the methacrylate and acrylic acids, respectively. The group includes synthetic glass and embedding materials, e.g. Technovit 4004 (Kulzer), Acrulite (Rubert), Perspex (ICI) (USA: Oroglas (Rohm and Haas)), Plexiglas (Roehm GmbH), as well as consolidants, coatings and adhesives, e.g. the Paraloids or Acryloids (Rohm and Haas), *acrylic* paints, and the cyanoacrylate adhesives. The acrylic polymers generally share qualities of glass-like clarity, with good light ageing properties and resistance to oxidation. Individual characteristics vary, depending on whether they are of acrylate or methacrylate composition. Methacrylate polymers tend to have a higher T_g than equivalent acrylate polymers. The higher methacrylate polymers and the acrylates will cross-link when exposed to ultraviolet light, the former more especially if exposed at temperatures close to their T_g; both will eventually become insoluble. Solvents tend to be released very slowly from the acrylic resin, sometimes taking months to complete evaporation. Of all the acrylics poly(methylmethacrylate) is most resistant to the effects of ultraviolet light. Barov (1986) describes the use of Technovit 4004 (Kulzer) for applications where a low-strength adhesive is required; he also mentions tests to assess its suitability as a filler.

Paraloid
Paraloid, also known as Acryloid in the USA (Rohm and Haas), is available in a number of different grades, each of which possesses different characteristics. Paraloid B-72, a copolymer of methyl acrylate and ethyl methacrylate, with a T_g of 40°C, has found a range of conservation applications over recent years; its popularity has grown with the acknowledgement of its good long-term ageing properties. It can be

safely used as an adhesive, consolidant and coating for both high- and low-fired wares. There are several *recipes* for its application, which suggest mixing it with various solvents and bulking agents. Koob (1986) has had success using acetone as the solvent, adding fumed colloidal silica (0.1% by weight) to improve its flow properties and to distribute stresses during the solvent evaporation. Paraloid B-72 can be susceptible to mould growth at high humidity.

The Paraloids B-67 and B-44 are less commonly used on ceramics, although there may be unexplored potential in their use for retouching. The former is an isobutyl methacrylate polymer with T_g of 50°, and the latter, harder resin is a methyl methacrylate polymer with T_g of 60°C. The thermoplastic properties of the Paraloids can be successfully utilized where alignment of stepped joints is necessary, and where flakes of glaze are to be laid back down and secured in place with the use of a heated spatula.

Reversibility

Paraloid B-72 is soluble in acetone, xylene, toluene, m-butanol, diacetone alcohol, methylene chloride, ethylene dichloride, trichlorethylene, ethyl acetate, methylethylketone, dimethyl formamide and Cellosolve.

Cyanoacrylates

This group of acrylic adhesives, commonly known as *superglues*, has been introduced commercially with a wide range of suggested applications. Although their use in conservation has so far been limited, they have been used as a means of *tacking* fragments of ceramics in situations where support by other means would not be possible. By tacking pieces together in this manner, it is then possible to introduce a second more suitable adhesive into the join. Owing to the speed with which they cure, they allow little time for error or any realignment of the join and so are not suitable for multiple breaks (Newey *et al.*, 1983).

Cyanoacrylates are composed of an alkyl-2-cyanoacrylate monomer that is then mixed with an acid to inhibit polymerization. Before being packaged in an applicator for use, other additives are incorporated such as plasticizers and thickeners. When applied to the break edge, the acid is neutralized by the hydroxyl groups in moisture which is usually present on most surfaces. The curing process begins immediately with a bond being formed in seconds. Curing is complete some hours later, resulting in a polymer of a high molecular weight. Since the adhesives are a relatively recent development, their long-term stability and compatibility with other resins have not been fully assessed. They are thought to lose strength after prolonged exposure to light, and to break down in alkaline conditions (Horie, 1987).

Reversibility

They are soluble in acetone, for a limited period of time after curing, and later only after prolonged soaking. They are also soluble in nitromethane and dimethyl formamide.

Acrylic paints

The ready-mixed pigmented acrylic paints available in small quantities in tubes, e.g. Cryla Colours (Rowney), Winsor and Newton acrylic paints, Liquitex (Binney and Smith) have found popular usage amongst archaeological conservators for retouching unglazed pottery. They are generally composed of an emulsion containing a copolymer of methyl methacrylate and either butyl acrylate or ethyl acrylate, combined with water, pigments, extenders, solvents and small amounts of other compounds. They can be mixed with water to obtain the desired consistency necessary for application and can be painted on by hand or with an airbrush. However, they tend to be difficult to abrade and cut back as they retain a rubbery consistency that may not bond adequately to the surface. Colour matching with acrylic paints requires some practice in order to overcome their tendency to alter tone upon drying.

Cellulose derivatives

Of the cellulose derived adhesives, cellulose nitrate (sometimes called nitrocellulose) is probably the only one which has enjoyed a wide usage as an adhesive and a consolidant for ceramics (especially archaeological earthenware) for a number of years. It is produced by the controlled reaction of nitric acid with cellulose, yielding a highly flammable cream or white-coloured thermoplastic material. The adhesive is generally made up as a solution of cellulose nitrate (20%) in a solvent (75%) such as acetone, ethanol, butyl acetate or amyl acetate; plasticizers (5%), usually aromatic esters, are added to enhance the flexibility (Horie, 1987). It has a clear water-white appearance, discolouring on ageing to yellow-brown. Examples include HMG (Guest), Durofix (Rawlplug), UHU Hart (Lingner), Duco Cement (Devcon) and Cement (Randolph).

Concerns have arisen regarding the stability of cellulose nitrate (Koob, 1982; Selwitz, 1988). Cellulose nitrate itself is known to be vulnerable to photochemical degradation, resulting in discoloration and increased flammability. The solvent and plasticizers may also contribute to the degradation of the adhesive, and their slow evaporation leads to a gradual embrittlement and a reduction in strength. However, recent work by Shashoua *et al.* (1992) has suggested otherwise, as demonstrated by comparative ageing tests of HMG adhesive with pure cellulose nitrate. Their research proved the adhesive to be superior, having enhanced resistance to embrittlement and discoloration; the authors attributed this to the plasticizer dibutyl phthalate. Despite the apparent uncertainty about its stability, cellulose nitrate is still used widely by many conservators in the belief that its advantageous working properties outweigh the potential negative aspects.

A point worth mentioning is the incompatibility of cellulose nitrate with epoxy adhesives. Rapid yellowing will occur when epoxy is used to join surfaces that have been previously bonded with a cellulose nitrate adhesive. Slight residues of cellulose nitrate are responsible for the effect, which is apparent within a few hours of the application of the epoxy. It is usually extremely difficult to achieve total removal of all traces of the adhesive.

Reversibility

It readily breaks down in acetone, even after prolonged ageing.

Polyesters

Polyester resins are thermosetting liquids which have been used as both adhesives and fillers. They consist of a mixture of an unsaturated polyester and styrene. A prepolymer of low molecular weight is mixed with a peroxide-based initiator. Also combined with the prepolymer is a reactive styrene solvent, an accelerator that catalyses the reaction and an inhibitor that prevents reaction until polymerization is required. During the exothermic curing reaction the temperature can rise excessively. Contact with air slows down the rate of cure, and the exposed surface has a tendency to remain tacky. This can be avoided by isolating the resin from oxygen using a polyester terephthalate film such as Melinex (ICI), or by adding 1% paraffin wax to the formulation. The wax separates out on the surface during curing, forming a barrier against the air, and preventing evaporation of volatile material from the mixture. The organic peroxide which initiates the reaction must be handled cautiously owing to its strong oxidizing potential. The reaction rate can be reduced by decreasing the amounts of the accelerator and initiator. Up to 12% shrinkage by volume can occur, though this can be reduced to some extent by controlling the temperature. The polymerization may continue for several months.

Various types of polyester have been developed, and have been used successfully as gap fillers in glass conservation (Jackson, 1982; Bradley and Wilthew, 1984; Davison and Jackson, 1985), though not so commonly for ceramics. Usually such polyesters are available as either laminating or embedding resins, e.g. Trylon's shallow cast embedding resin EM 400A and Tiranti's clear embedding resin. The former are designed to be built up in layers and are more brittle, while the embedding resins can be used in larger quantities but have to be enclosed in moulds to avoid the tacky surface. There are also products designed as marine or car fillers, e.g. David's P38 (David) and Plastic Padding Marine Filler (Plastic Padding), which consist of a polyester-based paste that cures after the addition of a hardener. These have been successfully used as gap fillers.

Although less commonly used as adhesives than some of the other resins, polyesters can be useful where a mechanical bond is required on rough or craggy edges (Larney, 1975a). Some of the more viscous polyesters with short curing times provide a quick-setting bond which will not be absorbed by porous material, so avoiding any risk of staining, e.g. Sebralit (Pisani) and General (General Industria Chimica). Polyesters will yellow on continued exposure to light, and become increasingly vulnerable to moisture attack.

The styrene component of the uncured resin is a highly toxic aromatic hydrocarbon solvent which can cause damage to the nervous system and liver, narcosis and temporary irritation of the respiratory system. It is also a suspected carcinogen. Organic peroxides may cause eye and respiratory irritations and many are sensitisers. All polyesters must be mixed and applied under effective fume extraction, since the fumes evolved during curing are unpleasant and harmful if exposure is prolonged. The uncured resin must not be allowed to come into contact with skin; gloves should be worn. Eyes must be protected from the risk of accidental splashes.

Reversibility

Aged polyesters become increasingly insoluble owing to cross-linking. Reversal is only possible by swelling, using a proprietary paint stripper or resin disintegrator.

Epoxy resins

These synthetic thermosetting resins have been widely used to bond and fill porcelains, stonewares and occasionally earthenwares. They are composed of a viscous resin component containing an epoxy ring, which hardens at room temperature by a cross-linking reaction, catalysed by a second component. The resin part is made in two stages. The first produces relatively long-chain molecules by condensation polymerization; typically the reaction occurs between epichlorohydrin and a polyhydric compound such as bisphenol A. The three-membered ring in epichlorohydrin is then opened to form an open chain with a hydroxyl group in it, and this forms the resin component of a two-pack system. In the second stage, the linear chains are cross-linked by additional polymerization reactions using a monomer, usually a di- or polyamine, as the catalyst. It is critical that the correct quantity of hardener is used, as too little will result in incomplete hardening, but an excess will cause the catalyst components to soften the resin, as well as reacting with the carbon dioxide in the air. Amines are toxic and contact can cause severe irritation of the skin; the vapours are also unpleasant and harmful.

There are many different kinds of epoxy available which share the properties of good adhesion and low shrinkage on curing. They have become increasingly important in the construction and engineering industry, and a consequence of this has been the increased availability of a wider range of products. Unfortunately the criteria which are deemed essential for resins in conservation, such as resistance to yellowing, are less important in industrial applications that concentrate on optimizing qualities of superior strength, chemical resistance, and resistance to heat. Recent developments have led to a greatly improved choice for conservation, with resins having superior ageing properties and durability. Studies have been made into their suitability for conservation (Tennent, 1979; Tennent and Townsend, 1984b; Bradley, 1984; Down, 1984; 1986). The majority, however, consist of resins incorporating bisphenol A and amine components, e.g. Araldite (Ciba-Geigy) and UHU Plus Endfest (Lingner), and are susceptible to yellowing. Such discoloration is the visible result of a complex, little understood process, involving the formation of chromaphores derived from the benzene part of the resin. The range of products available changes frequently as formulations are altered or replaced with upgraded versions, e.g. Araldite AY103/HY956 (Ciba-Geigy) which was originally water white but is now straw coloured. Products themselves may vary from batch to batch (Bradley, 1990a; 1990b). HXTAL NYL-1 (Conservation Materials) epoxy resin is specially designed for conservation and consists of a hydrogenated epoxy resin with a poly(oxypropylene) triamine hardener and imidazole accelerator. The excellent properties of light fastness and stability of HXTAL NYL-1 have been optimized at the expense of the curing time which can take up to seven days, resulting in extended treatment time and the potential risk of disalignment of joins during the curing period. Other epoxy resins that may be considered conservation quality and have been assessed as such include Araldite 2020 previously known as XW 396/397 (Ciba-Geigy), Epo-Tek 301-2 (Epoxy Technology) and Fynebond (Fyne Conservation Services) (Down, 1984; Tennent, 1991).

Epoxy foaming systems have been successfully used as a strong, lightweight rigid backing material for mounting tiles (Blackshaw and Cheetham, 1982) and for lifting objects.

As with all other resins, the manufacturers' health and safety instructions should be complied with. Epoxy hardeners are toxic and extremely sensitising to the skin and respiratory system. Individuals with allergies, dermatitis or any sensitisation should avoid exposure to epoxy resin systems. Contact with either of the components or uncured resin should be avoided by use of nitrile, neoprene or viton gloves (Clydesdale, 1990). The resin should be mixed and used under extraction; goggles should also be worn if there is any risk of splashes.

Reversibility

The resins can be swelled and broken down with dichloromethane or dichloromethane-based paint strippers. It is important to be aware that the swelling action can induce tensions along the break line which might prove potentially damaging. Although not recommended, epoxy resins will also break down when exposed to temperatures of 100–160°C.

Polyurethane resins

Polyurethane resins are products of an alcohol and an isocyanate group resin. The type of isocyanate involved determines the properties of the resins produced. Their main application is as retouching media, e.g. Torlife (Tor), but other types have been used as foams for backing mosaics and tiles, and for lifting archaeological ceramics. They tend to form good bonds with polar surfaces, as the isocyanate group reacts with moisture present on or in glazed surfaces.

The coatings have a number of advantageous properties in application. They mix well with pigments, and are easily applied. When white spirit is added as a solvent, the working time can be extended. They cure to give a hard glossy surface that responds well to abrasion and polishing. However, the cured resin is not stable in light, and can yellow quite rapidly after application.

The foams may be rigid or flexible and are produced by combining the isocyanate component with a polyester or polyether polyhydroxyl component. The polyester-type foams are less stable but have good mechanical properties, while the polyether type tend to last longer. These have been used in the past as a lifting material for small objects on excavation sites and also as a strong, lightweight backing material. Isocyanates are highly toxic (MEL: LTEL 8-hour TWA 0.02 ppm, STEL 15-minutes 0.07 ppm) and exposure to their vapours, during and following curing of the resin, can cause allergic reaction and sensitisation. In high doses the eyes, skin and respiratory system may be affected and the results of tests have suggested carcinogenic links. Isocyanate vapours can remain trapped within the bubbles of cured polyurethane foams, and care must be taken when breaking down such compositions. When handling the resin maximum protection must be provided by gloves and goggles; respirators should be worn together with adequate fume extraction (Bradley, 1986).

Reversibility
Although they become insoluble with age, the resins can be swelled with dichloromethane-based paint strippers and resin disintegrators.

Silicone-based polymers

There are numerous compounds that fall into the category of silicone-based polymers. They share the characteristic of having silicone, oxygen and organic groups in their chain structure. They include such compounds as silanes and silicone rubbers. The chemistry of both is complex; more detailed accounts are available elsewhere (Horie, 1987; Freeman, 1962).

Silanes are a class of silicon hydrides forming a homologous group and have the general formula Si_nH_{2n+2} (Uvarov and Isaacs, 1986). Although they have been used in stone conservation as a consolidant since the late 1960s (Dinsmore, 1987; Hanna, 1984; Moncrieff, 1976), they have only been used occasionally in conjunction with ceramics. They can be used to enhance the wetting properties and adhesion of various adhesives and consolidants, aiding penetration and increasing the adhesion of the polymer. Silanes have been successfully used to consolidate deteriorated stone prior to desalination (Larson and Dinsmore, 1984; Mangum, 1986). They have the ability to render the material water repellant, though not waterproof, achieving an almost invisible finish without completely filling the pores and making it possible to desalinate using poultices if necessary. Some initial shadowing will occur after application; this fades with time when all the solvent has completely evaporated. However, the treatment is irreversible and cannot be dissolved in solvents; consequently the use of silanes should only be considered as a last resort, when all other options have been ruled out and the survival of the object is threatened.

Silicone rubber, another silicone-based polymer, will be considered later in the section on mould-making materials.

The health and safety guidelines given in the manufacturers' technical data should be strictly complied with, owing to the toxic nature of these compounds.

Formaldehyde resins

The formaldehyde group of resins includes urea formaldehyde (UF), melamine formaldehyde (MF), and phenol formaldehyde (PF), which find applications in ceramics conservation as coatings for fillings. They are highly cross-linked network polymers, produced by the condensation reaction of two components resulting in a hard brittle coating which can be abraded and polished as required. Those used in ceramics conservation are usually two-pack systems, consisting of the resin component and an acid-based catalyst; examples include Rustins Plastic Coating (Rustins) and China Glaze (Phenoglaze). Rustins Plastic Coating consists of a UF-type resin mixed with solvents and an acidic hardener. The pH of the hardener is known to be incompatible with the blue pigments such as ultramarine, but not cobalt. China Glaze is a UF resin which is modified with an alkyl component (phthalic acid) but shows reduced stability in both dark and light situations which cause yellowing. Williams (1983) notes that it may have adverse reactions with oil paint. The resins are generally used in conjunction with a *thinner*, intended mainly as a brush cleaner, consisting of a cocktail of several solvents. Manufacturers guidelines on aspects of health and safety must be followed during use of any formaldehyde group resins.

Reversibility
Formaldehyde resins become increasingly less soluble after ageing, though will be disrupted by dichloromethane or acetone to some extent.

Alkyds
Alkyd resins form the basis for some paints which have been successfully used as an alternative to acrylic paints on archaeological and earthenware ceramics, e.g. Intenso Colours (Keep). They are produced by the reactions of polyhydric alcohols (polyols) with certain organic acids (drying oils). They generally have higher molecular weights than *oil paints*, and consequently tend to be more stable and resistant to yellowing, though they are susceptible to yellowing in the dark. White spirit and other hydrocarbons can be used as solvents to help their application. They set by evaporation of the solvent and gradual cross-linking. The advantage of this type of paint, as opposed to acrylics, is that they can be rubbed back with abrasive papers and polished or burnished as required. They are often particularly effective for retouching some earthenwares, though colour matching may demand some practice owing to the tendency to change tone on drying.

Oil paints
Although less commonly used by ceramics restorers nowadays, oil paints have been used in the past for

retouching. They consist of a pigment in drying oils, such as linseed, soya, tung or walnut, with a filler, and polymerization normally occurs as the paint dries. The naturally occurring fatty oils consist of a cocktail of long-chained molecules that are products of a reaction between glycerol and a fatty acid with a number of double carbon bonds. During the slow drying, oxidation occurs with oxygen diffusing in and causing cross-links to form. Eventually, with the continued occurrence of cross-linking, the coating will become increasingly brittle. Further reactions with impurities may cause discoloration and yellowing. Williams (1983) suggests the use of oilpaints to provide base colours, using them in conjunction with some other retouching media, though he states that some types of resin are incompatible with the oil, and also that the oil contributes to the rapid discoloration of the coating.

Supports and moulding materials

The selection of a suitable support takes into consideration a number of factors. Firstly, if the size of the missing area is small, a simple support may be adequate, but if a large area is to be backed, the support will have to be stronger and more durable. If there are undercuts, a flexible supporting material should be used so that it can stretch and pull away from around the object and the cast. The moulding material must also be compatible with both the filler and the material from which the object is made; some polyesters may require a separating agent to avoid adhesion between the resin and the mould, and some moulding materials may tint the resin, or stain the object.

Pressure sensitive tapes

Tape can be used in various applications, for example as a temporary support for the object while the adhesive cures, or as a backing for fillings whilst they set. It is best suited to backing small flat areas as the tape will not readily take up curved forms and tends to kink or cockle unevenly.

There are numerous types of pressure sensitive tapes available, some of which lend themselves to specific applications: for example, masking tape, which is one of the few tapes that will adhere to matt or unglazed surfaces. The adhesives with which the tapes are coated are viscous liquids derived from rubbers and resins with reduced molecular weights (Horie, 1987). Some of the pressure sensitive adhesives are not compatible with certain resins and may cause rapid discoloration. This effect has been noted with some epoxy resins that may turn to a pink-purple shade upon contact with the adhesive tapes. The reaction is usually apparent after 12 hours and can be frustrating if the contamination has penetrated the join. It is always worth testing compatibility if using a new or unfamiliar product.

Wax

Wax compositions can be used both as a modelling material, from which moulds may be taken, and as a support material to back up a missing area during application of a filler. They usually consist of a mixture of waxes from mineral and organic sources, coloured with dyes or pigments. Solid blocks of wax can be used for modelling, while sheets can make simple supports.

Sheets of wax, as designed for use by dentists, can be obtained in variable qualities, sizes and thickness, e.g. dental wax sheets by De Trey and Tenacetin by Associated Dental Products. The wax is simple to handle and apply, though easily distorted. It should not be allowed to come into contact with porous surfaces owing to the risk of staining. If necessary, the wax can be coated with a release agent such as poly(vinyl alcohol) (PVAL) (Newton and Davison, 1989). This is often quite difficult as the PVAL has a tendency to pool and must be brushed continuously in order to form a coating; the addition of a small amount of detergent helps to avoid this problem.

Where part of an object is missing and there is no reference object available from which to make a mould, modelling the missing area in wax may be the preferred option. Pryke (1991) assessed a number of commercial products for their modelling properties and ease of use.

Rubber latex

Rubber latex can serve as a cheap, readily available, highly flexible, moulding material. The rubber has a very low T_g, and consequently remains soft at room temperature. The commercial product, as used for mould-making, is derived from the sap of the rubber tree *Hevea brasiliensis*. It usually contains ammonia to give enhanced stability, and is pre-vulcanized by the addition of sulphur to produce a cross-linked product. Moulds can be reinforced, if necessary, by adding cotton flock, sawdust, or cotton gauze to the liquid latex. Such moulds will be stronger though less flexible. Talc may be used as a separating layer on matt or porous surfaces to ensure the removal of the rubber. It may also be necessary to back larger moulds with an additional plaster support casing. Petroleum jelly makes a reliable release agent between the plaster and the rubber. The rubber shrinks by around 8% when dried naturally. Contact with metals should be avoided as the ammonia constituent will react with them unless they have been pre-treated with a protective coating. Unstable surfaces, gilded, or cold-painted decoration should not be allowed to come into contact with rubber latex, as the latex may disturb and pull away the underlying fragile surface upon removal. Always test first and consolidate where necessary.

Rubber latex moulds have a limited life and will start to break down within a matter of months, reacting with air, resulting in loss of elasticity and strength, and deformation of shape. Mould rejection can sometimes occur with polyesters as a result of the exothermic reaction which occurs as the resin cures.

Silicone rubber

Silicone rubber, while not as flexible as rubber latex, can be used to produce good moulds with excellent detail. There are various types of silicone rubber; each is supplied with a separate catalyst that has to be mixed very thoroughly with the rubber prior to application to the object. The curing time may vary from a matter of minutes to several hours depending on the type of silicone rubber, and can sometimes be speeded up by warming. Some of the most easily applied silicone rubbers are *borrowed* from the dental profession, and consist of a thick paste or putty and separate catalyst that are mixed together by kneading in the palm of the hand (protected by disposable gloves), then pressed onto the object to make a one-part mould, e.g. Copol-sil (Anatomical Plastics), Provil (Bayers), Optosil (Bayers) and Reprosil (De Trey). Others, intended for industrial applications, demand more precise preparation and are useful for making multi-part moulds of complex forms. The consistency of the rubber may be altered by adding fillers such as fumed silica (to thicken), or silicone oil (to thin), though the latter tends to cause the rubber to tear.

Many of the impression rubbers are capable of reproducing a high level of detail and accuracy, and are useful for taking surface impressions, or for making simple one-part moulds. Some, however, possess a high oil content which can stain porous surfaces, and others contain colouring material that may migrate into the cast or the surface of the object from which the impression is taken (Shashoua, 1990a).

There are two types of room temperature vulcanizing (RTV) silicone rubber available, which cure by either condensation or addition reactions. The silicone rubbers which vulcanize by condensation, e.g. Silastic 3110 and 9161 (Dow Corning) and RTV-M533, 539 (Wacker), have the disadvantage of producing volatile by-products such as alcohols or acetic acid resulting in slight shrinkage. Their curing time cannot be altered by changing the proportion of the catalyst in the same way that it can with other types of silicone rubber. The small amount of catalyst used (2–5%) makes thorough mixing essential. There is some risk of these types of silicones sticking to the surface of the object, especially if porous, owing to capillary action, though a separating layer can avoid this to some extent. Instances of rubber adhering to glass have also been reported (Morgos *et al.*, 1984). Addition-type silicone rubbers, e.g. Silastic E RTV, Silastic J RTV (Dow Corning), Provil (Bayers), RTV-ME 622, RTV-ME 628 (Wacker), on the other hand, are free from such problems. A larger proportion of catalyst is added to the rubber, making mixing easier; curing can be speeded up by raising the temperature. There is no emission of volatile products, and consequently shrinkage is minimal. However, the catalyst in the addition-type silicones can be inhibited by certain substances, and some types of polyester cannot be used with rubbers of any sort. Silicone rubbers in general should not be used on porous surfaces as staining will occur owing to contamination with the silicone oils contained within the rubbers. It is advisable to make an initial test of the compatibility of the rubber and substrate where possible.

Silicone rubbers are resistant to solvents, though aromatic, aliphatic and chlorinated hydrocarbons (e.g. dichloromethane) will swell them. Depending on the specific type of rubber, several casts may be made from the mould before it starts to degenerate and break down. The life of the mould can be increased by heating in an oven to 120°C for 12 hours (Larsen, 1981).

Hot melt impression materials

There are various, less commonly used, thermoplastic compositions available that may be softened in hot, or boiling water, then pressed onto an object to take an impression of an area which resembles a missing part. These may vary from gelatinous compositions such as Formalose, to vinyl-based flexible systems such as Vinamold (Clearway Plastics). Vinamold has to be heated to 150–170°C before pouring at between 140–150°C; and the risk of thermal shock response by the object makes its use inadvisable. Williams (1983) describes the use of Para-bar (Cottrell) as a support material. It is a thermoplastic gelatinous material available as a dark block. The material is softened prior to application in boiling water and pressed onto the object immediately while still hot and pliable. It serves as a rigid backing material that can be used several times.

Plasticine

Plasticine (Harbutts) consists of calcium carbonate (whiting) and calcium oxide (lime), mixed with petroleum jelly and fatty acids to a putty-like consistency. Sulphur is sometimes added to the mixture to act as a preservative. It has a slightly greasy quality, which is undesirable for some applications where there is a risk of staining. There are alternatives available that are oil-free, e.g. Aloplast (Trylon), which is dark blue in colour, and sulphur-free for use on metals, e.g. Klean Klay no. 2 (Art Chemical Products, USA).

Plasticine makes a useful material to prop pieces as resins cure. It can also be used, if necessary, as a support material when taking casts and as an inferior modelling material. However, it distorts very easily and the quality of the impressions is not sharp. The grease content may also interfere with the material being cast. Dusting with French chalk is recommended by Larney (1975b) to aid release of the putty.

Clay

Clay can sometimes be used as a cheap, readily available alternative backing material to support fillings on site. However, it should not be used on low-fired, porous or coarse pottery, as removal of clay particles deposited on the object would be almost impossible.

Fillers

Mention of some gap fillers and casting materials, such as polyesters and epoxies, has already been made in the section covering resins in general. Some further consideration should be given to those products which, though designed for other uses, have been adopted as filling materials because of their very appropriate properties.

Plaster of Paris

Plaster of Paris consists of calcium sulphate hemihydrate powder ($CaSO_4.\frac{1}{2}H_2O$), produced by heating gypsum (natural hydrated calcium sulphate) to 120°C, driving off the water of crystallization. The name is derived from the prolific deposits of gypsum found around Paris (Rich, 1947). When mixed with water it sets by an exothermic reaction to form a hard white filling which has a similar density to fired ceramics: the specific gravity of gypsum is 2.32 and that of earthenware 2.4–2.6 (Grimshaw, 1971). There are two main groups of plaster: beta plaster and alpha plaster. The two vary in their physical properties, alpha plaster requiring less water to produce a mix that can be easily poured, and having superior strength and qualities of reproduction to beta plaster.

Several grades of plaster are manufactured, differing in their particle size, setting time, density, expansion and colour. These differences are dependent on the purity of the raw gypsum mineral employed and also on the calcination process. Plaster is a widely available material that is inexpensive, easy to use, fast setting, and suitable for casting, carving, abrading and retouching (Chase and Zycherman, 1981; Koob, 1987). Specialist plasters designed specifically for the dental profession tend to set very hard with minimal expansion, some producing very dense, brittle products when set; examples include Kaffir D and Crystacal R (British Gypsum). Fillings can be consolidated by coating with a synthetic resin such as Paraloid/Acryloid B-72 or cellulose nitrate.

The main disadvantages of using plaster as a filler are the brevity of its working time and its tendency to expand on setting; the quantity of water that has to be mixed, and the consequential drying time, can also be a drawback. Plaster can be resistant to removal by mechanical means, and may put the object at risk, especially if the harder grades have been used. A further problem can arise if a plaster filling is allowed to become damp at a later stage; sulphate salts may be absorbed by a porous ceramic body which could subsequently result in the formation of salt crystals and their associated harmful effects.

Plaster is often most successfully used in mould-making, particularly for making outer support or *mother moulds* to encase a softer, inner material such as silicone rubber or rubber latex. Soft soap, microcrystalline wax or white petroleum jelly can be used as a release agent.

Inhalation of plaster dust should be avoided when handling through use of appropriate respiratory protection (OES: LTEL 8-hour TWA 10 ppm).

Plaster-based proprietary fillers: Polyfilla

There are a number of proprietary fillers consisting of modified mixtures of plaster of Paris designed for painters and decorators as a filler for cracks in walls. Of these, Polyfilla (Polycell) is the most commonly used by ceramic conservators; it is widely available in hardware shops in the UK. The two most useful grades for filling ceramics are the interior grade Polyfilla and the Fine Surface Polyfilla. A third type, Exterior Polyfilla, is coarser, and occasionally used for specialist applications where a hard granular texture is required, for example when filling the back of tiles.

Polyfilla (interior grade)

This consists of a cellulose reinforced plaster of Paris, that is, a combination of various ingredients including calcium sulphate, cellulose ethers and retarding agents. The plaster is mixed with a small amount of water to give the desired consistency and can be strengthened by adding PVA emulsion to the wet mixture. It has the advantage of possessing a longer working time than plaster of Paris; neither is it prone to salt growth. It dries quickly with negligible shrinkage and can be easily cut back and rubbed down. Removal is possible by mechanical methods and softening with water. The disadvantages of Polyfilla (interior grade) are that it is relatively weak and is not very resistant to rough handling and abrasion; it has poor powers of adhesion with smooth surfaces. As with all Polyfillas the dense appearance makes it an inappropriate filler for translucent bodies.

Fine Surface Polyfilla

This is mainly a vinyl acetate copolymer, mixed with inorganic mineral fillers, thickeners and a biocide. It is supplied ready mixed and is used for gap filling very small areas, or patching blemishes and flaws on larger areas of filling. A very smooth surface can be achieved on which to apply a coating. However, since it is liable to shrinkage, the filler can only be used in thin layers; it also lacks adhesion on smooth and polished surfaces.

Other filling materials

There are a number of commercially available products that have been successfully used by restorers. These are usually two-part putties with pigments already added; some are epoxy based, e.g. Sylmaster (Syglas), Milliput (Milliput) and Pliacre (Philadelphia), while others are polyesters, e.g. Sebralit (Pisani), David's P38 (David) and Plastic Padding Marine Filler (Plastic Padding). They are quick and easy to use, consisting of a ready made paste, to which a hardener must be added. They have some drawbacks: often being inappropriately coloured, too thick to be satisfactorily applied, or extremely hard to cut back. Also the long-term compatibility and ageing properties of the resins with either the ceramic body or the retouching medium may not be satisfactory. Bradley and Green (1987) refer to an adverse effect when Milliput filler is coated with a urea formaldehyde resin (e.g. Rustins Plastic Coating). The combination of coating and filler is susceptible to yellowing particularly in the dark or in low light levels. This phenomenon was attributed to a constituent in the putty known as butylated hydroxy toluene (BHT).

Aggregates

When resins are used as fillings, it may be desirable to simulate the visual and tactile qualities of the adjacent ceramic areas. To achieve this materials can be added that act as inert bulking agents, making the resin more viscous and easier to apply. The aggregate may also be used to opacify the resin, to the correct level of translucency. The density of the filling can be matched as near as possible with that of the body, and, if necessary, the texture of the filling can be adjusted by combining coarse granular inclusions to imitate the area being filled. It should be remembered, however, that certain additives may affect the properties of some resins in an adverse (or advantageous) manner. Consequently when trying new combinations of resins and aggregates for the first time it is advisable to test them.

Titanium dioxide powder (TiO_2) A fine white insoluble pigment which occurs naturally in crystalline forms, including anatase and rutile. Produces a very dense white filling.

Barium sulphate ($BaSO_4$) Also known as *barytes*, a white crystalline insoluble powder which is opaque to X-rays. It gives a greyish white filling when mixed on its own with a resin.

Kaolin powder ($Al_2Si_2O_5(OH)_4$) Also known as *china clay*, and consisting of a natural and pure form of hydrated aluminium silicate.

Glass balls These are hollow microspheres of glass which produce a light, slightly translucent, gritty filling, e.g. Q-Cels (PQ), SP Glass Bubbles (SP Systems).

Hydrated magnesium silicate ($3MgO.4SiO_2.H_2O$) *Also known as talc* or *French chalk*. It is an insoluble mineral with a variable composition usually containing calcium, iron and aluminium. *Steatite* and *soapstone* are two variations. It produces a soft opaque filling which is easy to file and cut. Also useful when added to retouching media to fill irregularities and pits in uneven fillings.

Micro Balloons These are hollow spheres made of phenolic resin which can reduce the density of the filling and make it softer to carve and abrade once the filling has cured, e.g. Microspheres (Union Carbide), SP Microballoons (SP Systems).

Silica (silicon dioxide SiO_2) Fumed colloidal silica (aerosol silica) and micronized silica gel are both forms of silicon dioxide that differ in their physical properties and applications.

Fumed silica, formerly known as *pyrogenic silica*, is a very finely divided colloidal form of synthetic silica, manufactured as a product of burning silicon tetrachloride. It is available in a hydrophobic form, e.g. Tullanox 500 (Tulco) or a hydrophilic form, e.g. Cab-o-Sil, (Calbot), Aerosil 200, Aerosil TT600 (Degussa), depending on the manufacturing process. The hydrophobic form acts as a water repellant when mixed with adhesives in quantities of 3–10%. Fumed silica has also been shown to alter the properties of some resins (e.g. Paraloid, poly(vinyl acetate) and epoxies), improving their adhesion and altering their mobility, plasticity and thixotropy (Byrne, 1984; Koob, 1986). However, there is some suggestion that certain grades of fumed silica can cause yellowing of a significant level in certain normally stable epoxy resins (Tennent, 1991).

The micronized silica gels are generally used as matting agents, e.g. Gasil 23C (now discontinued) and Gasil 23D (Crosfield). These are forms of silica gel that have been modified to produce a high-purity amorphous silica. When added to retouching media the resulting coating takes on a dull matt appearance.

The manufacturers' health and safety instructions for handling should be complied with when using these types of silica.

Stone powders Finely ground powders derived from stones of various types such as marble, alabaster and onyx are frequently employed as aggregates in fillings for stone sculptures; they can occasionally be useful in achieving certain effects in ceramics.

Finishing materials

The surface of a freshly applied filling or area of retouch will usually require further work in order to *finish* it. This stage in the treatment may vary from intensive abrading and cutting back to remove irregularities, to a final light polishing on an area of retouching to buff it up to match the reflectance of an adjacent area of fired glaze.

Abrasives and polishes

Abrasives, in general, consist of fine particles of different size and hardness, depending on their derivation. To facilitate application, the particles usually have to be combined with a medium or support of some form. Air abrasive techniques demand air under pressure, sometimes combined with water, in order to achieve their effect. Polishes are usually a paste or a cream, made up of a cocktail of abrasive particles, solvents, waxes and emulsifiers. Supports or backing materials for abrasives may comprise flat sheets of paper, fabric or plastic, or attachments for special machinery, made from wood, metal rubber or fabric to be used with drills, grinding machines and polishers. The particles and any other necessary fillers are usually bonded to the support with synthetic or natural resins.

Silicon carbide Consists of a synthetic material produced when silica and carbon react at very high temperatures in an electric furnace (Organ, 1968). The raw material is then processed by grinding and sieving to give brittle particles of appropriate size and shape. The most common form of usage of silicon carbide in ceramics conservation is as sheets, for rubbing down fillings. It will scratch glazes if carelessly applied (hardness graded at 9.5; see Chapter 4).

Glass Made from bottle glass, which is crushed to give particles of various sizes and then bonded onto a paper backing. It is not as aggressive as silicon carbide paper since the particles are less hard (6.5–4.5). Finer grades of glass paper are known as *flour paper*.

Garnet A naturally occurring mineral that may be processed to give it improved abrasive powers. Available as an abrasive sheet, the particles being bonded to a heavy duty paper. It is sometimes useful for the initial stages of rubbing down large irregular fillings (7.5).

Quartz Occurs naturally in abundance as flint and sand. Particles are specially selected from inland natural deposits and used to make *sand paper* which is only occasionally used in ceramics conservation.

Aluminium oxide (Al_2O_3) Also known as alumina. Sometimes used in powder form for some air abrasive applications, but more commonly in sheet form. There are numerous grades of synthetic aluminium oxide available which range in purity. The finer grades of the Flex-i-grit (Moyco) range of abrasives consist of fine particles of aluminium oxide adhered with a flexible adhesive to a durable tear resistant Mylar backing, which is both waterproof and solvent resistant. Ultrafine (Hill), consists of a fine grade aluminium oxide mounted on a fabric backing. The finer grades of (8000-12,000) Micro-mesh cushioned abrasive (Micro-surface Finishing Products inc) are a similar system of aluminium oxide bonded to a latex coated cloth.

Kieselguhr Is derived from the deposited skeletons of very small plants or diatoms. It consists of hydrated silica (SiO_2) particles of relatively uniform size which can be further crushed to form a very mild abrasive powder (1.5–1). It is often the main abrasive constituent in polishing pastes. Solvol Autosol paste (Hammerite), is made up of a mixture of kieselguhr (40%), kerosene (30%), distilled water (15%), fatty acids (10%), an emulsifier (3%) and ammonia (2%). This product has been replaced by Solvol Autochrome which is a similar composition.

Sodium bicarbonate ($NaHCO_3$) Occasionally used as a mild abrasive for air abrasion in dental polishing equipment. However, it is water soluble and, if used to clean porous bodies, the object should be thoroughly rinsed afterwards to remove all traces of the material.

Diamond A crystalline form of carbon and one of the hardest known materials (10). In their crushed form, the fractured, dark particles have very sharp edges which are extremely abrasive and, when mounted on a point or burr in conjunction with a dental drill, can be used to cut into glazes or abrade hard corroded rivets.

Microcrystalline wax

This is a semi-synthetic wax with a microcrystalline structure, produced as a by-product from the refining of petroleum. The crystal particles are around 0.001–0.002 mm in diameter (paraffin wax is 0.1 mm) (Kuhn, 1986). It has a melting point between 55°C and 80°C. Microcrystalline wax, e.g. Renaissance Wax (Picreator), is sometimes used as a surface finish on the damaged glaze of stoneware objects; the wax will fill and disguise the groove of the scratch, making it less obtrusive. It is also sometimes used as a release agent for silicone rubber, latex rubber or plaster moulds.

Colouring pigments

Adhesives, fillings and coatings can be coloured using colouring agents. These will be based on either pigments or dyes. A pigment is an organic or inorganic material which is insoluble in most solvents, but which in a finely ground form can be added to a medium to give colour. Dyes are organic materials which are soluble in water or other liquids, and capable of producing an intense colour by being absorbed and retained, chemically combined within the substance. They are less commonly used in ceramics conservation owing to their intensity and ability to stain. They can, however, be useful for tinting filling materials.

Early pigments were naturally occurring minerals which could be ground to a powder. Many were oxides of various types, giving a range of yellows, browns, reds and blacks; soot and charcoal produced blacks; whites were obtained from chalk, shells and bone. The blues and greens, which were less common, were derived from copper and iron minerals, while brilliant reds and yellows came from mercuric and arsenic pigments. Organic pigments were extracted from fruit juice, flowers, and other vegetable products mixed with chalk or precipitated with alum (naturally occurring crystalline aluminium potassium sulphate) to make more permanent products. Exploration and travel from the sixteenth century onwards helped to widen the range of pigments available. Present day pigments are obtained from various sources: some are still derived from natural coloured earths and minerals, while others are of plant and animal origin, and more still (around 40,000) are synthetic products produced by the colour industry. A basic range of pigments suitable as colouring agents for retouching media and for tinting resins will be considered in this section.

Properties of pigments

Individual pigments possess a number of distinct characteristics which differentiate one from another, and make some a more suitable choice for a particular purpose. Each crystal particle is transparent and absorbs or reflects light selectively; some will absorb ultraviolet light. The colour of a pigment is determined by the wavelengths of the reflected light. This can be measured instrumentally and represented graphically as a spectral reflectance curve. Lighting conditions can alter the apparent colour of a pigment, and a pigment that closely matches the colour of an adjacent area of glaze in one light may appear quite different under other viewing conditions. This phenomenon is known as metamerism, and the only way to ensure perfect colour-matching under all lighting conditions is to select pigments with similar reflectance curves to that of the original colour to be matched. In practice this is unrealistic owing to the complex instrumental procedures that would be involved in examining each colour to be matched.

Individual pigments tend to deteriorate for different reasons, and their original colour may fade or become tinted. Factors affecting the permanence of pigments include light, atmospheric pollutants, the type of resin system used as the medium, and interaction between the pigments.

The transparency or opacity of a pigment depends on the thickness or thinness of the coating and the method of application. The quality known as the *body* is the tinting power or ability to colour a white ground. Intensity may vary from pigment to pigment, depending on the opacity and the particle size of the pigments. The weight per unit volume is proportional to the specific gravity of a pigment and determines whether it sinks or floats in a medium. The fineness of the pigment particles and body determine the working properties. Some coarsely ground pigments are difficult to work with and notoriously gritty, while others are oily and do not mix well. Traditionally pigments were hand ground and quite coarse compared with modern pigments, which are usually prepared by precipitation or ground in a grinding mill. Generally, the greater the transparency of the pigment, the larger the particle size needed to obtain a strong colour. Oil colours, which are partially set by the evaporation of volatile components and by oxidation, require pigments which possess a good disposition to drying.

Selected examples of pigments

Although there is a tremendous range of dry artist's pigments available commercially, only a relatively small number is necessary to imitate accurately the colours of ceramic surfaces (Larney, 1975b). Some of these are briefly considered in this section.

White

Titanium dioxide (TiO_2) Has already been mentioned as a useful aggregate for addition to fillings. This has been commercially produced since the 1920s. It is a microcrystalline, fine textured, dense, opaque white pigment which has good hiding power, with a high refractive index of 2.5–2.6. It occurs naturally in its pure form as anatase and rutile. Rutile titanium dioxide has been shown to play some part in slowing down the deterioration of certain resins by absorbing the harmful ultraviolet wavelengths responsible for cross-linking. Anatase titanium dioxide also blocks out ultraviolet light and delays the breakdown of some resins; it also, however, contributes to chain breaking and brings about a consequential loss of volatile materials, ultimately rendering the resin insoluble (Whitmore and Bailie, 1990; Horie, 1987). The pigment is manufactured from ilmenite ($FeTiO_3$), a black titanium ore (natural iron II titanate). It is a very stable substance that is unaffected by heat, ultraviolet, air, dilute acids and alkalis. It is compatible with all other pigments.

Black

Ivory black Produces the most intense black of all black pigments, and is probably the most commonly used. It was originally produced by processing the charred residue of burned ivory, though now is also produced from animal bones. It is compatible with all other pigments.

Lamp black Also known as *carbon black*, consists of 99% carbon, derived from the soot created by burning mineral oil, tar, pitch or resin. Lamp black is not as intense as ivory black and tends to have a blue tint to it, though it still has good hiding power. The fine light powder has been used for hundreds of years as a pigment. It is very stable, remaining unaffected by light or chemical reaction.

Brown

Raw umber A brown-coloured earth pigment containing manganese dioxide and iron oxides. It occurs commonly in nature, though it varies in quality; one of the superior grades comes from Cyprus. The raw product is processed by grinding to produce a fine durable pigment which is compatible with other pigments and mediums. Inferior grades which can contain impurities are less stable and liable to fading in ultraviolet.

Burnt umber Is produced by roasting raw umber to a dull red heat, converting the iron III hydrate to iron III oxide which is more red and slightly more transparent.

Red

Burnt sienna This pigment is produced by roasting (or calcining) raw sienna, a type of ochre, which derives its name from the city of Sienna in Italy where the high-quality pigment has been produced for hundreds of years. *Raw sienna*, which consists of hydrated iron III oxide with alumina and silica, is changed to iron III oxide during heating, giving a warm red-brown. In transmitted light the pigment looks reddish-brown to orange, and when mixed with white gives a pale pinky-orange shade.

Light red Also known as *iron oxide red*, is composed of almost pure iron III oxide. It is opaque, with good covering and tinting power, giving a bright warm red. When mixed with white it produces salmon-coloured tones.

Alizarin crimson Originally produced from the madder root, alizarin was the first of the natural dyes to be synthetically produced from a derivative of coal tar. It has greater stability in light than other organic red pigments, or the natural madder lake, owing to the absence of fugitive purpurin. The pigment itself is deep red in colour, yielding a ruby red tone when thinly applied, and rose pinks when mixed with white. It has generally good qualities of compatibility when mixed with other pigments, and does not react adversely with lead white, though its permanence may be affected when mixed with earth colours (Gettens and Stout, 1966).

Cadmium red This toxic pigment is produced by precipitating cadmium sulphate with sodium sulphide and selenium. The exact ratios and the conditions present during the precipitation process determine the colours that are produced; they can range from vermilion to deep maroon. It can be used as a substitute for vermilion. It consists of very small non-crystalline particles of high refractive index and is dense and opaque with good tinting powers and permanence.

Blues

Cobalt blue A pure bright blue permanent pigment produced by calcining cobalt oxide with aluminium hydrate. Colours may vary depending on the different methods of manufacture. The pigment particles are characteristically moderately fine. It is very stable, unaffected by strong sunlight, and insoluble in strong acids and alkalis. It is also used as a blue stain for glazes in fired ceramics (e.g. Delft blue).

French ultramarine This is a brilliant blue artificial pigment which was originally derived from the semi-precious stone lapis lazuli, but is now made artificially in a furnace process producing a material which is chemically identical to the natural pigment but much purer. It consists of sodium aluminium silicate and contains some sulphur. Acids will decompose and change the colour, releasing hydrogen sulphide, as in the case of catalysts in urea-formaldehyde-based retouching media and epoxy resins (Tennent, 1991). The particles give opaque shades of low refractive index, and have a tendency to flocculate in the retouching media. It is stable in light, high tempera-

tures and alkalis. Inferior ultramarine with sulphur impurities may sometimes cause darkening with lead and copper pigments.
Prussian blue The earliest synthetic pigment to be produced, consisting of ferric ferrocyanide made by oxidizing a mixture of iron II sulphate, sodium ferrocyanide, and ammonium sulphate. The pigment, which is extremely fine, is a deep dark blue, giving a transparent green-blue colour. It has good qualities of permanence in light and air, and is unaffected by dilute mineral acids, though it turns brown in alkalis.
Cobalt violet A synthetic pigment consisting of either anhydrous cobalt phosphate, or arsenate, or a mixture of the two. It is a clear semi-opaque pigment with a weak tinting strength, giving bluish or reddish violet colours that are stable and unaffected by most chemicals.

Greens

Viridian green A bright green pigment, consisting of hydrated chromium oxide, prepared by heating a mixture of alkali chromate with excess boric acid. The pigment gives a deep cool transparent emerald green colour; at full strength it can be very dark and almost blackish. It has large characteristic irregular particles with a medium refractive index.
Terre-verte (green earth) A naturally occurring pigment originating from a marine clays, with a complex composition. It gives shades of green from a pale greenish grey to a neutral yellow green. Terre-verte consists of a mixture of coarse rounded particles with angular silica and silicate particles. Light, air or chemicals do not affect the stability of the pigment; however, when strongly heated it will turn red-brown.

Yellows

Yellow ochre A natural earth pigment in the ochre range, consisting of silica and clay, coloured by hydrated iron oxide (limonite). Owing to its wide occurrence, it has been universally used by cultures for thousands of years. Other ochres range in colour from golden brown to red, depending on the amount and type of iron oxide. The particle size and composition of the pigment is variable. It is a permanent colour which is unaffected by dilute acids or alkalis.
Chrome yellow A toxic yellow pigment consisting of lead chromate, produced in large sheets by mixing solutions of lead acetate or nitrate with an alkali chromate or dichromate. It consists of a crystalline material of variable particle size giving colours from lemon yellow to orange. The pigment is known to discolour and become brown. A colour alteration may also occur when mixed with organic pigments.
Lemon yellow Also known as *barium yellow* and *permanent yellow*. It is a pale and weak yellow-green pigment produced by mixing solutions of neutral potassium chromate and barium chloride. It is soluble in dilute alkalis and mineral acids and decomposed by heat at high temperatures, and can discolour slightly in light, acquiring a green tint due to the formation of chromic oxide.

Metallic finishes

Gilding, lustres and burnishing can be imitated to a certain extent using a combination of the pigments mentioned above and other specialist materials.

Powder gold Available in a range of different shades. The powder consists of a high proportion of gold mixed with small amounts of silver and copper. The precise ratios of the ingredients determine the colour. Although expensive, a very small quantity (usually sold by the gram) will last a long time provided the powder is used carefully. When dusted onto resins, thin layers can be built up giving a controllable degree of density, and a fine non-granular quality. The applied gilding can be burnished.
Gold leaf Also available in different shades in a variety of forms. It is most commonly available in books of five or twenty-five leaves; each thin leaf (84 × 84 × 0.001 mm) is separated by a sheet of tissue. It is difficult to handle and apply, the sheets being so thin that they tear and are easily disturbed by slight draughts. *Transfer gold leaf* is easier to handle, being mounted on acid-free tissue in books of twenty-five sheets. It can be easily cut with scissors, unlike the loose gold leaf, then transferred onto the object, and can be burnished if necessary.
Tablet gold This consists of powdered gold mixed with gum arabic to form a solid block that is water soluble. When dry, the surface to which it has been applied can be burnished.
Bronze powder Composed of finely ground particles of bronze of various colours. It can be used to imitate metallic finishes, though the powders tend to have a granular quality and will tarnish in time unless they are well sealed from the atmosphere with a resin to prevent corrosion.
Bronze paint Made up of fine metallic particles dispersed in a resin, e.g. Classic Treasure Gold and Classic Liquid Leaf (Connoisseur). It is an inferior quality substitute that can be used to imitate gold. The paints should be mixed thoroughly before use as the particles tend to sink. In general, they give a dull granular finish, as the particles are not usually fine enough to imitate the lustrous qualities of gilding or lustre glazes.
Lustre pigments These are non-metallic powders consisting of very small transparent particles (0.006 mm) of mica coated with titanium dioxide or iron oxide. They have been developed mainly for industrial applications, e.g. Mearlite (Mearl). The powders can

be mixed with retouching media and pigments to imitate iridescent lustre glazes. The controlled thickness of the small mica platelets produces the lustrous appearance by refraction of light.

Graphite powder Consists of fine particles of carbon that can be used to impart a grey metallic sheen, particularly appropriate for some earthenwares with blackened burnished surfaces.

Part Four

15

Displaying and mounting ceramics

Private and public institutions responsible for displaying their collections for others to enjoy and study may occasionally be confronted with objects whose form, size and nature set limitations on the display arrangements. There will be situations when the safety and security of the objects may be threatened in some way, for example if objects are on open display; in such cases it may be necessary to fix the object to a surface. Alternatively, the interpretation of the object may be compromised if the object cannot be presented to reflect the purpose for which it was designed; for example pictorial floor tiles may have to be viewed as a panel on the wall, and the decorated flat surface of plates may only be appreciated to the full when displayed vertically.

This chapter will consider some of the more common problems which arise in the course of mounting a display of ceramic objects. The finer details of case design, furnishings, and lighting will usually be resolved by designers and exhibition organizers. The environmental specifications for these have already been covered in Chapter 3.

Objects on open display

In certain circumstances it may be desirable to display ceramics unprotected by cases. The most obvious occurrence of this is those collections in historic houses that are open to the public. The interiors are frequently displayed with objects and furniture arranged much as they were when the house was lived in. The safety of the objects will make considerable demands on security (Sandwith and Stainton, 1985). For temporary exhibitions, contemporary ceramics are often shown on open display to allow them to be appreciated from all angles, without the added visual distraction and physical restrictions of a show case. In the permanent collections of museums, very large and durable ceramics may sometimes be displayed in the open, when it may be impractical to place them in a display case. Occasionally the designers of a display may wish to give special consideration to those visitors who are visually impaired, and in such a situation it will be important that objects are available to be touched (Figure 15.1).

There are a number of important disadvantages to displaying ceramics in the open, the most obvious being the threat of theft. Any decision to display ceramics openly should take into account all the potential risks. The objects will probably be protected from theft if there is adequate human surveillance and a security system.

In both public collections and private homes, thought should be given to the siting of the object. Objects should not be displayed in busy thoroughfares, or in blind spots where they may not be visible to attendant staff; nor should they be placed on the edges of furniture where they could be knocked and damaged. Vibration of the furniture on which the objects are displayed, (caused for example by springy floors or heavy traffic) may result in movement and potential risk of damage as objects gradually *creep* towards the edge of a table or knock against another object. By attaching a small piece of chamois or felt to the base of the object with cellulose nitrate adhesive, or Paraloid (Acryloid) B-72 (acrylic copolymer of methyl acrylate and ethyl methacrylate), or poly(vinyl acetate) (PVA) emulsion, the friction between the polished surface and the object should be increased so that the effects of vibration are less significant (Halahan and Plowden, 1987). This also has the effect of avoiding damage to a polished piece of furniture by abrasion from the rough base of an object. If possible, display shelves should have a small lip at their edge to restrain any *creeping* objects. It is preferable not to

Figure 15.1 A Korean porcelain jar on open display for the appreciation of the visually impaired. Visitors with poor vision are invited, by a Braille label, to enjoy the tactile qualities of the surface of the jar. The jar is secured into a recessed plinth to avoid the risk of damage, and the neck has been sealed on the interior just below the shoulder to avoid the accumulation of rubbish (Victoria and Albert Museum, London).

place objects directly under hanging mirrors or paintings, particularly if the latter are secured to the wall with picture wire; not only is there a risk of the wire breaking, but it is possible that the painting or mirror might be removed while the ceramics are still below, inviting accidents. Locations near windows are also dangerous: sudden draughts, flapping curtains and blinds may be enough to unbalance a delicate porcelain object. Doors, both to rooms and on cupboards, can be an additional hazard to objects. Objects on open display will be exposed to environmental pollution, but in particular, those on ledges above heat sources are likely to be more affected owing to the circulation of dust and dirt in convection currents.

Further methods of making the objects on open display more secure from theft or vandalism involve the use of adhesives, weights or brackets, either in combination, or on their own. Any method of attachment still leaves the object vulnerable to accidental or intentional damage, and the possibility of the fabric of the object yielding before the attachment in the event of someone forcefully attempting to remove it. The application of the adhesive may in itself be undesirable and damage may be caused during its removal.

Weighing down a hollow vessel form involves filling the object with a heavy material, such as lead shot or sand. Such methods, which have been used in the past, should be avoided, as they subject the object to constant and considerable strain. In any case, the added weight may not prevent a determined individual from removing the object. The method should only be used in situations where there is no alternative method for anchoring the object and only when it shows no indication of cracks or other instability. The weighting material should be isolated from contact with the object by placing it in polythene and surrounding it with padding. A weighted object should never be moved as this will put it at risk; the weight should always be removed first.

Another method of securing the ceramic is to bond it to a suitable surface by means of a separating layer of laminated card, cut to fit the base of the object. Poly(vinyl acetate) (PVA) emulsion, Paraloid (Acryloid) B-72 (acrylic copolymer) or cellulose nitrate adhesive can be used to adhere the card to both surfaces. The laminated card should be of approximately six layers, and should be cut to a size that is very slightly smaller than the foot rim or base, forming a ring of card with the centre cut out (Figure 15.2). Removal of the object is easily effected by slicing through the card horizontally with a scalpel. Any remaining card or adhesive on the object or surface can be easily removed with warm water or acetone. The covers on jars can be similarly secured by adhering the lower surface of the flange of the cover to a ring of laminated card; this is then adhered to the rim of the jar. This method should not be used if the object is damaged, or if it has been restored with materials that might be affected. Tests should be carried out before attempting to adhere objects where there may be a risk of absorption of the adhesive into the body. This attachment method should not be used if there is any risk that the surface to which the object is to be bonded might be damaged by the adhesive or solvents (for example a polished wood surface). An alternative is to cover the surface of the furniture with a protective sheet of glass to which the object can be safely attached (Larney, 1971).

Where objects are to be placed on tall pieces of furniture, and the upper surface is above eye level, a sheet of chipboard cut to the correct size can be used to protect the surface. The board can be secured to a back wall with brackets so that it forms a safe rigid invisible wall shelf to which the ceramics can be attached using the laminated card method. If the display surface is below eye level and it is not possible to adhere the object directly to the surface of the furniture, alternative methods will have to be employed. It may be feasible to insert a disc of wood

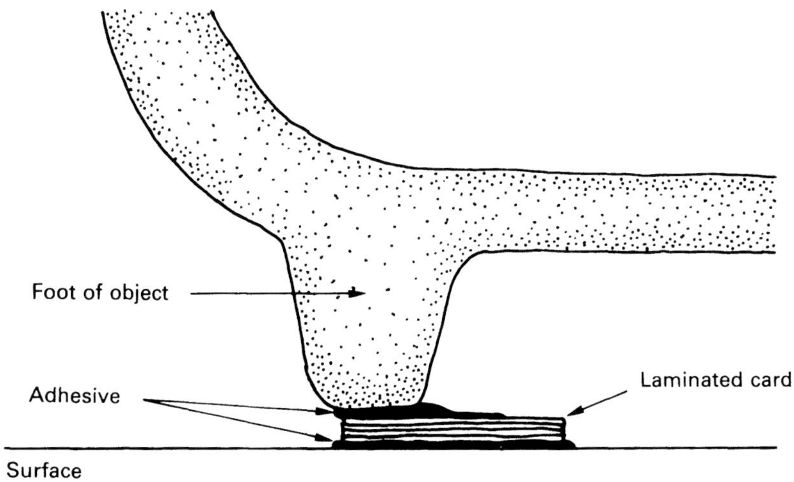

Figure 15.2 In section: diagram showing the arrangement for adhering a foot indirectly to a display surface using a separating ring of laminated card.

adhered to a disc of laminated card under the base of the pot, concealed by the foot rim, then attach a metal strap to the wood with short screws. The other end of the strap can be attached to the wall, or a board secured behind the piece of furniture.

Flat forms

Flat forms such as dishes and individual tiles with decorated horizontal surfaces are easier to view in a near vertical position so that their decorated surface is clearly displayed. Since this is not usually the position in which the maker intended the object to be seen, it will be necessary to prop it up. The main consideration when displaying an object in this way is avoidance of the potential stresses between the object and the support or prop. Direct contact between the ceramic and harder materials should be avoided by padding with softer insulating material, and ensuring that the support does not grip the object too tightly or scratch it.

There are many hangers available commercially that can be used to display small dishes safely on walls. They should be of the correct size to hold the plate firmly with no risk of stress or strain. The type which are made of Perspex (ICI) (poly(methyl methacrylate), also known as Oroglas (Rohm and Hass), and Plexiglas (Rohm GmbH) or metal with a plastic coating are preferable. However, all-metal hangers can be adapted and made safe by isolating the metal from the ceramic at points of contact with soft padding such as polyethylene foam, felt, chamois, leather or card. Damaged or previously restored objects should not be displayed on hangers, owing to the risk of stressing areas of weakness. Hangers that incorporate a spring mechanism are not recommended; they tend to grip the object too tightly and are also difficult to put on, or remove safely.

Small stands available at specialist suppliers will allow tiles and dishes to be propped almost vertically on horizontal surfaces (Figure 15.3). Again these should be made of plastic or wood, to prevent damage to the glaze at points of contact. They should also be the correct size, to avoid an oversized plate becoming unbalanced and toppling over, or a small plate from looking disproportionate and slipping out.

Small tiles may be displayed against a vertical backing board using specially made plastic clips or strong pins. The pins may be bent into an L shape, and inserted into a sleeve of polyethylene tubing to protect the tile edge from the metal (Figure 15.4). It is important to use pins which are of an appropriate diameter and length and which will not corrode, and to select tubing of the correct bore size. It may be preferable to nip off the pin heads to obtain the exact length required. The backing board should be soft enough to allow easy insertion of the pins. By carefully offering the tile up to the backing board and marking the proposed position, the best points for insertion of the pins can be judged. The holes should be made with the tile safely out of the way, so that the pins can be pressed firmly in place by hand. The bent ends of the pins can then be twisted outward while the tile is gently inserted into position, avoiding the risk of scratching their edge. Once in position, the ends are twisted back round in front of the tile to hold it and restrain it securely. Larger heavier tiles will demand a stronger support such as an L-shaped length of stainless steel rod, pressed into a drilled hole; the exposed shaft can again be sleeved with tubing. For large groups of tiles it may be more desirable to mount them up as a single panel.

Very large dishes may demand specially made support stands which need not be unduly complex.

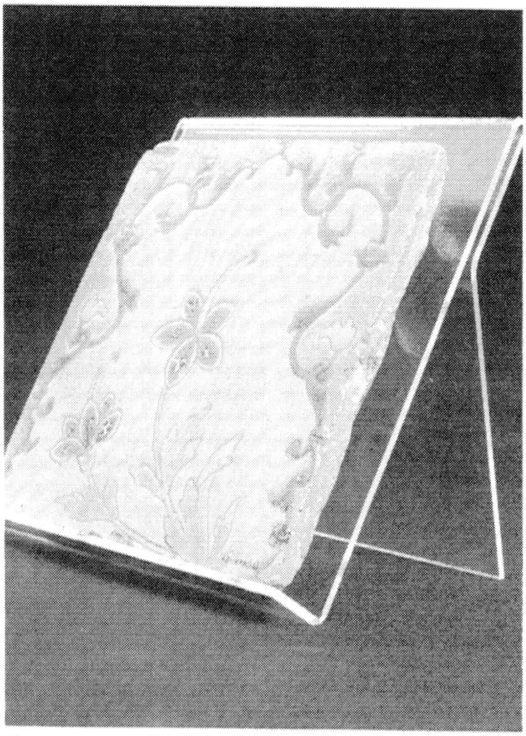

Figure 15.3 Small stand in use propping a tile into an almost vertical position so that it may be easily viewed.

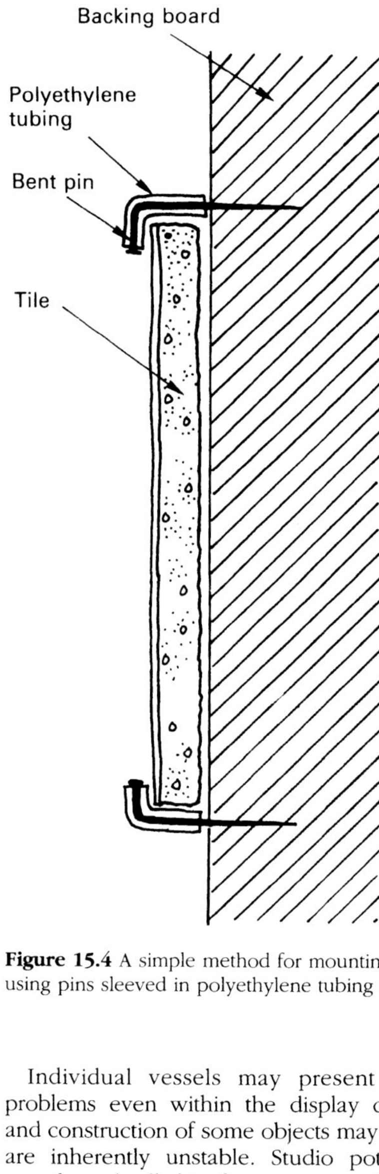

Figure 15.4 A simple method for mounting tiles vertically using pins sleeved in polyethylene tubing (in section).

Objects to be displayed on walls can be supported by three Perspex brackets shaped J in profile (Figure 15.5). The thickness and width of the brackets will depend on the size and weight of the dish, and their positioning will also have to be carefully planned using a paper template as a guide. For large dishes that are to be displayed vertically on a horizontal surface, it may be necessary to have a stand specially made which will provide the essential support to keep the object firmly held in position without risk of slipping, sliding, or overbalancing.

Vessel forms

It is probably fair to assume that the majority of ceramics will fall into the category of vessel forms that were designed as functional objects combining aesthetic considerations with practical requirements. Consequently many ceramics can be placed directly into an exhibition display without any need for special mounting aids. Ideally, they will be displayed in glass fronted cases, allowing the object to be viewed from all sides, including the base, so that manufacturers' marks are clearly visible.

Individual vessels may present very specific problems even within the display case. The form and construction of some objects may mean that they are inherently unstable. Studio pottery, damaged vessels and tall thin forms cannot always be relied upon to sit squarely on a flat surface, and may have a tendency to rock or lean, so that the slightest vibration might disturb their centre of gravity and cause them to fall over. It may be possible to stabilize the base of the vessel by adding small wedges or props. In the case of a temporary exhibition the problem might be simply resolved by using small pieces of laminated card cut to the appropriate size, and adjusted for depth either by shaving away unwanted lamination or by building up further layers using double-sided adhesive tape to stick the extra layers of card. The wedges can be temporarily attached to the base with an easily reversible adhesive which is compatible with the

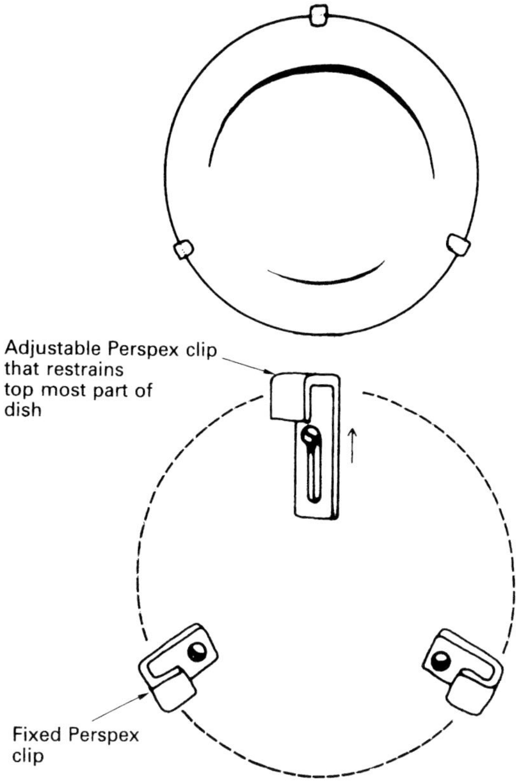

Figure 15.5 Basic arrangement for mounting a dish on a wall. The top clip is adjustable and can be moved upwards to facilitate the removal of the dish.

object. Self-adhesive pads and removable adhesive putty should be avoided since they may stain a porous body owing to their grease content, or pull away unstable glazes and friable surfaces. A more permanent, though still reversible, method is to make small pads of epoxy putty which can be placed as three small balls at strategic points under the object. The pot can be temporarily propped in the ideal position with card wedges while the epoxy cures and adheres to the base. The weight of the object will squeeze the epoxy into a supportive pad of the correct height. Silicon release paper may be used to avoid the pads adhering to the work surface. If necessary, it will be possible to remove the pads later either mechanically, or with epoxy softening solvents.

When fine lightweight vessels, or tall vessels with centres of gravity that endanger the object, are placed on polished surfaces, the risk of vibration from traffic or earth tremors should be considered. Even where display cases are fixed to the floor, prolonged exposure to vibration can cause objects to creep. If there is no restraining lip on the shelf edge the consequences may be disastrous. If the source of vibration cannot be removed, or the cases and shelves cannot be insulated, the object will have to be stabilized in some way (Agbabian *et al.*, 1991). Pliable wax-based compositions, e.g. Tackywax (Bards), have been successfully used in the USA to prevent the movement of ceramics on smooth or polished surfaces. The thermoplastic material can be manipulated with the fingertips and pressed into position on the base of the object. It will not only prevent creep of the objects but will also absorb vibration and shock from earth tremors. The material has been tested for adverse properties such as staining and irreversibility (Shashoua, 1990b). Another solution is to use support stands made from Perspex to suit the specific requirements of each object; the stands can also be adhered to the shelf (Figure 15.6). Other methods of attaching objects to the shelf will vary depending upon the nature of the surface as well as the object itself. In certain situations there may be no alternative except to bond the object directly to a glass surface using an easily reversible adhesive. The method has obvious disadvantages and dangers in terms of removal at a later date. A separating layer of laminated card, as discussed earlier, may offer a preferable solution, and should

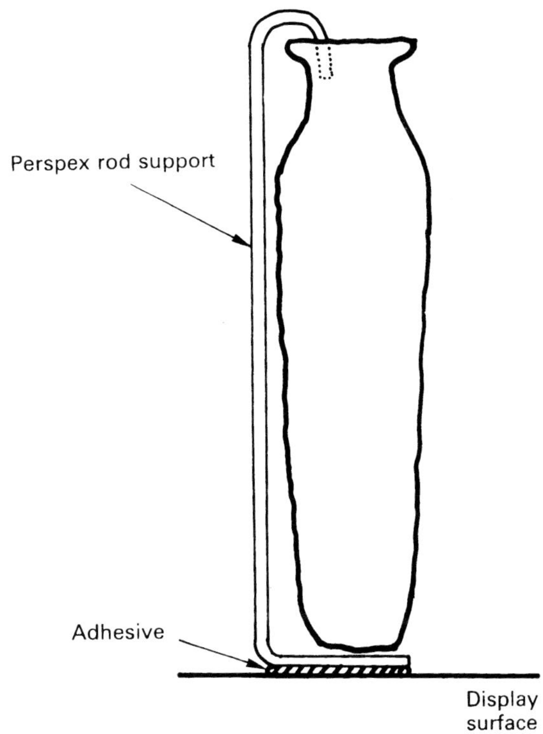

Figure 15.6 Side view of a method for supporting a precarious flask.

make removal easier. The method can be more or less invisible; consequently it is important that some record be made by noting the method of attachment and adhesives used. The information should be filed in the institution's location index, or with any other documentation relating to the object, in order to avoid confusion and any risk of the object being mishandled during attempts by uninformed individuals to remove it.

Composite objects

More unusual ceramics that are composed of several parts may sometimes be precarious and unstable. These include objects such as tulip vases, pagodas, candelabra, and comports (Figure 15.7). Unless they have been very skilfully made, so that each section fits precisely into another, they can present problems in

Figure 15.7 Composite objects, such as this Minton fountain, may demand special considerations when it comes to mounting them for display (Victoria and Albert Museum, London).

their care and display. Such assemblages may involve other types of materials as supports, such as wooden dowels, metal collars, rods, nuts and bolts. The more complex the object, the more precarious it may be, particularly as the various parts are unlikely to be in their original juxtaposition, because the object will probably have undergone previous undocumented disassembly and reassembly. Before such objects are put on display, they should be laid out in their dismantled state and their condition checked for stability and old restorations. Registration of all the various parts should be carefully assessed and any deteriorated padding material should be removed and replaced. Polyethylene foam, available in various grades, thicknesses and colours, can be useful to cushion vulnerable sections; small strips cut to the required shape and size can be stuck in position with PVA (poly(vinyl acetate) emulsion) or Paraloid (Acryloid) B-72, giving better location and avoiding the possibility of ceramic rocking against ceramic, resulting in cracking or chipping.

Composite objects should be dismantled prior to transportation over long distances (for example in the case of a loan to another establishment), in order to avoid damage by handling and vibration. In some cases, however, this may not be possible; a metal mount may be so securely attached using adhesives, fillers, nuts and bolts that the risks and time involved in taking the object apart may be too great. In such situations there may be no benefit in dismantling the object. Rusty nuts and bolts on objects should be loosened where necessary with an appropriate lubricant, taking care to avoid the risks of staining. Unless original, deteriorated washers should be replaced with new ones using a suitable inert material such as acid-free laminated card, Teflon, silicone rubber or chamois. Original washers, if degraded, either may be removed and stored for reference, or may be retained (after conservation by a specialist conservator) and reused with additional new washers as necessary.

It is even more important with composite objects to make certain that the display case is stable and not liable to any vibration.

Drawers and trays of small or fragmentary objects

Some collections may include considerable quantities of ceramics in an incomplete and fragmentary form. Often such material is considered to be of sufficient importance to be displayed in a manner which can be accessible to scholars and interested individuals. Although large chests, with shallow glass topped drawers, provide a means of storage and display that is more compact than display cases, they are not ideal. The motion and vibration caused by opening the drawers leads to movement of individual pieces and consequent impact damage. Efforts to avoid such damage using cotton wool or crumpled tissue paper can lead to further damage by pulling off loose fragments and flakes, or by obscuring some pieces from view. A more satisfactory though less flexible solution is to line the bottom of the drawers with a material such as polyethylene foam (Plastazote, (BXL)) that has *nests* specially cut out in the shape of each object. An intact sheet of the foam, placed beneath the objects, will give adequate padding between the lower surface of the object and the base of the drawer. Different densities, thicknesses and colours of foam are available, and the foam can be cut easily and precisely using a template of the object's profile. Obviously some fragments may be different thicknesses than others, in which case inserts of foam can be made in the nest to bring the object up to the desired height.

The main disadvantage of this method is that the display cannot be rearranged as and when new fragments are acquired or moved. An alternative system is to use pins to secure and restrain the individual fragments. This is best achieved using an inert backing material to line the drawer which will not warp or distort, and which is soft enough for insertion of pins. The board is then covered with fabric, or a thin sheet of polyethylene foam. The pins should be in different lengths and thicknesses depending on the object. They should be non-corrosive and their shafts should be sleeved in polyethylene tubing to protect the objects from abrasion. Four pins should generally be adequate to secure each fragment and avoid movement when the drawer is opened and closed. The shiny heads of the pins can be painted grey with acrylic paint to make them less obtrusive. Fragments may be similarly mounted up using bent pins in a vertical display if necessary (Figures 15.8, 15.9).

Figure 15.8 Tiles of different sizes displayed in a drawer (with its protective glass top removed). The tiles are not anchored and are free to move around with the motion of the drawer causing damage (note small chips on backing material) (Victoria and Albert Museum, London).

Figure 15.9 Tiles secured by restraining them with pins sleeved in polyethylene tubing. The pins are securely held, by insertion into a backing of rigid corrugated plastic, concealed by a thin layer of polyethylene foam. One tile has been removed to make room for a label (Victoria and Albert Museum, London).

Backing and mounting tiles

It may be desirable to mount tiles that were originally intended to be seen as a group, decorating a wall or floor, in one portable panel (Sturge, 1988; Cooper, 1992). Former methods of backing tiles have included the following:

1. Each tile had three or four loops of wire set in holes which had been drilled into the unglazed side and secured with plaster, resin or lead. Lengths of wire were then threaded through each loop and passed through two holes in a large wooden backing panel. The wires were then secured by twisting and bending the ends flat, then protecting the exposed fastening with gummed tape. Vulnerable tile edges were sometimes protected from rubbing against each other by taping round the edges with gummed tape, or by inserting card pads at the corners of the tiles.
2. Tiles were sometimes stuck with size or animal glue to a hessian covered backing board. Strips of card were used to lift up individual tiles to a common level where necessary.
3. Cardboard adhered to a wooden backing was also sometimes used; the tiles would be stuck directly onto the card.
4. Occasionally the reverse side of the tiles would be coated with plaster, which was then attached to wood or slate.

5 Often plaster alone was used as a backing material, making a very rigid support which was heavy and awkward to handle, difficult to reverse and potentially risky for the tiles owing to the possibility of salt migration from damp plaster.
6 Bolts were sometimes attached to the back of the tile with fibre glass tape strips saturated in epoxy. The tiles were then placed on a pierced backing board and secured in place with nuts.
7 Similarly, bolts were sometimes secured in holes drilled into the back of the tiles packed with plaster, resins or lead.
8 Polyurethane resin foaming systems, reinforced with aluminium mesh (Larney, 1971; Johnson and Bearpark, 1982), gave a rigid lightweight backing, but with poor ageing properties. The use of polyurethane resins is potentially hazardous to health unless all necessary precautions are closely observed.
9 Self-adhesive hangers, which stick to the back of the tile, have been used. However, the adhesive breaks down with age, causing tiles to become insecure and eventually drop off (Halahan and Plowden, 1987).

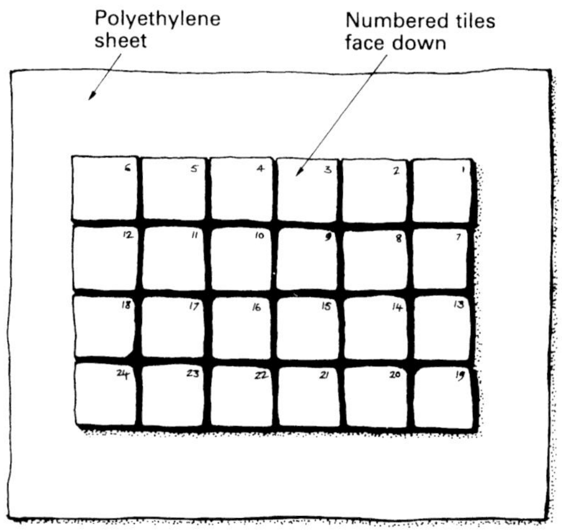

Figure 15.10 The tiles are laid out decorated side downwards, on a sheet of polyethylene.

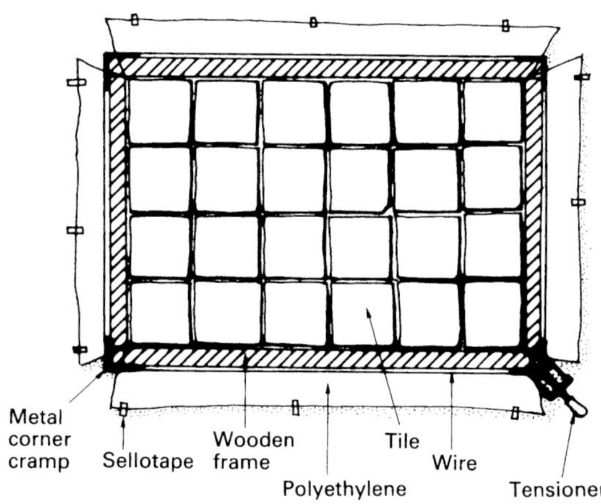

Figure 15.11 A wooden frame is clamped into position around the tiles, beneath the polyethylene.

Methods for supporting large mosaic panels have employed composite backing materials involving epoxy or polyester resins mixed with vermiculite, an expanded mica mineral, additionally reinforced with a steel weld mesh (Bradley, *et al.*, 1983).

In order for a tile backing system to be successful it must meet a number of desirable criteria: the system should be unobtrusive, strong and rigid, though light and easy to handle. In addition the individual tiles should not be put at any risk of damage. The method should be easy to apply, and reverse if necessary, without causing harm to the conservator. Finally, the materials used should have good ageing properties.

A method that has been successfully used at the Victoria and Albert Museum for backing tile panels which meets these criteria employs an epoxy foam resin system which provides a good means of support. The individual tiles are cleaned beforehand, all traces of any old backing or grouting are removed, and damaged tiles are bonded or consolidated where necessary. The reverse sides are clearly numbered with a chinagraph pencil to ensure the tiles are laid out in the correct sequence. Large panels are divided into smaller units, of around 120 × 120 cm, for greater ease of handling, and then placed face downward, evenly spaced, on a sheet of polyethylene that has been laid over a flat level surface. The polyethylene extends about 15 cm beyond the edge of the tiles, and acts as a separating sheet (Figure 15.10). A wooden frame, cut to size, is then clamped around the tiles under the polyethylene to act as a wall which will contain the foam (Figure 15.11). The wood should be 2 cm deeper than the tiles to allow sufficient depth for the foam. The joints between the tiles and also between the frame are then filled with Polyfilla, to prevent the foam seeping through to the front of the tiles. Leaving only the corners exposed, for contact with the foam, the backs of the tiles are protected with masking tape, which will act as an isolating barrier should reversal prove necessary at a later stage (Figure 15.12). Wooden blocks are placed at each corner of the panel, and along the sides at various points, to provide a means of attachment for fixings when the panel is eventually displayed. These mounting blocks should be of a depth which allows them to lie flush with the top of the frame. The foam is

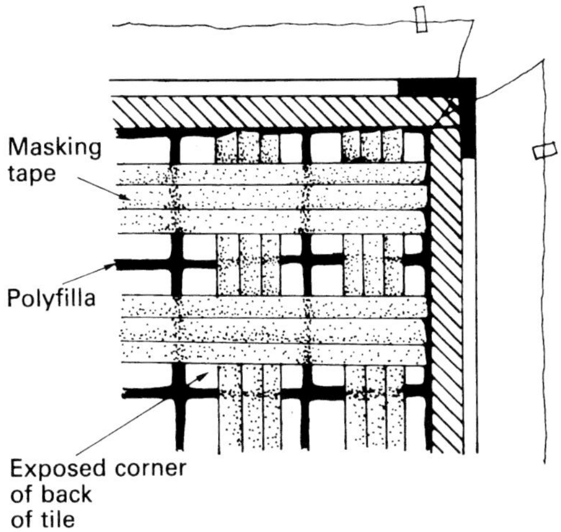

Figure 15.12 Detail showing separating layer of masking tape covering the tile backs, leaving the corners exposed. The tiles have been grouted with Polyfilla.

then mixed according to the manufacturers' instructions, taking care to ensure that the correct quantity to fill the required volume has been calculated. A small dab of the mixture is then put under each mounting block, to attach them securely to the panel, then the rest of the resin is carefully poured evenly over the back. A sheet of plate glass covered with polyethylene is then placed over the panel, resting on the frame, and weighed down in position. A small air space at one edge of the panel will allow air and excess foam to escape (Figures 15.13, 15.14, 15.15). Once cured, the frame is dismantled, and sharp edges and irregularities in the foam are removed with a hacksaw or file. The panel is then turned face up, and excess Polyfilla and grouting are removed with a riffler or a scalpel to a level slightly below that of the tiles. Any irregularities in the grouting are then filled with Polyfilla. The grouting may then be smoothed and levelled using scalpels and fine grade silicon carbide paper, and retouched as necessary. The completed panel is then attached to the wall with mirror plates.

Barov (1986) describes a variation on the above technique that also involves the use of an epoxy foam. An initial separating layer (5 mm) of an easily reversible acrylic paste is applied to the backs of the tiles. A stainless steel frame is then positioned on top followed by a final backing layer of foamed epoxy resin mixed with glass microballoons.

Another approach for mounting a group of medieval tiles is described by Cooper (1992), employing an undulating bed of polyester resin as a support for the irregular sized tiles. He describes how the tiles are arranged face down on a level surface in order to maintain the decorated surfaces in the same plane. Separating layers of rubber latex followed by clingfilm are applied before the final backing of polyester resin with glass fibre matting. Once cured, the polyester bed is removed and attached to an additional support of medium density fibreboard. The individual tiles are then adhered to the polyester using a silicone sealant.

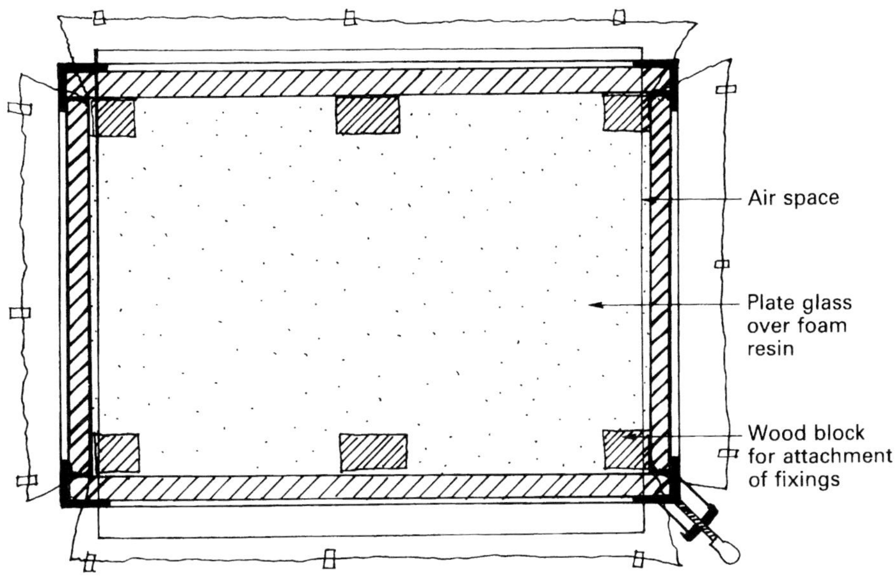

Figure 15.13 Foamed resin is poured onto the prepared tiles. A sheet of polyethylene covered plate glass is placed on top of the uncured foam, with an air space along two edges.

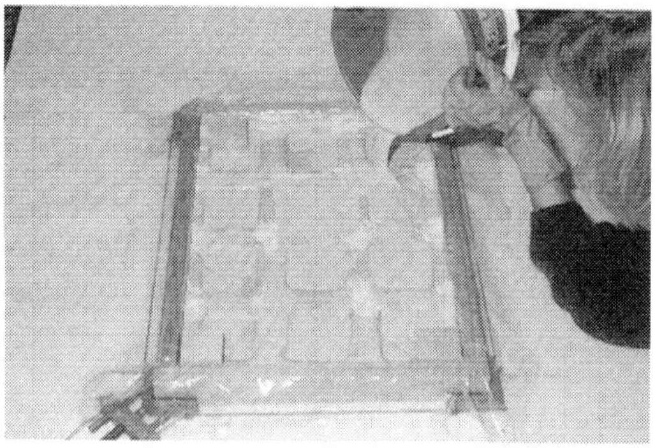

Figure 15.14 Foamed resin being poured onto the tile backs (Victoria and Albert Museum, London).

Figure 15.15 The foaming reaction continues, filling the space beneath the polyethylene covered glass (Victoria and Albert Museum, London).

Other methods of mounting tile panels involve the use of proprietary tile adhesives to secure groups of tiles to a backboard. A non-warping blockboard or medium density fibreboard should be used. Large architectural panels may require fixing directly and permanently to the wall using flexible adhesives with additional steel supporting brackets and restraints. Special lightweight fillings, of plaster-based compositions mixed with polystyrene granules and poly(vinyl acetate) emulsion, have been used to provide a strong matrix between the wall and object in such circumstances.

16

Emergency procedures

Individuals involved in managing the conservation or care of ceramics as a profession must be responsible for the well-being of both the objects and the people within the work space. Chapter 13 emphasized the importance of being vigilant concerning aspects of health and safety, and guarding against the possibility of accident or disaster when planning a conservation studio. The risk of accidents involving people or objects can only be minimized by taking steps to ensure that those areas devoted to the conservation, display, or storage of ceramics are well planned, and that colleagues are thoroughly versed in all aspects of safety and security. However, no matter how careful we are, unpredicted incidents can occur, often with devastating effects, and it is important to prepare ourselves for such eventualities.

This section will discuss how to plan for disasters or emergency situations by considering possible scenarios, and making preparations to enable an organized response to them. Both large and small institutions should formulate procedures for various types of emergency. Private restorers and collectors, in their own businesses, galleries or homes, should also take time to review their situation periodically.

All unforeseen events which result in damage to an object will be regarded as a disaster in this context. This includes the smallest one-off incidents, as well as major national disasters. The former are more common and usually consist of a single incident, caused by direct or indirect human involvement, resulting in damage to an object or small group of objects. Such incidents might include knocking a vase off a surface by catching it inadvertently with the cuff of a sleeve, or closing a cupboard door on a carelessly positioned object. On the other hand, major disasters are those emergency situations of a much larger scale, caused by external agents that are beyond our control. These include fire, explosions, natural disasters (e.g. wind, flood, earthquake and subsidence), civil unrest (e.g. riots, bombs and war), and vandalism. Such events will have the effect of overwhelming the day-to-day running of an institution.

General risk precautions

There are various inexpensive precautions that can be taken, not only to minimize the aftermath of such events, but also to give peace of mind before their occurrence. This initially includes assessing the risks by identifying the events that could cause a disaster, determining what sort of losses might occur and then formulating ways to reduce them.

It may be possible to *eliminate* the risk. For example, if some of the chemicals used in the studio are potential fire hazards, they could be substituted with something safer; or, if an entrance poses a particular security threat, then steps could be taken to install better doors, locks and alarms. In certain situations it may be worth letting someone else take the responsibility for the potential problem. In a large institution this might involve the work being carried out elsewhere, while for the private restorer risks could be avoided by simply saying 'no' to certain projects that might be a security risk.

The risk can also be *transferred* to an insurer. This involves having adequate insurance cover of building and contents, as well as cover for workers, so that the expenses which may be incurred can be claimed. The insurance policy should be as comprehensive as possible, based on up-to-date valuations. It should cover the full amount of potential damage, such as replacing the building, furnishings, equipment, objects, documentation, temporary storage for objects, relocation of premises and compensation for injured workers. The possibility of initial first-aid treatment of the objects immediately after the disaster, as well as their conservation later, should be allowed for in the policy, even if estimates for the work might exceed the value of similar historic objects or replicas of them. Professional advice should always be sought on such matters.

Procedural measures such as making contingency plans for disasters, combined with basic good housekeeping, can prevent or reduce the potential loss that might be caused by a disaster. Training and briefing personnel and making provision for all the essential emergency resources to be constantly available on standby should form a part of this. Documentation and records of objects should be kept complete and up to date with as much detail as possible. Each object can be marked or labelled with an inventory or accession number and the location recorded in a register. This might take the form of a simple tagging system and log book for the private conservator. Any claims for loss and damage will only be successful if the object has been thoroughly recorded. In larger institutions the curatorial department should hold the necessary registers which provide information on acquisition, provenance, current value, detailed descriptions, measurements, photographs and condition reports of the object. For a unique collection, such documentation should be duplicated and kept up to date, ideally with the copy being held elsewhere.

Finally, *physical* means of avoiding certain types of disaster should be reviewed often; for example, fire-fighting equipment and security systems should be installed and maintained regularly. Frequent training and refresher courses in the operation and use of fire-fighting equipment should also take place (Martin, 1977).

Minor accidents

The materials and techniques involved in the manufacture of individual ceramic objects will greatly influence their durability and susceptibility to different types of deterioration (see Chapter 2), but all ceramics share a common vulnerability to accidents involving impact, causing chips, cracks or breaks. The cause can often be attributed to a moment of human carelessness – loss of concentration and neglect of the rules of handling ceramics (see Chapter 3). In any accident or emergency situation, the first and foremost aim should be to prevent any further damage occurring to the broken object.

The freshly damaged object should be made safe. In a public area, such as a museum's gallery, a dealer's shop, or a busy studio, the immediate and surrounding vicinity of the damaged object should be isolated. When an object is dropped and shattered, small fragments have a tendency to travel far, especially on hard polished floors. Stray pieces can accidentally be stepped on and crushed irretrievably, or they may be accidentally kicked even further away. Before gathering up the pieces, it may be worth photographing the scene, particularly if the object is of value or if the circumstances of the accident may raise some query over insurance cover.

A safe place nearby should be selected before attempting to move the object. All the fragments should then be carefully collected and counted before placing them in a padded basket or tray. The broken edges should not be touched, as they may have a tendency to crumble and can be easily marked and stained by the transfer of grease and dirt from skin contact. Any small pieces should be placed in a small beaker or box to avoid loss. A really thorough search of the surrounding area should be made for small fragments that might have scattered under furniture or into dark corners. The temptation to check that all the pieces have been recovered by trying to piece the object back together should be resisted by anyone other a than trained conservator, as more damage can be caused by clumsily grinding friable edges together. Marking pieces by the attaching of sticky labels is not advisable as this can cause staining of unglazed surfaces, and removal may result in damage of insecure glaze or exposed body particles.

Following the incident, a debriefing session should help to determine the circumstances of the accident and to prevent such occurrences in future.

Major disasters

The idea of setting aside time to formulate a contingency plan for coping with a major disaster may not seem like a high priority, particularly when such a threat can seem remote during the day-to-day activities of the small studio or ceramics collection. However, like an insurance policy, such plans offer the long-term peace of mind that comes with the knowledge that should the unthinkable happen, the necessary preparation has been made to respond accordingly and cope with the situation.

Depending on the location, either in a geographical or in a local context, some of the different categories of disaster may be of a more obvious threat than others. If, for example, the crime rate in the neighbourhood is high, risks from vandalism and burglary should be considered, and in cities in countries undergoing political unrest, whether Belfast, Baghdad or Beirut, the risks of damage occurring as a consequence of bomb, bullet or brick will be a serious consideration. Collections in geographically vulnerable zones where risks from earthquake (Agbabian *et al.*, 1991), landslip, volcano, or flood are higher than normal should prepare for such eventualities.

Planning will involve considering the consequences of possible incidents and the most appropriate response to take in each case. It should be organized to include:

1 preparation ahead of the disaster
2 response during the disaster
3 actions to be taken after the disaster.

Preparing for disaster

The preparations which can be made before an emergency apply as much to a large organization as to a smaller establishment. Many of the steps which can be taken may appear very obvious, but can, in the event of a crisis, save valuable time and confusion. In a studio where there are a number of conservators working together, one person should be given the responsibility of informing and training others and of preparing and co-ordinating any recovery. The main types of details he/she will be concerned with are outlined below, though these will obviously vary to suit individual requirements.

Appointment of a disaster team

A group of responsible individuals should be elected, who will be involved with planning, training, co-ordinating and decision-making. Their roles should be clearly defined to avoid confusion and duplication in what might be a tense situation. It may be worth involving other professional colleagues or friends if extra help is likely to be needed. Each member of the disaster team should know their way around the building and be familiar with its layout and the location of objects. Training should involve rehearsing strategies for response in different situations including fire, flood or storm, bearing in mind that the disaster could strike during hours of darkness. Individuals should know which objects to move first, how to move them and where to move them to. Consideration should also be given to: how to respond if time is limited, how to organize and involve volunteer helpers, how to direct and instruct the fire brigade if access to the objects is limited only to them.

Emergency contacts

There should be a file listing the telephone numbers and addresses of useful people to contact and inform. These will include the private homes of colleagues, employees, and other professionals who can be relied upon to be on hand to help and advise. Listings might take the form of a *tree*, with the leader being responsible for contacting two people who then immediately contact two others and so on. Contact numbers for the local emergency services should also be in the file, including fire, police, ambulance, as well as gas technicians, security specialists, electricians, plumbers, and suppliers of essential specialist materials and equipment. Also, an up-to-date list of other institutions and clients will be of use. The file, whether on a simple card index system or a computer database, should be available to all senior staff, and all members of the disaster team. Senior staff should also keep a copy of the most important contact numbers at their homes.

Contact should be established with the local fire officer and fire station to discuss fire prevention as well as fire-fighting and salvage. The layout of the building and the vulnerable and valuable nature of the contents should also be discussed in some detail. It may also be worth involving the fire brigade in a rehearsal. Similarly the local crime prevention officer should be invited to advise on physical and electronic security against intruders. The possibility of additional police surveillance of the premises and rescued objects following the disaster should also be discussed.

Emergency equipment

A cupboard should be set aside to store a range of tools, materials and equipment to be used in emergencies. This should avoid wasting time attempting to gather the necessary items from everyday stocks after the disaster has struck. The store should be checked regularly by an appointed person, perishable items replaced and tools and equipment maintained in good working order.

Priorities for removal

Priorities should be agreed for saving items, so that objects of major value and importance may be removed before those of minor significance. Where applicable a list should be made, detailing the relevant location. In general, the objects should be given a high priority, followed by the relevant documentation. Last of all should be consumable supplies, which are of low value and easily replaced.

Identification of service points

A marked floor plan showing the location of main taps and switches for controlling the supply of the general services such as gas, electricity, oil and mains water should be held by members of the disaster team. They should use the plan to familiarize themselves with how to operate and shut down the supplies if necessary. Regular checks of stopcocks, gas mains, electricity mains, telephone lines and fuel tanks should take place to ensure that such services are secure from vandals but accessible to firemen in an emergency.

Temporary accommodation and transport to it

If the gallery, store or studio has been rendered unsafe and insecure by the disaster, it may be necessary to completely evacuate all objects, fixtures and fittings to a temporary site until all essential repair works are completed. If this is some distance away in another building, everything will have to be packed and transported. Contingency plans should be made for this eventuality.

Coping with a disaster

The precaution of planning for the disaster will be tested when what has so far been considered a hypothetical situation becomes a reality. Even with the most ingenious and imaginative foresight, the sequence of events which will occur cannot be predicted. The safety of individuals should always be paramount and even the most precious object should be abandoned if the price of its recovery may be in human suffering, or loss of life.

The emergency services will respond to the disaster with the professional efficiency that they are trained to exercise in all crisis situations. They cannot be expected to share with conservators the same level of respect and concern for the objects: their main objectives during the initial stages will be to locate and halt the cause of the destruction, and to prevent any further repercussions by making the area safe. It is probably unlikely that conservators will be able to do anything until the immediate crisis has halted, since the risks involved may be too great, and the unexpected nature of the situation, which is the essence of disasters, may enforce a delay on any recovery attempts.

First-aid treatment of objects may have to be carried out immediately on site by individuals under the supervision of trained conservators. As soon as conditions allow, each object should be quickly but carefully examined, so that a clear idea of priorities can be decided early on. Any information on the location that may be helpful later should be recorded at this stage using photographs, sketches and notes where appropriate.

The main categories of damage which are likely to have occurred to ceramics will be due to the following in various combinations:

1 mechanical damage due to impact
2 interaction with other materials
3 thermal damage due to the effects of rapid changes in temperature.

Mechanical damage due to impact

The damage which can arise from impact has already been considered above.

Interaction with other materials

When ceramics are unexpectedly brought into contact with alien substances, the consequences can range from insignificant to disastrous, this being determined by the precise nature of both the ceramic and the substance. Such substances may be either dry or liquid. Dry materials may be in the form of airborne particles such as smoke, or dust from structural disturbances within the building, or dry powders released from certain fire extinguishers to control electrical fires or burning solvents. Liquid materials include clean water from floods caused by leaking service pipes; or contaminated water from natural floods, loaded with dirt and mixed with other unwanted materials; or else other liquid chemicals including oil.

Dry contaminants

Those materials deposited *dry* upon the surface of a pot sometimes offer little threat to the object and may be removed initially by simple treatments such as brushing with a hog's hair brush, or using a vacuum cleaner with an appropriate attachment, or blowing it with a compressed air supply. This may be followed by washing, depending on the nature of the body. In the case of fire damage, the black carbon deposit on the surface may be difficult to remove and may penetrate deeper than just the surface, in which case treatment to obtain the original body colour may be complex, and may even involve refiring the object (Davison and Harrison, 1987; Bogle, in press). Those objects which are likely to demand a more intensive treatment, but whose condition is stable, should be put aside for inclusion in the programme of conservation which will begin in the months following the immediate crisis. Under no circumstances should any conservation be attempted during the immediate aftermath of a disaster in inadequately equipped surroundings where individuals are working under stress.

Wet contamination

Contact with liquids can have disastrous consequences for the object unless individuals are aware of the risks, and the action to take. Even water in its purest form can cause serious damage.

The range of problems which might be associated with the effects of the rising and receding waters of a flood illustrates the potential havoc that water can cause (Service, 1986). It is important to understand the ways in which water can affect not only the ceramic material, but also any other materials in close association, such as mounts, supports and restoration materials. While the majority of the damage that occurs in a flood will happen during or immediately after the disaster, certain types of deterioration, by their nature, will be delayed and not become apparent until later.

Immediate effects on ceramic materials

Vessel forms which have remained upright, or even on their sides, will probably retain amounts of water after the flood has drained away. This should be carefully emptied out, or siphoned off where the object is too large to safely lift, and any remaining sediment removed.

High-fired ceramics will only absorb very small amounts of water and, provided the surface is stable, they can be dried using paper towels. The surface of undamaged low-fired ceramics can be blotted dry with paper towels, but may take several days or weeks to dry completely. Some low-fired bodies will weaken when saturated with water, while unfired bodies will become hydrated and may soften and crack. Unfired decoration, such as earth pigments, unfired gold leaf, or lacquer, may detach from the surface as the binding media dissolve. Superficial material of ethnographic importance, such as burial earth or food residues, may also be dissolved by flood waters. Such objects should be allowed to dry in a well ventilated situation and any active deterioration stabilized by appropriate consolidation methods.

Porous bodies will become stained by contact with contaminated flood water. In the case of porcelain and stonewares, particles of dirt may settle on the surface or become trapped in flaws. Loose dirt and thick mud will become increasingly difficult to remove from textured or unglazed surfaces as it dries and hardens; it may be preferable to rinse it off with a hose or house plant sprayer while still damp, rather than risk staining and damage to the surface later.

Physical movement of the objects floating or submerged in moving waters may result in damage by impact as they knock against each other and against fixed fittings (Figure 16.1). This will result in chipping, cracking, breakage and loss. Any broken pieces should be recovered as far as possible, placed in labelled bags and kept safe with the object.

Salts present in some porous bodies will become mobile as the humidity within the ceramic pores increases, sometimes efflorescing on or near the surface, initiating the disruption of the surface and any decoration. Such objects should be kept damp until they can be desalinated.

Immediate effects on subsidiary materials

Old restorations may soften and dissolve in water if they are made from animal glue, causing bonds to weaken and fall apart (Figures 16.2, 16.3). Individual objects should be examined carefully before moving, then given maximum support during handling and placed carefully in padded containers together with any detached parts. The distance over which they are lifted should be minimal; the basket or box should be placed immediately beside the object. In certain situations it may be more appropriate to slide a piece of card or board underneath the object.

Plaster fillings or backings will rapidly absorb moisture, causing them to soften and swell, weakening the structures they were intended to support. Care should be taken when moving such objects that are partly supported by wet plaster fillings or backings. Plaster can also introduce soluble salts into the porous bodies and should be removed immediately where possible.

Metal mounts, rivets, dowels and fixings will corrode on contact with high humidity or water, causing staining. If mounts and fittings can be easily removed this should be done as soon as possible, so that the metal can be dried, and any corrosion treated by a metals conservator. However, the removal of dowels and rivets should not be attempted until circumstances allow. In the meantime the object

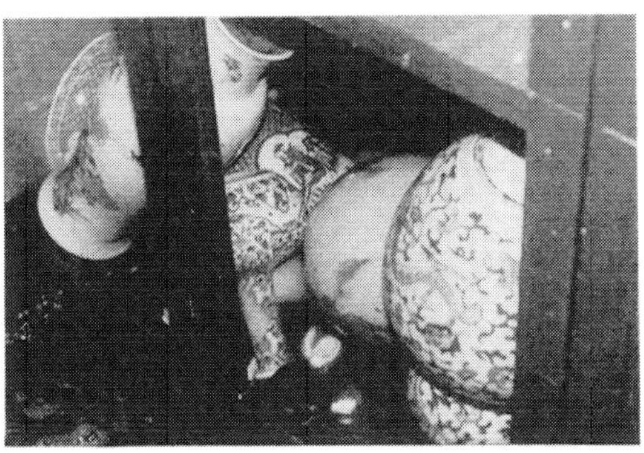

Figure 16.1 Objects in cases in a flooded store. The unsecured shelves of the cases were made of wood and floated with the rising flood waters, contributing to the damage (Victoria and Albert Museum, London).

Figure 16.2 Group of flood damaged Islamic ceramics that had been previously restored with water soluble adhesives (Victoria and Albert Museum, London).

Figure 16.3 Groups of shards, resulting from the disintegration of old restorations on repaired ceramics after contact with flood water (Victoria and Albert Museum, London).

should be dried as far as possible and set aside for immediate examination and possible treatment in the studio later (Thompson, 1984).

Warping or distortion of wet wooden supports, frames or backings will introduce stresses into the object which they hold and should be removed as early as possible.

Delayed effects

Some types of damage may not become apparent until later on; in some cases it may even be several weeks after the flood. Porous bodies contaminated by salts may not appear to be at risk until later when they gradually dry and the salts migrate towards the surface. Any metal components such as dowels or rivets may be concealed until evidence of metal corrosion manifests itself at the surface. Furthermore old restorations, which at the time of the rescue seemed sound, may weaken as the moisture content evaporates, with potential risk of accidents and further damage. The growth of mould may occur, nourished by organic dirt trapped in the pores of the body and on the exposed unglazed surfaces of earthenwares. It can also occur on unfired decoration of certain stonewares and porcelains; some oriental ceramics with lacquered surfaces may also be at risk of this type of biological attack (Figures 16.4, 16.5). Any unstable surface may have to be consolidated prior to removing the mould. Removal should be either by mechanical methods (for unstable and unfired surfaces), or where appropriate by washing. The object should then be allowed to dry thoroughly either in a well ventilated situation or in the warmth of a convection oven.

The only way to guard against such delayed effects is to carry out as thorough an examination as circumstances will permit during the recovery efforts. It is safer to exercise a greater degree of caution than normal if there is any doubt about the stability of a particular object, setting it aside for immediate examination as soon as time will allow.

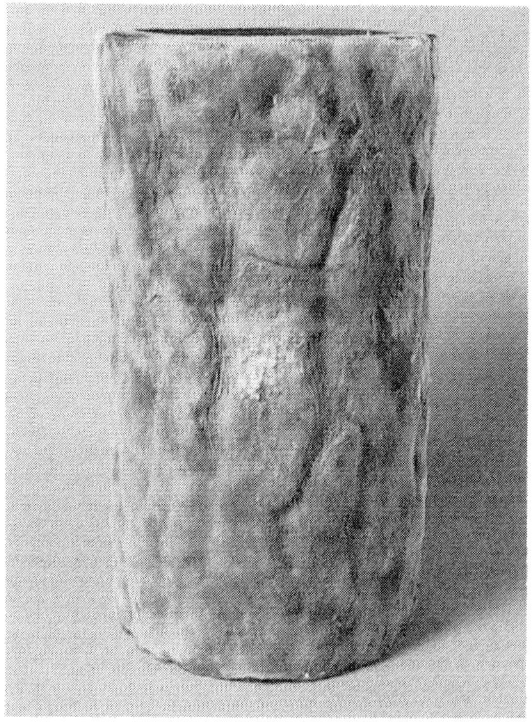

Figure 16.4 Stoneware vessel with a lacquered surface obscured by mould growth caused by a sudden increase in humidity as a result of a flood (Victoria and Albert Museum, London).

Thermal damage

The main type of damage that fire can directly cause to ceramics will be due to the effects of temperature. Other damage related indirectly to the fire will be the result of the atmosphere, such as gases, particulate contaminants and smoke. Mechanical damage may also occur arising from the destruction of other materials in the immediate vicinity.

The severity of the damage caused by the temperature changes will vary, depending on the rate at which the temperature rises, and the maximum temperature attained. Sudden temperature increases and localized fluctuations will cause uneven expansion and contraction of the body, resulting in cracking. If the temperature is particularly high, irreversible changes will occur: earthenwares will be heated beyond their original firing temperature, and will distort and melt; stonewares and porcelains may

Figure 16.5 The stoneware vessel after removal of the mould (Victoria and Albert Museum, London).

also deform; enamels and glazes may become fluid and undergo colour alterations. Such damage may not be repairable, as cracks may have sprung, causing distortions which will be impossible to correct. Any evidence for dating the object by thermoluminescence will be destroyed.

The combustion of a range of typical furnishings and fixtures will generate a thick dirty smoke which will blacken the surface of the object (Figure 16.6). In a reducing atmosphere where the air surrounding the object lacks oxygen, the metal oxides in the ceramic body will be altered as the oxygen is extracted, bringing about a change in colour. Carbon may also penetrate into the body in such conditions, blackening it. Old restoration materials will be altered by heat (Davison and Harrison, 1987), weakening and becoming embrittled and carbonized, making them extremely difficult to remove (Der Sarkissian and Goodberry, 1981).

Additional problems may be caused by the materials used to extinguish the fire. The use of water will exacerbate the damage caused by the fire by inducing the range of effects already described under wet contamination. The dry powders or sand or foam will all produce considerable mess before

Figure 16.6 A private collection of ceramics in the aftermath of a fire (courtesy L. Bogle).

putting out the fire, and their contact with a damaged object will complicate later treatment problems.

The immediate course of action in the aftermath of a fire will be to recover the objects regardless of their condition and remove them in labelled baskets, boxes or trays from the site of the fire. It may be difficult under such circumstances to salvage the fragments of broken objects, as many of the pieces may have been scattered onto surfaces littered with other similarly blackened debris. Decisions can be made later regarding the feasibility of restoration. Objects which appear whole should be handled very carefully as damage may not be obvious; cracks may separate once the object is moved. No immediate attempts should be made to clean blackened surfaces; these should be treated later.

After the disaster

The process of recovering, transferring and protecting the disaster-stricken objects will have helped to give an idea of the full extent of the problem. Provisional listings of the damaged items together with condition assessments should have been drafted out at the time of the recovery, on paper rather than mentally.

Time should be taken at this stage for thorough examination and documentation, both in note form and using photography, of the condition of the object, so that some idea of the scale of the conservation work can be gained for insurance purposes. Assistance may have to be sought from other professional colleagues in evaluating the full extent of the damage. It may also be worth considering the possibility of purchasing replacement objects if the time estimated for conservation is excessive. Where applicable, the owners should be contacted immediately and the situation clarified regarding liability and insurance. Solicitors will help advise on legal aspects should they arise.

Once the urgent administrative matters have been sorted out as far as possible, the priorities for treatment should be established, and any necessary extra help enlisted so that the work programme can begin.

Appendix I

Conservation associations and other bodies

American Institute for Conservation (AIC), 1717 K Street, NW Suite 301, Washington, DC 20008, USA.

Canadian Conservation Institute, 1030 Innes Road, Ottawa, K1A 0M8, Canada

Centre for Occupational Hazards, 5 Beekman Street, New York, NY 10038, USA

The Conservation Unit, Museums and Galleries Commission, 16 Queen Anne's Gate, London SW1H 9AA, UK

The Getty Conservation Institute, 4503 Glencoe Avenue, Marina del Rey, California 90292-6537, USA

Health and Safety Executive, Baynards House, 1 Chepstow Place, London W2, UK

Institute for the Conservation of Cultural Material (ICCM), PO Box 1638, Canberra, ACT, Australia

International Centre for the Study and the Preservation and Restoration of Cultural Material (ICCROM), 13 Via di S. Michele, Rome 1-00153, Italy

International Council of Museums (ICOM), Conservation Committee Working Group on Glass, Ceramics and Related Materials, Maison de l'Unesco, 1 Rue Miollis, F-75732 Paris Cedex 15, France

International Institute for Conservation, 6 Buckingham Street, London WC2N 6BA, UK

International Institute for Conservation – Canadian Group, Box/CP 9195, Ottawa, K1G 3T9, Ontario, Canada

Irish Professional Conservator's and Restorer's Association (IPCRA), Alison Muir (Secretary), c/o Ulster Museum, Botanic Gardens, Belfast BT9 5AB, UK

Scottish Conservation Bureau, Historic Scotland, Longmoor House, Salisbury Place, Edinburgh EH9 1SH, UK

Scottish Society for Conservation and Restoration (SSCR), The Glasite Meeting House, 33 Barony Street, Edinburgh EH3 6NX, UK

United Kingdom Institute for Conservation (UKIC), Ceramics and Glass Conservation Group, 6 Whitehorse Mews, 37–39 Westminster Bridge Road, London SE1 7QD, UK

Appendix II

Manufacturers

Aabbitt Adhesives Inc., 2403 N. Oakley Avenue, Chicago, Illinois 60647, USA

Albright and Wilson Ltd, PO Box 3, 210–222 Hagley Road West, Oldbury, Warley, West Midlands, B68 0NN, UK

Anatomical Plastics, 48 Hutton Close, Crowther Industrial Estate, Washington, Tyne and Wear, NE38 OAH, UK

Associated Dental products, Purton, Swindon, SN5 9HT, UK

BXL Plastics Ltd, ERP Division, 675 Mitcham Road, Croydon, Surrey, CR9 3AL, UK

Bard's Product Inc., 1825 Willow Road, Northfield, Illinois, USA

Bayer UK Ltd, Dental Products Group, Pharmaceutical Division, Bayer House, Strawberry Hill, Newbury, Berks, RG18 1JA, UK

Binney and Smith, 1100 Church Lane, P.O. Box 431, Easton, PA 18044-0431, USA

Binney and Smith (Europe) Ltd, Ampthill Road, Bedford, MK42 9RS, UK

British Gypsum, Industrial Products Division, Jericho Works, Bowbridge Road, Newark, Nottinghamshire, NG24 3BZ, UK

Blumøller Ltd., c/o Jenks Group, Sword House, Totteridge Road, High Wycombe, Buckinghamshire, HP13 6DP, UK

Calbot Corporation, 125 High Street, Boston, Massachusetts 02110, USA

Ciba-Geigy PLC, Hulley Road, Macclesfield, Cheshire, SK10 2NX, UK

Clearway Plastics Ltd, Unit A, Fishers Grove, Farlington, Portsmouth PO6 1SH, UK

Connoisseur Studio 36 Loom Lane, Radlett, Herts WD7 8AE, UK

Conservation Materials Ltd, 1395 Greg Street, Ste 110, Sparks, Nevada, 89431, USA

Crosfield Chemicals, PO Box 26, Warrington, Cheshire, England, WA5 1AB, UK

Daler Rowney Ltd, Southern Industrial Area, PO Box 10, Bracknell, Berkshire, RG12 8ST, UK

W. David and Sons Ltd, Manufacturers and Industrial Chemists, Ridgemount House, 1 Totteridge Lane, Whetstone, London N20 0EY, UK

De Trey Division, Dentsply Ltd, Hamm Moor Lane, Addlestone, Weybridge, Surrey, KT15 2SE, UK

Degussa Ltd., Winterton House, Winterton Way, Macclesfield, SK11 0LP, UK

Degussa AG, Weissfrauenstr. 9, Frankfurt 60311, Germany

(Devcon) ITW 3600 W Lake Ave, Glenview, IL 60025-5811, USA

ITW Devcon, Brunel Close, Park Farm, Wellingborough, NN8 3QX, UK

Dow Corning Co., 2200 Salzburg St, Midland, Michigan 48640-8590, USA

Dow Corning Ltd., Cardiff Road, Barry, South Glamorgan, CF63 2YL, UK

Duckhams Oil Ltd, 157–159 Mason Hill, Bromley, Kent, BR1 9HU, UK

Epoxy Technology Inc., Box 567, 14 Fortune Drive, Billerica, Massachusetts 01821, USA

Evode Ltd, Common Road, Stafford, ST16 3EH, UK

Fyne Conservation Services, Airds Cottage, St Catherines, Loch Fyne, Argyll, PA25 8BA, Scotland, UK

General Industria Chimica, Strada Cimitero S. Cataldo 141, 41100 Modena, Italy

GRP Factors, 2 First Avenue, Bluebridge Industrial Estate, Halstead, Essex, CO9 2EX, UK

Henry Marcel Guest Ltd, Collyhurst Road, Riverside Works, Manchester, M10 7RU, UK

Hammerite Products Ltd., Prudhoe, Northumberland, NE42 6LP, UK

Harbutts Ltd, The Mulberrys, Kembrey Park, Swindon SN2 6US, UK

Andrew Hill (distributor), PO Box 4, Aylesbury, Buckinghamshire, HP17 9UB, UK

Hoechst UK Ltd, Hoechst House, Salisbury Road, Hounslow, Middlesex, TW4 6JH, UK
ICI, Imperial Chemical House, Millbank, London, SW1P 3JF, UK
Jessops of Leicester, Jessop House, 98 Scudamore Road, Leicester, LE3 1TZ, UK
Jiffy Packaging Co. Ltd, Road 4 Industrial Estate, Winsford, Cheshire, CW7 3QJ, UK
John T. Keep and Sons, Ltd, PO Box 78, Croydon Road, Beckenham, Kent BR3 4BL, UK
Laporte Industries Ltd, PO Box 2, Moorfield Road, Widnes, Cheshire, WA8 0JU
Lingner and Fischer GmbH, Herrmann Str 7, 77815 Buehl, Germany
The Mearl Corporation, 217 N. Highland Ave, Ossining, NY 10562-2902, USA
Micro-Surface Finishing Products Inc., Box 818, Wilton, Iowa 52778, USA
The Milliput Company, Unit 5 & 6, The Marian, Dolgellau, Mid Wales, LL40 1UU, UK
Monsanto Polymers and Petrochemicals Co., 800 N. Lindbergh Blvd, St Louis, MO 63167-0001, USA
Moyco Industries Inc., Philadelphia, Pennsylvania 19132, USA
Philadelphia Resins Corporation, 130 Commerce Drive, PO Box 454, Montgomeryville, Pennsylvania, 18936, USA
Picreator Enterprises Ltd, 44 Park View Gardens, London NW4 2PN, UK
C.A. Pisani and Co. Ltd, Transport Avenue, Great West Road, Brentford, Middlesex, UK
The PQ Corporation, 1200 W Swedesford Rd, Berwyn, PA 19312-1071, USA
Plastic Padding Ltd, Watchmead, Welwyn Garden City, Herts, AL7 1JB, UK
Polycell Products Ltd, 30 Broadwater Road, Welwyn Garden City, Herts, AL7 3AZ, UK
Proctor and Gamble Ltd, Chemicals Division, PO Box 9, Hayes Gate House, 27 Uxbridge Road, Hayes, Middx, UB4 0JD, UK
Randolph Products Co., Carstadt, New Jersey, USA
The Rawlplug Co. Ltd, Skibo Drive, Thornliebank Industrial Estate, Glasgow, G46 8JR, UK
J. Rettenmaier and Sohne, 7091 Holzmuhle, Bei Ellwangen/Jagst, West Germany
Rhône-Poulenc Poleacre Lane, Woodley, Stockport, Cheshire SK6 1PQ, UK
Roehm GmbH, Kirschenallee, Darmstadt, Hessen 64293 Germany
Rohm and Haas Company, 6th and Market Sts, Philadelphia, Pennsylvania 19105, USA
Rohm and Haas (UK) Ltd, Lennig House, 2 Mason's Avenue, Croydon, CR9 3NB, UK
George Rowney and Co. Ltd, PO Box 10, Bracknell, Berks, RG2 4ST, UK
Rubert and Co Ltd, Acru Works, Demmings Road, Cheadle, Cheshire SK8 2PG, UK
Rustins Ltd, Waterloo Road, London, NW2 7TX, UK
Salient Development Services Ltd, (Phenoglaze), Unit 10, Vulcan Way, New Addington, Croydon, Surrey, CRO 9UG, UK
G.H. Smith and Partner, 28 Berechurch Road, Colchester, Essex, CO2 7QH, UK
SP Systems (Structural Polymer Systems), Love Lane, Cowes, Isle of Wight, PO31 7EW, UK
The *Sylglas* Co., Denso House, Chapel Road, London SE27 OTR, UK
A. Tiranti Ltd, 70 High Street, Reading, Berks, RG7 5AR, UK
Tor Coatings Ltd, Portobello Industrial Estate, Birtley, Chester-le-Street, Durham, DH3 2RE, UK
Trylon Ltd, Thrift Street, Wollaston, Wellingborough, Northants, NN29 7QJ, UK
Tulco Inc., 9 Bishop Road, Ayer, Massachusetts 01432, USA
Union Carbide, Noorderlaan 147, 2030 Antwerp, Belgium
Union Carbide, 39 Old Ridgebury Road, Danburry, Connecticut 06817, USA
Wacker-Chemie GmbH, Hanns-Seidel-Platz 4, Muenchen 81737, Germany
Winsor and Newton, Whitefriars Avenue, Harrow, Middlesex, HA3 5RH, UK
Zynolyte Products Co., Carson, California 96749-6244, USA

References

AGBABIAN, M.S., GINELL, W.S., MASRI, S.F. and NIGBOR, R.L. (1991) Evaluation of earthquake damage mitigation methods for museum objects. *Studies in Conservation*, 36, pp. 111–120.

ALLEN, K.W. (1984) Adhesion and adhesives – some fundamentals. In *Preprints of the Contributions to the Paris Congress on Adhesives and Consolidants*, edited by N.S. Brommelle, E.M. Pye, P. Smith and G. Thomson. London: International Institute for Conservation.

AMERICAN INSTITUTE FOR CONSERVATION (1979) *American Institute for Conservation of Historic and Artistic Works: Code of Ethics and Standards of Practice*. Washington: AIC.

AMOROSO, G.G. and FASSINA, V. (1983) *Stone Decay and Conservation*. Materials Science Monographs II. New York: Elsevier.

APPELBAUM, B. (1987) Criteria for treatment: reversibility. *Journal of the American Institute for Conservation*, 26, pp. 65–73.

ASHLEY-SMITH, J. (1980) Professionalism in conservation. *Conservation News*, (12), pp. 3–4.

ASHLEY-SMITH, J. (1982) The ethics of conservation. *The Conservator*, 6, pp. 1–5.

ASMUS, J.F. (1975) Use of lasers in the conservation of stained glass. In *Proceedings of International Institute for Conservation Stockholm Congress on Conservation in Archaeology and the Applied Arts*, edited by D. Leigh, A. Moncrieff, W. Oddy and P. Pratt. London: International Institute for Conservation.

BAILEY, A. and HOLLOWAY, A. (1979) *The Book of Colour Photography*. London: Ebury Press.

BAILEY, M.R. (1987) Infection and allergy in museums. In *Safety in Museums and Galleries*, edited by F. Howie. London: Butterworths.

BARLOW, M. (1994) An interim report concerning the long-term natural ageing of false glazes and fillers. *Conservation News*, (55).

BARNES, L. (1993) Mind the gap; conservation of a delftware bowl. *V&A Conservation Journal*, 7.

BAROV, Z. (1986) The use of methylmethacrylate as an adhesive in the conservation of two objects from the W.R. Hearst Collection. In *Preprints of the Contributions to the International Institute for Conservation Bologna Congress on Stone*, edited by N. Brommelle and P. Smith. London: International Institute for Conservation.

BAROV, Z. (1988) The reconstruction of a greek vase: the Kyknos Krater. *Studies in Conservation*, 33, pp. 165–177.

BAROV, Z. and LAMBERT, F. (1984) Mechanical properties of some fill materials for ceramic conservation. In *Preprints of International Council of Museums Committee for Conservation 7th Triennial Meeting, Copenhagen*, edited by D. de Froment. Paris: International Council of Museums.

BARTLETT, I. and ROWLES, S. (1987) Use of personal safety devices. In *Safety in Museums and Galleries*, edited by F. Howie. London: Butterworths.

BEETON, MRS I.M. (1861) *Book of Household Management*. London: S.O. Beeton.

BEETON, MRS I.M. (1915) *Book of Household Management*, revised edition. London: Ward Lock.

BEHRENS, G.A. (1989) Mechanical Cleaning of Ceramics with Air-Abrasive and Cavijet. Unpublished thesis for West Dean College, Ceramics Restoration Diploma.

BERGER, G.A. (1990) Inpainting using PVA medium. In *Preprints of the Contributions to the International Institute for Conservation Brussels Conference on Cleaning, Retouching and Coatings*, edited by J. Mills and P. Smith. London: International Institute for Conservation.

BERGERON, A. (1995) The Unbearable Lightness of Fillers (in French) in *Preprints of Association des Restaurateurs d'Art et d'Archeologie de Formation Universitaire 4th International Symposium, Paris.*

BIMSON, M. (1969) The examination of ceramics by X-ray powder diffraction. *Studies in Conservation*, 14, p. 69.

BLACKSHAW, S. and CHEETHAM, H. (1982) Foaming epoxy resin – a useful mounting medium for conservation. *Studies in Conservation*, 27, pp. 70–74.

BLACKSHAW, S. and WARD, S. (1983) Simple tests for assessing materials for use in conservation. In *Proceedings of the Symposium on Resins in Conservation*, edited by J.O. Tate, N.H. Tennent, and J.H. Townsend. Edinburgh: SSCR Publications.

BOGLE, L. (in press) The conservation of a collection of fire blackened ceramics. In *Proceedings of International Council for Museums Amsterdam Conference on Conservation of Glass and Ceramics*, edited by N. Tennent. London: James and James.

BOURGEOIS, B. (1993) La Restauration du Dinos du Peintre de la

Gorgone au Musee du Louvre. In *Preprints of International Council of Museums Committee for Conservation 10th Triennial Meeting, Washington DC, USA*.

BRADLEY, S. (1983) Conservation recording at the British Museum. *The Conservator*, 7, pp. 9–12.

BRADLEY, S. (1984) Strength testing of adhesives and consolidants for conservation purposes. In *Preprints of the Contributions to the International Institute for Conservation Paris Congress on Adhesives and Consolidants*, edited by N.S. Brommelle, E.M. Pye, P. Smith and G. Thomson. London: International Institute for Conservation.

BRADLEY, S. (1986) Health and safety: isocyanates. *Conservation News*, (30), p. 25.

BRADLEY, S. (1990a) Evaluation of Hxtal NYL-1 and Loctite 350 adhesives for glass conservation. In *Preprints of International Council of Museums Committee for Conservation 9th Triennial Meeting, Dresden*, edited by K. Grimstad. Los Angeles: Getty Conservation Institute, pp. 675–679.

BRADLEY, S. (1990b) *Evaluation of Hxtal NYL-1 Adhesive for Glass Conservation*. British Museum Conservation Research Report, no. 3.

BRADLEY, S., BOFF, R. and SHERE, P. (1983) A modified technique for the lightweight backing of mosaics. *Studies in Conservation*, 28, pp. 161–170.

BRADLEY, S. and GREEN, L. (1987) Materials for filling and retouching ceramics – hidden dangers. In *Preprints of International Council of Museums Committee for Conservation 8th Triennial Meeting, Sydney, Australia*, edited by K. Grimstad. Los Angeles: Getty Conservation Institute.

BRADLEY, S. and WILTHEW, S.E. (1984) An evaluation of some polyester and epoxy resins used in the conservation of glass. In *Preprints of Contributions to the International Council for Museums Committee for Conservation 7th Triennial Meeting, Copenhagen, Denmark*, edited by D. de Froment. Paris: International Council of Museums.

BREHENY, E. (1993) The conservation and preparation for display of a tin-glazed earthenware relief. *Scottish Society for Conservation and Restoration Journal*, vol. 4, no. 2.

BROWN, J.P. (1989) Hexcelite: a replacement for AJK/BJK dough. *Conservation News*, (40), p. 11.

BROWN-GOODE, G. (1895) The principles of museum administration. In *Report of Proceedings with Papers Read at the Sixth Annual General Meeting, Newcastle upon Tyne*. pp. 67–148.

BUIST, J. and GUDGEON, H. (1968) *Advances in Polyurethane Technology*. Maclaren.

BURGESS, D. (1990) *Chemical Science and Conservation*. London: Macmillan Education.

BURRELL, H. (1975) Solubility parameter values. In *Polymer Handbook*, edited by J. Brandrup and E.H. Immergut. Chichester: Wiley Interscience.

BUSH, P. and ZUBROW, E.B.W. (1986) The art and science of eating. *Science and Archaeology*, 28, pp. 38–43.

BUYS, S. and MURREL, V. (1990) Aptitude tests for young conservators. *Conservation News*, (42), pp. 29–32.

BYRNE, G.S. (1984) Adhesive formulations manipulated by the addition of fumed colloidal silica. In *Preprints of the Contributions to the International Institute for Conservation Paris Congress on Adhesives and Consolidants*, edited by N.S. Brommelle, E.M. Pye, P. Smith and G. Thomson. London: International Institute for Conservation.

CAIRNS, T. (1974) Thermoluminescence of clay and associated minerals. In *Applications of Science to the Dating of Works of Art*. Boston: Museum of Fine Arts.

CALVER, A. (1986) Scotchcast casting tape. *Conservation News*, (31), p. 12.

CARDEW, M. (1969) *Pioneer Pottery*. Longman

CASSON, M. (1977) *The Craft of the Potter*. London: BBC Publications.

CENTER FOR OCCUPATIONAL HAZARDS (1985a) *Solvents in Museum Conservation Laboratories*. New York: Center for Occupational Hazards.

CENTER FOR OCCUPATIONAL HAZARDS (1985b) *Ventilation for Conservation Laboratories*. New York: Center for Occupational Hazards.

CHARLESTON, R. (1981) *World Ceramics: an Illustrated History from the Earliest Times*. London: Hamlyn.

CHASE, W.T. and ZYCHERMAN, L.A. (1981) Choosing dental plasters for use in the conservation workshop. *Journal of American Institute for Conservation*, 21, pp. 65–67.

CHILD, R. (1988) Ethics in the conservation of social history objects. In *Preprints of United Kingdom Institute for Conservation 30th Anniversary Conference on Conservation Today*, edited by V. Todd. London: United Kingdom Institute for Conservation, pp. 8–9.

CIABACH, J. (1983) Investigation of the cross-linking of thermoplastic resins effected by ultra violet radiation. In *Proceedings of the Symposium on Resins in Conservation*, edited by J.O. Tate, N.H. Tennent and J.H. Townsend. Edinburgh: SSCR Publications.

CLYDESDALE, A. (1990) *Chemicals in Conservation – a Guide to Possible Hazards and Safe Use*. Edinburgh: Scottish Society for Conservation and Restoration.

COOPER, J. (1992) Mediaeval tiles. *Conservation News*, (49), pp. 15–17.

CORFIELD M. (1983) Conservation records in the Wiltshire Library and Museum Service. *The Conservator*, 7, pp. 5–8.

CORFIELD, M. (1988) Towards a conservation profession. In *Preprints of United Kingdom Institute for Conservation 30th Anniversary Conference on Conservation Today*, edited by V. Todd. London: United Kingdom Institute for Conservation. pp. 4–7.

CRONYN, J.M. (1990) *The Elements of Archaeological Conservation*. London: Routledge.

DAVIDGE, R.W. (1979) *Mechanical Behaviour of Ceramics*. Cambridge: Cambridge University Press.

DAVIDGE, R.W. and TAPPIN, G. (1967) Thermal shock and fracture in ceramics. *Transactions of the British Ceramics Society*, 66, 405 (119,122,127).

DAVISON, S. and HARRISON, P. (1987) Refiring archaeological ceramics. *The Conservator*, 11, pp. 34–37.

DAVISON, S. and JACKSON, P. (1985) The restoration of decorative flat glass: four case histories. *The Conservator*, 9, pp. 3–13.

DAVISON, S. AND JACKSON, P. (1988) Course notes for Institue of Archaeology Summer School course on Conservation of Archaeological Ceramics (unpublished).

DEASY, C.M. and LASSWELL, T.E. (1985) *Designing Places for People*. New York: Whitney Library of Design.

DELL, F. (1986) *The Airbrush Artist's Handbook*. London: Macdonald.

DER SARKISSIAN, M. and GOODBERRY, M. (1981) Treatment of a fire damaged ceramic plate. *Studies in Conservation*, 26, pp. 150–152.

DINSDALE, A., CAMM, J. and WILKINSON, W.T. (1967) The mechanical strength of ceramic tableware. *Transactions of the British Ceramics Society*, (8), p. 367.

DINSMORE, J. (1987) Considerations of the adhesion in the use of silane based consolidants. *The Conservator*, 11, pp. 26–29.

DORRELL, P.G. (1977) Photography of objects in conservation. *The Conservator*, 1, pp. 24–27.

DORRELL, P.G. (1989) *Photography in Archaeology and Conservation*. Cambridge: Cambridge University Press.

DOVE, S. (1984) Laponite R.D. as a gelling agent. *Conservation News*, (24), p. 16.

DOWMAN, E.A. (1970) *Conservation in Field Archaeology*. London: Methuen.

DOWN, J.L. (1984) The yellowing of epoxy resin adhesives: report on natural dark aging. *Studies in Conservation*, 29, pp. 63–76.

DOWN, J.L. (1986) The yellowing of epoxy resin adhesives: report on high intensity light aging. *Studies in Conservation*, 31, pp. 159–170.

DROWN, D. (1983) Record keeping – notes from a private conservator. *The Conservator*, 7, p. 17.

EASTAUGH, N. (1984) Gloss. *The Conservator*, (8), pp. 10–14

ELSTON, M. (1990) Technical and aesthetic considerations in the conservation of ancient ceramics and terracotta objects in the J. Paul Getty Museum: five case studies. *Studies in Conservation*, 35, (2), pp. 69–80.

ERHARDT, D. (1983) Removal of silicone adhesives. *Journal of the American Institute of Conservation*, 22, (1).

ESCRITT, J. and GREENACRE, M. (1972) Note on toxic gases in polyurethane foam. *Studies in Conservation*, 17, p. 134.

EVETTS, E. (1983) *China Mending: a Guide to Repairing and Restoration*. London: Faber.

FISHER, P. (1992) The Sophilos Vase, *The Art of the Conservator*, Chapter 10, edited by A. Oddy. London: British Museum Publications.

FITZHUGH, E. and GETTENS, J. (1971) Calclacite and other efflorescent salts on objects stored in wooden museum cases. In *Science and Archaeology*, edited by R. Brill. Massachusetts: Massachusetts Institute of Technology.

FLEMING, S.J. (1971) Thermoluminescent dating: principles and application. *Naturwissenschaften*, 58, pp. 333–338.

FLEMING, S.J. (1974) Thermoluminescence: glimmerings of the past. *New Scientist*, 28 March, pp. 1–7.

FLEMING, S.J. and SAMPSON, E.H. (1972) The authenticity of figures, animals and pottery facsimiles of bronzes in the Hui Hsien style. *Archaeometry*, 14, (2), pp. 237–244.

FLEMING, S.J. and STONEHAM, D. (1973) Thermoluminescent authenticity study and dating of Renaissance terracottas. *Archaeometry*, 15, (2), pp. 239–247.

FOSTER, K.P. (1987) Composition of colours in Minoan faience. In *Early Vitreous Materials*, British Museum Occasional Paper no. 56, edited by M. Bimson and I.C. Freestone. London: British Museum.

FRASER, H. (1979) *Glazes for the Craft Potter*. London: Pitman.

FRASER, H. (1986) *Ceramic Faults and their Remedies*. London: A & C Black.

FREEMAN, G.C. (1962) *Silicones: an Introduction to their Chemistry and Applications*. London: Iliffe.

GABASIO, M., EVIN, J., ARNAL, G.B. and ANDRIEUX, P. (1986) Origins of carbon in potsherds. *Radiocarbon*, 28, (2A), pp. 711–718.

GAUTIER, J. (1977) *Etude de ceramiques chypriotes provenant de Salamine*. Paris: Laboratoire de Recherche des Musées de France.

GEDYE, I. (1968) Pottery and glass. In *The Conservation of Cultural Property*. UNESCO Press.

GETTENS, R.J. and STOUT, G.L. (1966) *Painting Materials: a Short Encyclopedia*. New York: Dover.

GIBOTEAU, Y. (1995) The De-Restoration of Archaeological Pottery. In *Preprints of Association des Restaurateurs d'Art et d'Archeologie de Formation Universitaire 4th International Symposium, Paris*.

GIBSON, B.M. (1971) Methods of removing white and black deposits from ancient pottery. *Studies in Conservation*, 16, pp. 18–23.

GRAHAM, H. (ed.) (1966) *Vision and Visual Perception*. New York: Wiley.

GREEN, D. (1963) *Understanding Pottery Glazes*. London: Faber.

GREEN, L., FISHER, P. and BRADLEY, S. (1988) *Discoloration of Ceramics*. British Museum Conservation Research Report no. VII 13a.

GREGORY, R.L. (1979) *Eye and Brain* London: Weidenfield and Nicolson.

GRIMSHAW, R.W. (1971) *The Chemistry and Physics of Clays*. London: Benn.

HSE (1988) Ventilation in the Workplace. HMSO (EH22).

HSE (1990) Respiratory Protective Equipment – a Practical Guide for Users (HS(G)53).

HSE (1993) An Introduction to Local Exhaust Ventilation. HMSO (HS(G)37).

HALAHAN, F. and PLOWDEN, A. (1987) *Looking After Antiques*. London: Pan Books.

HAMER, F. and HAMER, J. (1986) *The Potter's Dictionary of Materials and Techniques*, 2nd edition. London: A. and C. Black.

HAMILTON-EDDY, E. (1984) Notes on basic health and safety precautions taken by the National Maritime Museum Conservation of Paintings Section. *The Conservator*, 8, pp. 31–34.

HAN, M.C. (1974) The effects of alpha dose and annealing temperature upon pottery dating by thermoluminescence. In proceedings of the seminar *Applications of Science to the Dating of Works of Art*. Edited by W.J. Young Boston: Museum of Fine Art.

HANNA, S.B. (1984) The use of organo-silanes for the treatment of limestone in an advanced state of deterioration. In *Preprints of the Contributions to the International Institute for Conservation Paris Congress on Adhesives and Consolidants*, edited by N.S. Brommelle, E.M. Pye, P. Smith and G. Thomson. London: International Institute for Conservation.

HANSEN, E. and AGNEW, N. (1990) Consolidation with moisture-curable isocyanates: polyureas and polyurethanes. In *Preprints of Contributions to the International Council for Museums Committee for Conservation 9th Triennial Meeting, Dresden*, edited by Kirsten Grimstad. Los Angeles: Getty Conservation Institute.

HARRIS, R. and SERVICE, S. (1982) Conservation of the centrepiece of the Sèvres Egyptian Service. *The Conservator*, (6), pp. 37–44.

HATCHFIELD, P. and CARPENTER, J. (1987) *Formaldehyde: how Great is the Danger in Museums?* Harvard University Art Museums.

HEUMAN, J. and GARLAND, K. (1987) A poultice technique for the removal of cellulose nitrate adhesive from textiles. *The Conservator*, 11, pp. 30–33.

HEY, M., ALTHOFER, H. and ORGAN, R.M. (1960) The limitations of polyethylene glycols: some advice and warning. *Studies in Conservation*, 5, pp. 159–162.

HODGES, H. (1963) Thin section analysis. Chapter 5 in *The Scientist and Archaeology*, edited by E. Pyddoke. London:

Phoenix.

HODGES, H. (1964) *Artifacts: an Introduction to Early Materials and Technology.* London: John Baker.

HODGES, H. (1975) The problems and ethics of the restoration of pottery. In *Proceedings of International Institute for Conservation Stockholm Congress on Conservation in Archaeology and the Applied Arts,* edited by D. Leigh, A. Moncrieff, W. Oddy and P. Pratt. London: International Institute for Conservation.

HODGES, H. (1986) The conservation treatment of ceramics in the field. In *Proceedings of International Institute for Conservation Mexico Congress on In Situ Archaeological Conservation,* edited by H. Hodges. Los Angeles: Getty Conservation Institute.

HODGES, H. (1990) Formation of crazing in some early Chinese glazed wares. In *Proceedings of International Institute for Conservation Kyoto Congress on The Conservation of Far Eastern Art,* edited by H. Mabuchi and P. Smith. London: International Institute for Conservation.

HOGAN, L. (in press) The conservation of Iznik pottery. In *Proceedings of International Council for Museums Amsterdam Conference on Conservation of Glass and Ceramics,* edited by N. Tennent. London: James and James.

HORIE, C.V. (1983) Reversibility of polymer treatments. In *Proceedings of the Symposium on Resins in Conservation,* edited by J.O. Tate, N.H. Tennent and J.H. Townsend. Edinburgh: SSCR Publications.

HORIE, C.V. (1987) *Materials for Conservation.* London: Butterworths.

HORIE, V. (1990) Solvent resistance of marking inks. *Conservation News,* (41), pp. 11–12.

HORLOCK-STRINGER, H. (1991) Correspondence. *Conservation News,* (45), pp. 16–17.

HOWIE, F. (ed.) (1987) *Safety in Museums and Galleries.* London: Butterworths.

HUGHES, D. (1987) The containment and ventilation of hazardous fumes in laboratories, workshops and studios. In *Safety in Museums and Galleries,* edited by F. Howie. London: Butterworths.

HUGHES, M.J., COWELL, M.R. and CRADDOCK, P.T. (1976) Atomic absorption techniques in archaeology. *Archaeometry,* 18, pp. 19–37.

HUNT, L.B. (1980) The gilding of European porcelain. *The Connoisseur,* June, pp. 106–113.

INSTITUTE FOR THE CONSERVATION OF CULTURAL MATERIAL (1986) *Code of Ethics and Guidance for Conservation Practice.* Canberra, Australia: Institute for the Conservation of Cultural Material.

INTERNATIONAL COUNCIL ON MONUMENTS AND SITES (1966) *The Venice Charter: International Charter for the Conservation and Restoration of Monuments and Sites.* Venice: International Council on Museums and Sites.

INTERNATIONAL INSTITUTE FOR CONSERVATION – AMERICAN GROUP (1964) Report of the Murray Pease Committee: International Institute for Conservation American Group Standards of Practice and Professional Relations for Conservators. *Studies in Conservation,* 19, pp. 116–121.

INTERNATIONAL INSTITUTE FOR CONSERVATION – CANADIAN GROUP (1989) *Code of Ethics and Guidance for Practice,* 2nd edition. Ottawa: International Institute for Conservation Canadian Group.

JACKSON, P.R. (1982) Resins used in glass conservation. In *Proceedings of the Symposium on Resins in Conservation,* edited by J.O. Tate, N.H. Tennent and J.H. Townsend. Edinburgh: SSCR Publications.

JACKSON, T. (1992) Personal respiratory protective equipment. *Conservation News,* (48), pp. 12–13.

JAQUELINE, P and MONEY, J. (1991) In the clear light of day. *Drawing and Graphics Today,* November.

JEDRZEJEWSKA, H. (1970) Removal of soluble salts from stone. In *Proceedings of International Institute for Conservation Congress on Conservation of Stone and Wooden Objects,* edited by G. Thomson. London: International Institute for Conservation.

JOHNSON, B. and BEARPARK, P. (1982) Conservation of mediaeval floor tiles at Norton Priory. *The Conservator,* (6), pp. 45–47.

JOHNSON, R.A., STIPP, J.J., TAMMERS, M.A., BONANI, G., SUTER, M. and WOELFLI, W. (1986) Archaeological sherd dating: comparison of thermoluminescence dates with radiocarbon dates by beta counting and accelerator techniques. *Radiocarbon,* 28, (2A), pp. 719–725.

JONES, A., JONES, J. and SPRIGGS, J. (1980) Results of a marker trial. *Conservation News,* (11), p. 6.

JONES, A., JONES, J. and SPRIGGS, J. (1985) Results of a second marker trial. *Conservation News,* (27), p. 37–38.

JORDAN, F. (1996) The practical application of tinted epoxy resins for filling, casting and retouching porcelain. *Conservation News,* (59).

KEENE, S. (1983) Conservation records – editorial introduction. *The Conservator,* 7, p. 4.

KHAZANOVA, I.A. (1981) Some problems concerning repeated restoration of antique painted vases. In *Preprints of International Council of Museums Committee for Conservation 6th Triennial Meeting, Ottawa, Canada.* Paris: International Council of Museums.

KING, R.H., RUPP, D.W. and SORENSON, L.W. (1986) A multivariate analysis of pottery from Southwest Cyprus using neutron activation analysis data. *Journal of Archaeological Science,* 13, (4), pp. 361–374.

KINGERY, W.D., BOWEN, M.K. and UHLMAN, D.R. (1975) *Introduction to Ceramics.* New York: Wiley.

KINGERY, W.D. and VANDIVER, P.B. (1986) *Ceramic Masterpieces: Art, Structure and Technology.* New York: Free Press.

KLEIN, W.K. (1962) Repairing and Restoring China and Glass; the Klein method, New York: Harper and Row.

KOOB, S. (1979) The removal of aged shellac adhesive from ceramics. *Studies in Conservation,* 24, pp. 134–135.

KOOB, S. (1982) The instability of cellulose nitrate adhesives. *The Conservator,* 6, pp. 31–34.

KOOB, S. (1984) The continued use of shellac as an adhesive – why? In *Preprints of the Contributions to the International Institute for Conservation Paris Congress on Adhesives and Consolidants,* edited by N.S. Brommelle, E.M. Pye, P. Smith and G. Thomson. London: International Institute for Conservation.

KOOB, S. (1986) The use of Paraloid B-72 as an adhesive: its application for archaeological ceramics and other materials. *Studies in Conservation,* 31, pp. 7–14.

KOOB, S. (1987) Detachable plaster restorations for archaeological ceramics. In *Recent Advances in the Conservation and Analysis of Artifacts,* Institute of Archaeology Jubilee Conservation Conference Papers, compiled by James Black. London: Summer Schools Press.

KUHN, H. (1986) *The Conservation and Restoration of Works of Art and Antiquities,* vol. I. London: Butterworths.

LACOUDRE, N. and DUBUS, M. (1988) Nettoyage et dégagement des agrafes au Musée National de Céramique à Sèvres. *Studies in Conservation*, 33, pp. 23–28.

LARNEY, J. (1971) Ceramic restoration in the Victoria and Albert Museum. *Studies in Conservation*, 16, pp. 69–82.

LARNEY, J. (1975a) Restoration of ceramics. In *Proceedings of International Institute for Conservation Stockholm Congress on Conservation in Archaeology and the Applied Arts*, edited by D. Leigh, A. Moncrieff, W. Oddy and P. Pratt. London: International Institute for Conservation.

LARNEY, J. (1975b) *Restoring Ceramics*. London: Barrie and Jenkins.

LARSEN, E.B. (1981) *Moulding and Casting of Museum Objects*. Copenhagen: School of Conservation, Royal Danish Art Academy.

LARSON, J. (1980a) The conservation of stone sculpture in historic buildings. In *Proceedings of International Institute for Conservation Vienna Congress on Conservation within Historic Buildings*, edited by N. Brommelle, G. Thomson and P. Smith. London: International Institute for Conservation.

LARSON, J. (1980b) The conservation of terracotta sculpture. *The Conservator*, 4, pp. 38–45.

LARSON, J. (1990) The treatment and examination of painted surfaces on 18th century terracotta sculptures. In *Proceedings of International Institute for Conservation Brussels Congress on Cleaning, Retouching and Coatings*, edited by J. Mills and P. Smith. London: International Institute for Conservation. pp. 28–32.

LARSON, J. and DINSMORE, J. (1984) The treatment of polychrome mediaeval English stone sculpture in the museum environment. In *Preprints of the Contributions to the International Institute for Conservation Paris Congress on Adhesives and Consolidants*, edited by N.S. Brommelle, E.M. Pye, P. Smith and G. Thomson. London: International Institute for Conservation. pp. 167–170.

LAZZARINI, L. and LOMBARDI, G. (1990) Bentonite for cleaning and desalination of stones. In *Preprints of Contributions to the International Council for Museums Committee for Conservation 9th Triennial Meeting, Dresden*, edited by K. Grimstad. Los Angeles: Getty Conservation Institute.

LEACH, B. (1976) *A Potter's Book*. London: Faber.

LESKARD, M. (1987) The packing and transportation of marine archaeological objects. In *The Conservation of Marine Archaeological Objects*, edited by C. Pearson. London: Butterworths.

LOCKEREN CAMPAGNE, VAN, K. and VEEN-SLAGEER, VAN DER, M. (1996) 'Golden' water-based acrylic media. *Conservation News*, (59).

LUCAS, A. (1932) *Antiques, their Restoration and Preservation*, 2nd edition. London: Arnold.

LING, D. (1991) Laponite poulticing. *Conservation News*, (46), pp. 10–11.

MACLEOD, I.D. and DAVIES, J. (1987) Desalination of glass, stone and ceramics recovered from shipwreck sites. In *Preprints of International Council of Museums Committee for Conservation 8th Triennial Meeting, Sydney, Australia*, edited by K. Grimstad. Los Angeles: Getty Conservation Institute.

MAISH, P.J. (1994) Silicone rubber staining of terracotta surfaces. *Studies in Conservation*, 39, pp. 250–256.

MANGUM, B.J. (1986) On the choice of preconsolidant in the treatment of an Egyptian polychrome triad. In *Proceedings of International Institute for Conservation Bologna Congress on Stone*, edited by N. Brommelle and P. Smith. London: International Institute for Conservation.

MARCONI, A. (1989) Attuali evidenze scientifiche sul rischio derivante dall'uso di fibre minerali e non, naturali e artificiali. *Giornale degli Igienisti Industriali*, 14, pp. 27–43.

MARSDEN, O. (1963) *Solvents Guide*. Cleaver Hulme.

MARTIN, J.H. (1977) *The Corning Flood: Museum under Water*. Corning Museum.

MECKLENBURG, M. (ed.) (1991) *Proceedings of Conference on Art in Transit: Studies in the Transportation of Paintings*. Washington DC: National Gallery of Art.

MELLAN, I. (1970) *Industrial Solvents Handbook*. New Jersey: Noyes Data Corporation.

MIBACH, E.T. (1975) The restoration of coarse archaeological ceramics. In *Proceedings of International Institute for Conservation Stockholm Congress on Conservation in Archaeology and the Applied Arts*, edited by D. Leigh, A. Moncrieff, W. Oddy and P. Pratt. London: International Institute for Conservation.

MILLS, J.S. and WHITE, R. (1987) *The Organic Chemistry of Museum Objects*. London: Butterworths.

MONCRIEFF, A. (1971) Polyurethane foaming resins. *Studies in Conservation*, 16, p. 119.

MONCRIEFF, A. (1975) Problems and potentialities in the conservation of vitreous materials. In *Proceedings of International Institute for Conservation Stockholm Congress on Conservation in Archaeology and the Applied Arts*, edited by D. Leigh, A. Moncrieff, W. Oddy and P. Pratt. London: International Institute for Conservation.

MONCRIEFF, A. (1976) The treatment of deteriorating stone with silicone resins; interim report. *Studies in Conservation*, 21, pp. 179–191.

MONCRIEFF, A. and WEAVER, G. (1983) *Science for Conservators. Book 2: Cleaning*. London: Crafts Council.

MOORE, W.R. and MURPHY, M. (1962) Viscosity of dilute solutions of poly(vinyl acetate). *Journal of Polymer Science*, 56, p. 519.

MORGOS, A., NAGY, J. and PALOSSY, L. (1984) New silicone rubber mould-making materials: the addition type silicone rubbers. In *Preprints of Contributions to the International Council for Museums Committee for Conservation 7th Triennial Meeting, Copenhagen, Denmark*, edited by D. de Froment. Paris: International Council of Museums.

NAVARRO, J. (1989) Jacks and clamps. *Conservation News*, (40), pp. 31–32.

NAVARRO, J. (1990) The use of flow promotors with Ablebond 342-1 in the restoration of glass and ceramics. *Conservation News*, (43), p. 25.

NEWEY, C., BOFF, R., DANIELS, V., PASCOE, M. and TENNENT, N. (1983) *Science for Conservators. Book 3: Adhesives and Coatings*. London: Crafts Council.

NEWEY, H., DOVE, S. and CALVER, A. (1987) Synthetic alternatives to plaster of Paris on excavation. In *Recent Advances in the Conservation and Analysis of Artifacts*, Institute of Archaeology Jubilee Conservation Conference Papers, compiled by James Black. London: Summer Schools Press.

NEWTON, R. and DAVISON, S. (1989) *Conservation of Glass*. London: Butterworths.

NORTON, F.H. (1958) Clay deposits as a means of identifying pottery. In proceedings of the seminar *Applications of Science to Examination of Works of Art*. Boston: Museum of Fine Art. New York: Arno press.

OAKLEY, V. and McGREEVY, J. (1995) A condition survey of the ceramics collection at the Ulster Museum. *V&A Conservation Journal*, 16, pp. 13–15.

ODDY, A. (1989) Care of ceramics in Japan. *Conservation News*, (40), pp. 18–19.

OLIVE, J. and PEARSON, C. (1975) The conservation of ceramics from marine archaeological sources. In *Proceedings of International Institute for Conservation Stockholm Congress on Conservation in Archaeology and the Applied Arts*, edited by D. Leigh, A. Moncrieff, W. Oddy and P. Pratt. London: International Institute for Conservation.

ORGAN, R.M. (1961) Conservation of cuneiform tablets. *British Museum Quarterly*, 23, pp. 52–57.

ORGAN, R.M. (1968) *Scientific Conservation of Antiquities*. Washington DC: Smithsonian Institute.

PADFIELD, T., ERHARDT, D. and HOPWOOD, W. (1982) Trouble in store. In *Proceedings of International Institute for Conservation Washington Congress on Science and Technology in the Service of Conservation*, edited by N. Brommelle and G. Thomson. London: International Institute for Conservation.

PADGHAM, C. and SAUNDERS, J. (1975) *The Perception of Light and Colour*. London: Bell.

PALEOS, C.M. and MAVROYANNAKIS, E.G. (1981) Conservation of ancient terracotta sherds by alkoxysilanes. In *Preprints of International Council of Museums Committee for Conservation 6th Triennial Meeting, Ottawa, Canada*. Paris: International Council of Museums.

PARSONS, W.M. and CURL, F.H. (1963) *China Mending and Restoration*. London: Faber.

PASCOE, M. (1980) Toxic hazards from solvents in conservation. *The Conservator*, 4, pp. 25–28.

PATERAKIS, A.B. (1987a) A comparative study of soluble salts in contaminated ceramics. In *Preprints of International Council of Museums Committee for Conservation 8th Triennial Meeting, Sydney, Australia*, edited by K. Grimstad. Los Angeles: Getty Conservation Institute.

PATERAKIS, A.B. (1987b) Deterioration of ceramics by soluble salts and methods for monitoring their removal. In *Recent Advances in the Conservation and Analysis of Artifacts*, Institute of Archaeology Jubilee Conservation Conference Papers, compiled by James Black. London: Summer Schools Press.

PATERAKIS, A.B. (1990) A preliminary study of salt efflorescence in the collection of the ancient agora, Athens, Greece. In *Preprints of International Council of Museums Committee for Conservation 9th Triennial Meeting, Dresden*, edited by K. Grimstad. Los Angeles: Getty Conservation Institute.

PATERAKIS, A.B. (1993) The consolidation and desalination of ceramics impregnated with calcium acetate. In *Preprints of International Council of Museums Committee for Conservation 10th Triennial Meeting, Washington, DC, USA*.

PAYTON, M. and PAYTON, G. (1981) *The Observer's Book of Pottery and Porcelain*. London: Frederick Warne.

PEARSON, C. (1987) *Conservation of Marine Archaeological Objects*. London: Butterworths.

PERLMAN, I. and ASARO, F. (1969) Pottery analysis by neutron activation. *Archaeometry*, 11, pp. 21–52.

PERRY, R. (1983) The Tate Gallery Conservation Department Records. *The Conservator*, 7, pp. 13–16.

PLENDERLEITH, H.J. and WERNER, A.E. (1974) *The Conservation of Antiquities and Works of Art*, 2nd edition. London: Oxford University Press.

PRYKE, L. (1991) Wax modelling. *Conservation News*, (46), p. 12.

PUHRINGER, J. (1990) Salt action and material testing. In *Preprints of International Council of Museums Committee for Conservation 9th Triennial Meeting, Dresden*, edited by K. Grimstad. Los Angeles: Getty Conservation Institute.

PUMFREY, G. (1993) Extruding a wax handle. *Conservation News*, (50).

RADO, P. (1969) *An Introduction to the Technology of Pottery*. London: Pergamon Press.

RADO, P. (1975) The effect of detergents on porcelain. In *Proceedings of International Institute for Conservation Stockholm Congress on Conservation in Archaeology and the Applied Arts*, edited by D. Leigh, A. Moncrieff, W. Oddy and P. Pratt. London: International Institute for Conservation.

RAMSAY, P. and THOMSON, D. (1990) Pens for museum documentation. *Conservation News*, (43), pp. 12–14.

RATHGEN, F. (1905) *The Preservation of Antiquities*, translated by G.A. Auden and H.A. Auden. Cambridge: Cambridge University Press.

RHODES, D. (1977) *Clay and Glazes for the Potter*, 2nd edition. London: Pitman.

RICH, J.C. (1947) *The Materials and Methods of Sculpture*. Oxford: Oxford University Press.

RICHARD, M.I. (1990) Packing delicate art objects for transit. In *Proceedings of International Institute for Conservation Brussels Congresson on Cleaning, Retouching and Coatings*, edited by J. Mills and P. Smith. London: International Institute for Conservation.

RICHEY, W.D. (1975) Chelating agents – a review. In *Proceedings of International Institute for Conservation Stockholm Congress on Conservation in Archaeology and the Applied Arts*, edited by D. Leigh, A. Moncrieff, W. Oddy and P. Pratt. London: International Institute for Conservation.

RIS-PAQUOT (1876) *Manière de restaurer soi-même les faience, porcelaines*, 2ième edition. Paris: Libraire Raphael Simon.

ROBSON, M.A. (1988) Methods of restoration and conservation of Bronze Age pottery urns in the British Museum. In *Early Advances in Conservation*, Occasional Paper no. 65, edited by V. Daniels. London: British Museum Press.

ROMAO, P., ALARCAO, A. and VIANA, C. (1990) Human saliva as a cleaning agent for dirty surfaces. *Studies in Conservation*, 35, pp. 153–155.

ROSENQUIST, A.J. (1961) New methods for the consolidation of fragile objects – wood, ivory, metals, etc. *Studies in Conservation*, 6, pp. 136–137.

SANDWITH, H. and STAINTON, S. (1985) *The National Trust Manual of Housekeeping*. Harmondsworth: Penguin Books in association with The National Trust.

SANK, M. (1994) The imitation of lustre and iridescence in three restoration cases studies. *Conservation News*, (55).

SAVAGE, G. and NEWMAN, H. (1976) *An Illustrated Dictionary of Ceramics*. London: Thames and Hudson.

SAYER, G. (1951) *The Potteries of China*. London: Routledge and Keegan Paul.

SAYRE, E.V. (1958) Studies of ancient ceramic objects by means of neutron bombardment and emission spectroscopy. In Proceedings of the seminar *Applications of Science to Examination of Works of Art*. Boston: Museum of Fine Art. New York: Arno Press

SEASE, C. (1981) The case against using soluble nylon in conservation work. *Studies in Conservation*, 26, pp. 102–110.

SEASE, C. (1987) *A Conservation Manual for the Field*

Archaeologist. Los Angeles: University of California.

SELWITZ, C. (1988) *Cellulose Nitrate in Conservation,* Research in Conservation no. 2. Los Angeles: J. Paul Getty Publications.

SERVICE, S. (1986) Pots under water at the V&A Museum. *Conservation News,* (30), pp. 25–26.

SHASHOUA, Y. (1990a) *Evaluation of Amsil Silicone Rubber Impression Material.* British Museum Conservation Research Report no. 10.

SHASHOUA, Y. (1990b) *Evaluation of Tackywax as a Display Aid for Glass and Porcelain Objects.* British Museum Conservation Research Report no. 37.

SHASHOUA, Y., BRADLEY, S. and DANIELS, V. (1992) Degradation of cellulose nitrate adhesive. *Studies in Conservation,* 37, (2), pp. 113–119.

SHASHOUA, Y. and WILLS, B. (1994) Poliflexsol polyester resin: its properties and applications to conservation. *The Conservator,* (18).

SHAW, K. (1971) *Ceramic Glazes.* Elsevier.

SHELLEY, M. (1987) *The Care and Handling of Art Objects: Practices in the Metropolitan Museum of Art.* New York: Metropolitan Museum of Art.

SHEPARD, A.D. (1980) *Ceramics for the Archaeologist.* Washington: Carnegie Institute.

SHERMAN, E. (1987) Museums and the Health and Safety Inspectorate. In *Safety in Museums and Galleries,* edited by F. Howie. London: Butterworths.

SHORER, P. (1971) Conservation and restoration of Romano-British wall plaster. *British Museum Quarterly,* 35, pp. 200–205.

SLADE, R.C. (1987) Fire safety. In *Safety in Museums and Galleries,* edited by F. Howie. London: Butterworths.

SMITH, P. (ed.) (1991) *Croner's Health and Safety at Work.* Croner Publications.

SMITH, S. (1994) Filling and painting of ceramics for exhibition in the British Museum – is it acceptable? In *Restoration: is it acceptable?* Occasional Paper no. 65, edited by A. Oddy. London: British Museum Press.

SMITH, S. (in press) Deterioration and conservation of Bronze Age pottery. In *Proceedings of International Council for Museums Amsterdam Conference on Conservation of Glass and Ceramics,* edited by N. Tennent. London: James and James.

SPYRIDOWICZ, K. (in press) In *Proceedings of International Council for Museums Amsterdam Conference on Conservation of Glass and Ceramics,* edited by N. Tennent. London: James and James.

STAMBOLOV, T. (1968) Notes on the removal of iron stains from calcareous stone. *Studies in Conservation,* 13, pp. 45–47.

STANIFORTH, S. (1985) Retouching and colour matching – the restorer and metamerism. *Studies in Conservation,* 30, pp. 101–111.

STOLOW, N. (1986) *Conservation and Exhibitions: Packing, Transport, Storage and Environmental Considerations.* London: Butterworths.

STRAHAN, K. and BOULTON, A. (1988) Chinese ceramic quadrupeds: conservation and restoration. In *Proceedings of International Institute for Conservation Kyoto Congress on The Conservation of Far Eastern Art,* edited by H. Mabuchi and P. Smith. London: International Institute for Conservation.

STURGE, T. (1988) The removal of a tiles façade from Leicester's railway station. In *Preprints of United Kingdom Institute for Conservation 30th Anniversary Conference on Conservation Today,* edited by V. Todd. London: United Kingdom Institute for Conservation. pp. 4–7.

TAYLOR, S. (1987) Consolidation of earthenware. *Conservation News,* (33), pp. 24–25.

TENNENT, N. (1979) Clear and pigmented epoxy resins for stained glass conservation: light aging studies. *Studies in Conservation,* 24, pp. 153–164.

TENNENT, N. (1982) The selection of suitable ceramic retouching media. In *Proceedings of the Symposium on Resins in Conservation,* edited by J.O. Tate, N.H. Tennent and J.H. Townsend. Edinburgh: SSCR Publications.

TENNENT, N. (1991) *An Epoxy Resin Update.* Text of lecture delivered to UKIC Ceramics and Glass Conservation Group Meeting on Adhesives and Consolidants. Available from author at Department of Chemistry, University of Glasgow, Glasgow G12 8QQ, UK.

TENNENT, N. (in press). In *proceedings of International Council for Museums Amsterdam Conference on Conservation of Glass and Ceramics,* edited by N. Tennent. London: James and James.

TENNENT, N. and TOWNSEND, J. (1984a) Factors affecting the refractive index of epoxy resins. In *Preprints of International Council of Museums Committee for Conservation 7th Triennial Meeting, Copenhagen,* edited by D. de Froment. Paris: International Council of Museums.

TENNENT, N. and TOWNSEND, J. (1984b) Photofading of dyestuffs in polyester and acrylic resins. In *Preprints of Contributions to the International Council for Museums Committee for Conservation 7th Triennial Meeting, Copenhagen, Denmark,* edited by D. de Froment. Paris: International Council of Museums.

THIACOURT, P. (1868) *L'Art de restaurer les faience, porcelains etc.,* 2nd edition. Paris: August Aubry.

THOMAS, R. (1988) Interim report on calculating rate of flow of consolidation of porous bodies. In *Preprints of United Kingdom Institute for Conservation 30th Anniversary Conference on Conservation Today,* edited by V. Todd. London: United Kingdom Institute for Conservation.

THOMPSON, J.M.A. (1984) *Manual of Curatorship: a Guide to Museum Practice.* London: Butterworths.

THOMSEN, S. and SHASHOUA, Y. (1991) *Evaluation of Kneadable Putty Rubber as a Mechanical Cleaning Agent for Ceramic and Paper Surfaces.* British Museum Conservation Research Report no. 1991/45.

THOMSON, G. (1968) *The Museum Environment,* 2nd edition. London: Butterworths.

TITE, M.S. and BIMSON, M. (1986) Faience: an investigation of the microstructures associated with the different methods of glazing. *Archaeometry,* 28, pp. 69–78.

TOPPING, P.G. (1986) Neutron activation analysis of later prehistoric pottery from the Western Isles of Scotland. *Proceedings of the Prehistoric Society,* 52, (5), pp. 105–129.

TORRACA, G. (1975) *Solubility and Solvents for Conservation Problems.* Rome: ICCROM.

TOWNSEND, J. (1986) Light fastness of marker pens. *Conservation News,* (30), pp. 6–7.

TOWNSEND, J. (1990) Labelling and marker pens. *Conservation News,* (42), pp 8–10.

UNITED KINGDOM INSTITUTE FOR CONSERVATION (1981) *Guidance for Conservation Practice.* London: United Kingdom Institute for Conservation.

URBANI, G. and TORRACA, G. (1965) *Nuovi Supporti Per Affreschi*

Staccati. 1st Centrale del Restauro, Rome, pp. 23–36.

UVAROV, E.B. and ISAACS, A. (1986) *A Dictionary of Science.* Harmondsworth: Penguin.

VANDIVER, P. and KINGERY, W.D. (1985) Variations in the microstructure and microcomposition of pre-Song, Song and Yuan dynasty ceramics. In *Ceramics and Civilisation: Ancient Technology to Modern Science*, vol. 1. Columbus, Ohio: The American Ceramic Society.

VARLEY, H. (ed.)(1980) *Colour.* London: Mitchell Beazley.

WALDRON, H.A. (1987) The toxicology of materials used in restoration and conservation. In *Safety in Museums and Galleries*, edited by F. Howie. London: Butterworths. pp. 75–84.

WATKINSON, D. (1975) An investigation into possible electro and ion exchange methods for removal of soluble salts from pottery. Institute of Archaeology thesis available on microfiche.

WATKINSON, D. (ed.)(1987) *First Aid for Finds*, 2nd edition. London: Rescue and UKIC Archaeology Section.

WATKINSON, D. and LEIGH, D. (1978) Polyurethane foam: a health hazard. *Conservation News*, (6), pp. 7–8.

WELLS, S. (1975) *Mend Your Own China and Glass.* London: Bell.

WHEELER, G.S. and WYPYSKI, M.T. (1993) An unusual efflorescence on Greek ceramics. *Studies in Conservation*, 38, pp. 55–62.

WHIR, R. (1977) *Restaurieren von keramik und Glas.* Munchen: Verlag Georg D.W. Callwey.

WHITE, M. (1981) *Restoring Fine China.* London: Batsford.

WHITMORE, P.M. and BAILIE, C. (1990) Studies on the photochemical stability of synthetic resin-based retouching paints: the effects of white pigments and extenders. In *Proceedings of International Institute for Conservation Brussels Congress on Cleaning, Retouching and Coatings*, edited by J. Mills and P. Smith. London: International Institute for Conservation.

WICKHAM, M. (1978) *Pottery Science – the Chemistry of Clay and Glaze Made Easy.* London: Pitman.

WILLIAMS, B., WILLIAMS, W. and MCMILLAN, J. (1985) Notes on some clays used for pottery in ancient Nubia. In *Ceramics and Civilization: Ancient Technology to Modern Science*, vol. 1, edited by W.D. Kingery. Columbus, Ohio: The American Ceeramic Society.

WILLIAMS, N. (1980) Pottery restoration: an account of spinning technique used in the British Museum. *The Conservator*, 4, pp. 34–37.

WILLIAMS, N. (1983) *Porcelain Repair and Restoration.* London: British Museum Publications.

WILLIAMS, N. (1987) Conservation of a large Clazomenian sarcophagus lid. In *Recent Advances in the Conservation and Analysis of Artifacts*, Institute of Archaeology Jubilee Conservation Conference Papers, compiled by James Black. London: Summer Schools Press.

WILLIAMS, N. (1988) Ancient methods of repairing pottery and porcelain. In, *Early Advances in Conservation*, Occasional Paper 65, edited by V. Daniels. London: British Museum Publications.

WILLIAMS, N. (1989) *The Breaking and Remaking of the Portland Vase.* London: British Museum Publications.

WISSLER, M. (1983) *China Mending for Beginners.* London: Bishopsgate Press.

WOOD, N. and KERR, R. (1992) Graciousness to wild austerity: aesthetic dimensions of Korean ceramics explored through technology. *Orientations*, 23, (12), pp. 39–44.

WOOD, N., WATT, J., KERR, R., BRODRICK, A. and DARRAH, J. (1992) An examination of some Han dynasty lead-glazed wares. In *Science and Technology of Ancient Ceramics 2, Proceedings of the International Symposium (ISAC '92)* edited by Li Jiazhi and Chen Xianqiu. Shanghai, China.

WOODS, A. (1982) Thin sections in ceramic technology – an introduction. In *Microscopy in Archaeological Conservation.* United Kingdom Institute for Conservation Occasional Paper no. 2.

YAP, C.T. (1986a) Chinese porcelain: genuine or fake? *Physics Bulletin*, 37, (5), pp. 214–215.

YAP, C.T. (1986b) A non-destructive scientific technique of detecting modern fake reproductive porcelains. *Oriental Art*, 32, (1), pp. 48–50.

Index